Structural Analysis in the Social Sciences 1

Intercorporate Relations

Within the last decade, researchers studying business organizations have come to realize that corporate behavior cannot be explained in terms of the actions of individual firms alone, and that in order to understand how businesses operate it is necessary to explore the relationships among them. This volume constitutes the first compilation of work by leading international scholars who have adopted a structural approach to the study of business, taking relations among companies as the fundamental unit of analysis, and examining the behavior of individual firms within this framework.

In their introduction to the volume, the editors analyze the historical and intellectual context of this rapidly growing area of research. The essays that follow include position statements by leading spokespersons for the two major structural perspectives on intercorporate relations – the resource dependence and social class views; national studies of the comparative historical development of intercorporate structures in Britain, France and Germany; essays on markets, money, and relations between corporations and cities; analyses of business structures in Europe, Latin America, Japan and the US; and a chapter on transnational business relations.

The volume as a whole will demonstrate to a broader public the significance and value of a structural approach to business studies, and will appeal to sociologists, organization theorists, business scholars, economists, political scientists, and business historians.

Structural Analysis in the Social Sciences

Series Editor: Mark Granovetter

Intercorporate Relations: The Structural Analysis of Business is the first volume of a Cambridge University Press series, *Structural Analysis in the Social Sciences*, which will present approaches that explain social behavior and institutions by reference to relations among such concrete social entities as persons and organizations. This contrasts with at least four other popular strategies: (1) reductionist attempts to explain by a focus on individuals alone; (2) explanations stressing the causal primacy of abstract concepts such as ideas, values, mental harmonies and cognitive maps (what is now called 'structuralism' on the Continent should be sharply distinguished from structural analysis in the present sense, though Claude Lévi-Strauss's early work on kinship is much closer to it); (3) technological and material determinism; (4) explanations that take 'variables' to be the main concepts of analysis, as for the 'structural equation' models that dominated much 1970s sociology, where the 'structure' is that connecting variables rather than concrete social entities.

The methodological core of structural analysis is the 'social network' approach but the series will also draw on a large body of work in areas such as political economy, conflict, human ecology, social psychology, organizational analysis, social mobility, sociology of science and biosociology, among others, that is not framed explicitly in network terms, but stresses the importance of relations rather than the atomization of reductionism or the determinism of ideas, technology or material conditions. The series will consist of edited and single-authored volumes; each will broadly synthesize one area of study and demonstrate the value of a structural perspective. Though this perspective has become extremely popular and influential in all the social sciences, it does not have a coherent identity, and no series yet brings together such work under a single rubric. It is my hope that the *Structural Analysis* series will, by doing so, bring the achievements of structurally oriented scholars to a wider public, and thereby encourage others to approach their theory and research in this very fruitful way.

Mark Granovetter

Intercorporate Relations

The Structural Analysis of Business

Edited by

Mark S. Mizruchi

Department of Sociology
Columbia University New York, New York

Michael Schwartz

Department of Sociology
State University of New York at Stony Brook

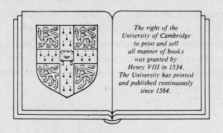

The right of the
University of Cambridge
to print and sell
all manner of books
was granted by
Henry VIII in 1534.
The University has printed
and published continuously
since 1584.

Cambridge University Press

Cambridge

New York   New Rochelle   Melbourne   Sydney

Published by the Press Syndicate of the University of Cambridge
The Pitt Building, Trumpington Street, Cambridge, CB2 1RP
32 East 57th Street, New York, NY 10022, USA
10 Stamford Road, Oakleigh, Melbourne 3166, Australia

© Cambridge University Press 1987

First published 1987

Printed in Great Britain at the University Press, Cambridge

British Library cataloguing in publication data

Intercorporate relations:
the structural analysis of business. –
(Structural analysis in the social sciences).
1. Industrial organization
I. Mizruchi, Mark S.   II. Schwartz,
Michael   III. Series
658.1   HD31

Library of Congress cataloguing in publication data

Intercorporate relations.
(Structural analysis in the social sciences)
Includes index.
1. Corporations.   2. Directors of corporations.
3. Capitalists and financiers.   4. Functionalism
(Social sciences)   I. Mizruchi, Mark S.   II. Schwartz,
Michael, 1942–   .   III. Series.
HD2741.I585   1987   338.7   87–6388

ISBN 0 521 33503 5

SE

Contents

Figures

Tables

Introduction

The structural analysis of business: an emerging field

Mark S. Mizruchi and Michael Schwartz

As recently as the early 1970s, organizational theory was principally focussed on the internal workings of organizations, and on the analysis of internal factors as the sources of organizational behavior. The bulk of the field utilized either human relations theory, which connected internal structure to worker morale and productivity, or neo-Weberian analysis, which sought to understand the impact of internal power relations on organizational behavior. This work tended to assume unchanging organizational structures invulnerable to outside forces. Contingency theory, though it escaped the static assumptions of previous work, maintained the focus on the internal workings of the organization.

This neglect of the environmental context limited the analytic leverage of organizational theory and led to misleading and incorrect descriptions of corporate behavior. The human relations approach, for example, sought to connect managerial strategy with worker productivity, but it ignored the supply of labor in its analysis. As Pfeffer and Salancik (1978) later argued, however, scarce labor usually implies less compliant workers and more accommodating management. Human relations evaluations of the effectiveness of various managerial strategies were therefore flawed, since the outcomes of each strategy would vary depending on the supply of labor, a variable which was not addressed in their research.

There were, of course, exceptions to this general trend. Works which emphasized the context within which organizations operated included Selznick's (1949) classic study of the TVA, Thompson's (1967) seminal work on organization-environment relations, and the unorthodox contingency theory advanced by Lawrence and Lorsch (1967; see also Zald, 1970). These works addressed the environment as something that affected an organization's behavior, but they did not press ahead to a fully structural view, in which an organization is viewed as interacting with its environment – molding it as well as being molded by it – and in which the structure of relations – rather than individual organizations – is the unit of analysis.

By the mid-1970s, the inability of existing perspectives to explain visible changes in the structure of business relations, combined with the impact of

3

multinational investment, government bribery scandals, and corporate crises, induced theoretical disenchantment and calls for more focussed concern on profit-making corporations and intercorporate structures (Perrow, 1972, Hirsch, 1975a).

In this context, Zeitlin's (1974) article, "Corporate ownership and control," which demolished the empirical and theoretical underpinnings of managerial theory, marked a turning point in the field. Managerialism's central tenet, that large corporations were invulnerable to major environmental constraint, had been an underlying premise of internalist organization theory. With this removed, researchers moved rapidly into interorganizational analysis. Paul Hirsch (1975b), for example, demonstrated the viability of this approach in a seminal study comparing the recording and pharmaceutical industries. Hirsch showed that these industries, although very similar in concentration and firm size, were differentially profitable due to the contrasting ways in which each industry managed its environment. Whereas the pharmaceutical industry's close partnership with the medical profession was a major reason for its success in the period following World War II, the recording industry's inability to control the highly competitive and easily entered radio industry was a major factor in its inconsistent performance. This research, together with a number of other pathbreaking studies (e.g. Pfeffer, 1972, Allen, 1974), clarified both the importance of organizational environments and the influence of organizations over their environments (see Aldrich, 1979 for a literature review; Perrow, 1979, chapter 7 presents an excellent overview of the logic of this work).

While organization theory was migrating as a discipline into a concern with corporate environments, a group of researchers centered around Harrison White and his associates (see, e.g., White, Boorman, and Breiger, 1976), began adapting the theory and methods of network analysis, which had been originally restricted to the study of small groups, to address larger structural issues. As studies of business organizations focussed more on the environment, many authors began to look beyond individual organizations to sets and systems of organizations (Aldrich and Whetten, 1981; Burns and Buckley, 1976). Instead of focussing on individual firms, researchers began treating industries (Burt, 1983) and interorganizational networks (Galaskiewicz, 1979; Laumann, Marsden, and Galaskiewicz, 1977; Laumann and Pappi, 1976; Turk, 1977) as their units of analysis. The environment, instead of being treated as an amorphous mass, became itself the object of analysis, and this readjusted focus found a methodological and theoretical fit with network analysis. Network analytic techniques, and the structural theorems they embodied, became basic tools of organizational analysis, and business structure research became an important area of network analysis.

Two widely-employed approaches that have emerged from this focus on organizational environments, the population ecology and transaction cost models, are compatible with but distinct from structural analysis.

A major tenet of the population ecology model is that organizations which are best suited to particular environments survive while organizations that are ill suited perish (Aldrich, 1979; Hannan and Freeman, 1977). In a profit-making context, this view implies that those companies which fit neatly into environmental niches will ultimately produce comparable commodities at lower cost or superior commodities at comparable cost. Environmental fit therefore produces economic efficiency and corporate prosperity.

Recently, several proponents of the population ecology model have begun to incorporate structural concepts into their analyses (Aldrich, 1982; Carroll, 1984; Hannan and Freeman, 1986; see also McPherson, 1983). However, most studies within the population ecology perspective have tended to deemphasize the power relations which enable certain organizations to dominate others, regardless of the fit between the corporations and their environments. Dominant companies, or groups of companies, however, can systematically alter an inhospitable environment. Chandler (1977),[1] for example, presents General Motors as an example of a corporation that survived and prospered because its multidivisional structure allowed it to pursue such strategies as market segmentation and frequent model changes, which fit neatly into its market environment. Without questioning the undoubted importance of the multidivisional form, other scholars (Yago, 1983; Whitt, 1982; Whitt and Yago, 1986; Du Boff and Herman, 1980) have demonstrated, however, that General Motors did not initially fit well with its environment. Densely populated cities, the absence of decent roads, and a host of less definable problems (including air pollution) all made the automobile an inefficient substitute for street railways, and by the early 1920s, when the company was still young, these problems had produced market saturation, industry-wide recession and corporate crisis. Nor was the solution to these problems found in an alteration of the firm to better fit with its environment. Instead, the considerable resources of the auto industry and its allies (including major lenders and the DuPont corporation, which controlled GM) were invested in altering the environment. On the one hand, the auto industry purchased over 400 street railways, converted them to buses and generally neglected them, thus handicapping the competition that could have exploited the poor fit between autos and cities. On the other hand, successful lobbying produced legislation which led to a multibillion dollar highway system that made America more hospitable to the automobile. Finally, the industry successfully resisted pollution control efforts. In short, despite some notable exceptions, studies within the population ecology framework have failed to examine the power that corporations have *in relation to* their competitors, customers, suppliers, and the society at large. This power can guarantee survival despite a poor fit with the environment.

Williamson's (1975) transaction costs model shares with structural analysis a focus on relations among companies (transactions) as the fundamental units of analysis. According to Williamson, corporations will adopt the multidivisional form or vertically integrate when the costs of transactions with customers and suppliers exceed the costs of administration and production under the firm's rubric. This approach constitutes an advance over traditional market approaches, since it explicitly defines the conditions under which the use of markets is the most efficient production strategy for particular firms, and consequently predicts when they will decline or disappear as mechanisms of corporate–environment interaction. But Williamson's argument, like Chandler's, is wedded to the concept of "efficiency" – the idea that changes in corporate behavior are impelled by the pursuit of – and almost always result in – the most efficient structure as measured by market performance. [2] Though Williamson's model does not exclude the survival of an inefficient firm, it nevertheless contains the implicit conclusion that, at any given time, a firm's (or economy's) behavior is by and large efficient relative to available alternatives. Structural analysis, as Leifer and White cogently argue in this volume, seeks to understand why firms behave as they do without assuming that this behavior is efficient. The efficiency assumption removes from view the sort of actions which the auto industry undertook in pursuit of (relatively inefficient) survival, because it searches for competitive advantage only in the market. The acquisition of street railways or lobbying for highway legislation are beyond the horizon of transaction cost analysis. A transaction cost analysis of the growth of General Motors (and Ford and Chrysler) must therefore (misleadingly) attribute the automobilization of America to the internal structure of G.M. (See also Burt, 1983, for a demonstration of how concentration of production facilitates industry profitability without necessarily increasing efficiency.)

As with population ecology, transaction cost analysis focusses on environments as major determinants of corporate activities, and it identifies important processes which condition corporate behavior. Its limitations, however, derive from its concern with only one mechanism of corporate-environment interaction: the market. It focusses exclusively on the ways in which firms alter their internal workings as a consequence of their success or failure in marketing their products and purchasing their supplies. While these dynamics are always critical and sometimes paramount to business behavior, they are not the sole determinants of the shape and behavior of the intercorporate network, or its constituent institutions. In fact, as Granovetter (1985) points out in a detailed critique of Williamson's argument, nonmarket relations of trust between customers and suppliers may make interfirm transactions less problematic than intrafirm transactions, even in situations in which Williamson's model would predict the establishment of internal hierarchies. While the structural analysis of business frequently begins with an analysis of markets, it proceeds to a consideration of the full array of relations among companies (and between companies and other actors), including those which proceed from, and subsequently modify and recast, market relationships. The impact of markets, therefore, cannot be properly understood outside of the ensemble of intercorporate ties in which they are embedded. And the behavior of the business community requires an understanding of these networks in all their complexity.

The third intellectual current which fed the stream of new research was derived from political sociology, which had been dominated after World War II by pluralist analysis of political decision-making and voting behavior (Seybold, 1980). Beginning with C. Wright Mills' *The Power Elite* and continuing through the research of G. William Domhoff (1967, 1983), politically active young academics became increasingly sensitive to the importance of business–government relations in determining the trajectory of American political–economic life. The mass movements of the 1960s guaranteed that these ideas would become an ongoing scholarly concern of activist-academics, former activists who became academics, and of other scholars influenced by them. The publication in 1966 of Paul Baran and Paul Sweezy's massively influential *Monopoly Capital* not only demonstrated the intellectual viability of Marxist political economy, but also redirected the attention of many political sociologists away from a narrow concern with political policy. The new generation of scholars had an abiding interest in structures within the business community which facilitated or prevented unified action (by individuals and/or corporations) *vis-à-vis* the rest of society. These concerns with the actions of the business community as a whole intermingled with those of organizational theorists to assure that issues of class formation and intercorporate power became major topics in the sociology of business.

Thus, three trends, the development of an interorganizational framework in organizational analysis, the application of network analysis to macrosociological topics, and the increasing attention paid to organizations by political sociologists, have combined to produce a new field of inquiry, the structural analysis of business.

The structural analysis of business is by no means a monolithic field. Still in its formative stages, there are many competing views on the direction in which it should move. But there is one fundamental principle which unites all of those working within this perspective: the belief that social processes can best be explained by examinations of the concrete interpersonal and organizational relations in which actors are embedded, rather than by concepts such as norms and values or aggregations of responses to survey items based on individual attributes. Structural analysts believe that by looking at the structure of relations among actors, we can understand the content of those relations (Berkowitz, 1982; Burt, 1982; Marsden and Lin, 1982; White, Boorman, and Breiger, 1976).

In the study of organizations, the structural approach suggests that by understanding the structure of relations among organizations, and among individuals who span organizational boundaries, we can learn a great deal about the behavior of those organizations, as well as their internal workings. Conversely, the principle states that we cannot fully understand what goes on inside organizations without knowledge of the organization's position within the structure of interorganizational relations. In addition, the structural approach emphasizes the importance of networks among individuals who span organizational boundaries, and whose connections affect the behavior of organizations.

Within these general principles, there have developed a variety of approaches to the structural analysis of business. In some areas, such as the study of markets, structural analysis has offered an alternative to – and critique of – predominant modes of study. These contrasting approaches seek to understand market transactions in the context of other (including stockholding, friendship, and political power) relations among the actors. In other areas, such as the analysis of coordinated action among large corporations, structural analysis has itself developed competing paradigms.

This variety is reflected in the contents of this volume. The two main competing perspectives in the field, the resource dependence and social class approaches, are described by their leading spokespersons. Many of the subsequent chapters are derived from one of the two perspectives, or employ elements of both. Others present a single structural alternative to conventional views, including fresh approaches to the analysis of markets, to the measurement of the money supply, and to the analysis of interurban relations.

Our purpose in assembling this volume is primarily expository. We wish to alert social scientists to the already considerable accomplishments, as well as the vast intellectual potential, of the structural approach to the study of business organizations. Each author has already produced significant research in the area and is still actively committed to viability of the paradigm. The articles are intended to demonstrate to other scholars the usefulness and validity of this approach. Part I attempts to define the theoretical substance of the field. Part II presents empirical analyses of national and international business structures which test and modify major analytic issues in the area. The remainder of this introduction describes the role each essay plays in the description and the shape of the field and signalling its future contributions.

Part I: Theoretical perspectives

Although the structural approach originally developed as a critique of internalist modes of thought within the social sciences, the emergence of this perspective has given rise to new controversies which have themselves illuminated the area. The most central of these debates concerns the fundamental nature of intercorporate relations in advanced capitalist societies. The lines have been roughly drawn between the resource dependence and social class perspectives. (See Useem, 1980 and Glasberg and Schwartz, 1983 for reviews of these controversies.)

Resource dependence theorists view companies as the primary actors in the business community; corporate leaders act principally as agents of the organizations with which they are affiliated. Social class theorists view corporations as tools of a dominant social class whose interests both embody and transcend those of any particular organization. The empirical predictions made by the two models are often similar, as several authors (Mizruchi, 1982; Ornstein, 1984; Palmer, 1983) have pointed out, since resource dependence theorists acknowledge the existence of leadership discretion and social class theorists acknowledge the autonomous dynamics of corporate processes. (There has even been an attempt to synthesize the two models (Mizruchi, 1987).) As a result, much of the dispute between proponents of the two perspective centers around divergent interpretations of the same data. Nevertheless, the two positions lead to contrasting conclusions about the capacity of the business community to act in a united fashion and about the relations between individuals and organizations within advanced capitalist societies.

In the first chapter, Jeffrey Pfeffer attempts to sort out the claims of the two positions, searching particularly for issues on which the two models diverge. He begins with a pointed and lucid expression of the basic tenets of the resource dependence model: the fundamental importance of organizations in advanced industrial societies; the fact that these organizations are not autonomous, but rather are interdependent with other organizations; and that these organizations attempt to manage (and limit) environmental uncertainty. He argues forcefully that organizational interests are more significant in determining organizational behavior than are family or class interests, and that resource interdependencies are the major source of interaction and conflict within the business community. He concludes that the class-wide interests of corporate leadership, however well understood or articulated, cannot achieve intercorporate unity because of the structural conflict created by resource dependencies.

Michael Soref and Maurice Zeitlin present a major new synthesis of recent developments in the social class perspective. They argue that intercorporate unity is possible, both because of unequal power relations among companies and because the network ties of corporate leaders allow them to overcome – at least episodically – the contradictions of interest among companies. They posit that the system of interlocking directorates is an indicator of a consolidated process of "intraclass integration, coordination, and control." While they agree with Pfeffer that there are significant sources of conflict among firms – particularly between industrial and financial companies – they argue that the development of a new class type, the finance capitalist, who owns and/or leads both banks and nonfinancial corporations, successfully suppresses these divisions and therefore facilitates significant coordination in the business community as a whole.

These chapters provide a clear expression of the differences between the two positions. But beyond this they allow us to perceive the ways in which the controversy between these perspectives has determined the important topics which researchers have addressed empirically and analytically. Chapter 6, by James Bearden and Beth Mintz, chapter 8, by Enrique Ogliastri and Carlos Dávila, and chapter 10, by Meindert Fennema and Kees van der Pijl, all directly address the dispute over the relative importance of interpersonal (or class) and interorganizational (or resource dependence) networks in determining the shape of corporate behavior. Chapter 5, by Donald Palmer and Roger Friedland, chapter 7, by John Scott, and chapter 9, by Koji Taira and Teiichi Wada, directly address the dialectic of conflict and coordination in national and local economies.

Though the structural perspective has arisen at least in part from discontent with market-centered theories of business behavior, it also attempts to understand the central role played by markets in corporate action. Eric Leifer and Harrison White underscore the distinction between their analysis of markets from the standard "information-oriented" approach, which views all producers as independent of each other and in full command of the information necessary to calculate the demand for their product. These models, according to Leifer and White, cannot account for how markets reproduce themselves over time – that is, how the consequences of individual marketing choices of individual firms result in a similar profile of companies, products and market share after each selling cycle. Information-oriented analyses assume that the most efficient firms survive (and that markets persist when several companies are equally efficient). This characterization nicely fits Chandler's analysis, outlined above. Leifer and White present a structural approach, in which individual producers have unique niches, or roles, within their industry's production system. In this approach, each producer decides how much to produce by examining the performance of its competitors in the prior production period, taking into account difficulties of attempts to invade another's niche. Leifer and White argue that companies know their own particular volume–revenue curve and its relation to those of other producers within the industry (that is, its position in a structure of intraindustry relations), but they do not know the abstract demand for a mythical or modified article they have not yet marketed. For this reason, production decisions are made on the basis of the performance of actually existing competitors instead of "information about the market." They thus introduce intrasectoral relationships as a key factor in the production decisions of individual companies. The authors illustrate their model by showing how a single producer determines his or her unique production volume and market price. At the same time, they demonstrate that markets can be conceptualized independently of the concept of demand and argue that corporate behavior can be better predicted using this approach than the standard economic model.

With similar disrespect for standard economic wisdom, Wayne Baker develops a structural description of money. Because of rapid advances in transaction technology, a growing number of money substitutes have appeared which make the traditional definition of money (cash plus demand deposits) increasingly problematic, and render federal monetary policies increasingly unworkable. Economists have tackled these conceptual and practical dilemmas by focussing upon the traits of the different financial instruments which contend for acceptance, an approach which once again directs attention exclusively to the market relationships in which these traits can be observed.

Using earlier work (Baker, 1984) which demonstrates the viability of dividing the interconnected network of financial actors into a core, composed of banks and other financial institutions, and a periphery, composed of noncommercial economic actors such as students, clerks, retirees, etc., Baker proposes a new definition based on the structural role played by the institutions which issue the contending instruments. Using financial futures assets as his analytic locale, Baker shows that the core actors tend to hold assets which are "close" to money because they become substitutable for existing money, while peripheral actors tend to hold assets which are further from money in this critical sense. Within the core, the central types of institutions are similarly more able to establish substitutability for their instruments; less central types have less success. This finding suggests that there is a core of actors in the business world which is able to define what constitutes money – and, by implication, how much money exists in the economy at a particular point in time – because of their central role in the complex overlaid networks of interfirm and interpersonal interactions. Once again, the key to understanding economic phenomena lies in simultaneous analysis of market and nonmarket relationships. A striking implication of this argument is that, without revamping its understanding of how various financial instruments become defined as money, the Federal Reserve may be powerless to regulate the money supply.

In chapter 5 Donald Palmer and Roger Friedland focus on the structure of relations among cities. Traditional theories of interurban relations have emphasized the dominance of the largest cities (central places), which serve as centers for financial decision-making and corporate administration, over smaller cities, which engage in more specialized manufacturing processes. They assume that the characteristics of cities determine the type of organizations that locate in them – once again based on the logic of markets. In these models, interurban relations can be understood primarily in terms of the "economic activities that organize the relationships between them" –

activities that are general to all technologically advanced societies. Drawing on a new data source, Palmer and Friedland argue that relatively recent changes, such as the concentration of capital, the separation of ownership from control, and the adoption of the multidivisional organizational form, have rendered a pure market approach inadequate for understanding industrialized Western societies. Combining elements of both the resource dependence and social class models, they focus on three network structures – the intraorganizational, interorganizational, and intraclass – arguing that the conscious decisions of the executives of business organizations have an increasingly large impact on the character and viability of the cities they serve. For example, the adoption of the multidivisional form has increased the distance between corporate headquarters and the firms' manufacturing plants, and therefore decreased the role that a corporation plays in employing people in its headquarters city or in nearby communities. This development has vast implications for corporate responsibility toward local communities, since opportunities for capital mobility are increased while corporate dependence on particular cities declines.

These three chapters each apply structural analysis to a new area, using the logic that relations among economic actors involve an understanding of the ensemble of social relations which constitute the overlaid structures in their environment. Leifer and White argue that we cannot understand even an apparently straightforward market relationship without analysis of the relations among all firms which compete in the market. The relational structures on both sides of the transaction ultimately influence both the extent to which the market itself is viable and the nature of the interchanges which take place across it. Baker sees the creation, expansion, and contraction of the money supply as an expression of a complex network of power relations among financial actors. These relations must be understood before we begin to see what money actually is, and before we can analyze the variations in the money supply. Palmer and Friedland see the relations among cities as founded upon the structural backbone of business interconnections among urban centers. As these multidimensional relations among businesses change, so do the types of relations which individual urban centers maintain with one another.

Part II: National and international business structures: a comparative perspective

The second section of the volume focuses on structures of intercorporate and business–government relations from a comparative and international perspective. A considerable volume of research on the structure of the US corporate elite has accumulated in recent years (Domhoff, 1983; Mintz and

Schwartz, 1985; Mizruchi, 1982; Moore, 1979; Useem, 1984), but most of this research has chosen to focus either on the interorganizational or the interpersonal level. The analysis of the interface between interpersonal and intercorporate structures is a neglected but critical topic which is central to the debate over the relative importance of organizations and individuals in corporate behavior. Chapter 6 represents a pioneering attempt to deal with this issue. Using a classic article by Breiger (1974) as their point of departure, James Bearden and Beth Mintz examine the two networks which are created when individuals share seats on the same corporate boards – the network of board interlocks among corporations and the network of shared boardships among executives. All studies of corporate interlock networks in industrialized Western societies have found financial firms – usually banks – to be the most central units (see, e.g., Dooley, 1969; Bunting, 1976; Mariolis, 1975; Mintz and Schwartz, 1985; Mizruchi, 1982; Sonquist and Koenig, 1976; Scott, 1979; Stokman, Ziegler and Scott, 1985). Bearden and Mintz once again confirm this finding, but they also report an apparent paradox: bankers are not the most central individuals. This surprising result fits neatly into Soref and Zeitlin's argument that while banks are the pivotal institutions in the modern business world, the dominant individuals are not necessarily bankers, but also class-conscious industrial leaders who sit on bank boards.

Despite a considerable amount of research on the causes and consequences of corporate interlocks (Allen, 1974; Burt, 1983; Galaskiewicz *et al.*, 1985; Koenig, Gogel, and Sonquist, 1979; Ornstein, 1984; Palmer, 1983; Pennings, 1980; Ratcliff, 1980), there is still a paucity of knowledge on why particular national interlock networks have taken specific forms. Though Bunting and Mizruchi (1982), Roy (1983), and Mizruchi (1982) have examined the development and changes in the US network during the twentieth century, there has been virtually no research examining the sources of variation among different countries. In chapter 7, John Scott compares the British, German, and French intercorporate systems and relates these differences to the particular set of historical circumstances peculiar to each nation. Scott identifies three different routes to capitalist national development: the *entrepreneurial* system (Britain), in which development was generated primarily by small, family-owned firms which grew with internally generated funds; the *hegemonic* system (Germany), based on an alliance of large banks and commercial enterprises through shared loan consortia, stockholdings, and director interlocks; and the *holding* system (France), distinguished by a series of separate "interest groups," centered around specific financial and family interests. Reviewing recently collected data, Scott shows how the corporate networks within these countries reflect their specific paths of development, thus demonstrating the contemporary impact of differing structural histories.

The study of macro social change has been consistently preoccupied with the relationship between economic development and class structure. This is reflected in the ongoing controversy among development theorists over the relationship between economic development and the structure of national business communities (see, e.g., Frank, 1967; Evans, 1979). Latin American nations have been an important focus in this controversy because of their status as developing countries, and a large sector of scholarly opinion accepts Walton's (1977) conclusion that as economic development progresses, power becomes more fragmented and less centralized. Enrique Ogliastri and Carlos Dávila examine this thesis through the lens of a comparative analysis of business and political elites in eleven Colombian cities at various stages of industrialization. They show that the increased development of local economies leads to resource dependencies on the industrial and financial center in Bogotá, which, in turn, leads to a system of structurally significant intercorporate relations, just as resource dependence theory predicts. It also produces a group of important entrepreneurs, whom Ogliastri and Dávila call polyvalents, whose economic vision transcends their particular firms and localities (notice the similarity between this concept and that of the finance capitalists discussed by Soref and Zeitlin in chapter 2). These polyvalents play an important role in integrating local economies into the broader Colombian political economy. Ogliastri and Dávila conclude that, contrary to the prevalent view, both concentration of power and interurban dependency are greatest in the larger, more economically developed cities.

As a consequence of the eclipse of its economic hegemony, the United States has increasingly paid scholarly attention to Japanese society as an example of a successful free market economy. Much has been made of the apparently superior managerial practices of Japanese firms, particularly their stress on job security and strong identification with the organization, with the idea that such management practices are to a great extent responsible for Japan's economic success, and thus worthy of emulation by US firms (Ouchi, 1981). Koji Taira and Teiichi Wada argue that there is more to Japan's economic "miracle" than good internal management. They identify and analyze the system of relations among corporations, business associations, government, and elite universities which allows for coordinated action, particularly between business and government. Taira and Wada describe the typical career life-cycle of members of the Japanese corporate elite, beginning with education at one of a small number of prestigious universities, proceeding to a position in a government agency, and culminating in an executive position in a major corporation and membership of an important business policy organization. Because performance in the public sector gives an individual credentials for later employment in the private sector, ambitious government officials are structurally constrained to fit their decision-making into the dynamics of corporate interest. This structural pressure is further refined by the over-laid impact of complex family structures which facilitate cohesion across public–private boundaries and transmit elite status to succeeding generations.

In the past two decades, as corporations have become multinational in scope, it has become increasingly difficult to understand the functioning of business in a particular country without locating that nation's role in the world economy. Yet most studies of intercorporate structures, including the comparative studies presented in this volume, have taken national business communities as their units of analysis. The usefulness of an international focus is demonstrated in chapter 10 by Meindert Fennema and Kees van der Pijl. Fennema and van der Pijl argue that the decline of US domination of the world economy has corresponded to the decline of the strength of US manufacturing capital *vis-à-vis* financial institutions, notably banks. As capital accumulation became more internationalized during the 1970s, corporations and business leaders of advanced capitalist countries established a complex network of formal relations with one another, including a dramatic increase in cross-national interlocking directorates, multinational lending consortia, and the formation of the Trilateral Commission, a policy formation body committed to the concept of world industrial expansion and American economic dominance. Fennema and van der Pijl argue that the economic recession of the late 1970s contributed to the rise in the power of financial institutions and exacerbated the contradictions between the dynamics of international economic expansion and control of inflation at home. This, in turn, contributed to both the decline of US dominance and the collapse of the integrative mechanisms which gave expression to it, and formed the quasi-visible background to the economic policies and the more aggressive foreign policy of the United States in the early 1980s.

The empirical analyses presented here are united by a concern with the effect of interorganizational structures on the behavior of individual firms with the network. The implication of Scott's article is that individual corporations in the European economy are influenced and constrained by the structure of interlocks in which they are embedded. Ironically, since this structure is itself a reflection of previous historical developments, Scott is, in fact, describing a recursive constraint in which new actions reproduce old structures and sustain them in a manner not unlike the process outlined by Leifer and White in Part I.

Bearden and Mintz offer a different version of the same argument. The two intersecting networks they analyze cannot be disentangled, and yet their different structures force us to confront once again the intersection of the resource dependence and social class perspectives. The centrality of banks expresses the role of investment capital as the preeminent business resource and symbolizes the constraints placed on individual corporations by the sectoral interests of banks. The fact that many inner circle members are not themselves bankers gives a strong sense of the disjunction between the collective goals of corporate leaders and the structural needs of banks, thus underscoring the independent impact of class interest within the constraints of resource dependencies. The contrasting, yet intersecting constraints which emerge from this help to explain the richness and variety of corporate behavior.

Taira and Wada offer yet a third perspective on the same phenomenon. They juxtapose an elaborate set of personal networks, which extend far beyond the corporate community, with corporate networks, represented by groupings of firms with historical ties. Once again, the delicate interaction which characterizes these intertwined networks is the critical feature which constrains and directs the activities of particular firms and groups of firms.

And finally, Fennema and van der Pijl utilize the same logic to examine the broadest facet of the modern world's economic trajectory. There we see the effect of changes in relations between financial and nonfinancial corporations on both international economic relations and national domestic and foreign policies.

New directions

The chapters of this volume illustrate the strengths of the structural approach to the analysis of business organizations, while providing us with a sense of the directions in which the field is moving.

First, the ongoing confrontation between the resource dependence model and the class model remains an engine for creative and integrative analysis. Several chapters, notably those by Palmer and Friedland and Bearden and Mintz, have employed both perspectives simultaneously. Though the underlying division suggests that no synthesis could satisfy both sides, the search for a unifying framework in which one perspective incorporates the most important insights of both models appears to be a fruitful area for continuing work.

One such attempt is that of Mizruchi and Koenig (1986), who argue that political groupings – a lay expression of class cohesion – within the business community may occur along dimensions which express the degree of resource dependence among major industries. Employing the input–output tables discussed by Pfeffer and the concept of interindustry "constraint" developed by Burt (1983), Mizruchi and Koenig have found a positive association between the level of constraint and the extent to which members of different industries contribute to the same congressional candidates. This study demonstrates the utility of the structural approach in predicting business political behavior.

A second area of further research involves the search for effective intervention to ameliorate or prevent the negative consequences of what Schumpeter called the "creative destruction" of capitalism. The economic decline of the northeastern United States in the 1970s and 1980s, triggered by the geographic and sectoral out-migration of basic industry, has produced a wide range of prescriptive suggestions and policies, nearly all premised on the assumption that corporate locational decisions are strictly market-driven (see, for example, Magaziner and Reich, 1982). Recent analyses (see, e.g., Bluestone and Harrison, 1982; Yago, Korman, Wu, and Schwartz, 1984) demonstrate the inadequacy of these views and they reveal the necessity of understanding the full impact of the corporate environment in analyzing and ameliorating this and other functional economic problems, that is, the need for a structural analysis of economic decline. These two examples offer a taste of the intellectual leverage which structural analysis may provide over critical issues in business structure research. The essays in this volume offer a multitude of others.

NOTES

1 Chandler is not generally considered a population ecology theorist (see Fligstein, 1985). However, his discussion of General Motors is consistent with a population ecology interpretation of the firm's success.
2 This discussion of Williamson does not mean that the concept of transaction costs cannot be employed in a structural analysis. On the contrary, Aldrich (1982), Cook et al. (1983), Galaskiewicz (1985), and Marsden (1983) have all examined transaction costs within a structural framework. Our point is that the domain assumptions of Williamson's model differ from those of structural analysis.

REFERENCES

Aldrich, Howard E., 1979. *Organizations and Environments.* Englewood Cliffs, NJ: Prentice-Hall
    1982. "The origins and persistence of social networks: a comment." In Peter V. Marsden and Nan Lin (eds.), *Social Structure and Network Analysis.* Beverly Hills: Sage, pp. 281–93
Aldrich, Howard E., and David A. Whetten, 1981. "Organization sets, action sets, and networks: making the most of simplicity." In Paul C. Nystrom and William H. Starbuck (eds.), *Handbook of Organizational Design.* New York: Oxford University Press, pp. 385–408
Allen, Michael P., 1974. "The structure of interorganizational elite cooptation: interlocking corporate directorates." *American Sociological Review,* 39: 393–406
Baker, Wayne E., 1984. "The social structure of a national securities market." *American Journal of Sociology,* 89: 775–811
Baran, Paul, and Paul Sweezy, 1966. *Monopoly Capital: An Essay on the American Economic and Social Order.* New York: Monthly Review Press
Berkowitz, S. D., 1982. *An Introduction to Structural Analysis: The Network Approach to Social Research.* Toronto: Butterworths

Bluestone, Barry, and Bennett Harrison, 1982. *The Deindustrialization of America: Plant Closings, Community Abandonment and the Dismantling of Basic Industry*. New York: Basic Books

Breiger, Ronald L., 1974. "The duality of persons and groups." *Social Forces*, 53: 181–90

Bunting, David, 1976. "Corporate interlocking: Part II – The modern money trust." *Directors and Boards*, 1 (Summer): 27–37

Bunting, David, and Mark S. Mizruchi, 1982. "The transfer of control in large corporations: 1905–1919." *Journal of Economic Issues*, 16 (December): 985–1003

Burns, Tom R., and Walter Buckley (eds.), 1976. *Power and Control: Social Structures and their Transformations*. Beverly Hills: Sage

Burt, Ronald S., 1982. *Toward a Structural Theory of Action: Network Models of Social Structure, Perception, and Action*. New York: Academic Press
    1983. *Corporate Profits and Cooptation: Networks of Market Constraints and Directorate Ties in the American Economy*. New York: Academic Press

Carroll, Glenn R., 1984. "Dynamics of publisher succession in newspaper organizations." *Administrative Science Quarterly*, 29: 93–113

Chandler, Alfred D., Jr., 1977. *The Visible Hand: The Managerial Revolution in American Business*. Cambridge, Mass.: Harvard University Press

Cook, Karen S., Richard M. Emerson, Mary R. Gillmore, and Toshio Yamagishi, 1983. "The distribution of power in exchange networks: theory and experimental results." *American Journal of Sociology*, 89: 275–305

Domhoff, G. William, 1967. *Who Rules America?* Englewood Cliffs, NJ: Prentice-Hall
    1983. *Who Rules America Now? A View for the 1980s*. Englewood Cliffs, NJ: Prentice-Hall

Dooley, Peter C., 1969. "The interlocking directorate." *American Economic Review*, 59: 314–23

Du Boff, Richard B., and Edward S. Herman, 1980. "Alfred Chandler's new business history: a review." *Politics and Society*, 10: 87–110

Evans, Peter, 1979. *Dependent Development*. Princeton University Press

Fligstein, Neil, 1985. "The spread of the multidivisional form among large firms, 1919–1979." *American Sociological Review*, 50: 377–91

Frank, Andre Gunder, 1967. *Capitalism and Underdevelopment in Latin America*. New York: Monthly Review Press

Galaskiewicz, Joseph, 1979. *Exchange Networks and Community Politics*. Beverly Hills: Sage
    1985. *The Social Organization of an Urban Grants Economy*. Orlando, Fla.: Academic Press

Galaskiewicz, Joseph, Stanley Wasserman, Barbara Rauschenbach, Wolfgang Bielefeld, and Patti Mullaney, 1985. "The impact of class, status, and market position on corporate interlocks in a regional network." *Social Forces*, 64: 403–31

Glasberg, Davita Silfen, and Michael Schwartz, 1983. "Corporate ownership and control." *Annual Review of Sociology*, 9: 311–32

Granovetter, Mark, 1985. "Economic action and social structure: the problem of embeddedness." *American Journal of Sociology*, 91: 481–510

Hannan, Michael T., and John H. Freeman, 1977. "The population ecology of organizations." *American Journal of Sociology*, 82: 929–64
  1986. "Where do organizational forms come from?" *Sociological Forum*, 1: 50–72
Hirsch, Paul M., 1975a. "Organizational analysis and industrial sociology: an instance of cultural lag." *American Sociologist*, 10: 3–10
  1975b. "Organizational effectiveness and the institutional environment." *Administrative Science Quarterly*, 20: 327–44
Koenig, Thomas, Robert Gogel, and John Sonquist, 1979. "Models of the significance of interlocking corporate directorates." *American Journal of Economics and Sociology*, 38: 173–86
Laumann, Edward O., Peter V. Marsden, and Joseph Galaskiewicz, 1977. "Community influence structures: replication and extension of a network approach." *American Journal of Sociology*, 83: 594–631
Laumann, Edward O., and Franz U. Pappi, 1976. *Networks of Collective Action: A Perspective on Community Influence Systems*. New York: Academic Press
Lawrence, Paul, and Jay Lorsch, 1967. *Organizations and Environment*. Cambridge, Mass.: Harvard University Press
Magaziner, I. C., and Robert B. Reich, 1982. *Minding America's Business: The Decline and Rise of the American Ecomony*. New York: Harcourt, Brace, Jovanovich
Mariolis, Peter, 1975. "Interlocking directorates and control of corporations: the theory of bank control." *Social Science Quarterly*, 56: 425–39
Marsden, Peter V., 1983. "Restricted access in networks and models of power." *American Journal of Sociology*, 88: 686–717
Marsden, Peter V., and Nan Lin (eds.), 1982. *Social Structure and Network Analysis*. Beverly Hills: Sage
McPherson, Miller, 1983. "An ecology of affiliation." *American Sociological Review*, 48: 519–32
Mills, C. Wright, 1956. *The Power Elite*. New York: Oxford University Press
Mintz, Beth, and Michael Schwartz, 1985. *The Power Structure of American Business*. University of Chicago Press
Mizruchi, Mark S., 1982. *The American Corporate Network, 1904–1974*. Beverly Hills: Sage
  1987. "Why does business stick together?: an interorganizational theory of class cohesion." In G. William Domhoff and Thomas R. Dye (eds.), *Power Elites and Organizations*. Beverly Hills: Sage, pp. 204–18
Mizruchi, Mark S., and Thomas Koenig, 1986. "Economic sources of corporate political consensus: an examination of interindustry relations. *American Sociological Review*, 51: 482–91
Moore, Gwen, 1979. "The structure of a national elite network." *American Sociological Review*, 44: 673–92
Ornstein, Michael D., 1984. "Interlocking directorates in Canada: intercorporate or class alliance?" *Administrative Science Quarterly*, 29: 210–31
Ouchi, William G., 1981. *Theory Z: How American business can meet the Japanese challenge*. Reading, Mass.: Addison-Wesley
Palmer, Donald, 1983. "Broken ties: interlocking directorates and intercorporate coordination." *Administrative Science Quarterly*, 28: 40–55

Pennings, Johannes M., 1980. *Interlocking Directorates*. San Francisco: Jossey-Bass

Perrow, Charles, 1967. "A framework for comparative organizational analysis." *American Sociological Review*, 32: 194–208

  1972. *Complex Organizations: A Critical Essay*. Glenview, Ill.: Scott, Foresman

  1979. *Complex Organizations: A Critical Essay*. Second edition. Glenview, Ill.: Scott, Foresman

Pfeffer, Jeffrey, 1972. "Size and composition of corporate boards of directors." *Administrative Science Quarterly*, 17: 218–28

Pfeffer, Jeffrey, and Gerald R. Salancik, 1978. *The External Control of Organizations: A Resource Dependence Perspective*. New York: Harper and Row

Ratcliff, Richard E., 1980. "Banks and corporate lending: an analysis of the impact of the internal structure of the capitalist class on the lending behavior of banks." *American Sociological Review*, 45: 553–70

Roy, William G., 1983. "The unfolding of the interlocking directorate structure of the United States." *American Sociological Review*, 48: 248–57

Scott, John, 1979. *Corporations, Classes and Capitalism*. London: Hutchinson

Selznick, Philip, 1949. *TVA and the Grass Roots*. New York: Harper

Seybold, Peter, 1980. "The Ford Foundation and the triumph of behavioralism in American political science." In Robert F. Arngrove (ed.), *Philanthropy and Cultural Imperialism*, Chicago: G. K. Hall

Sonquist, John A., and Tom Koenig, 1976. "Examining corporate interconnections through interlocking directorates." In Tom R. Burns and Walter Buckley (eds.), *Power and Control: Social Structures and their Transformation*. Beverly Hills: Sage

Stokman, Frans N., Rolf Ziegler, and John Scott, 1985. *Networks of Corporate Power: An Analysis of Ten Countries*. Cambridge, England: Polity Press

Thompson, James D., 1967. *Organizations in Action*. New York: McGraw-Hill

Turk, Herman, 1977. *Organizations in Modern Life: Cities and Other Large Networks*. San Francisco: Jossey-Bass

Useem, Michael, 1980. "Corporations and the corporate elite." *Annual Review of Sociology*, 6: 41–77

  1984. *The Inner Circle*. New York: Oxford University Press

Walton, John, 1977. *Elites and Economic Development: Comparative Studies on the Political Economy of Latin American Cities*. Austin: University of Texas Press

White, Harrison C., Scott A. Boorman, and Ronald L. Breiger, 1976. "Social structure from multiple networks – Part I: blockmodels of roles and positions." *American Journal of Sociology*, 81: 730–80

Whitt, J. Allen, 1982. *Urban Elites and Mass Transportation: The Dialectics of Power*. Princeton University Press

Whitt, J. Allen, and Glenn Yago, 1986. "Means of movement: the political economy of mass transportation." In Michael Schwartz (ed.), *The Business Elite as a Ruling Class*. New York: Holmes and Meier

Williamson, Oliver E., 1975. *Markets and Hierarchies: Analysis and Antitrust Implications*. New York: Free Press

Yago, Glenn H., 1983. "Class politics, mass transit and the city: Frankfurt/Main and Chicago." In *Comparative Social Research*, Volume 5. Winthrop, Mass.: JAI Press, pp. 299–338

Yago, Glenn H., Hyman Korman, Sen-Yuan Wu, and Michael Schwartz, 1984. "Investment and disinvestment in New York, 1900–1980." *Annals of the American Academy of Political and Social Science*, 75 (September): 28–38

Zald, Mayer N. (ed.), 1970. *Power in Organizations*. Nashville, Tenn.: Vanderbilt University Press

Zeitlin, Maurice, 1974. "Corporate ownership and control: the large corporation and the capitalist class." *American Journal of Sociology*, 79: 1073–119

Part I

Theoretical perspectives

1

A resource dependence perspective on intercorporate relations

Jeffrey Pfeffer

The literature on organizations has been dominated by a rationalistic, individualistic perspective and, for the most part, has denied both the reality of organizations as institutions (Zucker, 1983) as well as the embedded and at times quasi-political character of organizational action and choice (Granovetter, 1985). Thus, for instance, much of the writing in the 1950s and 1960s, particularly that emanating from schools of administration, emphasized the primacy and efficacy of managerial action. The behavior of organizations was to be understood in terms of concepts such as leadership, managerial values, style, culture, and strategy (Miles and Snow, 1978). The emphasis on proactive, intentional managerial action remains a prominent, if not dominant, theme in contemporary writing as well (Bourgeois, 1984; Peters and Waterman, 1982).

Such a focus has two consequences. First, attention is directed inside the organization in seeking explanations of organizational practices and decisions. If managerial intention and choice are prepotent, it is inevitably to managerial decision-making that one must look to understand organizations. Such a focus continues to dominate the managerial literature on organizations as well as much of the social science literature more generally. It fits prevailing social ideologies emphasizing the individual, rational choice and decision-making, and managerial accountability as well as being consistent with cognitive biases that tend to lodge causation in individuals rather than in their environments (Nisbett and Ross, 1980).

Second, this focus tends to deny the institutional reality of organizations. Organizations are seen as settings – settings in which class interests are developed and articulated (Palmer, 1983), settings in which managerial, individual work gets done and decisions made, settings in which power and resources are created and allocated (Pfeffer, 1981). As March and Olsen (1984: 734) noted, "From a behavioral point of view, formally organized social institutions have come to be portrayed simply as arenas within which . . . behavior, driven by more fundamental factors, occurs."

The resource dependence perspective (Aldrich and Pfeffer, 1976; Pfeffer and Salancik, 1978) was developed in part both to direct attention back to the social context of organizations to explain behavior, and to develop an analysis of organizations that began from the premise that organizations were real and had an existence and purpose apart from serving as settings and apart from the various people who were in them at any point in time. The perspective has probably been more successful in developing a coherent position on the first issue than the second, but both are important foci of attention.

There had been growing attention to the open systems nature of organizations (Katz and Kahn, 1966; Thompson, 1967; Yuchtman and Seashore, 1967). If organizations were open systems, necessarily transacting with environments in order to acquire resources and dispose of outputs, then the possibility of interorganizational power emerging from these systems of exchange exists, as well as the likelihood that this interorganizational power would be used to influence decisions and behaviors. "Corporate policy, therefore, could not be seen strictly as an expression of executive attitudes; it was a product of negotiation between a company's leadership and major actors in the environment" (Glasberg and Schwartz, 1983: 313).

Furthermore, the resource dependence perspective treats organizations as units of analysis and, on occasion, argues that organizational action is more than a product of individual intent. Thus, there is both some concern for how interorganizational power becomes intraorganizational power and transforms organizational actions (Pfeffer and Salancik, 1978: ch. 9), and also recognition that organizations are at once coalitions of interests but also produce activities which do not necessarily perfectly fit the interests of any participants. Once so created, such activity patterns persist as they become institutionalized. Thus, the resource dependence perspective has defined organizations as settings "in which groups and individuals with varying interests and preferences come together and engage in exchanges" (Pfeffer and Salancik, 1978: 26), but has also recognized that "once established, patterns of interaction are likely to persist" (p. 26). Organizations are viewed as markets for influence and control, but once such power relations get established, there is a continuity in organizational action. Moreover, the perspective treats contextual imperatives as affecting the organization, and analyzes interorganizational behavior in terms of the requirements for survival and acquiring resources that affect the organization as a unit.

The basic argument of the resource dependence perspective, then, is: (1) the fundamental units for understanding intercorporate relations and society are organizations; ours is a society of organizations (Presthus, 1978); (2) these organizations are not autonomous, but rather are constrained by a network of interdependencies with other organizations; (3) interdependence, when coupled with uncertainty about what the actions will be of those with which the organization is interdependent, leads to a situation in which survival and continued success are uncertain; and, therefore, (4) organizations take actions to manage external interdependencies, although such actions are inevitably never completely successful and produce new patterns of dependence and interdependence. Furthermore, (5) these patterns of dependence produce interorganizational as well as intraorganizational power, where such power has some effect on organizational behavior. Organizations tend to comply with the demands of those interests in their environment which have relatively more power, and those inside the organization who can successfully cope with these external contingencies come to have comparatively more power within the organization. This perspective sees the question of who controls the organization, for what ends, as both problematic and critical (Mintzberg, 1983).

Contrast with the class perspective

Resource dependence differs in some subtle but important ways from two other perspectives that have been used to analyze intercorporate relations, economics and the intraclass perspective. The differences with economics emerge primarily in the resource dependence perspective's emphasis on reducing uncertainty and interdependence through activities which either organize networks of relations or which bring dependencies inside the organization, regardless of considerations of profit or efficiency for the most part. Of course, efficiency is not always a straightforward concept, and as Burt (1980a) has shown, power in an interorganizational network is empirically related to the profits that can be earned as a result of that power. Thus, the distinctions between power and efficiency may be less than they at first appear, though certainly the causal mechanisms as well as the social legitimacy of achieving profit through one's position in a network of power relations is very different from profit presumably achieved through the efficient organization of economic exchange.

Resource dependence is distinguished from the intraclass or social class model of intercorporate relations by the emphasis on actions serving the interests of and being organized by organizations rather than families, individuals, or a social class. As Palmer has noted: "According to the interorganizational approach, organizations are entities that possess interests . . . According to the intraclass approach, individuals within the capitalist class or business elite are actors who possess interests. Organizations are the agents of these actors" (1983: 40–2). The social class approach sees organizations as instruments used by members of the capitalist class or by families (Mizruchi, 1983). Organizations are settings in which members of an elite class interact and develop common perspectives (e.g. Domhoff, 1974). Thus, the social class approach is, in many respects, reductionist in orientation, "inclined to see political [and organizational] phenomena as the aggregate consequences of individual behavior" (March and Olsen, 1984: 735). The resource dependence perspective, in contrast, sees organizations as elemental or fundamental building blocks of social structure (see also Coleman, 1974). Individuals and their interests are largely controlled by and encompassed in formal organizations. Rather than having organizations act as agents of individuals, families, or a social class, individuals and other aggregates serve as agents of organizations.

A second distinction is in the sense in which intent and rationality is imputed in the two approaches. The class perspective is more consciously rational in its approach – individuals possess interests, and organize themselves to pursue those interests (e.g. Whitt, 1980; Dunn, 1980). There is a strong element of intentionality in the language as well as in the empirical work deriving from this prediction. Although the resource dependence perspective also has elements of strategic action embedded in its argumenta-tion, it is somewhat less consistent on this issue, and argues that organizations act as if they are seeking to manage dependence, without necessarily assuming some conscious, overarching intent or purpose. Indeed, intention as a concept is itself more problematic in a perspective that takes the reality of organizations, with their political and institutionalized elements, more seriously.

Of course, any distinction between the perspectives depends importantly on how class gets defined and operationalized. Mizruchi (1983), reviewing this controversy, noted that "for Marx, the original definition of class was based on ownership vs. non-ownership of the means of production" (p. 10). Others have viewed class membership as deriving from other criteria such as kinship or family relations. As long as class is defined in this fashion, there remain clear distinctions between the resource dependence and class perspectives, because it is possible to empirically investigate whether or not firms are family or managerially controlled and the consequences for firm behavior, as well as the degree of family involvement in management and the coordination of family interests. However, some (e.g. Mizruchi, 1983: 22) go further and argue that "class can be viewed as a function of one's position in the productive process, irrespective of social background." At that point, of course, class position becomes defined in terms of organizational position, and the possibility of there being any discrepancy between organizational and family or class interests is removed. For purposes of discussion, we assume the distinction made between family and ownership versus organizational interests.

There are many similarities in the predictions made by the two perspectives. Nevertheless, two major points of contrast appear to be: (1) the issue of whether it is organizations or individuals or family interests that are preeminent in understanding organizational behavior; and (2) whether resource interdependencies and constraints act to create differences in interests and conflict within the system of organizations or, rather, whether there are class-wide interests that transcend the parochial concerns of resource exchanges and the interorganizational power differences that can emerge from such exchanges. The first distinction has been made by Mizruchi (1983: 8), who noted in describing the class perspective that "corporations are seen as tools which are used for the maximization of profits of controlling groups whose interests transcend those of an individual firm." To explore this first issue, we need to consider the extent to which the social system has, indeed, become a society of organizations and, more importantly, how or whether organizations effect a subordination of individual, familial, or class interests.

The second distinction has been prominent in writers from the social class perspective who have sought to demonstrate that although there may be economic competition, there is not much political competition across organizations (e.g. Whitt, 1980); that the capitalist class can organize itself and its interests through vehicles such as the family office (Dunn, 1980); and that there is a structure of interests and linkages within the class that can be explained by class-wide rather than parochial concerns and that transcends organizational boundaries. In examining this second issue, we need to consider whether or not there is evidence that resource exchange patterns do predict intercorporate behavior, and whether such predictions appear to reflect more parochial, transaction-specific or more system-wide interests.

Of course, family and organizational interests are often coincident, which makes distinguishing the resource dependence from the class perspective sometimes difficult. One way of beginning to make such a distinction is to argue that the fundamental issue is whether the organization's managers are firmly embedded in the corporation, with few alternative ties or interests, or whether they face competing demands deriving from membership in other social structures such as family groups. This distinction is at times captured in the differences between organizations that are controlled by ownership groups or by professional managers. Thus, Palmer and his colleagues (Friedland and Palmer, 1983; Palmer, Friedland, Jennings and Powers, 1984) have sought to argue for the importance of the class perspective by demonstrating that family-controlled firms are different from non-family-controlled firms in things such as the location of plant sites and the choice of organizational form, even after controlling for other variables.[1] This formulation frames the issue in terms of who controls the dominant coalition (Mintzberg, 1983; Perrow, 1979).

But the resource perspective argues that it is the patterns of transactions and resource flows, not issues of family or class solidarity, or even managerial interests, that are the most critical in analyzing interorganizational behavior. The question of who controls the organization, who constitutes its dominant coalition, is of interest, of course, but this is more a result of patterns of resource exchanges than a cause of such exchanges. Because of the need to acquire resources from the environment and to stabilize such exchanges, organizations are externally controlled and constrained. Responses to these external constraints follow organizational imperatives, and produce internal differentiation and power differences, rather than being produced by them.

One other introductory comment is in order. It seems clear that the intraclass perspective is more focussed strictly on business corporations or profit-making entities, whereas the resource dependence approach is general in its application across a variety of organizational types (e.g. Randall, 1973). In their description of class cohesion theory, Glasberg and Schwartz (1983) noted the importance of profits as a motivating force, while clearly bank control and bank hegemony theories apply to private sector enterprises. In a study consistent with resource dependence predictions, Randall (1973) found that state employment service offices in Wisconsin were more likely to adopt a human resource/training rather than free employment agency orientation to the extent the area they served had smaller employers (giving the office relatively more power) and to the extent that there were competing community action agencies in the area which could absorb the human resource funds if the employment office failed to adopt the appropriate response. Thus, the resource dependence approach readily encompasses the explanation of behavior from organizations of any type.

Organizations and interests

The resource dependence perspective asserts that organizational actions are taken in organizational, rather than individual, class, or familial interests. If we assume that there are such interests not coincident with organizational interests in all cases, then the question is posed: how do organizations operate to assure the primacy of their interests in decision-making? A related, but I suspect less controversial, issue is the extent to which organizations have come to dominate the institutional landscape so that the question of whether formal organizations determine the definition of interests and behavior even becomes relevant.

A society of organizations

Presthus (1978: 58) noted that, by 1970, only about 10 per cent of the US workforce worked for themselves; the remaining 90 per cent were employees of an organization. Presthus went on to claim that about half of these employees worked in organizations that could be characterized as bureaucratic. Whether the US is indeed becoming a society of large, bureaucratic organizations or not is itself not a settled question. On the one hand, there is evidence that the concentration of both assets and employment in manufacturing is increasing. Thus, Blair (1972) reported that the proportion of assets controlled by the 200 largest manufacturing organizations increased from 45.8 per cent in 1929 to 60.4 per cent in 1968. Granovetter (1984) noted that the proportion of persons working in establishments of fewer than 20 persons in manufacturing declined from 14.4 per cent in 1909 to 6.5 per cent in 1977, while by 1977 about 75 per cent of the workforce in manufacturing were employed in establishments with more than 100 employees. At the same time, Granovetter has noted that employment in manufacturing as a percentage of the total economy has declined, and that retail, wholesale, and service establishments are on the whole smaller on average. Of course, public sector employment has increased, and most public organizations are both large and bureaucratic. Although many firms have more than one establishment, it is the case that probably one-half of the workforce is employed in firms with fewer than 100 employees.

It is clear that the growth of the large corporation is primarily a phenomenon of the twentieth century. The size of the largest corporations has increased much more rapidly than the size of the workforce, and, consequently, more of the assets and more employment are now lodged in truly giant organizations than in the past. As Williamson (1975) has noted, transactions can be organized by market mechanisms or by hierarchy – organizations. Why there is increasing reliance on organizational rather than market forms of control, and why, indeed, the size distribution of various industries and sectors looks the way it does are both important issues, but well beyond the scope of this chapter. What is important is that large organizations are an increasingly important part of the social landscape, but that there are a large number of smaller organizations as well that are significant in accounting for the growth in employment.

For our purposes, however, it really does not matter how many of the workforce are employed in organizations of one size class or another. What is important is that a highly differentiated size distribution of organizations has emerged, and where one is located in this distribution is consequential for one's status as well as material well-being. Stinchcombe (1965: 169) has argued, "Organizations as well as individuals have ranks, and these ranks are defended with substantial resources." Organizations differ in terms of their prestige and reputations. *Dun's Review* and now *Fortune* both publish rankings of the best managed firms. Clearly, one's status as an employee and particularly as a manager is enhanced by being associated with a firm known for the quality of its management and performance. Aldrich and Weiss (1981), examining income for a sample of small business owners, found that workforce size is a powerful predictor of income. The literature on managerial compensation (e.g. McEachern, 1975) has considered whether size or performance was a more important determinant of the salaries of top managers, but in no case is the assertion made that size is unimportant in affecting salary. It is clear that the correlation between organizational size and salary is less in the US than in Japan (Clark, 1979), where the relationship is very, very strong. Nevertheless, it is fair to state that one's prestige and income are both importantly determined by (a) the organization in which one works, and its size, reputation, performance, and prestige, and (b) one's position in that organization. Thus, to understand inequality and stratification, one must understand the processes by which people are sorted in and by organizations (Pfeffer, 1977; Baron, 1984; Granovetter, 1981). By the same token, holding organizational position constant, it is better, in terms of both money and prestige, to be associated with a larger than a smaller organization, and one that is more successful. Thus, one's position in society is, in large measure, a consequence of one's position in the society of organizations.

What this means is that people have power because of their organizational position. When John McArthur was appointed Dean of the Harvard Business School, he received numerous offers to join boards of directors, something experienced to a lesser degree by deans of other major business schools. One could argue that these offers of directorships reflected his general business wisdom, skill, and intelligence, rather than his organizational position. This argument, however, is inconsistent with the discontinuity in which such offers accrued – much more rapidly after the position was assumed than before. Certainly assuming that position did not instantaneously increase his wisdom, skill, and business acumen. A somewhat more plausible argument is that the position signaled (Spence, 1974) to the world that this individual possessed certain skills and abilities. Although this signaling or visibility function is consequential, it seems fair to state that there are many positions in organizations that convey power just because of occupying the position, and this power is translated into power in an intercorporate or interorganizational network. At that point, it seems reasonable to assert that the interorganizational power is a property of the position and the organization, not of the particular individual who happens to occupy the position at that moment.

To have power because of one's organizational position ties one psychologically as well as materially to that organization. One's prestige and income are affected by the success of the organization and one's ability to maintain one's position in it. Thus, we would expect individuals to be interested in furthering the interests of their organizations.

And organizations clearly do have interests in a variety of public policy as well as more narrowly defined, economic issues. The growth of political action committees (PACs), the opening of Washington offices by numerous major corporations, and the extensive growth in the Washington legal practice associated loosely with lobbying and representation activities all provide evidence that organizations both recognize political interests and are willing to devote some consequential resources to pursuing those interests. As Epstein (1969) noted: "American business corporations have been, *are*, and, in the foreseeable future, will undoubtedly continue to be involved in the political process. This involvement results from the corporate presence in a pluralistic democracy in which diverse social interests seek to enhance their economic positions *vis-à-vis* each other" (p. 6). What this means is that in this organizational society, organizations, including business corporations, are distinct entities active and involved in the political and public policy formulation process. Organizations have definable interests and act to pursue them.

The primacy of organizational interests

Individuals and families have interests, too, and there may be interests shared among members of a social class. Thus, it is useful to consider some of the ways in which organizational interests come to be preeminent. This argument is not meant to imply that organizational perspectives are always prepotent, and that individuals or other groups never act in ways contrary to organizational concerns, but rather, for the most part, one can reasonably argue that an organizational perspective on problems, issues, and decisions will tend to prevail. Empirically, there is almost no research which directly addresses the fundamental issue – is there evidence which suggests that individual, familial, or class interests rather than organizational concerns explain behavior and, particularly, intercorporate or interorganizational behavior? One way of examining this issue, albeit somewhat indirectly, would be to see whether intercorporate activity – such as mergers, joint ventures, or the structuring of boards of directors – differed depending on the ownership structure of the firm. A second line of inquiry would involve finding instances in which family or class interests could be identified as separate from organizational interests, and tracing which set of perspectives seemed to account for organizational actions. In the absence of direct evidence, indirect evidence and argument are all that can be offered at present.

The issue of organizational versus class or family interests has at times been raised under the separation of ownership and control question. Berle and Means (1932) were among the first to argue that with the dispersion of stock ownership among numerous small holders, a small group of self-perpetuating managers assumed power. Owner capitalism was replaced, they asserted, by managerial capitalism, and the issue became what goals these managers would pursue. The fact of the separation of ownership from control in the large corporation is itself a finding which is not generally agreed upon. Zeitlin (1974) has reviewed the evidence mustered by both sides on whether ownership is increasingly separated from control. The importance of this controversy, according to Zeitlin (1974: 1075), is because "a class theory of contemporary industrial society, based on the relationship between the owners of capital and formally free wage workers, 'loses its analytical value as soon as legal ownership and factual control are separated'" (Dahrendorf, 1959: 136).

As Zeitlin has noted, there are tremendous conceptual and empirical problems involved in resolving the ownership/control issue, including how large a proportion of stock is necessary to exercise effective control and whether such stock ownership, if dispersed among members of a family, still constitutes a controlling interest.[2] The issue of the separation of ownership versus control, however, is not really the relevant concern. The fact of the distribution of ownership comes to be important only if ownership structure makes a difference in the operation of the enterprise. Unless nonowning managers behave differently from owners, then whether or not the firm is owner-controlled or manager-controlled is empirically irrelevant.

One reason why managers may behave the same as owners is the structure of managerial compensation. Principals (owners) have incentives to structure compensation systems so that agents (managers) will act according to the wishes and interests of the principals. Two ways of doing this are by tying compensation levels directly to goals of interest to the owners – e.g. by having compensation based on profits and by building into compensation performance bonuses payable only if firm performance achieves some certain level – and by providing managers with a significant portion of their compensation in the form of stock options, so that their ownership income is itself significant enough to produce a correspondence of goals. On the second point, Lewellen (1968, 1971, 1972) examined compensation first for the period 1940–63 and subsequently extended the study to include the 1964–69 period (after a change in the tax laws that made stock options less attractive). He computed the ratio of stock-related income (capital gains and dividends) to the salary and bonus portion of managerial compensation. This ratio went from 1.0 in the early 1940s to 6.5 in the early 1960s. With extreme values deleted, the ratio increased from 0.8 to 2.7 (1971). Even after the tax law changes of 1964, Lewellen (1972) found that stock options remained an important source of income. The Conference Board (1970) reported that 65 per cent of all manufacturing firms offered executive bonus plans by the late 1960s. McEachern (1975: 25) noted, "it appears that the overall trend in the design of compensation plans is towards aligning the manager's interests with those of the stockholders."

Furthermore, if firms are tightly externally constrained, then their behavior will be determined by these constraints, regardless of the preferences of goals of those running such firms. Thus, under conditions of external constraint, managers and owners will behave similarly. The two most commonly discussed constraints are (1) product market competition and (2) capital markets and the market for corporate control. In a world of stringent product market competition, natural selection pressures will ensure that all firms operate as efficiently as possible and, by implication, similarly. "The forces of competition in the product market will not permit the manager to stray far from the norm of profit maximization if the firm is to remain viable" (McEachern, 1975: 35). Of course, product market competition is limited, particularly in industries dominated by a few large firms.

However, even in the absence of product market competitive pressure, firms may be constrained if there is an efficient market for corporate control. Manne (1965), Meade (1968), and Marris (1967) were among those who argued that if managers did not use the assets of their firms efficiently, the share prices of those firms would be depressed. Thus, an outsider could take over the firm more easily because of the depressed price, run the firm more efficiently, and make a profit as shares rose in value to reflect the more effective operation of the enterprise. Hindley (1970) and Kuehn (1969) both found that firms experiencing contests for control had relatively lower market values compared to net assets when contrasted with firms not subject to such takeover attempts. However, both also observed that there were numerous firms not subjected to contests for control which also had relatively low ratios of market to asset value. Thus, they concluded there was some discipline from the market for corporate control, but that this discipline was not necessarily tightly constraining.

A third set of constraints is composed of precisely those described in resource dependence theory (Pfeffer and Salancik, 1978). These authors list a number of conditions that would affect the extent to which an organization was subject to external control (1978: 44), as well as a number of mechanisms through which organizations attempt to avoid external pressures and demands. If resource dependence theory is correct, then firms subject to the conditions specified should operate more similarly to each other and in accordance with the constraints. However, resource dependence theory makes predictions which are not as simple or unidimensional as those of standard market competition theories. To be constrained is to be subject to complying to the demands of those providing the constraint, but those groups could include government organizations, worker organizations, stockholders, customers, suppliers, or providers of financial capital, among others. The specific behavior that would be observed would be a function of who the constraining set of external organizations were and what their specific demands were for the focal organization. Thus, the resource dependence prediction is that firms equally constrained by the *same* external agents should operate more or less similarly, and, indeed, engage in similar patterns of intercorporate relations. Thus, the distinction between management-controlled and owner-controlled firms may be irrelevant either because compensation structures ensure a correspondence of interests or because external product market, financial market, or interdependence-derived constraints delimit discretion in any event.

There is little empirical evidence yet available to address this issue of whether or not interorganizational relations differ by control type. There is evidence that there is less interlocking in boards of directors of family-controlled corporations (Allen, 1976; Burt, 1980b) than in other corporations. But, there is also evidence that the concentration of control not only in a kinship group but also in a management group is associated with less interlocking as well (Dooley, 1969; Pfeffer, 1972a). Burt (1980b: 559) argues that these two findings taken together support the idea "that interlocking is intended as cooptation." The loss of control from cooptation is greater the more concentrated the control, and there is less need to coopt external support because of the more secure position of those with more corporate control. The fact that there is more interlocking among management-controlled than owner-managed firms thus does not definitively indicate an effect of ownership on intercorporate behavior. What is needed is a comparison of firms with similar degrees of concentration of control to resolve this issue.

The professionalization of management and organizational control

To this point, the argument has been that organizational interests are preeminent because of a system of external constraints imposed on those who run organizations – compensation systems that produce congruity of interests, and product, capital market, and interorganizational constraints. Yet, these are not the only factors acting to produce conformity to organizational interests on the part of managers. The very idea of organization, or at least the rational–legal bureaucratic form of organization, is oriented toward eliminating "all unwanted extraorganizational influences upon the behavior of members. Ideally, members should act only in the organization's interests" (Perrow, 1979: 4). Although, as Perrow noted, the rational–legal bureaucratic form is never completely realized, the extent of organizational control over all members, including owners and managers, is extensive.

Writers in the class perspective have recognized the fact of organizational socialization and control, and have sought to counterpose these forces with arguments about mechanisms that produce class-wide identification and solidarity. Thus, Domhoff (1974, 1975), in particular, has examined clubs and associations as vehicles in which people from different organizations come together to develop a common perspective and frame of reference. There is, of course, nothing in the resource dependence perspective that would argue that persons do not develop networks of association, and indeed, the perspective argues quite forcefully that the development of such interorganizational networks and other linkages is an important activity. The issue becomes whether such associations and linkages develop a perspective that transcends parochial, organizational interests, or rather whether such associations and organizations merely facilitate the advancement of organizational interests in ensuring the supply of resources.

Organizational control is accomplished first through the professionalization of management and the structure of managerial careers in organizations. Managers, be they members of capitalist families or from working-class origins, are increasingly subject to a similar pattern of training and career experiences which will tend to produce similarity in outlook and perspective. In the late 1960s, about 16,000 MBA students were being produced each year and the professional degree in business was still comparatively novel. By the early 1980s, barely fifteen years later, more than 60,000 MBAs were being graduated each year, and increasingly CEOs of major US corporations had MBA degrees. The practice of management was being codified, professionalized and institutionalized. In the process, the managerial point of view was being inculcated in future managers. Corresponding to the increase in degree-granting business education was an explosion in the number and attendance at executive programs and managerial training sponsored by both organizations and universities, as well as trade associations and companies which were in the seminar business. Again, this proliferation of management training tended to ensure that most high-level managers would have exposure to the basic concepts that had evolved in the professionalization of management. Thus, managers regardless of their background are increasingly exposed to a similar set of analytical techniques and, more importantly, socializing experiences conducted in universities and in organizational training programs.

The effect of this increasing professionalization of management is, it appears, to reduce the effects of socioeconomic origins on managerial career attainment. Pfeffer (1977) studied 215 MBA and 156 bachelor's degree graduates from a large, prestigious public school of business administration. He found:

> The effect of social class on current compensation is much larger for those with the bachelor's degree. In the case of those respondents obtaining only the bachelor's and MBA degrees, the coefficient is almost twice the size for the bachelor's degree subsample . . . Graduate education in business, then, is an important avenue for social mobility, particularly for those persons not coming from the highest socioeconomic backgrounds.
> (1977: 703–4)

In an unpublished study using graduates from the early 1960s from Stanford's business school, Pfeffer found no significant effect at all of socioeconomic origins on subsequent career attainment. Professional schools, and certainly business schools, are powerful socializing influences (Schein, 1968). Student values and attitudes change during the course of study, and the net result is that those exposed to professional business education emerge more similar and with diminished effects of background.

The socialization accomplished in school and training programs pales in significance compared to the socialization which occurs on the job. Kotter (1982), in a detailed case study of 15 general managers, concluded that the idea that managers were generalists who could manage anything was not true. General managers required a lot of detailed knowledge of both the industry in which they worked and the firm, including relationships with enough people inside and outside the organization to get things done. Thus, they tended to rise within the industry and within the company:

> Once settled in, they stayed put. On the average, 90 per cent of the time in their careers was spent in the industry in which they were engaged at the time of the study . . . On the average, 81 per cent of the time in their careers was spent with their present employers . . . they specialized in a particular industry and in a particular company.   (1982: 46)

In a study involving the composition of top management groups, Murray (1985) reported that the 1,425 managers he examined in the food and petroleum industries had, on average, twenty years of experience in their firm. To spend the bulk of one's career and a large number of years in a single organization is to learn that place, its mores, values, and decision premises so well that they become internalized. Thus, through long periods of association, the organization's standard operating practices and procedures become taken for granted, accepted, and internalized.

This socialization is facilitated by the system of bureaucratic control which has emerged in the large US corporation: "bureaucratic control is embedded in the social and organizational structure of the firm and is built into job categories, work rules, promotion procedures, discipline, wage scales, definitions of responsibilities, and the like. Bureaucratic control establishes the impersonal force of 'company rules' or 'company policy' as the basis for control" (Edwards, 1979: 131).

Bureaucratic control institutionalizes the control process. Zucker (1977: 726) has argued: "internalization, self-reward, or other intervening processes need not be present to ensure cultural persistence because social knowledge once institutionalized exists as a fact, as part of objective reality, and can be transmitted directly on that basis." In an experiment on the transmission, maintenance, and resistance to attack of a microculture, Zucker observed that giving subjects the induction that they were in an organization increased all three effects and, furthermore, giving them a formal position increased the institutionalization of the culture even more. To the extent that controls are institutionalized, they are taken for granted, unobtrusive, and implicit in the definition of organizational reality which comes to be shared. Moreover, this control, particularly at the higher organizational levels, involves the adoption of organizational values and decision premises: "In the lowest-level jobs, employers tend to stress rules orientation most heavily ... At the upper levels, employers appear to reserve rewards for those who have internalized the enterprise's goals" (Edwards, 1979: 151).

The control system and control process is ubiquitous in its effects. Bureaucratic control is exercised on all organizational members, including (and, perhaps, particularly) those at the very highest management levels. Indeed, the higher one goes in an organization, the more pervasive control becomes. March and March (1977: 379) have noted that "In general, social and organizational control systems reduce the variance in controlled characteristics and thereby make differentiation within a controlled group more difficult." In their study of the careers of Wisconsin school superintendents, March and March noted that, in large measure, careers could be modeled as a random process. They concluded:

> most of the time most superintendents are organizationally
> nearly indistinguishable in their behaviors, performances,
> abilities, and values. This is partly a consequence of the filters by
> which they come to the role, partly a consequence of the
> ambiguity of inference in educational settings, partly a
> consequence of the long-run stability of . . . activities and
> organization, partly a consequence of a lifetime spent in
> educational institutions.   (1977: 405–6)

These same factors apply to corporate officers, who are filtered carefully over a long career, who have spent a long time in a specific industry, organization and, often, in a limited number of functions (Kotter, 1982), and who operate in organizations that are often fairly stable in terms of technology, size, market position and, most importantly, cultural and operating premises.

Of course, family members are not going to be subject to the same degree of filtering and screening. If your name is on the company, there are clear advantages in terms of one's career progress. However, there is still some filtering and, more importantly, the family members are exposed to the institutionalized controls and shared definitions and cultures which characterize bureaucracies. They may be less susceptible to the homogenizing influences of career filtering, socialization, and bureaucratic control, but there is still some influence of these effects.

Executives, like other organizational members, occupy roles which have associated with them role expectations and pressures (Gross, Mason, and McEachern, 1958; Kahn *et al.*, 1964). They act on the basis of information that is provided largely by others and which they acquire in informal contacts and meetings (Mintzberg, 1973). They exist in a world of interdependence, complexity, and ambiguity. What this means is that the behavior of those in high-level organizational positions is importantly constrained by the role expectations, informational influence, and socialization experiences they share. And this means that the organization for which they work has probably been largely successful in inculcating its values and decision premises.

Thus, the question "In whose interests do organizational leaders act?" is most likely to be answered, "The organization's interests." Enormous resources are expended ensuring that organizational members act on behalf of the organization. It is likely that these efforts are substantially successful for the reasons enumerated in this section.

Intercorporate relations as products of dependence and constraint

The resource dependence perspective is premised on two themes: that organizations are the primary social actors and that intercorporate relations can be understood as a product of patterns of interorganizational dependence and constraint. Having addressed the first issue – the primacy of organizational interests – it is now time to address the second. The key issue is whether there is a unified set of class interests that is transorganizational, extending across organizations, or whether organizational interests and actions are more fractionated. Given that different organizations sit in different positions in the network of interorganizational exchange, a resource dependence perspective would suggest at least some degree of conflict of interest. On the other hand, the social class perspective suggests a commonality of interests formed by common schooling, membership in social clubs, and sitting on overlapping and interlocking civic as well as corporate boards of directors. Thus, the question becomes "To what extent can intercorporate relations be accounted for by patterns of resource interdependence?" or "To what extent do they reflect class interests and the homogeneity implied by this overarching conception?"

To relate intercorporate relations to patterns of resource dependence, it is first necessary to develop some measures of dependence that can be used, *a priori*, to predict where intercorporate relations are more likely to develop. There is certainly a temptation in this approach, as with many other theories, to infer dependence from the pattern of intercorporate relations that does, in fact, develop. Yet, for the most part, studies in this tradition have avoided this particular pitfall.

Following Hawley (1950), Pfeffer and Salancik (1978) identified two forms of dependence: symbiotic, in which the output of one organization is the input to the other (e.g. banks as suppliers of capital to corporations; manufacturers as suppliers of products to retailers), and commensalistic, in which the organizations compete in the same niche (e.g. manufacturing firms competing for the same markets). The early research took a relatively simple approach to measuring resource dependence. In the case of symbiotic interdependence, the greater the proportion of the transactions between sectors or types of organizations, the greater the dependence was presumed to be. In the case of organizational dependence on banks, measures of the capital structure, such as the proportion of debt, were used to infer variations in dependence. In the case of commensalistic or competitive interdependence, the argument was made that such dependence was greatest and most problematic at intermediate levels of market concentration. When markets were very highly concentrated, the few major competitors could monitor each other's behavior and develop stable conjectural variations, or estimates of what each would do. When there were many competitors, each became a price taker, and since no firm or even set of firms could affect the market, there was a decoupling in the actions of each, so there was no longer direct interdependence. Rather, it was when concentration was intermediate that interdependence was both highest and was most likely to be addressed through forming intercorporate relations.

Since these early studies, progress has been made on measuring dependence by conceptualizing patterns of transactions across economic sectors in network terms and then using the concept of structural autonomy (Burt, 1982) to assess the constraint imposed by these transactions. Burt (1983) has argued that intercorporate relations will be pursued to reduce constraints on profits and, therefore, that understanding the pattern of constraint is very important in predicting patterns of interorganizational relations. Burt (1983) argued that there were two aspects which determined constraint or its converse, autonomy – the relationship among the actors jointly occupying a position in the network, and the relationship between these actors and those in the sectors with which they transacted. Burt (1983: 9) maintained that "profits are obtained by exploiting transactions."

> the establishments in an industry are free to obtain high profits (i.e., enjoy high structural autonomy) to the extent that their pattern of market transactions ensures low competition with one another while simultaneously ensuring high competition among their suppliers and consumers. Their ability to obtain high profits is severely constrained by their market transactions with establishments in a particular other sector to the extent that the bulk of their buying and selling is with establishments in that sector and the establishments in that sector are coordinated as a single corporate hierarchy so as to pursue their own interests collectively.
>
> (Burt, 1983: 13)

It is clear that Burt's definition and network operationalization of structural autonomy are consistent with, though more developed than, the earlier formulation in which dependence was defined as the proportion of transactions with some other entity and the control (or monopolization) that entity possessed (Pfeffer and Salancik, 1978). What Burt's formulation enables one to do is to move from an input–output table for the economy, or from any other pattern of transactions across organizations and sectors, to derive where constraints are likely to be greatest and, therefore, to predict, a priori, where interorganizational relations to manage these constraints are most likely to occur.

The resource dependence approach has been used to examine a number of forms of intercorporate and interorganizational relations. For the most part, the evidence is consistent with the predictions of the theory, though there are obviously issues and problems remaining to be resolved. In reviewing these forms of intercorporate relations, we will again try to contrast the resource dependence approach with the intraclass approach, to the extent that this alternative has been used in the particular subject domain.

Board of director interlocks

The structure of corporate boards and, in particular, the use of interlocks to manage resource dependence has probably been the most empirically examined form of intercorporate relation. Pfeffer (1972a: 222) argued: "business organizations (and other organizations) use their boards of directors as vehicles through which they coopt, or partially absorb, important external organizations with which they are interdependent." In a random sample of 80 large corporations, Pfeffer (1972a) found that the proportion of inside directors was negatively related to both national and local regulation and the debt/equity ratio, while the percentage of board members from financial institutions was positively correlated with the debt/equity ratio. Also, the percentage of attorneys on the board was positively related to the debt/equity ratio and to the corporation being regulated at a national level. In a subsequent study of hospital boards of directors, Pfeffer (1973) used questionnaire data from the chief hospital administrator to examine the function of the board as well as its composition in terms of its context. He found that the function the board was expected to serve was to be partly explained by its ownership and sources of funding and, in turn, the dimensions of board size and composition could be explained by the function the board was expected to serve as well as its social context. Thus, for example, "the proportion of directors from financial organizations was . . . directly correlated with the size of the budget of the hospital . . . the proportion of the capital budget obtained from private donations . . . and inversely related to choosing board members for regional or subgroup representation" (Pfeffer, 1973: 359). In a study of the board of director composition of 96 electric utilities, Pfeffer (1974) found that the proportion of persons from manufacturing organizations was positively related to the proportion of persons in the state employed in manufacturing and the importance of sales to industrial customers, with the converse being true for the proportion of directors with agricultural affiliations. Thus, with respect to the management of symbiotic interdependence, Pfeffer reported a consistent set of results indicating that persons needed to manage such interdependence would be more likely to be found on boards of organizations which faced relatively more significant interdependence.

Pfeffer and Salancik (1978) also examined the use of board of director interlocks to reduce competitive uncertainty. They found that "the amount of competitor interlocking is positively related to the level of concentration and negatively related to the difference in concentration from an intermediate level" (1978: 166). Recall that commensalistic interdependence was argued to be highest at intermediate levels of concentration, so that one would expect the most horizontal interlocking under that condition.

The results of these original studies have not always been replicated in subsequent analyses. Allen (1974) did not find a relationship between capital structure and the degree of financial interlocking, nor did Pennings (1980). Pennings also failed to find a relationship between the difference in industrial concentration from a median value and the extent of horizontal interlocking, though he did find a moderate positive association between concentration level and interlocking. Burt (1980b) examined three forms of cooptive relations – ownership, direct interlocking, and indirect interlocking – through financial institutions. He found that there was no tendency for capital-intensive firms to directly interlock with financial institutions. However, there was a tendency for capital-intensive firms to own finance establishments. Thus, Burt (1980b: 577) concluded:

> As explanation of the observed tendency for capital-intensive firms not to extensively interlock with financial institutions, then, these data suggest that such firms have no special need for interlocks with financial institutions. They have already extended their cooptive corporate actor networks to the finance sector by directly owning establishments there.

Burt (1983; Burt, Christman, and Kilburn, 1980) reported that the pattern of directorship ties followed patterns of market constraint as defined by his network measure:

> the absence of directorate ties was contingent on market constraint . . . Where a sector had no effect on profits in a four-digit industry, the simultaneous absence of ownership ties, direct interlock ties, and indirect financial interlock ties occurred five times as often as would be expected . . . to occur in the economy generally . . . the quantitative frequency with which establishments in industry and sector were connected by

> directorate ties is a function of the severity of the market
> constraint posed for industry profits . . . Directorate ties were
> most frequent in industries where control over industry prices
> would have been most uncertain (i.e., in moderately competitive
> industries).   (1983: 167–8)

Burt also reported that there was some association between successful
cooptation of market constraints and organizational profitability, an association observed by Pfeffer (1972a) as well.

Since Burt's results generally paralleled the earlier findings of Pfeffer, using
a much more sophisticated methodology and conceptualization of interlock
ties, one might conclude that there is evidence consistent with the resource
dependence view of intercorporate relations. However, two qualifications
need to be made explicit. First, as Burt (1983) has noted, there was variation in
the pattern of directorship ties that could not be accounted for by market
constraint, and Pfeffer's analyses also indicated a reasonable amount of
unexplained variance. Thus, it seems fair to argue that resource
interdependencies and market constraints are predictors of directorship
patterns and practices, but are not the only determinant.

Second, Koenig, Gogel, and Sonquist (1979) and Palmer (1983) found that
most accidentally broken interlock ties were not reconstituted. Koenig,
Gogel, and Sonquist observed a reconstitution rate of only 6 per cent for single
interlock ties, and Palmer argued that only about 15 per cent of the ties in his
data could be construed as vehicles for coordination. Thus, since so few ties
are reconstituted when accidentally broken, the argument is made that
interfirm coordination could not be a major purpose of director interlocking.
However, resource interdependence exists and is defined primarily in terms of
intersectoral, rather than interfirm, transactions. Many resources, such as
capital, are fungible. Thus, if a tie between a firm and a specific bank is
accidentally broken and a new tie is established with another bank, that will
appear as a tie that is not reconstituted in these studies, though from the
perspective of resource dependence theory, the connection to a source of
capital, albeit a different source, has been maintained.[3]

In order for the renewal of director interlocks data to be inconsistent with
resource dependence theory, it would be necessary to observe that
reconstitution was not more likely to the extent that the firms were
interdependent, and that when new ties were established, these relations did
not follow patterns of market constraint or resource interdependence.
Palmer, Friedland, and Singh (1986) do provide some evidence on the first
point, finding that neither competitive constraint nor interindustry (transactions interdependence) constraints account for the reconstitution of broken
ties. Burt's (1980b) analysis of the different forms of cooptive relations, and
the issue of the renewal of ties with other firms but in the same industry, means
that although these results are not consistent with the resource dependence
perspective, they are not necessarily strong evidence against it either.

Mergers and joint ventures

Directors tie firms together, but only loosely, through the flow of information and social obligations established by such ties. More inclusive and resource intensive ways of addressing resource interdependencies are through either the absorption of such interdependence, as in the case of a merger, or through the partial absorption of such interdependence by creating a joint subsidiary or joint venture. As Burt (1983: 70) has noted, "The most direct strategy for eliminating a source of market constraint would be to purchase an establishment within the constraint sector."

In comparison to the large number of studies of interlocking directorates, there have been very few studies of mergers or joint ventures undertaken from the resource dependence perspective. Pfeffer (1972b) studied 854 mergers during the period 1948–69. He found that the proportion of mergers occurring between industries (in terms of either numbers of mergers or assets acquired) was significantly correlated with the proportion of transactions occurring between the two industries. Furthermore, the relationship between merger intensity and transaction intensity held when profitability, concentration, and the number of firms in the industry were statistically controlled. Examining the proportion of mergers occurring within the same industry, Pfeffer (1972b: 389) found that there was a positive association with the proportion of intraindustry transactions and a negative association with the difference in concentration from a median value.

Pfeffer and Salancik (1978: 121–2) extended this analysis to consider whether purchase or sales interdependence was more strongly related to patterns of merger activity on an industry by industry basis. Anticipating to some extent Burt's arguments on constraints, they maintained that in a relatively concentrated environment, in which the firm had market power with respect to customers, mergers would be more important in reducing purchase interdependence, while when market power was lower, mergers would be more focused on reducing sales interdependence. Examining the correlations between the different types of interdependence and patterns of merger activity, they found some evidence consistent with these arguments. Burt (1980a), examining the same merger data using his network model of constraints on profits, also observed a tendency for merger patterns to follow patterns that would be expected if a merger was a cooptive relation used to manage interorganizational constraint arising from transaction patterns. He noted:

> If firms in industry J suffer a constraint to their structural
> autonomy from firms in industry I . . . the odds of a significant
> merger relation . . . more than double . . . If firms in industry J
> suffer negligible constraint from firms in industry I, the odds are
> nine to one there will be no significant merger relations from J to I.
> (1980a: 919–20)

Joint ventures, in which two or more parent organizations pool some portion of their resources to create an additional independent entity, are another form of cooptive interorganizational relation. The organizations that found the joint venture are tied together through the shared resources and, more importantly, through the joint responsibility for managing the joint venture. Pfeffer and Nowak (1976), analyzing Federal Trade Commission data on patterns of joint venture activity, found results which corresponded in important respects to the results just discussed for mergers. They observed a statistically significant association between transactions interdependence among industry sectors and the pattern of joint venturing across sectors. Also, as in the case of mergers, there was a tendency for joint venture activity to be more strongly related to patterns of purchase interdependence in the case of more highly concentrated industries, while joint venturing was more related to sales interdependence when concentration was intermediate in range and competitive uncertainty was greater. And, again as in the case for mergers, forming joint subsidiaries with other firms in the same industry was related to concentration being intermediate. Although the amount of variation explained in joint venturing was somewhat less than that accounted for in the case of mergers, the same pattern of results was observed.

Burt (1983) has indicated that patterns of charitable contributions can be explained by examining the system of network constraints on profits. Burt observed that there was a strong positive correlation between expenditures on advertising and on corporate philanthropy. The incentive to engage in either of these cooptive relations, where the cooptation is presumed to be of the household sector, varies with "the extent that the sector in which the firm operates depends on consumption by people to maintain demand for its product and provides structural autonomy enabling the firm to do something about institutionalizing that demand so as to eliminate a source of uncertainty in its profits" (Burt, 1983: 200).

Burt observed a positive relationship between his measure of incentive to engage in cooptive relations and expenditures on advertising and philanthropy, with a stronger effect observed in the case of advertising. Moreover, this effect was observed even after tax incentive effects were statistically controlled.

The evidence suggests that patterns of interorganizational cooptive relations of numerous forms can be accounted for, at least in part, by the patterns of resource interdependence firms face and the constraints that such interdependencies impose. Moreover, there is evidence that these results hold for hospitals as well as for business firms, and hold when transaction patterns and constraints are conceptualized in more sophisticated, network terms. Thus, there is some evidence that, as expected by resource dependence theory, intercorporate relations do follow patterns of resource interdependence. The failure to consistently find effects on profits or effectiveness of engaging in

cooptive relations has been interpreted by Burt (1983) as indicating that, for
the most part, cooptive relations are maintained where they are needed so that
there is not a great deal of variation in the success of cooptive strategies.

Corporate political activity

Because different firms in different sectors face different patterns of constraint
and resource interdependence, we would expect both different patterns of
cooptive relations to develop as well as to observe differences in point of view
on issues of public policy and politics. It is in this domain in which resource
dependence and the intraclass perspective make different predictions, since
the intraclass perspective hypothesizes a fundamentally unified set of business
interests not tied to patterns of transactions.

Resource dependence research has not yet empirically examined corporate
involvement in politics systematically, though the theoretical mechanisms are
in place to do so. Pfeffer and Salancik (1978: 214) for instance imply that those
organizations that are most dependent on the government for either
purchases, subsidies, or regulation are more likely to make campaign
contributions and be active in the political process. To the extent that
measures of corporate political involvement were available, it would be
possible to examine this form of cooptive activity in a manner analogous to
Burt's examination of advertising and philanthropy as related to dependence
on the household sector. Pfeffer (1972b) did present evidence that indicated
that diversification activity was related to dependence on the government,
with the argument being that governmental interdependence was more
difficult to manage, thereby providing an incentive to diversify activities to
reduce such dependence.

The class position on corporate involvement in politics has argued that: (1)
groups of corporations and families have both the mechanisms and the
capacity to organize themselves into cohesive, unified groups; there are not
divisions within the corporate community, but rather a community of
interests which transcends parochial interests; and (2) there is a social
structure of the business elite which provides evidence of class-wide or
transcendent organization and rationality.

Evidence for the first position comes primarily from Dunn's (1980) analysis
of the family office and its particular manifestation in the case of the
Weyerhaeuser family, and Whitt's (1979, 1980) study of five transportation
issues in Calfornia. Whitt argued that although there may be economic
competition among business units, such competition does not necessarily
become political competition. Whitt examined five transportation-related
referenda in California during the 1962–74 period. He noted: "the pattern of
the contributions is striking. Even though there is good reason to expect that,
for each issue, some companies would favor it and some would oppose it, the

money in every case is virtually *all on one side or the other of the issue*" (1980: 105–6, emphasis in original). Three of the propositions, including two with strong business support, failed to pass. The indication of business organization is the pattern of contributions (with virtually all business financial contributions being on one side or the other of the issue) and the strong correlation between measures of size (stake) and the amount contributed.

Whitt's results are interesting, but they stand in stark contrast to other studies of whether or not competition exists within business over political issues. Bauer, Pool, and Dexter (1968) examined, for instance, American business response to reciprocal trade legislation in the mid-1950s. They did not look at contributions, but rather at letter-writing and other attempts to persuade Congress. They found, first of all, a clear link between attitudes toward foreign trade issues and self-interest: "We found clear linkages between tariff attitudes and self-interest . . . Prospects of loss had more impact than prospects of gain . . . any single criterion of self-interest seemed to have more effect on smaller than on larger firms. The interest structure of larger firms is more complex, and they are therefore less dependent on any single factor" (Bauer, Pool and Dexter, 1968: 152). They further noted that action, such as writing to Congress, was a function of self-interest (1968: 221). The overwhelming conclusion from the Bauer, Pool, and Dexter study is of political competition among industries and among firms of different sizes, with a clear realization of economic self-interest and a willingness to act on this self-interest.

Other anecdotal examples also make the point. At the time of the proposal for deregulation of the airlines, the industry itself was split over the proposal, with some airlines testifying in favor of deregulation and others opposing it. Some steel firms want to merge with other firms and argue that foreign competition provides a justification, while other steel firms are desirous of being protected from such foreign competition. Thus, splits have occurred within the steel industry in terms of action to raise barriers to the importation of foreign steel. Railroads and truckers have been on opposite sides of truck weight-limit regulations (Stigler, 1971), and the history of truck regulation indicates that the railroaders and the truckers have even on occasion shot at each other. Railroads and pipeline companies have been on opposite sides of the issue of whether to build facilities to carry coal slurry (liquefied coal). And the list goes on. Although it is certainly possible to find issues which follow Whitt's model, it is also possible to find a number of issues in which in terms of testimony, letter-writing, and lobbying activity, there is evidence for political as well as economic competition among business interests.

And there is ample evidence of squabbling even within families, let alone within the capitalist class as a whole. Describing the agreement to sell Superior Oil to Mobil, *The Wall Street Journal* (Getschow and Petzinger, 1984: 1) noted: "the sale of Superior, which has more reserves than any other independent in the country, is the result of emotional upheaval more than economic inevitability. Feuding among the founder's heirs, miscues by a desperate management and a legacy of internal conflict all converged to cost the company its long-prized independence." Similar factors contributed to the takeover of Getty Oil by Texaco. Although the acquiring companies' motives were consistent with resource dependence predictions (the acquisition of a critical resource, crude oil supplies, at favorable economic terms), the acquired companies' vulnerability was the result of conflicting interests and struggles among a group that had enough shares to, potentially, ensure continued independence and control if they had been able to act in concert.

Of course, not all class theorists have necessarily asserted a uniformity of business interests in all events (e.g. Roy, 1981). But, if there are cleavages and conflicts within the capitalist class, and even within capitalist families, and at such times such conflicts follow economic dependence contours, then the class perspective looks like resource dependence predictions in slightly different language. The class perspective has been most often articulated and defined in terms of commonality of interests, and it would seem that this is a critical empirical point of distinction with other approaches for explaining inter-organizational behavior.

The examination of the social structure of the business elite has also not really resolved the issue of a community of interests versus the pursuit of more parochially defined economic interests. Both Moore (1979) and Useem (1979) have identified a structure to the elite, pointing to the existence of an inner group with more directorships and more involvement in other institutions of governance, and an outer group with fewer connections which is somewhat more parochial in orientation. Yet Moore's analysis defines network clusters in terms of nominations, not necessarily in terms of similarity of interests of those within the issue group. Useem (1982) seems to suggest that although most businessmen are not members of this national elite, those who are take an overall business perspective on public policy issues and screen out those who would adopt a more parochial approach. Thus, Useem's argument is that it is possible to identify a national business elite which does seem to have common interests that transcend parochial concerns. It should be clear, however, that his data are much more persuasive for the first part (that there is a structure to the national business leadership) than for the second, that those within this elite act as a unit. Moreover, even if the premise were accepted, it provides at least tacit recognition that while there are organizations included in some national network which is undoubtedly influential, many organizations and many individuals are not in this network. Thus, answering the question "Is there a unified business or class interest?" confronts us with the question: "How unified and how inclusive do such networks have to be to provide an affirmative response?"

Conclusion

Research on intercorporate relations has grown tremendously in the last fifteen years. Yet it seems clear that a great deal of work remains to be done. Theorists working from a resource dependence point of view have made some progress in examining a number of forms of intercorporate relations such as mergers, joint ventures, and boards of directors, but other forms, such as political activity, corporate philanthropy, and trade association membership and activities have been largely unexamined thus far. The available evidence seems to suggest that resource dependence notions do explain some, but far from all, of the variation in patterns of intercorporate activity. Furthermore, as Pfeffer and Salancik (1978) have suggested, resource dependence does not require (though it does not exclude) assumptions of conscious, coordinated, foresightful activity on the part of large collections of organizations. Many of the mechanisms discussed by resource dependence theory may occur through the process of executive succession and those factors that affect who is chosen and how frequently succession occurs (Pfeffer and Salancik, 1978: ch. 9).

It is important to recognize, as Bauer, Pool, and Dexter (1968) did some years ago, that in large, complex organizations there will be a multitude of interests and interdependencies present. Thus, to argue that organizations rather than individuals, families, or classes are the important elements for understanding social action is not to imply inevitably or perfectly coordinated action within those organizations. It is possible that organizations have, at once, both narrowly parochial interests and broader interests in economic stability and macroeconomic policies. It is quite possible that the first set of interests is obtained through more proximate forms of cooptive, interorganizational relations (such as mergers, joint ventures, and director interlocking), while the second type of more general interest is obtained through cooperative action in industry or trade associations as well as through political activity. Organizational interests do not necessarily always contradict, or always coincide. To predict the extent of coordinated activity, this approach would argue that examining the patterns and correspondence of resource interdependencies and market constraints would permit beginning to answer the question of under what circumstances coordinated action is likely to occur as opposed to witnessing the pursuit of more parochial objectives.

Finally, there must be within systems of organizations, as there are within organizations, tensions between the socialization and communication practices which tend to produce common views and attitudes and the particular roles, information, and rewards which tend to produce conflict and disagreement. Just as organizations themselves are neither completely political nor completely free of conflict, so intercorporate relations would be expected to observe similar degrees of a mixture between conflict and consensus. What the resource dependence perspective does is focus on both the power-dependent basis of conflict and action and help diagnose both the content of such action and the conditions under which it is likely to occur.

NOTES

The comments of Donald Palmer on an earlier version of this chapter are gratefully acknowledged.

1 Since this chapter deals with intercorporate relations, or relations among organizations, the issue of predictions of the class perspective and the resource dependence perspective on behaviors within organizations, such as the design of structures or the location of production facilities, is not considered in any depth. Such issues would be the subject for another chapter on the prediction of the internal structuring and behavior of organizations.
2 For those who believe that family members always act in concert in some common interest, the recent conflicts at Superior Oil (Keck family) and Getty Oil (Getty family), which resulted in these firms being subject to takeovers by other concerns, offer dramatic counter examples.
3 See Stearns and Mizruchi (1986) for a treatment of this issue.

REFERENCES

Aldrich, Howard E., and Jeffrey Pfeffer, 1976. "Environments of organizations." In Alex Inkeles, James Coleman, and Neil Smelser (eds.), *Annual Review of Sociology*, 2: 79–105. Palo Alto, Calif.: Annual Reviews

Aldrich, Howard E. and Jane Weiss, 1981. "Differentiation within the United States capitalist class: workforce size and income differences." *American Sociological Review*, 46: 279–90

Allen, Michael P., 1974. "The structure of interorganizational elite cooptation: interlocking corporate directorates." *American Sociological Review*, 39: 393–406
  1976. "Management control in the large corporation: comment on Zeitlin." *American Journal of Sociology*, 81: 885–94

Baron, James N., 1984. "Organizational perspectives on stratification." In Ralph Turner (ed.), *Annual Review of Sociology*, 10: 37–69. Palo Alto, Calif.: Annual Reviews

Bauer, Raymond A., Ithiel de Sola Pool, and Lewis Anthony Dexter, 1968. *American Business and Public Policy: The Politics of Foreign Trade*. New York: Atherton Press

Berle, Adolph, Jr., and Gardiner C. Means, 1932. *The Modern Corporation and Private Property*. New York: Macmillan

Blair, John M., 1972. *Economic Concentration: Structure, Behavior, and Public Policy*. New York: Harcourt, Brace, Jovanovich

Bourgeois, L. J., 1984. "Strategic management and determinism." *Academy of Management Review*, 9: 586–96

Burt, Ronald S., 1980a. "Autonomy in a social topology." *American Journal of Sociology*, 85: 892–925

1980b. "Cooptive corporate actor networks: a reconsideration of interlocking directorates involving American manufacturing." *Administrative Science Quarterly*, 25: 557–82

1982. *Toward a Structural Theory of Action: Network Models of Social Structure, Perception, and Action*. New York: Academic Press

1983. *Corporate Profits and Cooptation: Networks of Market Constraints and Directorate Ties in the American Economy*. New York: Academic Press

Burt, Ronald S., Kenneth P. Christman, and Harold C. Kilburn, Jr., 1980. "Testing a structural theory of corporate cooptation: interorganizational directorate ties as a strategy for avoiding market constraints on profits." *American Sociological Review*, 45: 821–41

Clark, Rodney, 1979. *The Japanese Company*. New Haven, Conn.: Yale University Press

Coleman, James S., 1974. *Power and the Structure of Society*. New York: Norton

The Conference Board, 1970. *Top Executive Compensation*. New York: The Conference Board

Dahrendorf, Ralf, 1959. *Class and Class Conflict in Industrial Society*. Stanford University Press

Domhoff, G. William, 1974. *The Bohemian Grove and Other Retreats: A Study in Ruling Class Cohesiveness*. New York: Harper and Row

1975. "Social clubs, policy-planning groups, and corporations: a network study of ruling-class cohesiveness." *Insurgent Sociologist*, 5: 173–84

Dooley, Peter C., 1969. "The interlocking directorate." *American Economic Review*, 59: 314–23

Dunn, Marvin G., 1980. "The family office: coordinating mechanism of the ruling class." In G. William Domhoff (ed.), *Power Structure Research*. Beverly Hills, Calif.: Sage, pp. 17–45

Edwards, Richard C., 1979. *Contested Terrain: The Transformation of the Workplace in the Twentieth Century*. New York: Basic Books

Epstein, Edwin M., 1969. *The Corporation in American Politics*. Englewood Cliffs, NJ: Prentice-Hall

Friedland, Roger, and Donald Palmer, 1983. "The geographic structure of the industrial corporation." Paper presented at the Annual Meeting of the American Sociological Association, Detroit

Getschow, George, and Thomas Petzinger, Jr., 1984. "Keck family's feud, more than economics, sealed Superior's fate." *Wall Street Journal*, March 13: 1, 6

Glasberg, Davita Silfen, and Michael Schwartz, 1983. "Ownership and control of corporations." In Ralph H. Turner (ed.), *Annual Review of Sociology*, 9: 311–32. Palo Alto, Calif.: Annual Reviews

Granovetter, Mark, 1981. "Toward a sociological theory of income differences." In Ivar Berg (ed.), *Sociological Perspectives on Labor Markets*. New York: Academic Press, pp. 11–47

1984. "Small is bountiful: labor markets and establishment size." *American Sociological Review*, 49: 323–34

1985. "Economic action and social structure: the problem of embeddedness." *American Journal of Sociology*, 91: 481–510

Gross, N., W. S. Mason, and A. W. McEachern, 1958. *Explorations in Role Analysis: Studies of the School Superintendency Role*. New York: John Wiley

Hawley, Amos H., 1950. *Human Ecology: A Theory of Community Structure.* New York: Ronald Press

Hindley, Brian, 1970. "Separation of ownership and control in the modern corporation." *Journal of Law and Economics,* 13: 185–221

Kahn, Robert L., Donald M. Wolfe, Robert P. Quinn, and J. Diedrick Snoek, 1964. *Organizational Stress: Studies in Role Conflict and Ambiguity.* New York: John Wiley

Katz, Daniel, and Robert L. Kahn, 1966. *The Social Psychology of Organizations.* New York: John Wiley

Koenig, Thomas, Robert Gogel, and John Sonquist, 1979. "Models of the significance of interlocking corporate directorates." *American Journal of Economics and Sociology,* 38: 173–85

Kotter, John, 1982. *The General Managers.* New York: Free Press

Kuehn, D. A., 1969. "Stock market valuations and acquisitions: an empirical test of a component of managerial utility." *Journal of Industrial Economics,* 17: 132–44

Lewellen, Wilbur G., 1968. *Executive Compensation in Large Industrial Corporations.* New York: National Bureau of Economic Research
   1971. *The Ownership Income of Management.* New York: National Bureau of Economic Research
   1972. "Managerial pay and the tax changes of the 1960's." *National Tax Journal,* 25: 111–31

Manne, Henry G., 1965. "Mergers and the market for corporate control." *Journal of Political Economy,* 73: 110–20

March, James C., and James G. March, 1977. "Almost random careers: the Wisconsin school superintendency, 1940–1972." *Administrative Science Quarterly,* 22: 377–409

March, James G., and Johan P. Olsen, 1984. "The new institutionalism: organizational factors in political life." *American Political Science Review,* 78: 734–49

Marris, Robin, 1967. *The Economic Theory of "Managerial" Capitalism.* London: Macmillan

McEachern, William A., 1975. *Managerial Control and Performance.* Lexington, Mass.: D. C. Heath

Meade, J. E., 1968. "Is 'The New Industrial State' Inevitable?" *Economic Journal,* 78: 372–92

Miles, Raymond E., and Charles C. Snow, 1978. *Organization Strategy, Structure, and Process.* New York: McGraw-Hill

Mintzberg, Henry, 1973. *The Nature of Managerial Work.* New York: Harper and Row
   1983. *Power in and Around Organizations.* Englewood Clifts, NJ: Prentice-Hall

Mizruchi, Mark S., 1983. "An interorganizational theory of social class: a synthesis of the resource dependence and social class models of intercorporate relations." Paper presented at the Annual Meeting of the American Sociological Association, Detroit

Moore, Gwen, 1979. "The structure of a national elite network." *American Sociological Review,* 44: 673–92

54   *Jeffrey Pfeffer*

Murray, Alan I., 1985. "Top management group composition and firm performance." Unpublished Ph.D dissertation, Stanford University, Graduate School of Business, Palo Alto

Nisbett, Richard, and Lee Ross, 1980. *Human Inference: Strategies and Shortcomings of Social Judgment.* Englewood Cliffs, NJ: Prentice-Hall

Palmer, Donald, 1983. "Broken ties: interlocking directorates and intercorporate coordination." *Administrative Science Quarterly,* 28: 40–55

Palmer, Donald, Roger Friedland, P. Devereaux Jennings, and Melanie Powers, 1984. "Testing a political economy model of divisionalization in large US corporations." Paper presented at the Academy of Management Meetings, Boston

Palmer, Donald, Roger Friedland, and Jitendra V. Singh, 1986. "The ties that bind: organizational and class bases of stability in a corporate interlock network." *American Sociological Review,* 51: 781–96

Pennings, Johannes M., 1980. *Interlocking Directorates.* San Francisco: Jossey-Bass

Perrow, Charles, 1979. *Complex Organizations: A Critical Essay,* 2nd edn. Glenview, Ill.: Scott, Foresman

Peters, Thomas J., and Robert H. Waterman, Jr., 1982. *In Search of Excellence,* New York: Harper and Row

Pfeffer, Jeffrey, 1972a. "Size and composition of corporate boards of directors: the organization and its environment." *Administrative Science Quarterly,* 17: 218–28

  1972b. "Merger as a response to organizational interdependence." *Administrative Science Quarterly,* 17: 382–94

  1973. "Size, composition and function of hospital boards of directors: a study of organization–environment linkage." *Administrative Science Quarterly,* 18: 349–64

  1974. "Cooptation and the composition of electrical utility boards of directors." *Pacific Sociological Review,* 17: 333–63

  1977. "Towards an examination of stratification in organizations." *Administrative Science Quarterly,* 22: 553–67

  1981. *Power in Organizations.* Marshfield, Mass.: Pitman

Pfeffer, Jeffrey, and Phillip Nowak, 1976. "Joint ventures and interorganizational interdependence." *Administrative Science Quarterly,* 21: 398–418

Pfeffer, Jeffrey, and Gerald R. Salancik, 1978. *The External Control of Organizations: A Resource Dependence Perspective.* New York: Harper and Row

Presthus, Robert, 1978. *The Organizational Society,* rev. ed. New York: St. Martin's Press

Randall, R., 1973. "Influence of environmental support and policy space on organizational behavior." *Administrative Science Quarterly,* 18: 236–47

Roy, William G., 1981. "The vesting of interests and the determinants of political power: size, network structure, and mobilization of American industries, 1886–1905." *American Journal of Sociology,* 86: 1287–310

Schein, Edgar H., 1968. "Organizational socialization and the profession of management." *Industrial Management Review,* 9: 1–16

Spence, A. Michael, 1974. *Market Signaling*. Cambridge, Mass.: Harvard
    University Press
Stearns, Linda Brewster, and Mark S. Mizruchi, 1986. "Broken-tie reconstitution
    and the functions of interorganizational interlocks: a reexamination."
    Administrative Science Quarterly, 31: 522–38
Stigler, George J., 1971. "The theory of economic regulation." *Bell Journal of
    Economics and Management Science*, 2: 3–21
Stinchombe, Arthur L., 1965. "Social structure and organizations." In James G.
    March (ed.), *Handbook of Organizations*. Chicago: Rand McNally, pp.
    142–93
Thompson, James D., 1967. *Organizations in Action*. New York: McGraw-Hill
Useem, Michael, 1979. "The social organization of the American business elite
    and participation of corporation directors in the governance of American
    institutions." *American Sociological Review*, 44: 553–72
    1982. "Classwide rationality in the politics of managers and directors of large
    corporations in the United States and Great Britain." *Administrative Science
    Quarterly*, 27: 199–226
Whitt, J. Allen, 1979. "Toward a class-dialectical model of power: an empirical
    assessment of three competing models of political power." *American
    Sociological Review*, 44: 81–100
    1980. "Can capitalists organize themselves?" In G. William Domhoff (ed.),
    Power Structure Research. Beverly Hills, Calif.: Sage, pp. 97–113
Williamson, Oliver E., 1975. *Markets and Hierarchies: Analysis and Antitrust
    Implications*. New York: Free Press
Yuchtman, E., and S. E. Seashore, 1967. "A system resource approach to
    organizational effectiveness." *American Sociological Review*, 32: 891–903
Zeitlin, Maurice, 1974. "Corporate ownership and control: the large corporation
    and the capitalist class." *American Journal of Sociology*, 79: 1073–119
Zucker, Lynne G., 1977. "The role of institutionalization in cultural persistence."
    American Sociological Review, 42: 726–43
    1983. "Organizations as institutions." In Samuel B. Bacharach (ed.), *Research
    in the Sociology of Organizations*. Greenwich, Conn.: JAI Press, Vol. 2, pp.
    1–47

2

Finance capital and the internal structure of the capitalist class in the United States

Michael Soref and Maurice Zeitlin

A handful of immense banks, concentrating within their coffers the bulk of the assets and deposits of the entire banking system and providing much of the loans and credits for industry, are the decisive units in the circulation of capital in contemporary capitalist economies.[1] With this consolidation of oligopoly in banking itself, the amount of loans and credits granted by the leading banks actually determines the amount of money deposited with them, because what they lend flows back to them as deposits. They can, within fairly wide limits, "vary at will the supply of credit or short-term capital available at any given time" and thus determine the price of (or rate of interest on) loan capital.[2] As C. Wright Mills (1942: 46) aptly remarks, "not violence, but credit may be a rather ultimate seat of control within modern societies."

The leading banks are also structurally interconnected – through long-standing business associations, financial arrangements, interlocking directorates, and overlapping and interpenetrating ownership – with the top nonfinancial corporations. Thus, if our originating question is how this affects the dynamics of contemporary capitalism, this article focusses, in particular, on the inner structure of the capitalist class itself, and involves the following questions: Do the interconnections between the major financial institutions (banks, insurance companies, and other financial firms) and large industrial corporations constitute institutional means of intraclass power? Do the men who sit simultaneously in the managements of both of them play a distinctive role in the corporate world? Are they, in a phrase, "a special social type, in contrast to the other officers and directors of the largest corporations and banks?" (See Zeitlin, 1974: 1103, 1110; also 1976: 900–1.)

The contending theories

"Historically," as a US congressional antitrust subcommittee notes, "*interlocking relationships between bank managements and the directors of other corporations have been of special significance* [because of the potential] . . . misuse of the power to control money and credit from financial institutions" (see US Congress, 1965: 164; also Federal Trade Commission, 1951; US Congress, 1978.) In recent years, several sociologists and economists have conducted informative but essentially descriptive studies and "network analyses" of interlocking directorates.[3] But the critical theoretical issues and empirical questions in this article have been all but entirely neglected, primarily, perhaps, because they cannot be posed within the regnant academic paradigms in the social sciences.[4]

Remarkably, despite its explicit focus on the impact of the large corporation on contemporary society, even managerial theory simply discounts, when it does not ignore, the major bank as a decisive locus of economic power, and its authors (e.g. Galbraith, 1967: 68) dismiss the "bankers" themselves with witticisms concerning their ostensible "dwindling social magnetism." For although banking functions persist, these functions are supposedly no longer vital in "the new industrial state" or "post-capitalist society." Rather, in managerial theory, because the large corporation exists in a state of splendid – and self-perpetuating – autonomy, generating earnings "wholly under its own control," and running "on its own economic steam," it no longer depends on "financial capital."[5] "Management thus becomes," as Berle and Means (1967: xiv–xv) put it, "in an odd sort of way, the uncontrolled administrator of a kind of trust, having the privilege of perpetual accumulation." Freed from the dictates of capital and the control of its major shareowners, and thereby of the imperatives of profit maximization, the large corporation is thus, in managerial doctrine, the embodiment of economic rationality. The large corporation's management (or "technostructure"), deriving its "decisive power" not from capital but from *organization,* is said to administer social investment much as if it were a "purely neutral technocracy," allocating "the income stream on the basis of public policy rather than private cupidity."[6]

Sociological analyses of the large corporation, whether or not they explicitly accept such managerialist notions, tend to have the same implicit premises. In the "interorganizational paradigm," for instance, the large corporation is also conceptualized essentially as merely one sort of complex organization operating "within a larger environment comprised of other organizations" (see Allen, 1974: 393, 403; 1976). In this paradigm, too, the imperatives of capital accumulation and the private ownership of capital are not considered of decisive relevance. Instead, what impels the interaction of the large corporations is an "interorganizational" dynamic based on their efforts to "avert threats to their stability or existence" as autonomous organizations and to anticipate and control "environmental contingencies" (see Thompson, 1967: 35; Allen, 1974: 393; also Pennings, 1980: 7–10). It is also this same dynamic that accounts, in particular, for the pattern of interlocking among the large corporations and major banks.[7]

Thus, although managerialism dismisses or ignores interlocking directorates, and the men who fill them, both among large corporations and between them and the major banks,[8] while "interorganizational theory" actually *focuses* on these interlocks, the paradox is that they share the identical paradigmatic presupposition: the major banks and large corporations are assumed to be, as Ratcliff observes (1980b: 557), more or less "distinct islands of self-interest." Neither theory attaches any significance to the so-called "outside interests" (let alone controlling interests) of ownership, or considers the possibility that the so-called "outside directors" who interlock the big banks and top industrial corporations are bearers of decisive *extra-organizational powers.* Both theories assume that the management of the large corporation or leading bank is, in Galbraith's phrase (1967: 88, 409), "invulnerable to external authority," and "selects itself and its successors as an autonomous and self-perpetuating oligarchy." For both theories, the basic unit of analysis is the "firm," i.e. the corporate *organization* itself, as it interacts with other organizations to maximize its security and minimize its uncertainty.

In our conception of class theory, however, the top nonfinancial corporations and leading banks are considered, in Zeitlin's words (1974:1079), "units in a class controlled apparatus of appropriation; and the whole gamut of functionaries and owners of capital participate in varying degrees, and as members of the same social class, in its direction." This means that the relevant analytical unit in an adequate explanation of the significance of the interlocking directorate is not merely the corporation or the bank as an "organization" or even as a "firm," but rather the internal structure of the *class* that owns and controls them both. Our central proposition, then, is that it is not a process of autonomous self-selection or of "interorganizational elite cooptation" that underlies the pattern of interlocking and the selection of the interlocking directors themselves, but rather a process of intraclass integration, coordination, and control.

For, if managerialism poses a false problem and provides a false solution, the ascendancy of the large corporation surely has altered the structure of the capitalist class, to the extent that, within the large corporation itself, the ownership of capital has become partly dissociated from the control of production. "With the dispersion of shares," as Rudolf Hilferding long ago observed (1910: 155–6),

> capitalist property has been converted increasingly into a limited form of property which merely gives its owners simple title to surplus value without in itself permitting them to intervene decisively in the productive process . . . The effective control of production is in the hands of persons who provide only a part of the capital involved. The owners of the means of production no longer exist in isolation, but rather constitute an economic

association [*Gesellschaft*] in which the individual has a right only to an aliquot share [i.e. proportional to the stockholding] of the profits.

The critical theoretical issue, then, is how the dissociation of these once unified functions of capital affects the inner structure of the capitalist class. This, in turn, necessitates recognizing and specifying the different locations occupied in the accumulation (and appropriation) process by various types of "owners" and "managers," and analyzing their implications. In fact, the so-called "managers," themselves do not constitute a homogeneous category of functionaries identically situated in the accumulation process or in the capitalist class itself. The crucial empirical question is thus how the various types of higher executives – those leading *functionaries of capital* – are related to the principal *capital-owners* themselves in the actual ensemble of intraclass social relations.

If the large corporation has partly dissociated the functions of capital ownership and corporate control, it has also unified functions of capital that were dissociated before the corporation's ascendancy – functions that used to constitute *"a qualitative division"* both of "the total capital" and of "the entire class of capitalists." As Marx (1967, III: 379, 372–8, italics added) argued a century ago, "interest-bearing capital as such has . . . productive capital for its opposite." the "money-capitalist" confronts the "industrial capitalist . . . as a special kind of capitalist," that is, they confront each other "not just as legally different persons but as *persons playing entirely different roles in the reproduction process.*" In their hands, "the same capital really performs a two-fold and wholly different movement. The one merely loans it, the other employs it productively." The "capitalist working on borrowed capital" ends up with only a "portion of profit," i.e. "profit minus interest." Thus, in Marx's time, as he saw it (1952: 86), "money capitalists" and "industrial capitalists" constituted, as did "merchant capitalists" also, "rival fractions . . . of the appropriating class." They were, in our conceptual terms, separate and opposed "class segments" occupying – despite their common ownership of the means of production – relatively distinct locations in the processes of accumulation and appropriation of capital, and, consequently, possessing inherently contradictory interests.[9]

Under the domain of large corporations and major banks, and the consequent interpenetration of industrial, commercial, and loan capital, however, there emerges a new historical form of capital and, with it, a new coalesced class type: "finance capital" and the "finance capitalist." The big banks and top industrial corporations, as we noted earlier, have both proprietary and organizational interconnections. The big banks are not only major creditors of the top corporations, but also simultaneously own or administer some of their principal shareholdings. And the top corporations (which in the United States are themselves being transformed into "conglomerates" spanning all economic sectors) tend, in turn, to own or control substantial blocks of stock in the leading banks.

Aside, however, from such reciprocal institutional shareholdings and financial connections, the big banks and top nonfinancial corporations also tend to have the very same individuals and families among their principal owners. In the United States, for example, such prominent wealthy families as the Mellons, Rockefellers, Stillmans, Duponts, Fishers, Weyerhausers, Rosenwalds, Motts, Fords, and Hannas have identifiable principal ownership interests in some of the largest industrial corporations *and* leading commercial banks (see Zeitlin, 1974: 1102; Black and Goff, 1969; Domhoff, 1983: 60–3; Dunn, 1979; Knowles, 1973; White, 1978). But, in all likelihood, these wealthy families are merely well-documented instances of the general tendency of the principal capital-owning families to have interests overlapping finance, industry, and commerce. They thus illustrate the critical theoretical question of the extent to which it is at all valid to think of the various firms to which these families are attached as independent "organizations," whatever their formal or legal status. Rather, these firms tend, as Ratcliff perceptively puts it (1980b: 557), to be "interconnected points of decision-making within larger networks of class interests." The big banks, other financial institutions, and top nonfinancial corporations tend, that is, in Zeitlin's words (1976: 901), to be "units in, and instrumentalities of, the whole system of propertied interests controlled by these major capitalist families" and their entire class. (See the fine analysis, using a similar approach to Scotland and England, by Scott, 1979, and Scott and Griff, 1984.)

Under these circumstances, the interlocking directorates tying together the major banks and top nonfinancial corporations take on a crucial political–economic role in integrating the simultaneous and potentially contradictory financial, industrial, and commercial interests of the wealthiest families, whose various investments span these ostensibly separate sectors. Those who sit at the conjoined managerial helms of the big banks or other financial institutions and top industrial corporations as the functionaries of "finance capital" are, to this extent and in this limited sense – by virtue of their simultaneous administration of loan and productive capital – themselves "finance capitalists." In short, we suggest that the interlocking of the leading banks or other financial institutions and top industrial corporations is an organizational expression of the inner transformation of the capitalist class itself. In Zeitlin's words (1974: 1102): "neither 'financiers' extracting interest at the expense of industrial profits nor 'bankers' controlling corporations, but finance capitalists on the boards of the largest banks *and* corporations preside over the banks' investments as creditors *and* shareholders, organizing production, sales, and financing, and appropriating the profits of their integrated activities."

With this coalescence of banking and industrial capital, however, the contradictions between them are not eliminated, nor are the claims of the former to a share of the profits extracted by the latter. Rather, this form, i.e. "finance capital," now contains as "constitutive contradictions" within itself, the contradictory interests once dividing qualitatively different, coexisting segments within the capitalist class. In Hilferding's (1910: 299) ironic imagery: "Industrial capital is the Father that sired commercial and banking capital as its Son, and money as the Holy Spirit. They are three but only one in finance capital" (see also Poulantzas, 1975: 130). Put more mundanely, in the words of a leading econometrician (Kuh, 1963: 16), the "financial policies of industrial enterprises should be meshed with their investment behavior, but exactly how remains an open question."

"Meshing" these potentially contradictory investments, then, is the special double role of the finance capitalist, who, as James O'Connor observes, "combines and synthesizes the motives [and functions] of the merchant, industrialist, and banker."[10] As the representative of the nonfinancial corporation's lenders and bondholders, the finance capitalist must favor higher interest rates, but as the representative of its principal shareowners, he must strive to assure maximum industrial profits. In other words, the coalescence of banking and industrial capital produces a *self-contradictory intraclass location*: thus, the individual higher executives who personify this coalescence must continually try, in practice, to reconcile the irreconcilable – these contradictory interests of loan and productive capital. If this reconciliation can never be assured, interlocking directorates between the leading banks and top nonfinancial corporations are nonetheless the singular "interorganizational means of administration" with which to attempt it.

To the extent that propertied individuals and families have major investments and principal shareholdings both in financial institutions and industrial corporations, they have a special and heavy stake in trying to harmonize their broad policies and reconcile the contending interests involved in them. And to the extent that actual participation in management is necessary (and it may not be) for them to be able actively to shape a business strategy that they think will best accommodate their own specific self-contradictory interests, they should also seek (and be sought) to occupy precisely those directorships that interlock the leading financial and industrial corporations. Faced with the need to coordinate the business strategies of the various business units in which they have substantial interests in order to try to maximise this entire *system's* profits, irrespective of the profits earned by each of its separate financial or industrial units, these men of property may well wish to provide an added measure of assurance that such coordination actually occurs in practice, by sitting personally on the boards of these companies.[11]

For these reasons, our major hypotheses are as follows.

(1) Finance capitalists, defined here in the limited sense as directors who sit simultaneously on the boards of top industrial corporations and major banks or other financial institutions, should tend, by virtue of the greater number of directorships held, to have a more extensive role than other directors in coordinating the policies of the top industrial corporations.

(2) Finance capitalists should also tend, in particular, to have a more extensive role in coordinating the policies of those top industrial corporations that are the dominant and most centrally located ones in the economy.

(3) Finance capitalists should thus also be more likely than other directors to be drawn from the nation's leading propertied families.

Data, concepts, indicators

We analyze these interrelationships based on data gathered on the men occupying the directorships of the top 200 United States industrial corporations of 1964, ranked by sales (on the "*Fortune 500*" 1965 list). Data for 1964 were utilized both because of the comparisons such data allow to the findings of related studies and because several of these studies also provided relevant data to supplement our own analysis. There have been at least nine studies of corporate control of large nonfinancial corporations in the United States, spanning the period from 1959 through 1970. Of these studies, five presented case by case evaluations of the locus of control in specific corporations, and were thus useful secondary sources for our own analyses of corporate control. Two of the latter studies were based on 1964 data and one on 1963 data (see James and Soref, 1981: 5; Soref, 1979: 219–37).

From the top 200 industrials, 40 were selected as "sampling units." The 200 industrials were ranked by the number of their directors, and divided into 20 strata, from each of which two companies were selected, without replacement. Then from these 40 companies 300 directors were selected. The two-stage sampling design introduced the possibility of a bias toward directors of companies with large boards. Thus, the stratified sampling was done to minimize any such bias.

The unweighted sample was a sample of directorships, i.e. of the "offices" or positions, not of directors. A sample of directors would be taken from a list of directors on which every individual appeared only once. In our sample, however, a man who sat on the board of three different top 200 industrials, i.e. who held three directorships, had three times the probability of being selected as a man having only a single directorship on a top 200 industrial. Accordingly, cases were weighted for the quantitive analysis, so that a man having one directorship was assigned a weight of unity, a man with two top 200 directorships was assigned a weight of 0.5, and so on. For most tabulations, the total N is 235 from a sample size of 273. (For details on procedures, see Soref, 1979: 87–94.)

Information on the various directorships occupied was drawn from such standard sources as *Who's Who in America, Who's Who in Commerce and Industry, Poor's Register of Corporations, Executives and Directors, Moody's Manual,* and *Who's Who in Canada.* To qualify as a "finance capitalist" in the present analysis, a director of a top 200 industrial also had to be either a partner of a leading investment bank or a director of one of the top 50 commercial banks, top 50 insurance companies, or of another major financial company: 47 of the 235 directors in the sample were classified as finance capitalists.

The directors who belonged to a leading propertied family were identified. We defined three types of propertied families, two by specific information on their capital ownership *in the 40 industrials analyzed,* whom we call "dominant owners" and "outside owners," and one by information on their "membership" in the national status-community of the very rich, whom we call members of the "establishment." Conceptually, all three types of propertied families belong to the capitalist class, specifically the segment based on the ownership and control of the nation's leading corporations.

The "principal owners" in the present analysis are defined by their personal or family holdings *in the 40 industrials analyzed.* Soref carried out a secondary analysis of the ownership and control of each of these companies as of the mid-1960s, based on information provided on them in several studies (Burch, 1972; Chevalier, 1970; Kotz, 1978; Larner, 1970; Lundberg, 1968; Pederson and Tabb, 1976; Sheehan, 1967; Villarejo 1961/2), as well as in various government publications and periodicals. Soref scrutinized citations concerning his sample companies and all source articles cited by the other authors; he also consulted the periodical files of the North American Congress on Latin America, and we are grateful to NACLA for its kindness in making these accessible. To ascertain the control of several companies, Soref also consulted the *SEC Official Summary,* the *Foundation Directory,* company and family histories, and various biographical reference works.

A "dominant owner" was a director who either personally had a principal holding in or belonged to a family that controlled an industrial corporation in our sample of 40. An "outsider owner" was a director identified as the representative of another company (whether financial or nonfinancial) with a controlling interest in an industrial corporation in our sample of 40, when the locus of control of the controlling company itself was not ascertained.

"Dominant owners" included among our directors, for example, were Samuel Mosher, August A. Busch, Jr., and Thomas Mellon Evans. In 1958, when he was chairman of the board, Mr. Mosher reportedly held 75 per cent of the voting securities of Signal Company. The 1965 proxy gave Mr. Mosher only 11.3 per cent of Signal's stock (*Fortune,* 1958; Chevalier 1970: appendix II). But Burch (1970: 47) found that the Mosher family held at least 39.6 per cent, as of the mid-1960s. Mr. Busch, chairman of the board of Anheuser-Busch, Inc., is the grandson of Adolphus Busch, the brewery's co-founder.

Business Week reported (1968: 104) that the combined Anheuser and Busch family holdings exceeded 40 per cent, and, according to an earlier report in *Time* (1955: 85), Mr. Busch himself held 22 per cent. Among his listed financial directorships were those in General American Life Insurance and First National Bank of St. Louis. Mr. Evans (a Mellon relative) probably personally controlled the Crane Company, with 16.8 per cent of the voting stock and 15.6 per cent of the voting securities, according to the 1965 proxy report. (A member of the original owning family, Emily Crane Chadbourne, also had a substantial Crane holding. Larner, citing the 1964 proxy report, notes that she held 11.1 per cent of Crane's stock, but Mr. Evans was clearly "in charge," according to insiders [e.g. Sheehan, 1967: 182]).

Examples of "outside owners" included among our directors are Plato Malozemoff in Continental Oil, and Arthur K. Walton and Charles M. Odorizzi on the board of Whirlpool. Mr. Malozemoff, president of Newmont Mining, probably represented its 4.15 per cent interest (reported in the 1965 proxy) in Continental Oil. Mr. Walton, a Sears vice-president, represented the Sears group's substantial interests in Whirlpool, which amounted in 1965 to at least 7.5 per cent (held among Allstate, Sears savings and profit-sharing pension fund, the Sears Foundation and Allstate Foundation, according to Moody's). Sears also held 27 per cent of Whirlpool's 4.25 per cent cumulative convertible preferred stock, according to the 1965 proxy report. Mr. Walton had been with Sears since 1931 and represented it in several of its subsidiaries also. Among Mr. Walton's listed financial directorships were the Sears Bank and Trust Company. Mr. Odorizzi, and executive vice-president of RCA, which he joined in 1949, probably represented its substantial interest in Whirlpool. Villarejo (1961/2) found that RCA held 18.65 per cent of Whirlpool's stock but subsequently RCA disposed of a significant portion of this holding; in 1962 it sold about a million of its Whirlpool shares and still held about 165,000 shares, or 3.1 per cent, as of 1965, according to data in the SEC Official Summary. Sears and RCA were not the only elements involved in the control of Whirlpool; other directors in the sample representing substantial ownership interests, but not enough to be classified as "dominant" owners, were a member of a Cleveland financial family (Boynton Murch), and a member of one of Whirlpool's founding families (Steve Upton).

Now, of course, many of the directors of the 40 industrials in our sample who were not identified as dominant or outside owners *of these 40 industrials* probably belonged to capital-owning families that had principal ownership interests elsewhere. That some directors were from prominent owning families was immediately obvious to a relatively informed observer, among them, for example, Thomas Watson, Jr., Gilbert W. Humphrey, and Ogden Phipps. Mr. Watson sat on the board of *Time* and Messrs. Humphrey and Phipps on that of Texaco, two of our sample of 40 industrials. The three sons of Thomas Watson, Sr., who presided over IBM's rise, held in the mid-1960s perhaps 6 per cent of the stock of IBM, of which Thomas, Jr., was chairman.

His brothers Arthur and Richard were also in IBM's top management, and the Watsons probably held the company's controlling interests (see Burch, 1970: table 3.1; Rodgers, 1974: 235–46). Mr. Humphrey's father, George M. Humphrey, was the leader of a coalition of four Cleveland families (Hanna, Humphrey, Weir, Love) that, as of the mid-1960s, controlled several major industrial companies, including Chrysler, Consolidation Coal (which merged in 1965 with Continental Oil), National Steel, and M. A. Hanna Co., as well as National City Bank of Cleveland (see Black and Goff, 1969; Burch, 1972; Chevalier, 1970). Mr. Humphrey is also married to a Hanna, Louise Ireland. Ogden Phipps, chairman of Bessemer Securities, is the grandson of Henry Phipps – a partner of Andrew Carnegie and the founder of the family fortune. Bessemer Securities is a "family office" that holds and manages the Phipps stock portfolio, which came to some $550 million in 1967. Other Phipps assets are held by other such family offices (see Mahon, 1978: 4; Dunn, 1979: 9).

Despite the fact that these three directors, i.e. Messrs. Watson, Humphrey, and Phipps, are members of three of the nation's most prominent capitalist families, they were *not* defined here as dominant or outside owners, because they neither held nor represented identifiable principal ownership interests in any of the 40 industrials in our sample. Obviously, then, to the extent that such men of property appeared among the directors of the 40 industrials but were not identified as such by our limited analyses and procedures, the latter underestimate the number of directors who were, in fact, principal owners of capital. It was simply not feasible for us to investigate such other ownership interests systematically; it was already a formidable research task to specify the ownership interests involved in the 40 industrials and the connections of their directors to these interests.

As something of a surrogate for such research, however, we utilized publicly available information that allowed us, we believe, to identify the directors belonging to the integrated core of older, more established families of the capitalist class, whose diversified holdings probably span finance and industry. For want of a better term, we call them, as we mentioned earlier, members of the "establishment." The three criteria used to identify a director as a member of the "establishment" were: (a) listing in the *Social Register*, (b) attendance at one of a few exclusive preparatory schools, or (c) membership in one of a few exclusive men's clubs. These schools and clubs are considered by G. William Domhoff (1970: 21–4) as usually indicative of "upper class" membership.[12] Using these criteria, Messrs. Watson, Humphrey, and Phipps, as well as Mosher, Busch, and Evans, but not Malozemoff or Odorizzi, qualified as members of the "establishment." All told, 100 of the 235 directors qualified as members of the "establishment," while only 23 qualified as principal (dominant or outside) owners. And, as will be seen in the following analysis, 14 men were both principal owners and members of the establishment.

Using such criteria as attendance at an exclusive school, membership in such a club, or a *Social Register* listing to indicate whether or not a director belonged to an established propertied family obviously may have resulted in the inclusion in the "establishment" of some men whose families, though prominent and enjoying considerable "status," were not among the nation's principal capital-owning families. We may be sure, however, that the vast majority of such families belong to a self-conscious national status group high within the American capitalist class. As Weber (1949: 187–8) long ago pointed out (stimulated in part by his observations during his trip to the United States in 1904), "status groups are normally communities" self-defined by a "social estimation of honor," but, if the relationship between social honor and property varies, and there may even be a tension between their claims, historically property tends to be the basis of such communities of "social honor . . . property as such is not always recognized as a status qualification, but in the long run it is, and with extraordinary regularity." In any case, even when the "pretensions of sheer property" and of social honor may stand opposed to each other, the *institutions* of the establishment, in Baltzell's apt phrase, "carry authority" and serve as gatekeepers for admission to the community of families of old, established wealth, at the core of the capitalist class.

The "inner group" and finance capitalists

The interlocking directorate, as C. Wright Mills rightly remarks, "is no mere phrase: it points to a solid feature of the facts of business life, and to a sociological anchor of the community of interest, the unification of outlook and policy, that prevails among the propertied class." The men who sit at the interlocking managerial helms among the top corporations are, then, in a very concrete sense the leading organizers of the corporate system of "operating classwide property" (Mills, 1956: 122–3). Compared with other higher executives, the authority of the directors in this "inner group" ranges further, and their responsibility is far broader, whether in attempting to protect and enhance the common interests of the same principal owning families dispersed among the interlocked corporations or to reconcile the opposed interests of the contending major investors involved in them.[13] In short, the men in this inner group bear a special class burden: they have a disproportionate responsibility for managing the common affairs of the entire "business community."

We suggest that finance capitalists, because they preside over the contradictory confluence of loan and productive capital, also play a special role in coordinating and integrating the class-wide interests embodied in the top industrials. And insofar as their occupancy of multiple industrial directorships is an indicator, this is precisely what we find: among the directors who sit on the board of only a single industrial, a mere 15 per cent are finance capitalists; in sharp contrast, a majority of those who hold multiple seats (51 per cent of those who sit on two industrial corporation boards and 59 per cent of those who sit on three or more boards) are finance capitalists. Thus, they predominate in the "inner group." The same pattern repeats itself if we take into account the relative assets size of the industrial corporation: the more seats a director occupies in the biggest industrials among the top 200, with assets of a $0.5 billion or more, the more likely that he is a finance capitalist: of the 116 directors without a seat in a $0.5 billion or bigger corporation, 15 per cent are finance capitalists; of the 108 with a single such seat, 21 per cent, and of the dozen who hold seats in two or more of the biggest industrials, 52 per cent are finance capitalists.

Conversely, the contrast is also sharp between finance capitalists and other directors in the number of directorships they hold in the top 200 industrial corporations, especially the largest of them; the finance capitalists are far more likely than other directors to hold multiple directorships of both kinds: 34 per cent of the finance capitalists but only 8 per cent of the other directors hold seats on the boards of two or more of the top 200. By no means as sharp but still substantial is the difference in the seats held in the largest corporations, ranked by assets: 62 per cent of the finance capitalists compared with 48 per cent of the other directors in the sample hold directorships in industrial corporations having assets of a $0.5 billion or more.

In manufacturing, certain "key" industries might be said to constitute the industrial nucleus of all manufacturing, because of both their close technical and market interdependence (Averitt, 1968: 38–44). They consist of the manufacturing industries that produce the most important capital goods; that have backward and forward linkages to other industries (i.e. accounting for a high proportion of their output and input) or have a high price-cost effect on them; that are characterized by considerable "technological convergence" (e.g. machine tools, chemicals, electronics); or are leading "growth" or innovative industries. Thus, given their place "in the hierarchy of economic importance," the corporations in the "key" industries "at the heart of manufacturing" (Averitt, 1968: 2–3) might also be expected to have their boards disproportionately engrossed by finance capitalists, and this is more or less what we find: the more corporate boards in the "key" industries a man sits on, the more likely it is that he is a finance capitalist. Of the men who hold either no seats or a single seat on the board of a company in a "key" industry, 15 per cent are finance capitalists, but of those with two such seats, 29 per cent, and of those with three or more such seats, 44 per cent are finance capitalists. Conversely, finance capitalists are far more likely to sit on multiple boards in "key" industries than are other directors of the top 200 industrial corporations: for instance, of the 47 finance capitalists, 17 per cent hold two and 19 per cent hold three or more directorships in companies in "key" industries but of the 188 other directors, 11 per cent hold two and only 6 per cent hold three or more such "key" directorships.

In sum, finance capitalists not only establish a form of "personal union," as Hilferding called it, between the leading financial institutions and top industrial corporations, but also are the preeminent embodiment of the interlocking community of interest formed among the top industrial corporations themselves. They are thus uniquely located to try to coordinate and harmonize the policies of the financial institutions and industrial corporations in order to maximize the net return of the entire system of large-scale production and investment under their command.

"Bureaucracy" and property in the managerial realm

But who are they, in sociological terms? Leaving aside their personal predilections, their individual character, talents, and skills, what sort of men are socially selected and recruited to exercise the decisive powers in the interlocking managerial realms of finance and industry? Do these finance capitalists represent "a special social type" (Zeitlin, 1974: 1103, 1110) compared with the other industrial directors? No single indicator is sufficient to answer this question, but information concerning their own propertied interests and their place within the nation's community of established families of property is surely critical.

We find that, by both their concrete ownership interests in the corporations they direct and their membership in the "establishment," the finance capitalists stand out as distinctively men of property. The overwhelming majority (69 per cent) of the 47 finance capitalists are in the establishment as compared with just over a third (36 per cent) of the 188 other industrial directors. Similarly, the finance capitalists are roughly three times more likely than other directors to be principal owners of "their" corporation. Conversely, 32 per cent of the 100 establishment directors but only 11 per cent of those who are not in the establishment are finance capitalists; and 41 per cent of the 23 principal owners are finance capitalists compared with 18 per cent of the 212 nonowners among the directors.

How, then, does the combination of a man's being both a principal owner of a corporation of which he is a director *and* belonging to an established family affect the chances that he will also be a finance capitalist? Is this "establishment owner" more likely than other directors to occupy the strategic seat of power of a finance capitalist? And, conversely, what is the relative likelihood that a finance capitalist as compared with an ordinary industrial director will be an establishment owner? As tables 2.1 and 2.2 show, once again the finance capitalist stands out as a distinctive class type: the "establishment owners" are the most likely of all directors to be finance

Table 2.1 *Percentage of directors of the top 200 industrial corporations who are finance capitalists, by establishment membership and corporate ownership*

	Finance capitalists	(N)
Establishment owners	45	(15)
Nonestablishment owners	35	(9)
Establishment nonowners	30	(85)
Nonestablishment nonowners	9	(127)
All directors	20	(236)[a]

[a]Rounding error in weighted cases.

Table 2.2 *Percentage of finance capitalists and other directors of the top 200 industrial corporations who are in the establishment or principal owners, both, or neither*

	Establishment outside owners	Nonestablishment outside owners	Estab lishment dominant owners	Nonestablishment dominant owners	(N)
Finance capitalists	7	6	7	0	(47)
Other directors	1	1	4	2	(188)
All directors	2	2	4	2	(236)[a]

	Establishment owners	Nonestablishment owners	Establishment nonowners	Nonestablishment nonowners	(N)
Finance capitalists	14	6	55	25	(47)
Other directors	4	3	32	61	(188)
All directors	6	4	36	54	(236)[a]

[a]Rounding error in weighted cases.

capitalists and the nonestablishment nonowners, by far, are the least; indeed, proportionately five times as many of the former as the latter are finance capitalists: 45 per cent of the establishment owners but only 9 per cent of the nonestablishment nonowners are finance capitalists. Conversely, each of the types of directors that are either in the establishment or are principal owners, or both, have a much higher proportion among finance capitalists than among ordinary industrial directors, but the nonestablishment nonowners overwhelmingly predominate among the ordinary directors: some three-fourths of the finance capitalists are either principal owners or in the establishment, but some three-fifths of the other industrial directors are *neither*.

As we have seen, the finance capitalists and the "inner group" overlap considerably, for the men in the "inner group" – sitting as they do at the center of a web of interlocking directorates among the top industrials themselves – are probably charged with serving not only the particular interests of specific companies or families, but the broader community of interest of the principal owners with investments among the variously interlocked industrial corporations. But for this same reason, we might expect that the men in the inner group will also be drawn more heavily than single-firm directors from propertied families. Mere "business administrators," however gifted and fitted for such responsibility they might be, are not as likely to be entrusted with such broad class responsibility, we suggest, as are men whose family's own privileges and prerogatives rest on their extensive principal ownership of the top industrials.

Consequently, it is necessary to control for the number of directorships held while comparing the relative intraclass situation of finance capitalists and other industrial directors. For it is possible that it is not their location at the conjoined financial and industrial managerial helms but rather their longer reach throughout the interlocked top industrials alone that accounts for the apparent intraclass specificity of the finance capitalists. Put differently, the "null hypothesis" is that it is not that they are finance capitalists but rather that they are in the inner group that explains the difference in propertied interests between them and ordinary industrial directors. If this reasoning is correct, then with the number of directorships in the top 200 industrial corporations held constant, finance capitalists should be indistinguishable in their property ownership from ordinary industrial directors, while inner group members should stand out in comparison with single-firm directors as distinctively men of property.

As the series of tables which follow shows conclusively, however, this is not what happens. Rather, compared with other industrial directors, the finance capitalists consistently stand out as belonging to established propertied families or as being among the principal owners of the industrial corporations of which they are directors. With the number of directorships held constant, finance capitalists are far more likely than ordinary industrial directors to be establishment members or principal owners, and, conversely, members of the establishment and principal owners are also far more likely to be finance capitalists than nonestablishment members and nonowners. On the other hand, it is also correct, as we expected, that in comparison with single-firm directors, the men with multiple directorships are generally more likely to be members of the establishment or principal owners both among finance capitalists and among other industrial directors. And the converse relationship also tends to hold: among the men in the inner group, the proportion of

Table 2.3 *Percentage of finance capitalists and other directors of the top 200 industrial corporations who are in the establishment, by the number of top 200 directorships held*

	Number of top 200 directorships		
	One	Two Plus	Total
Finance capitalists	61 (31)	84 (16)	69 (47)
Other directors	36 (174)	33 (14)	36 (188)
All directors	40 (205)	60 (31)[a]	43 (236)[a]

[a] Rounding error in weighted cases.

Table 2.4 *Percentage of directors of the top 200 industrial corporations who are finance capitalists, by establishment membership and the number of top 200 directorships held*

	Number of top 200 directorships	
	One	Two plus
Establishment	23 (82)	74 (18)
Nonestablishment	10 (123)	21 (12)
All directors	15 (205)	53 (31)[a]

[a] Rounded error in weighted cases.

finance capitalists is generally higher, both among establishment and non-establishment directors and among owning and nonowning directors, than among single-firm directors (see tables 2.3–2.6).

Finally, as table 2.7 reveals, when we examine the combination of establishment membership and principal ownership, while holding the number of directorships constant, the pattern is again repeated: both among single-firm and multifirm directors, the proportion of "establishment owners" is far larger among finance capitalists than among ordinary industrial directors; similarly, the proportion of "nonestablishment nonowners" is far smaller among finance capitalists than among ordinary directors. And to clinch the point, the *smallest* proportion of "*non*establishment *non*owners" by far is found among *the finance capitalists in the inner group;* a mere 9 per cent of the latter are in that category compared with 62 per cent among the single-firm nonestablishment nonowner ordinary industrial directors.[14]

The same pattern reappears when we consider the relative centrality and economic power of the industrial corporation, even in this already rarefied atmosphere of the top 200: established families of property and principal

Table 2.5 *Percentage of finance capitalists and other directors of the top 200 industrial corporations who are principal owners, by the number of top 200 directorships held*

| | Single top 200 directorships | | | |
	Outside	Dominant	All principal owners	(N)
Finance capitalists	10	10	19	(31)
Other directors	1	6	7	(174)
All directors	2	6	9	(205)

| | Two or more 200 directorships | | | |
	Outside	Dominant	All principal owners	(N)
Finance capitalists	20	2	22	(16)
Other directors	7	3	10	(14)
All directors	14	3	17	(31)[a]

[a]Rounding error in weighted cases.

Table 2.6 *Percentage of directors of the top 200 industrial corporations who are finance capitalists, by corporate ownership and the number of top 200 directorships held*

| | Number of top 200 directorships | |
	One	Two plus
Principal owners	33 (18)	70 (5)
Nonowners	13 (187)	49 (25)
All directors	15 (205)	53 (31)[a]

[a]Rounding error in weighted cases.

Table 2.7 *Percentage of finance capitalists and other directors of the top 200 industrial corporations who are in the establishment or principal owners, both, or neither, by the number of top 200 directorships held*

	Single top 200 directorship				
	Establishment owners	Nonestablishment owners	Establishment nonowners	Nonestablishment nonowners	(N)
Finance capitalists	13	7	48	32	(31)
Other directors	5	2	32	62	(174)
All directors	6	3	34	57	(205)
	Two or more top 200 directorships				
	Establishment owners	Nonestablishment owners	Establishment nonowners	Nonestablishment nonowners	(N)
Finance capitalists	16	6	69	9	(16)
Other directors	0	10	33	56	(14)
All directors	8	8	52	32	(31)[a]

[a] Rounding error in weighted cases.

Table 2.8 *Percentage of directors of the top 200 industrial corporations who are finance capitalists, by establishment membership and "key" industrial directorships*

	Directorships in corporations in "key" industries	Directorships in corporations in other industries
Establishment	33 (76)	29 (24)
Nonestablishment	8 (88)	16 (48)
All directors	20 (164)	20 (72)

owners are much more likely to have their members or representatives located at the interlocking financial–industrial helms, both in the "key" manufacturing industries and others, and in the larger and smaller of the top 200 industrials. And, again, the converse also holds in each of these cases: finance capitalists are drawn far more heavily than ordinary industrial directors from the establishment and from among active principal owners. Because of space limitations, we have not presented the tables showing these same relationships by the assets size of the corporation in which the directorships are held, but the pattern closely parallels that shown for companies in "key" and other industries (see tables 2.8–2.11).

Table 2.9 *Percentage of directors of the top 200 industrial corporations who are finance capitalists, by corporate ownership and "key" industrial directorships*

	Directorships in corporations in "key" industries	Directorships in corporations in other industries
Principal owners	42 –(16)[a]	40 (8)
Nonowners	18 (148)	18 (64)
All directors	20 (164)	20 (72)

[a]Rounding error in weighted cases.

Table 2.10 *Percentage of finance capitalists and other directors of the top 200 industrial corporations, in "key" and other industries, who are in the establishment*

	Directorships in corporations in "key" industries	Directorships in corporations in other industries	Total
Finance capitalists	79 (33)	48 (15)	69 (47)[a]
Other directors	39 (131)	30 (57)	36 (188)
All directors	47 (164)	34 (72)	43 (236)[a]

[a]Rounding error in weighted cases.

These relationships are recapitulated, once again, for the various combinations of establishment membership and principal ownership. In the "key" industries and in other manufacturing, in the corporations with assets of a $0.5 billion or more and in the smaller ones, the finance capitalists stand out sharply in comparison with other directors as peculiarly men of property: indeed, while the vast majority of the ordinary industrial directors in these categories are neither members of established propertied families nor principal owners, this is true of only a small fraction of the finance capitalists (except among those in *non*-"key" industries). The contrast in the intraclass situations of the finance capitalists in the "key" industries and in other manufacturing is thus especially striking: in the "key" industries, which constitute the industrial nucleus of all manufacturing, the overwhelming majority (88 per cent) of the finance capitalists are either in the establishment or are principal owners, but in the other industries this is so for only slightly less than half (48 per cent) of the finance capitalists (see tables 2.12 and 2.13.[15])

Table 2.11 *Percentage of finance capitalists and other directors of the top 200 industrial corporations, in "key" and other industries, who are principal owners*

| | Directorships in corporations in "key" industries | | | |
	Outside	Dominant	All principal owners	(N)
Finance capitalists	16	4	20	(33)[a]
Other directors	2	5	7	(131)
All directors	5	5	10	(164)

| | Directorships in corporations in other industries | | | |
	Outside	Dominant	All principal owners	(N)
Finance capitalists	7	14	21	(15)[a]
Other directors	0	8	8	(57)
All directors	1	9	11	(72)

[a]Rounding error in weighted cases.

Table 2.12 *Percentage of finance capitalists and other directors of the top 200 industrial corporations in "key" and other industries, who are in the establishment or principal owners, both, or neither*

| | Directorships in corporations in "key" industries | | | | |
	Establishment owners	Nonestablishment owners	Establishment nonowners	Nonestablishment nonowners	(N)
Finance capitalists	11	9	68	12	(33)
Other directors	4	3	35	58	(131)
All directors	5	4	41	49	(164)

| | Directorships in corporations in other industries | | | | |
	Establishment owners	Nonestablishment owners	Establishment nonowners	Nonestablishment nonowners	(N)
Finance capitalists	21	0	28	52	(15)
Other directors	5	3	25	68	(57)
All directors	8	2	25	64	(72)

Table 2.13 *Percentage of finance capitalists and other directors of the top 200 industrial corporations who are in the establishment or principal owners, both or neither, by the assets size of the corporations in which they held directorships*

	Assets of $0.5 bn plus				
	Establishment owners	Nonestablish-ment owners	Establishment nonowners	Nonestablish-ment nonowners	(N)
Finance capitalists	10	5	59	26	(29)
Other directors	2	2	34	62	(90)
All directors	4	3	40	53	(119)[a]

	Other corporations				
	Establishment owners	Nonestablish-ment owners	Establishment nonowners	Nonestablish-ment nonowners	(N)
Finance capitalists	20	8	50	22	(18)
Other directors	6	4	30	61	(98)
All directors	8	4	33	55	(116)

[a]Rounding error in weighted cases.

Conclusion

This empirical analysis has been guided by our theory of the relations between various conceptually defined types of "managers" of major financial institutions and top industrial corporations and their "owners" under conditions of the high concentration, centralization, and coalescence of both loan capital and productive capital in the large corporation. With the consequent emergence of the self-contradictory historical form of "finance capital," a specific class type or distinctive class segment also emerges, namely, the "finance capitalist," representing and embodying it in the interlocked directorates of the biggest banks and other financial institutions and the top industrial corporations.

As we probed systematically into the comparative intraclass situations of the various types of directors of the top industrials, we found that the finance capitalists, sitting at the interlocked helms of financial and industrial corporations, do indeed have a special and extensive directorial role and constitute a genuine class type within the higher industrial world and in the capitalist class itself. These leading organizers of the corporate system of classwide property and private appropriation, presiding over the coalescence of financial and industrial capital, and bearing the specific intraclass burden of coordinating and attempting to reconcile the self-contradictory interests inherent in the interpenetrating ownership and interlocking directorates of the major financial institutions and largest industrial corporations, are drawn heavily, and disproportionately compared with other industrial corporation directors, from among the nation's established families of property and principal owners of capital. They are the virtual personification of the fusion of the family and property systems in the so-called bureaucratic and interorganizational managerial realm of the large corporation.[16]

From the standpoint of managerial theory, in general, and of "interorganizational theory" in particular, the findings in this chapter are inexplicable, and directly contradict some of their most basic assumptions and central propositions. In both, the large corporation appears as no more than another complex organization in an uncertain environment constituted of other organizations, and administered by propertyless "managers" who even take on a semblance of being a "purely neutral technocracy" or "technostructure." Neither the private ownership of capital nor the imperatives of capital accumulation determine their conduct or the dynamics of the large corporation and its interrelations with other corporations and major financial institutions. In short, neither theory would predict the systematic findings presented here and neither theory can account for them. For we have shown conclusively that not "organization" but capital, and not the "mere administrator" or bureaucratic manager, but the finance capitalist, representing and personifying the coalescence of financial and industrial capital, exercise the decisive power in the nation's top industrial corporations. Not a process of supposed "interorganizational elite cooptation" but rather discrete, specific intraclass relations and concrete propertied interests explain the selection and recruitment of the men who fill the strategic seats of power interlocking the managerial helms of the leading financial institutions and largest industrial corporations in our country.[17]

NOTES

1 As of 1964, the 100 largest commercial banks in the United States held 46 per cent of all the deposits of the 13,775 commercial banks in the country. The 14 largest alone held 24 per cent of all commercial bank deposits. See the Patman Report, 1966, p. 804. Germany's dominant "Big Three," the Deutsche, the Dresdner, and the Commerz, have long dominated its banking system. In England, the same is true of the "Big Five": Lloyds, Westminster, Midland, Barclays, and National Provincial; they already controlled three-fourths of all funds deposited in British banks by the eve of World War II (Eaton, 1949: 143). The United States, despite its concentration, is unusual in the *number* of competing banks. England has 11 clearing banks and 24 "joint stock" banks, and Canada has 8 chartered banks, for instance, compared to the nearly 14,000 in the United States (Nadler, 1968: 167; also see Sayers, 1962).

2 Strachey, 1956: 273–5, concerning the theory of John M. Keynes. Limited research on the relationship between banking concentration and interest rates in the United States shows that, when regional and local market conditions and differences in

loan characteristics are held constant, there is a significant relationship between banking concentration in metropolitan areas and loan rates. The Chicago Federal Reserve Board's own studies have shown that "the greater the number of banks or the lower the percentage of deposits held by the largest bank in the study, the lower were effective interest rates charged on loans . . . Higher banking concentration was also associated with greater pre-tax earnings on assets" (Fischer, 1968: 369).

3 For a review of the issues and evidence presented in several of the most influential studies, see Glasberg and Schwartz, 1983.

4 Earlier formulations of these questions and several hypotheses on the "inner group" and "finance capitalists" in the United States appear in Zeitlin, 1974, 1976. Cf. also Mintz and Schwartz, 1983; Ratcliff, 1980a, 1980b; Soref, 1980.

5 Galbraith, 1967; Berle and Means, 1967: xiv–xv. Berle's phrase was "financial capital," which he used as a synonym for "loan capital," *not* with the specific conceptual content we elaborate below concerning "finance capital."

6 Galbraith, 1971: xix; Berle and Means, 1967: 313. Galbraith's concept of "technostructure" was adumbrated three decades earlier by Berle and Means' "technocracy."

7 Allen, 1976; Pfeffer, 1972; Pennings, 1980: 67, 107ff; these authors are rather vague about the meaning and implications of "financial interlocks." A very recent systematic analysis of the corporate network of American business also rejects this interorganizational paradigm, and argues instead that "hegemonic relations organized around the interests of financial institutions are the main organizing principles of the business world" (Mintz and Schwartz, 1985: 249).

8 Gordon (1966: x), for instance, simply notes, in a new preface to his study of American corporations in the late 1930s, that there is extensive interlocking between the banks and corporations, and suggests that this is a "far cry from what was once meant by 'financial control,'" but suggests no possible implications. "Interorganizational" theorists often make reference to the "interorganizational *context*," as well as "characteristics of the organization," but the "unit of study . . . [is] construed as an individual organization," and the "context" as other organizations. See Pennings, 1980: 9–10. The so-called "interorganizational context" never involves even the concrete interests of principal shareowners and major investors, let alone the class and intraclass relations within which these "organizations" – the major corporations – operate.

9 For analyses of the historical and social relevance of class segments, see Zeitlin, 1984; Zeitlin, Neuman, and Ratcliff, 1976; Zeitlin and Ratcliff, forthcoming. Although Weber, unlike Marx, focusses in his conception of class on so-called "market relations" rather than "production relations," he also differentiates the propertied according to the specific form in which they appropriate their portions of the social product, and underlines the contradictions between the industrialist on the one side, and "the rentier . . . and the banker" on the other; the latter's "cash boxes," writes Weber, are filled with "'unearned' gains" taken from "the pockets of the manufacturers" (Weber, 1946: 181–6, 301).

10 O'Connor, 1968: 31, referring to "corporate capital," which he substitutes for the term "finance capital," because, he says, the latter is often confused with bank capital, i.e. the notion that the banks control the corporations or dominate the economy. Hilferding occasionally appears to lapse into this, perhaps because of the specific situation at the time in Germany, when the ascendancy of the big banks

seemed indisputable. But whatever his occasional tendency to speak of industry as under bank control, this is not the overall theoretical thrust of *Das Finanzkapital*. Lenin's formulation of the concept of finance capital (1967: I, 710–11) was borrowed explicitly, with slight modification, from Hilferding. We think that referring, as O'Connor does, to the decision-makers in simultaneous charge of the leading banks and large nonfinancial corporations as "corporate capitalists" deflects attention from the critical theoretical focus on the contradictions inherent in the coalescence of loan and productive capital.

11 "Men" because very few women yet occupy these corporate commanding heights, and only two (one of whom was Vera Heinz on the board of Heinz) did in our sample of 40 top industrials of 1964.

12 Domhoff developed the lists of (a) clubs and (b) preparatory schools to fill in the gaps which would be left by exclusive reliance on the (c) *Social Register*. He tried to narrow down the lists of clubs and preparatory schools to those composed almost entirely of establishment members (thus excluding Andover and Exeter from the list of preparatory schools, for example). We classified a director as belonging to the establishment if he met any *one* of the three criteria, i.e. (a) clubs, (b) preparatory schools, or (c) *Social Register*. We used the 1965 edition of the *Social Register Locator* to check *Social Register* listings for the sample. The *Social Register Locator* is a master list of the names listed in the various *Social Register* volumes. There is a volume for each of twelve cities. As Domhoff (1967: 21) suggests, men listed only in the Washington, DC edition of the *Social Register* were not classified as members of the establishment. Domhoff also used the "blue books" of several other cities (the *Detroit Social Secretary*, the *Houston Social Register*, the *Los Angeles Blue Book*, the *New Orleans Social Register*, and the *Seattle Blue Book*), but these volumes were unavailable. Our procedure also deviated from Domhoff's in that we did not check listings for parents, siblings, or wives. These deviations probably resulted in a few misclassifications. E. Digby Baltzell (1958; 1964) considers private schooling an even better index of "upper class" membership than the *Social Register*. Information on schooling came from entries on directors in *Who's Who in America*, or *Who's Who in Commerce and Industry* (or other collective biography information). In some cases, the only biographical information available was in *Poor's Register of Corporations, Executives, and Directors*, which gives only information on college attendance. Membership in specific exclusive clubs is perhaps *the* mark of acceptance into the establishment (Domhoff, 1967: 18–20, 35–6). The list of clubs covered most of the country, unlike the *Social Register* criterion and the preparatory school criterion (the schools on Domhoff's list are concentrated in the northeast); most of the nation's big cities had at least one club on Domhoff's list of forty clubs. Directors' *Who's Who* biographies generally listed directors' club memberships. Directors for whom there was only a *Poor's* entry and who were not listed in the *Social Register* were classified as nonestablishment, even though there was no way to know whether or not they belonged to a club on Domhoff's list or had attended a preparatory school on Domhoff's list. Domhoff set out two additional criteria for membership in the upper class, which we did not use (1970: 24–7). We found that the number of directors misclassified as nonestablishment did not justify the additional efforts. See Soref 1976: 362; 1979: 282–3, for an estimate of false negatives.

13 The *term* "inner group" has been around for decades in the United States, and recurs, for instance, throughout US Congress, 1965. But Zeitlin and his students first conceptualized and elaborated a theory of the internal relations of the capitalist class and the inner group's place in intraclass business leadership and political hegemony. See Zeitlin, Ewen, and Ratcliff, 1974a and 1974b; Zeitlin, Neuman, Ratcliff, and Ewen, 1974; Zeitlin, 1976: 900–1. Since then, Useem (1978; 1979; 1980; 1984) has taken our theory of the inner group as the basis of his own fine work. Cf. also Domhoff, 1983: 70–2; he presents evidence on the inner group, and wrongly attributes the original concept and propositions on intraclass differentiation to Useem.

14 The numbers in the relevant cells are too small to compute reliable percentages in order to show the converse relationships here.

15 Here, too, the converse relationships cannot be shown because the numbers in the relevant cells are too small to compute reliable percentages.

16 Mintz and Schwartz (1985) analyze the role of financial institutions in intercorporate relationships but do not consider the role of the capitalist class itself or of the place of specific segments within it. They argue, however, that "class can be introduced into this analysis" by focussing both on the "inner group" and "finance capitalists" and integrating such an "analysis of individuals with the theory of finance capital . . ." Based on Zeitlin's elaboration of that theory for analysis of the internal structure of the capitalist class, and related empirical analyses (Zeitlin, 1974, 1976; Zeitlin, Neuman, and Ratcliff, 1976; and Ratcliff, 1980a and 1980b), Mintz and Schwartz (1985: 253-4) conclude, by

> combining . . . inner-group analysis with the theory of finance capital,
> that business leadership accrues to a special social type: a cohesive group
> of multiple directors . . . who sit on bank boards as representatives of
> capital in general . . . [D]ecisions on capital allocation are affected by
> the needs of this inner group of finance capitalists . . . and conditioned
> by the class networks they create and inhabit.

Thus, if finance capitalists are constrained and limited in their conduct by the imperatives of capital accumulation and by the centrality of banks in this process, "they must also make real choices about which investment options to pursue [as Ratcliff has stressed] . . . Without their input, capital would be allocated in different ways and in response to different pressures. Like everyone else, the capitalist class makes decisions but not under conditions of its own choosing." Cf. also Glasberg, 1985.

17 Analysis of the internal structure of the dominant class in Chile by Zeitlin and Ratcliff (forthcoming) has yielded findings that are strikingly like the ones reported here. Based on the analysis both of far richer data on ownership and on a detailed and systematic analysis of kinship relations among the families of the higher executives and principal owners of capital in the nation's top Chilean-owned and controlled corporations and banks, they also find that finance capitalists constitute a special class type, both in terms of the extensiveness of their role in coordinating the common affairs of their class and in their integration within its central core of principal capital-owning families.

REFERENCES

Allen, Michael P., 1974. "The structure of interorganizational elite cooptation: interlocking corporate directorates." *American Sociological Review* 39 (June): 393–406

Averitt, Robert T., 1968. *The Dual Economy.* New York: Norton

Baltzell, E. Digby, 1958. *Philadelphia Gentlemen: The Making of a National Upper Class.* New York: Macmillan
1964. *The Protestant Establishment.* New York: Random House

Berle, Adolph, Jr., and Gardiner C. Means, 1967. *The Modern Corporation and Private Property.* New York: Harcourt, Brace and World (originally published in 1932 by Macmillan)

Black, Edie, and Fred Goff, 1969. *The Hanna Industrial Complex.* Berkeley: NACLA

Burch, Phillip H., Jr., 1972. *The Managerial Revolution Reassessed.* Lexington, Mass.: Heath

Business Week, 1968. "Brewing his own formula for success." July 13: 104–6

Chevalier, Jean-Marie, 1970. *La structure financière de l'industrie américaine et le problème du contrôle dans les grandes sociétés américaines.* Paris: Cujas

Domhoff, G. William, 1967. *Who Rules America?* Englewood Cliffs, NJ: Prentice-Hall
1970. *The Higher Circles: The Governing Class in America.* New York: Random House
1983. *Who Rules America Now? A View for the '80s.* Englewood Cliffs, NJ: Prentice-Hall

Dunn, Marvin, 1979. "The family office as a coordinating mechanism within the ruling class." *Insurgent Sociologist* (Fall-Winter): 8–23

Eaton, John, 1949. *Political Economy.* New York: International Publishers

Federal Trade Commission, 1951. *Report of the Federal Trade Commission on Interlocking Directorates.* Washington, DC: Government Printing Office

Fischer, Gerald C., 1968. *American Banking Structure.* New York: Columbia University Press

Fortune, 1958. "West-Coast Wheeler Dealer." November: 69

Galbraith, John K., 1967, 1971. *The New Industrial State.* New York: New American Library (also, "Introduction", 2nd edn, 1971. New York: Houghton Mifflin)

Glasberg, Davita S., 1985. "The role of finance capital and the social construction of corporate crisis." *Insurgent Sociologist,* 13 (1–2): 39–51

Glasberg, Davita S., and Michael Schwartz, 1983. "Ownership and control of corporations." *Annual Review of Sociology,* 9: 311–32

Gordon, Robert A., 1966. *Business Leadership in the Large Corporation.* Berkeley: University of California Press (originally published in 1945 under the auspices of the Brookings Institution)

Hilferding, Rudolf, 1910. *Das Finanzkapital: Eine Studie über die jungste Entwicklung des Kapitalismus.* Berlin: Verlag J. H. W. Dietz (1947 reprint of the original edition)

James, David R., and Michael Soref, 1981. "The unmaking of the corporation president: profit constraints on managerial autonomy." *American Sociological Review*, 46 (February): 1–18

Knowles, James, 1973. *The Rockefeller Financial Group*. Warner Modular Publications, Module 343

Kotz, David M., 1978. *Bank Control of Large Corporations in the United States*. Berkeley: University of California Press

Kuh, Edward, 1963. *Capital Stock Growth: A Micro-Econometric Approach*. Amsterdam: North Holland Press

Larner, Robert J., 1970. *Management Control and the Large Corporation*. Cambridge, Mass.: University Press, Dunellen

Lundberg, Ferdinand, 1968. *The Rich and the Super Rich*. New York: Bantam

Mahon, Gigi, 1978. "War of fortunes: the wealthy Phipps clan is rent by strife." *Barrons*, July 31: 4, 5, 16

Marx, Karl, 1952. *The Civil War in France*. Moscow: Foreign Languages Publishing House
   1967. *Capital*. Vols. I–III. New York: International

Mills, C. Wright, 1942. "Review of the social life of a modern community." *American Sociological Review*, 7 (April): 264–71. In I. L. Horowitz (ed.), *Power, Politics and People: The Collected Essays of C. Wright Mills*. New York: Oxford University Press, 1963, pp. 39–52
   1956. *The Power Elite*. New York: Oxford University Press

Mintz, Beth, and Michael Schwartz, 1985. *The Power Structure of American Business*. University of Chicago Press

Nadler, Paul S., 1968. *Commercial Banking in the Economy*. New York: Random House

O'Connor, James, 1968. "Finance capital or corporate capital?" *Monthly Review*, 20 (October): 3–35

[Patman] Staff Report, 1966. "Bank stock ownership and control." In US Congress, House Committee on Banking and Currency, Domestic Finance Committee, 90th Congress, 1968, *Commercial Banks and their Trust Activities*. Washington, DC: Government Printing Office (cited as Patman Report)

Pederson, Lawrence, and William Tabb, 1976. "Ownership and control of large corporations revisited." *Antitrust Bulletin* (Spring): 53–66

Pennings, Johannes, 1978. "Interlocking relationships: the case of interlocking directorates." Paper presented at the meeting of the American Sociological Association, San Francisco, August
   1980. *Interlocking Directorates: Origins and Consequences of Connections among Organizations' Boards of Directors*. San Francisco: Jossey-Bass

Pfeffer, Jeffrey, 1972. "Size and composition of corporate boards of directors: the organization and its environment." *Administrative Science Quarterly*, 17 (June): 218–28

Poulantzas, Nicos, 1975. *Classes in Contemporary Capitalism*. London: New Left Books

Ratcliff, Richard E., 1980a. "Banks and the command of capital flows: an analysis of capitalist class structure and mortgage disinvestment in a metropolitan area." In Maurice Zeitlin (ed.), *Classes, Class Conflict, and the State*. Boston, Mass.: Little, Brown, pp. 107–32

1980b. "Banks and corporate lending: an analysis of the impact of the internal structure of the capitalist class on the lending behavior of banks." *American Sociological Review*, 45 (August): 553–70

Rodgers, William, 1974. *Think: A Biography of the Watsons and IBM*. New York: Mentor

Sayers, R. S. (ed.), 1962. *Banking in Western Europe*. London: Oxford University Press

Scott, John, 1979. *Corporations, Classes and Capitalism*. London: Hutchinson

Scott, John, and Catherine Griff, 1984. *Directors of Industry: The British Corporate Network 1904–1976*. Cambridge, England: Polity

Sheehan, Robert, 1966. "There's plenty of privacy left in private enterprise." *Fortune* (July): 224–5, 327, 328, 334, 343, 348

1967. "Proprietors in the world of big business." *Fortune*, June 15: 178–83, 242

Soref, Michael, 1976. "Social class and a division of labor within the corporate elite: a note on class, interlocking, and executive committee membership of directors of US industrial firms." *Sociological Quarterly*, 17 (Summer): 360–8

1979. "The Internal Differentiation of the American Capitalist Class." PhD dissertation, Department of Sociology, University of Wisconsin, Madison

1980. "The finance capitalists." In Maurice Zeitlin (ed.), *Classes, Class Conflict, and the State*. Boston, Mass.: Little, Brown, pp. 62–82

Strachey, John, 1956. *Contemporary Capitalism*. New York: Random House

Thompson, James D., 1967. *Organizations in Action*. New York: McGraw-Hill

Time, 1955. "The baron of beer." July 11: 82–6

US Congress, Senate Subcommittee on Anti-Trust and Monopoly, 1965. *Interlocks in Corporate Management. Staff Report to the Anti-Trust Subcommittee of the Committee on the Judiciary*. House of Representatives, 89th Cong., 1st sess. Washington, DC: Government Printing Office

US Congress, Senate Committee on Governmental Affairs, 1978. *Interlocking Directorates among the Major US Corporations*. Washington, DC: Government Printing Office

Useem, Michael, 1978. "The inner group of the American capitalist class." *Social Problems*, 24 (February): 225–40

1979. "The social organization of the American business elite and participation of corporation directors in the governance of American institutions." *American Sociological Review*, 44 (August): 553–71

1980. "Corporations and the corporate elite." *Annual Review of Sociology*, 6: 41–77

1984. *The Inner Circle: Large Corporations and the Rise of Business Political Activity in the US and UK*. New York: Oxford University Press

Villarejo, Don, 1961/2. "Stock ownership and control of corporations." New England Free Press reprint of a two-part article published in *New University Thought*, Autumn 1961 and Winter 1962

Weber, Max, (1921) 1946. "Class, status, party." In Hans Gerth and C. Wright Mills (eds.), *From Max Weber*. New York: Oxford University Press, pp. 180–95

White, Shelby, 1978. "Cradle to grave: family offices manage money for the very rich." *Barron's*, March 20: 9, 18, 20–1

Zeitlin, Maurice, 1974. "Corporate ownership and control: the large corporation and the capitalist class." *American Journal of Sociology*, 79 (March): 1073–1119

   1976. "On class theory of the large corporation." *American Journal of Sociology*, 81 (January): 894–903

   1984. *The Civil Wars in Chile (or the Bourgeois Revolutions that Never Were)*. Princeton University Press

Zeitlin, Maurice, Lynda Ann Ewen, and Richard E. Ratcliff, 1974a. "New princes' for old? The large corporation and the capitalist class in Chile." *American Journal of Sociology*, 80 (July): 87–123

   1974b. "The 'inner group': interlocking directorates and the internal differentiation of the capitalist class in Chile." Paper presented at the annual meeting of the American Sociological Association, August

Zeitlin, Maurice, W. Lawrence Neuman, and Richard E. Ratcliff, 1976. "Class segments: agrarian property and political leadership in the capitalist class of Chile." *American Sociological Review*, 41 (December): 1006–29

Zeitlin, Maurice, W. Lawrence Neuman, Richard E. Ratcliff, and Lynda Ann Ewen, 1974. "Politics and the capitalist class in Chile: the 'inner group' and the state." Paper presented at the annual meeting of the American Sociological Association, August

Zeitlin, Maurice, and Richard E. Ratcliff, forthcoming. *Landlords and Capitalists: The Dominant Class of Chile*. Princeton University Press

3

A *structural approach to markets*

Eric M. Leifer and Harrison C. White

Structural analysis focusses upon the patterns of relationships among social actors. This emphasis rests on the often unspoken postulate that these patterns – independent of the content of the ties – are themselves central to individual action. Moreover, structural analysis posits that the constraints associated with positions in a network of relationships are frequently more important in determining individual action than either the information or attitudes people hold (Berkowitz, 1982: 8).

Structural context is represented by patterns of ties of varying content, and the analyst's interest is in how individual behavior serves to reproduce the structural context (Burt, 1982). The discovery of "self-reproducing" structural contexts has occupied structural analysts in such diverse areas as kinship systems (White, 1963), organizational structures (Kanter, 1977), world systems (Snyder and Kick, 1979; Love 1982; Breiger, 1981) and abstract social structures (Lorrain and White, 1971). In this endeavor structures are "explained" when their self-reproducing properties – and therefore their continued existence – are analytically understood.[1]

This approach contrasts sharply with information-oriented approaches, which explain the existence and/or continuation of a particular structure by showing how it is more "efficient" (in terms of a set of defined goals) than any available alternative (Williamson, 1975). Only efficient structures are likely to be empirically observed, because inefficient structures would perish through natural selection or be made more efficient through the "maximizing" efforts of interested individuals. Structural approaches, on the other hand, identify a self-perpetuating system of structural constraints, without stepping within the kind of information framework needed to assess efficiency.

Structural analysis is often criticized because it excludes maximization and efficiency considerations, and hence lacks a solid basis for explaining how individual actors choose among the alternatives available to them. Though some notable efforts have been made to include maximizing considerations (Boorman, 1975; Winship, 1978; Burt, 1982), we will argue that to do so risks violating a basic thematic of structural analysis: *structures exist and reproduce themselves in part because the information needed to pursue maximization and efficiency* is not available. In other words, an individual frequently does not know in advance which option will produce, for example, the highest profits or the lowest costs. In these circumstances, *the only tangible guidance available to the actor is that which can be inferred from the patterns and outcomes which emerge from relations among actors.* That is, the individual makes his or her choice by observing the fate of others who have faced similar, but by no means identical choices. Maximization, if relevant, is defined only within the limited *social* framework of existing outcomes. Other alternatives may not appear or may be left unexplored simply because no useful evidence about them can be generated. Individuals rely on existing outcomes for guidance, and in doing so generate new outcomes to rely on. *Reproducibility*, rather than efficiency, *is the main issue*.

In this chapter, we present a recent model of production markets (see White, 1981a, 1981b, 1987; Leifer, 1985) that adopts the orientation of structural analysis. It shows how manufacturers of a particular product decide on the volume of their production and the prices they charge in a setting where they have a distinct reputation (i.e. their product is perceived and treated by their potential customers as being different from that of the competition in the market).

The vexing problem manufacturers must resolve is how they "fit into" the market, or, more to the point, how their customers would have them fit in. The producer would, of course, like to know how consumers would respond to volume and price changes, as well as how other producers would respond to such changes.

However, the requisite "demand curves" are almost never available and game-theoretic efforts to second guess competitors' reactions must rely on implausible assumptions. In the real world businesses cannot know how consumers or competitors will respond to a particular change in volume or price. Our proposed structural model pulls the producer out of the mythical information setting in which everything is known and has the individual entrepreneur seeking guidance purely on the basis of the *observed* outcomes for all the producers in his or her market in the prior production period. The various outcomes are treated as a menu of fates (i.e. roles, or niches), to select from in the coming period. Producers "maximize" within this very limited social framework. They assess future possibilities by observing competitors' past pricing volume strategies, and find their place amongst the competitors by assessing these possibilities against their own production costs. The parallel action of competitors will influence each producer's fate that is observed in the next production period.

Our concern here is with the circumstances in which a viable market is produced, one where the summation of producers' choices serves to reproduce the role structure from the previous production period, and it is then used in a subsequent period with the same effect. When these circumstances materialize, the producers become locked into a self-fulfilling framework in which their unique fate (role) is perpetuated from period to period.

We begin our exposition with a speculative discussion of how Tony's frozen pizza operation uses its experience (and that of its competitors) to make choices about pricing and volume of production – and, hence, total revenues. We then sketch the formal model that underlies the speculation, moving from the interests of Tony to an interest in the conditions under which markets can function and reproduce themselves. Finally, we shift to the comparative issue, developing a topology of markets to show how inequality of revenue outcomes results from different cost and valuation contexts. We conclude with a discussion contrasting our structural approach with the information approaches found in the economic and business literature.

Tony's dilemma

Tony produces and distributes frozen pizzas at the national level. Every three months he evaluates the market performance of his frozen pizzas and makes a decision about his volume (y) of production and his suggested retail price[2] for the coming quarter – and hence his projected revenue (W).[3] Tony uses his knowledge of the frozen pizza market to make this decision.

The market for Tony is populated by other frozen pizza producers that Tony knows by name and reputation. A brand name is attached to the frozen pizzas of each producer, and these give the producers distinct public images. Totino's and Jeno's, for example, are high-volume, inexpensive party pizzas. Stouffer's, on the other hand, sports a "French crust" (homebased in Ohio) and finds its way into more intimate gatherings at a higher price and a much lower volume. Celeste implants itself in the middle range, a favorite in middle-class families where neither parent has much time to cook.

These reputations are quite stable, and, combined with the distinctive reputation of his own pizza, create a powerful constraint on Tony's choices. At least for the next three months, Tony assumes these reputations are not likely to change. Even in the long run, however, Tony is very uncertain about what would happen if he tried to induce a change in the reputation of his frozen pizza and therefore change his niche; and he is equally uncertain about how he would go about doing this. Tony perceives himself as locked in a structure of distinct "niches" over which he has little control.

The reputation of each frozen pizza brand can be represented in two dimensions: volume and revenue. Market shares are quite stable. The lower "quality" frozen pizzas command a large proportion of the market, while high "quality" pizzas account for a small percentage. These reputational–price differences are sharp and stable. Stouffer's costs more than Totino's, and this difference is an acknowledged feature of the "market" Tony has come to know. Tony accepts the fact that consumers are willing to pay different prices for different brands of frozen pizzas, without needing to understand the dynamics of consumer behavior. In textbook terms, Tony is operating in a "differentiated" market.

Quality differentiation poses a formidable problem for Tony's production and pricing decisions. Tony cannot take "price" as a given, since there is no single price in the market, but a unique price for each brand of goods. He could, of course, simply reuse the price he received in the prior period, but this has some potential drawbacks. First, in doing so he may be ignoring significant changes in the conditions of his market and this could result in major problems. Second, Tony would be evading the basic question (which he might reflect on, but a researcher would insist on) of why he occupies the particular niche that he occupies. That is, a good business person should seek to change niches, if it is possible and profitable to do so. Finally, Tony could not safely assume his current price would be accepted if he changed his production volume (explained below).

Hence, his own production figures for the previous quarter offer Tony only a little guidance concerning the possibilities he faces. Outside of simply repeating his past period decision for both price and volume, no obvious guidelines for action appear present. The uniqueness of Tony's niche and the niches of other frozen pizza producers makes it unclear how Tony can use his own past, or the pasts of others, for guidance for the future.

Fortunately, Tony's knowledge of the "market" goes beyond the mere description of each producer's "niche" and his own production figures. *Tony knows how the niches are tied together.* There is a particular order to them. In Tony's market, low "quality" (that is, price) is tied to high production volumes (though in other markets, like disposable diapers, it may be the opposite). This he takes as a basic fact of the market he is in. This fact is crucial in his production volume and pricing decisions. If Tony successfully increased his market share, his public reputation would undergo a change also. He would become a mass market pizza maker and, in this market, the perceived quality of his product would decline. Thus Tony cannot make his volume decision independent from his price decision. The two are interrelated, as they are both tied to a distinct set of reputations, or niches, that are sustainable in this particular market.

This arrangement – or menu – is not secret; every pizza maker, market analyst, and non-casual observer of the business knows it well. The menu simply consists of the basic prices, sales volume and – hence – revenues of frozen pizza producers in the prior production period. These figures are published routinely in trade publications and business indexes, and reflected locally in retail prices and shelf space allocations. The menu that Tony observes is provided in figure 3.1. The orderliness of this menu is found in the

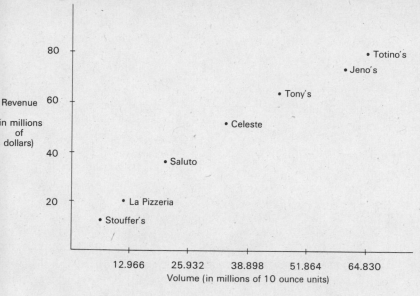

3.1 A menu of fates. The (annual) volume, revenue outcomes for seven frozen pizza producers. The menu defines the possibilities awaiting the producers in the next production period.

fact that each production volume is associated with a unique revenue (i.e. price), insofar as the producer's outcomes fall on an "orderly" (though not usually linear) curve.

The menu of producer outcomes is the only tangible evidence for the possible niches that are sustainable within the frozen pizza market. To step outside this tangible menu would involve considerations of reputation formation, consumer psychology and producer reactions that hold few prospects for sure-footed guidance for Tony. Tony uses the observed fates of other frozen pizza producers as his "opportunity set," because his knowledge of the market goes no further.

The rest is simple. Tony has a good idea of his (variable) production costs over a range of volumes. He assesses these costs against the assumed revenue opportunities in the market, and selects the production volume and appropriate asked revenue (price) that maximizes his return (profits). This can be done with a graph and ruler, as illustrated in figure 3.2. In a stable market, with each producer operating like Tony, the individual maximizing decisions lead each producer to choose the same niche as the previous period. The producer therefore reproduces the same opportunity set (menu of possibilities). This is then used for guidance in the next period, yet this does not arise through mechanically repeating past (y, W) actions; *each enterprise assesses its situation in each cycle and reaffirms that its niche in a structure of*

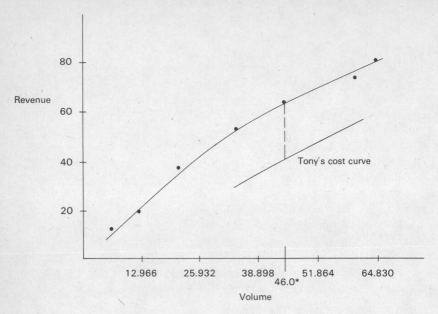

3.2   Tony's optimization problem. Tony assesses his production costs against the volume, revenue opportunities defined by actual outcomes of frozen pizza producers in the prior production period. Tony chooses the production volume, and associated price, which optimizes the difference between revenue and cost (i.e. profit).

niches is where it is best suited. The frozen pizza producers' belief in the market is self-fulfilling, but it is a useful and reasonable belief, since without it they would lack any tangible guidance in choosing a production–pricing strategy.

The market is a simple affair for Tony, which he can use with no mathematical effort. From Tony's point of view, the reliance on tangible price and volume data – not just his own, but also his competitors – is reassuring. The ease of using these data enhances their appeal, particularly in com- parisons to the largely fictional (difficult to utilize) curves of the econometrician. Tony has little incentive to abandon his particular view of the market as long as it seems to work for him – that is, as long as he is making money.

Exploring the conditions under which markets work, in the sense of market behavior reproducing market structure, requires going beyond Tony's simple point of view. The analytic underpinnings of Tony's market must be developed, so we can understand how distinct roles are sustained and orderliness is reproduced. We do this in the next section (for a more thorough treatment, see White, 1981a or Leifer, 1985).

Reproducing structures

The producer

Tony, and each of the other pizza manufacturers, uses the data of observed volume (y), revenue (W) outcomes from the prior production period to construct a schedule of possibilities for the next period. We refer to this schedule as a $W(y)$ schedule. It is a shared construct among all the producers; they are a closed "clique" in the sense that they know each other's outcomes and use them to define their own possibilities.[4]

Each producer, however, has his or her own cost curve. These differences in the cost of production mean that the various pizza makers will come to different volume and revenue decisions. Tony, for example, calculates how much it would cost him to manufacture the number of pizzas that a competitor produces ($C(y)$). He compares his cost with their revenues (assuming that if he entered their niche, he would be forced [or allowed] to charge their price) and computes his total anticipated profit *in that niche*. If some niche other than his own offers a greater return he must consider a change. The desirability of particular niches will be different for producers with different manufacturing costs than Tony.

In mathematical form, the volume decision is resolved by solving the maximization problem below:

$$\max_{y} \ W(y) - C_i(y) \tag{1}$$

where $C_i(y) =$ producer i's total production cost for volume y and $W(y) =$ total revenues for volume y ($W(y)$ is not unique to producer i, but rather is a menu shared by all producers). Equation 1 is a mathematical representation of the process illustrated in figure 3.2.

We will approximate the cost curves of the different producers as a family of similar and simple shapes. First, all producers experience the same economies of scale where c is a shape parameter that taps economies ($c < 1$) or diseconomies ($c > 1$) of scale, and q is a scale parameter. To account for differences in the scale of costs, we introduce a cost index g_i that is unique for each producer i.[5] The cost curves are given the following form:

$$\text{Costs}_i = C_i = qy^c g_i{}^d \tag{2}$$

where d allows the range of cost differentiation fixed by the cost indices (g_i) to be stretched or shrunk, and can be positive or negative.[6] The need for this stretching or shrinking of cost differences between producers will become apparent when we show how cost differences have to be related to consumer valuation differences for a stable market to be possible.

Maximizing profits (equation 1) is assured when the well-known marginal condition is met:

$$\frac{dW}{dy} = \frac{dC}{dy}$$

(In words, when the slope of the cost curve equals the slope of the revenue curve, marginal cost equals marginal revenue. This can be seen in figure 3.2.)   (3)

along with the second order condition (ensuring a maximum as opposed to a minimum):

$$\frac{d^2W}{dy^2} < \frac{d^2C}{dy^2}$$ (4)

In addition, producers require positive profits to produce. These conditions provide a complete specification of the producer's behavior.[7] In the real world, each manufacturer can (without fancy mathematics) approximate the profit-maximizing solution for his or her cost curve and pursue that niche.

The consumer

There is another side to markets, the consumer side. There is always some mystery associated with consumer behavior in differentiated markets, because consumers are so often willing to pay substantially higher prices for a product whose superiority cannot be "objectively" established. The producer never looks directly inside the mysterious consumer.[8] Yet consumer behavior in aggregate plays a fundamental role in shaping producer outcomes.

A desirable feature of our model is that producers never have to look past the outcomes of other producers to see the consumer side. The role of the aggregate consumer can be represented as follows. The consumer, for whatever reason, values the different goods (brands) differently, that is, is willing to pay a higher price for some brands than others. As a group, consumers also value different quantities of each good differentially, for example, they may be willing to pay only 50 per cent more for two pizzas than one. This aggregate taste can be expressed mathematically as a collective value consumers receive from the goods of producer i:

$$\text{Value}_i = S_i = r y^a h_i^b$$ (5)

Here r is a scale parameter; the exponent a relates quantity (y) to value; h_i is a unique "value" index for the good of producer i; and b is a parameter that determines the spread for these indices across producers (it can only be positive, due to the convention of assigning a higher value index to producers whose products are perceived as more valuable).[9]

The consumer makes comparisons across products, and insists that value received bears some relation to dollars given out for each product. If one producer's total offering has less value for the consumer than another's, then the consumer will insist on paying less for the total output. A product which successfully occupies a niche in a differentiated market must sell for a price appropriate to its (perceived) quality; it must confer the same "value per dollar" as other products. Hence in a stable market, the same ratio (θ) of value per dollar holds across all goods, or

$$\theta = \frac{S_i}{W_i} = \frac{S_j}{W_j} \qquad \text{for all goods of producers } i, j \qquad (6)$$

The stage is set now for showing how the differences in costs and differences in valuations provide the materials for building a stable market. Tony's cost position *vis-à-vis* the other producers and the valuation his pizzas receive *vis-à-vis* other frozen pizzas will "voluntaristically" restrain the niches he can occupy in the market. These positions are set in the g and h indices, respectively.

Tying the sides together

We have now given mathematical expression to both the cost and value elements in differentiated markets. In order for an equilibrium $W(y)$ schedule consistent with these elements to exist, the ordering of producers on costs must be the same as the ordering of their goods on value, though these orderings can be stretched and shrunk or even reversed. This means that either: (1) the producer whose product commands the highest value has the highest costs, the second highest value has second highest costs, etc., or (2) the producer who commands the highest value has the lowest costs, the second highest has the second lowest, etc.

We call this constraint the *coherence condition*, as the constraint is that the two orderings must cohere. Without this coherence the behavior of the producer and consumer sides could not be tied together in a reproducible market, as we will show below. The fact that the elusive "value" to the consumer must be related to production costs is somewhat reassuring. We see this as a reasonable hypothesis about real world economics: *a sustainable market cannot be built among a set of products whose valuations are unrelated to their costs.*

Mathematically, we proceed as follows. The abstract property that lies at the basis of both cost and value differentiation can be called quality. Let n_i be the quality index for producer i. The coherence condition insures that:

$$n_i = g_i = h_i \text{ for all } i \qquad (7)$$

So let g and h be vectors of indices. The producers insist that (from equations 2 and 3):

$$\frac{dC}{dy} = cqy^{c-1}g^d = \frac{dW}{dy} \qquad (8)$$

i.e. maximum profit. The consumer insists that

$$S = \theta W = ry^a h^b \Rightarrow h = (\theta W/ry^a)^{1/b}$$

$$\frac{dW}{dy} = \frac{cqy^{c-1}(\theta W)^{d/b}}{r^{d/b}y^{ad/b}} = cqy^{((bc-ad)/b)-1}(\theta W/r)^{d/b} \tag{9}$$

i.e. competitive value per dollar. Only a market where equations 8 and 9 hold will satisfy both producers and the consumer. The coherence condition implies that the solution for h in equation 9 can be substituted for g in equation 8, producing an equation where the abstract quality index disappears. By rearranging the terms in this equation and integrating, a solution can be obtained for W (revenue) in terms of y (volume). The $W(y)$ equation is:

$$W = ((cq(b-d)/(bc-ad))(\theta/r)^{d/b}y^{(bc-ad)/b} + K)^{b/(b-d)} \tag{10}$$

or $W = (Py^e + K)^f$ with the appropriate substitution for P, e, and f. Given the context of differentiated costs and valuations (equations 2 and 5, with 7) that characterizes a particular market, the ratio θ, and the historically determined constant of integration K, observed producer outcomes should fall on the $W(y)$ schedule of equation 10. Producers, of course, "see" only the discrete outcomes, and not the $W(y)$ equation.

The crucial interdependence between volume and quality sensed by producers like Tony can be derived by solving the following problem:

$$\frac{d(\text{profits})}{dy} = \frac{dW}{dy} - \frac{dC}{dy} = f(Py^e + K)^{f-1}Pey^{e-1} - cqy^{c-1}n^d = 0$$

to obtain (with substitution for P, e, and f):

$$n^{b-d} = (cq\theta(b-d) \ / \ (r(bc-ad))y^{c-a} + K(\theta/r)^{(b-d)/b}/y^{a(b-d)/b}) \tag{11}$$

Given the range of quality indices and contextual parameters, this equation yields the optimal production volumes for producers in a market. (Note that these volumes cannot be obtained through a closed form solution unless K happens to equal zero.)

Interpretation

The alert reader might suppose that equations 10 and 11 would relieve a producer like Tony from the task of observing outcomes of other producers. This is not the case, however. The quality index "n" will be meaningless to Tony since he is aware of only his own costs, so equation 11 cannot be used to find his optimal volume. The $W(y)$ equation (10) looks more promising, since "n" does not appear in it. Even assuming Tony knows the cost and value parameters in equations 2 and 5, however, he could not obtain an analytical solution for his (y,W) decision (with equation 3) because there are two indeterminacies K and θ, which require observational data to obtain. These indeterminacies imply that the schedule of niches that emerges in any given market will not be uniquely determined by the cost and value context (equations 2 and 5). A range of schedules is possible that all "work" in the sense of both satisfying the producer and consumer sides and being reproduced through the behavior of these sides. Tony, or researchers, cannot predict the exact shape or scale of a schedule in a specific market. *No amount of analytical finesse can relieve Tony of his social interdependence on other producers in defining his "opportunity set," or relieve the researcher of a dependence on data.*

The indeterminacies fit neatly with, and strengthen the case for, our portrait of real world market behavior. In an ongoing market for frozen pizzas (or other products), there are established, discernible niches – for example, a cheap, quick, doughy product may occupy the bottom end of the spectrum, just below the less inexpensive, slightly more time-consuming, very cheesy entry. While it is possible to conceive of an infinity of new products (say a cheaper cheesy pizza), it is impossible to calculate their impact on the current niche structure. It is far simpler to estimate the consequences of invading (or remaining in) an existing niche. That is, producers correctly (from a mathematical *and* practical perspective) rely on the current structure as a frame for decision-making, basing future choices on data derived from the current circumstances of themselves and their competitors.

This raises a new substantive and analytic issue. If both Tony and the researcher must look at producer outcomes for guidance and parameter estimates, how should this schedule be interpreted? Only a discrete set of outcomes is observed, yet it represents a continuous $W(y)$ schedule. What is the meaning of such a schedule, above and beyond the discrete producer outcomes it is based upon?

To illustrate this issue mathematically, we note that parameter K in equation 10 can take on non-zero values. If the continuous $W(y)$ schedule had a reality independent from the discrete producer outcomes, one would be led to the implausible conclusion that producing nothing ($y=0$) might yield positive revenue. We are therefore tempted to limit the range of the continuous $W(y)$ schedule to the close vicinity of the actual producer outcomes.

Yet even within a limited range the interpretation of a continuous schedule is not unambiguous. The equation for this schedule (equation 10) has parameters b and d, θ and K, and possibly r and q, which depend upon a specific set of producers (ns) for their values. A different set of producers (and thus quality index range) would yield different values for b and d, as well as the other parameters above. Therefore, though producers could assume that any point on the continuous $W(y)$ schedule represents a viable niche, this assumption stands in tension with the dependence of the $W(y)$ schedule on a specific set of producers.

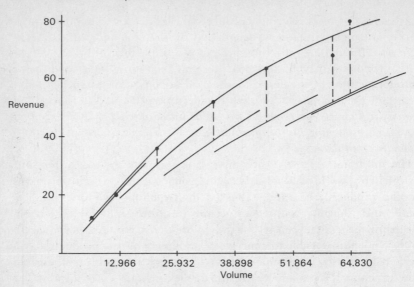

3.3   A self-reproducing market. Each producer uses the shared menu of
fates (market outcomes) to select a volume and associated price for the
next production period. In a self-reproducing market, their selections
will reproduce the menu of fates they used for guidance. That is, they
will reselect the niche they occupied in the prior period.

Producers assume they could be anywhere on the $W(y)$ schedule while
simultaneously realizing that the schedule itself is built from their own
uniqueness. The only situation where these dual beliefs do not stand in
contradiction is when the $W(y)$ schedule leads them to reselect their prior
niche, and hence reproduce the schedule. We believe that this is a key to
understanding the real world conservatism of producers: they have little
tangible motivation to step outside of their niche in a reproducible market.

Tony produces in a market that continually reproduces itself through the
actions of Tony and the other producers, and the mysterious consumer. The
production has a structural context, which both guides it and is reproduced by
it. To illustrate this reproduction process, figure 3.3 shows some partially
simulated data from the frozen pizza market. Each producer is producing at
an optimum volume, and therefore chooses to remain in the same niche after
each production period. The volumes and revenues suggested by this context
serve to reproduce the context (assuming reacceptance by the consumer). The
reproduced context can then serve for guidance in the next production period,
and so on. Tony is locked into this reproducible structure by his self-fulfilling
behavior. He has little incentive to step outside this structure into a setting of
ex ante information and expectations.

A possible new entrant into the market, however, must be concerned with the viability of the untested positions. A continuous schedule implies that any position is viable, yet the schedule itself may have little meaning outside of the set of distinct producers around which it is constituted. To address the issue of *potential* niches, we must look at constraints on aggregate volume and revenue flows.

Aggregating differentiation

We must treat aggregate demand in a different way from traditional theory, because we accept qualitative distinctions among the various entries in the market. However, the frozen pizza industry (and other similar sectors) does constitute a market in the sense that entries or exits that affect aggregate flows will affect existing producers in the market. It makes sense, therefore, to ignore the uniqueness of each producer's goods, and to speak of an aggregate demand, even if this total demand depends very much on the specific products offered. If, for example, the cheap, quick, doughy pizza were pulled from the market and replaced by an equally cheap and quick cheesy entry, the aggregate demand might change upward or downward. Therefore, we can speak of aggregate demand, but we must be sensitive to its dependence on the particular schedule of products offered.

The aggregate mechanism is expressed in a satiation parameter, γ, which operates on aggregate value in the following way:

$$\text{Total value} = V = (\Sigma_i S(y(n_i), n_i))^{\gamma} \tag{12}$$

Hence a γ of less than one means the sum of value obtained from separate goods is discounted. This discounting, however, will affect the ratio of value per dollar (θ) through a complex feedback path (see White, 1981a). To illustrate the connection between θ and γ, assume that the market is operating at a level where the total value to the consumer is equal to the total revenue flow ($W = \Sigma_i S(y(n_i))$). The θ_0 associated with this special case is derived in the following manner:

$$V = (\Sigma_i S(y(n_i), n_i))^{\gamma} = (\theta \Sigma_i W(y(n_i)))^{\gamma} = \theta^{\gamma} W^{\gamma} = W$$

$$\Rightarrow \text{breakeven theta} = \theta_0 = W^{(1-\gamma)/\gamma} \tag{13}$$

Thus while γ is not found in the $W(y)$ schedule (equation 10), its influence operates through θ and hence can affect the scale of flows in a market.

Entry and exit will be very noticeable events in such markets involving named producers and significant shifts in the market schedule faced by all producers. The ultimate shape of the market is contingent not only on a specific set of unique producers, but also on the aggregate flows they generate. The continuous $W(y)$ schedule that links discrete producers, mathematically given in equation 10, is a fragile construct that has a clear interpretation only when it functions so as to reproduce itself across periods. Should the producer be guided to shift niches, or a new producer contemplate entering the market, their acceptance would be dependent upon factors only vaguely understood.[10]

One strength of our model is that it gives considerable leverage over such possible changes. The tools outlined here allow predictions of the consequences of a change in costs or valuations as well as the effects of entry, exit or niche changes. These predictions are illustrated and discussed in Leifer (1985).

A topology of reproducible structures

Our model can also be used to explore the variety of possible reproducible market structures. Markets can vary widely in the degree to which producers are *spread out* in their costs of production (*d*) or in the value of their goods to consumers (*b*). They can also vary in the consequences of *shifting* their volumes on production costs (*c*) or value to consumers (*a*). Variation on these spread and shift dimensions correspond to considerable variation in market operation.

There is, therefore, no single type of market, but instead a whole topology of market contexts. Some cost and valuation contexts will not sustain a reproducible market. For example, in some contexts, the perceived comparative value of the products, combined with the cost structures associated with them, lead to an "unravelling" of the $W(y)$ schedule by encouraging producers to seek a corner solution. In these circumstances, we expect that markets do not appear. Conversely, our model predicts reproducible markets where none were thought possible in economic theory, for example in circumstances where it would cost less to produce more – a situation common in real markets. Among reproducible markets, variations will be found in the inequality of outcome (volumes, revenues, profits) between producers, and on basic aspects of market functioning.

In an earlier paper, White (1981a) maps out the cost and valuation contexts that can sustain reproducible markets. Here we focus on a portion of these contexts – those in which it costs more to make higher quality goods – and explore the possible range of inequalities among producers. Though the analytic results we offer are dependent upon a number of simplifying assumptions and specific functional forms, they provide an intriguing glimpse into the variety of reproducible market structures one should expect to find in comparative studies of markets.

For present purposes, the topology of reproducible market structures can be represented in two dimensions. The first dimension concerns spreads or, more precisely, a ratio of spreads. This ratio (*b/d*) compares the spread of goods in value to consumers with their spread on costs of production. If the spreads are equal ($b/d = 1$) this means, for example, that if one product costs twice as much to produce as another, consumers perceive it as twice as valuable. A ratio of greater than one ($b/d > 1$) means that goods are more differentiated on value to consumers than they are on the manufacturing costs for producers, and a ratio of less than one implies the reverse.

In the frozen pizza market, the ratio is greater than one, since valuation differences are large relative to cost differences. Using a number of guesses in the absence of reliable data, and methods developed elsewhere (Leifer, 1985), we have placed the b/d ratio for the frozen pizza market around 2.5. (For example, Stouffer's pizza may cost 1.2 times as much as Jeno's to produce, while conferring 1.5 times the value.)

The second dimension concerns shifts. It too turns out to be a ratio. This ratio (a/c) compares the consequences of shifting production volumes on value to consumers and costs to producers. Stated simply, if overall production were doubled, it might increase production costs by 75 per cent (considering economies of scale). If consumer values increased by 90 per cent for the doubled output, however, then our ratio is greater than one ($a/c > 1$). If an increase in production volume increases the dollar value to consumers as much as it increases dollar costs to producers, then our ratio (a/c) is one.

We have placed the ratio for the frozen pizza market around 1.89 with $c = 0.9$ (unit costs would decrease slightly with an increase in production volume) and $a = 1.7$ (value to consumers would increase sharply with an increase in producer volumes).

These two dimensions – the spread ratio (b/d) and the shift ratio (a/c) – define the axes of a topology of market structures. We will focus only on regions that can sustain viable markets in the upper right quadrant. This quadrant is shown in figure 3.4. The frozen pizza market is a solitary point in this quadrant. One can imagine, or discover through comparative efforts, a multitude of diverse markets in different regions of the quadrant. Each market would have its own inequalities and sensitivities, as we will now map out.

We limit our attention to the prime regions for stable markets. These correspond to the "STABLE" areas in figure 3.4. In the market region "UNRAVELS" there is a tendency for producers to select corner solutions in their production decisions, and hence "unravel" the volume–revenue schedule as all producers move toward the same "corner." In the market region "EXPLODES" there is a potential (in certain parameter configurations) for explosive growth[11] because companies are monetarily rewarded for increased production. In either instance, though relative niches can be found, there is no stability in the niches sought across production periods. Each company migrates at each decisional juncture. For a more detailed explanation of stable and unstable regions, see White (1981a).

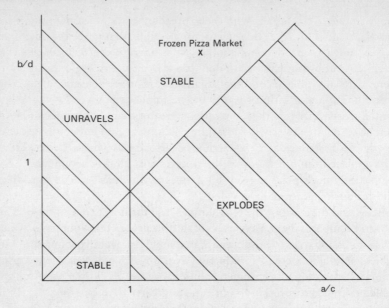

3.4 A topology of market contents. The parameters associated with cost and value contexts define a two-dimensional topology of market contexts. The dimensions are the ratios of spreads on value over spreads on cost between goods, and volume shift consequences on value over volume shift consequences on costs.

Within the stable market region – where firms are constrained to maintain their niches – it turns out that inequality in market (revenue) share depends primarily on the ratio which we call *g*.

$$g = \frac{(b/d)-1}{(a/c)-1}$$

In the shaded region, *g* is constant across lines passing through (1,1), though it is not defined on (1,1) as here the denominator of *g* is zero. As will become evident, (1,1) is a highly peculiar point in the topology of reproducible markets. It is the point where the spreads and shifts are the same for the producer and consumer sides.

To mathematically explore inequality as a function of *g*, some simplifying assumptions are necessary. We assume that *K* (see equation 10) is zero, and that producers are spread uniformly across the entire range of *n* (see equations 2, 5, and 7). With these assumptions, an equation for the Gini index, a widely used measure of inequality, which ranges between 0 (equality), and 1 (maximum inequality) can be derived. The Gini Index, *G*, is equal to:

$$\text{Gini} = G = \frac{1}{1 + \dfrac{2}{(g-1)d}}$$

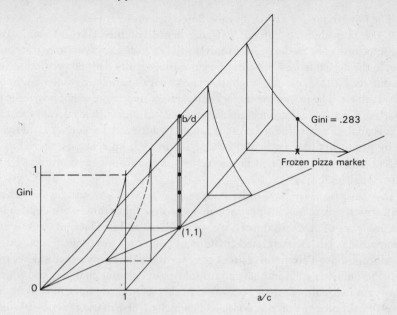

3.5   Outcome inequality. Gini measures of revenue outcome inequality
are graphed over the topology of stable market contexts. Inequality
approaches 1 along the vertical $a/c = 1$ (though it is not defined over
$a/c = 1$). Equality holds where $a/c = b/d$ (i.e. Gini $= 0$). The point $(1,1)$
is a "black hole" where the lines of maximal inequality and equality
intersect.

Due to the appearance of d in the equation for G, interpretation for
inequality in the topology of market structure is the clearest for the limiting
cases of 90° and 45° lines running through $(1,1)$. Approaching the 90° line
(where $a/c = 1$), g heads toward infinity so G heads toward 1, or maximal
inequality. Approaching the 45° line, g heads toward 1 so G heads toward 0, or
equality. Intermediate values of G between these two limiting lines will, of
course, depend on d, but given a constant d, one gets a gradual transition from
maximal inequality to equality as one rotates from the 90° to 45° line through
$(1,1)$. Hence there is the full gamut of possibilities for inequality in market
share or profits across markets. Figure 3.5 graphs these possibilities, for
$d = 1$.[12]

To get some intuitive feel for this measure, consider that inequality in pay in
a typical business hierarchy of managers might be about 0.2, inequality in
earned income in a Western society might run about 0.4, and the Gini for
inequality in some major forms of property, say agricultural land in
traditional societies or capital ownership in ours, could go as high as 0.8 or
more.

The Gini index for actual revenue outcomes in the frozen pizza market is 0.283, a considerable but not extreme degree of inequality. Though the assumptions used to derive the analytical Gini index results are not strictly met in the actual frozen pizza market, the analytically derived prediction for inequality is 0.255, close enough to suggest that the analytic results might be quite robust. The frozen pizza market is demarcated in the sea of possibilities charted in figure 3.5. Each location in figure 3.5 carries with it a distinct reality that is analytically sliced from many angles by interested onlookers and lived in by producers like Tony and others. Figure 3.5, however, is offered as a potent illustration that real life diversity may share a common underlying processual logic.

In this section, we have moved a long way from Tony and his operating concerns. Tony makes his production decisions in the framework defined by the decisions of other producers, whose products and production options are comparable, but differentiated, from his. Tony and the other frozen pizza producers share a common context of costs and valuations which shapes the way their market will function and respond to exogenous changes, and which shape the inequality in their outcomes. In this section, we have moved to the level of a topology of market contexts in which diverse markets can be placed. The basic structuralist credo holds at this level with equal force: position in a topology of market contexts constrains the functioning of a market, just as position in a market constrains ("voluntaristically") the decisions of producers.

Discussion

The model presented here defines the structural context of producers by referring to the relations among producer outcomes. The shape and location of the structural context of market activity are dependent on specific sets of producers, and cannot be defined apart from them. The structural context of a schedule of niches sums up market possibilities and thereby provides a guide for producer behavior. In a viable market, producer behavior is guided in such a way that it functions to reproduce the structural context from which it derives. Our model provides the conceptual and mathematical conditions for self-reproducing structural contexts, and thus delimits the variety of markets which can be empirically observed. Reproducibility therefore becomes the central issue in characterizing markets and understanding market behavior. In this section, we contrast this structural approach with the information orientation which dominates economic analyses of markets.

Information approaches are driven more by the questions producers ask than the way they go about answering them. Each producer, in a differentiated market, wants to know the unique demand curve for his product. That is, he wants to know how much he can sell at any given price. Furthermore, the producer's questions are asked in *ex ante* terms – he wants to know what *will* happen. Given this question, economists and marketing consultants have focussed on the kinds of information and theories needed to provide an answer. Firm-specific demand curves can be estimated from prior firm outcomes, yet this estimation depends on the assumption that the demand curve *does not change (or changes predictably) over time* (Intriligator, 1978), *and such estimation ignores interdependencies between producers.*

If these interdependencies are to be taken into account, assumptions must be made about how other producers *will* react to the focal companies' price–quantity decision, and further assumptions must be made about the cross-product elasticities which guide the consumers' selection among producer offerings. An *ex ante* focus on all these interdependencies requires much more information and many more theories to define the possibilities that face each producer. An answer to the simple question asked by producers therefore invariably requires invoking a whole series of assumptions which inspire little confidence because they are based on mathematical convenience rather than empirical plausibility. A definitive answer has therefore not been found, and if left to be provided by the theory of games, it does not look like one will be found (see Shubik, 1982; Smith, 1982).

One might wonder why the producer's simple question is so central if the solution is intractable, or at best dependent on such arbitrary assumptions? Producers, after all, seem to function in the absence of a clear answer, and few would claim that markets must be fully understood (in the form of explicit theory) in order to operate.

A solution to this dilemma comes from recognizing the link between the producer's question and the idea of efficiency. If we view the producer as situated in a visible spectrum of evaluatable alternatives, efficiency can become a relevant concern. The wider the range, the more relevant is the idea of efficiency in rationalizing actions (see Granovetter (1985) for a critique of the centrality of efficiency in economic thought). Answers to the question of what will happen must cover all real world possibilities for efficiency to be relevant. The producer's ultimate choice must be set against a backdrop of possible, yet less desirable, behaviors. This circumstance simply does not occur in the real world.

The problem with focussing on the hypothetical producer's question is that it stands in the way of discovering any distinct reality associated with a "market." Firm-specific demand curves divert attention from markets altogether. Yet the producer's reputation, behavior, and possibilities may be defined, as we have claimed, purely from the standpoint of the producer's relation to other producers in a "market." These relations are knowable (observable) only *ex post*, from market structure, or what has worked in past periods. An "orderly" market structure therefore reflects the interdependencies in the market, *ex post*. When the producer is viewed from the standpoint of the market, these "ex post" interdependencies – already observed in the previous production period – replace speculated gaming interdependencies and cross-product elasticities – which are assumed in some *a priori* manner.

The producer's position and possibilities are defined in terms of these *ex post* interdependencies that make up market structure. This central feature of structural analysis is lost when we lock ourselves inside a hypothetical producer's *ex ante* point of view and attempt to depict *ex ante* possibilities that lie outside of observed *ex post* interdependencies. In our structural approach, producer behavior can be understood only from the point of view of the market. The "market" assumes a distinct reality of its own, and it provides guidance to producers. Rather than being a consequence of solutions to producers' *ex ante* speculations, it is an empirical premise derived from past production periods.

In stepping outside a hypothetical producer's *ex ante* point of view, efficiency ceases to be well defined. A wide range of market structures becomes possible for any particular set of producers, the particular structure that appears being partly determined by historical accident (K) and scale indeterminacies (θ). The varying structures will be associated with varying levels and dispersions of profits across producers. In most cases, producers will make positive profits; and different profit levels will exist across producers as stable features of the market. The "zero profit" criteria for "equilibrium" markets that economists insist upon has no place in the proposed structural approach. The positions of producers in a market, with their distinct profitability implications, must be treated as givens. For this treatment of position to be useful, positions must be stable, else the structural context of interrelated positions could not provide a useful source of guidance.

Reproducibility, not efficiency, is the relevant issue in structural analysis. The range of possibilities is defined by the structures in which position holders operate. It does not extend beyond these *extant* structures, as would be needed to assess the abstract efficiency of a structure. Given the narrow and well-defined range of possibilities that defines a reproducible structure, the behavior of position holders is self-fulfilling. It functions to maintain their position within the structure. Figure 3.4 showed that not all imputed market structures are reproducible in this sense. Clearly if the behavior of "position holders" serves to undermine positions and structure, then the reality of "position" and "structure" as observer constructs must be suspect.

In our model, markets are real structures with definite boundaries. Producers are position holders whose behavior reaffirms their position in the market, marked by a distinct reputation in the "culture" associated with a market. Positive and unequal profits are facts-of-life institutional details for most markets. This treatment of markets as real structures contrasts sharply with the (neoclassical) economist's treatment of markets as a convenient analytical device for drawing inferences about the "economy," or systems of markets. It also contrasts with most applied economics treatments (e.g. Porter, 1980), which treat markets as loosely defined arenas for strategic (*ex ante*) ploys. Our model tries to combine some of the analytical rigor of the economist with some of the institutional realism of the business professor. Markets become a realistic device that can be used by concrete producers and studied by researchers.

NOTES

Financial support from the University Research Council of UNC is gratefully acknowledged. This chapter has benefited from the extensive editorial efforts of Mark Granovetter, Mark Mizruchi, and Michael Schwartz.

1 It should be stressed that, unlike functionalism, structural analysis does not assume that a social arrangement is self-reproducing. Integral structural contradictions can produce ongoing conflict and change – or even destruction – of a social institution. This point is elaborated below.

2 We assume Tony treats the retail customer as the "consumer," as opposed to the distributors and/or retail outlets which buy pizzas directly from him. Tony allows a standard markup for these outlets in arriving at the price he will charge them, and thus absorbs the costs and benefits from market fluctuations. Other arrangements are certainly possible. Defining the "consumer" must involve careful consideration of the distribution channels for a product, with regard to the pricing, packaging, and marketing responsibilities of each concern that handles the product.

3 Since revenues equal price times volume, this is analytically identical to describing the dimensions as volume and price. In our formulation, we use y (volume) and W (revenue).

4 In advocating structural over information approaches, our argument largely rests on the "publicness" of information and not its presence or absence. The advantage of the proposed structural approach is that it assumes actors act on the basis of information that is readily obtainable, through informal communications, trade association publications, marketing reports, and the like. (We do not assume a producer knows the other producers' costs, which are not easy to obtain – and presents difficulties for the researcher in estimating parameters for a market.) Information approaches, in adopting an *ex ante* point of view, tend to freely assume the availability of "private" information that has no tangible existence in the producer's operating world.

5 We treat cost differences as exogenously determined. They could result from the use of different production techniques, factors of production, labor rates, locations, etc. If one envisions, however, the formation of a market as a trial and error process, where products and images are put before the consumer and either received or rejected, initial cost differences might be related to initial role perceptions of the producers. That is, the producer who perceives he is slipping into

a definite market role (e.g. as a high-quality producer) may alter his product or its image (e.g. packaging), and hence its costs, in a way that conforms to the perceived role. Cost differences, and their relation to valuation differences (see below), cease to be so mysterious when viewed in this light.

6 To get unique estimates for g and d, the range of g_i must be arbitrarily fixed. The interval selected for the lowest and highest g will determine how d is interpreted (e.g. if a "large" interval is selected, then a "small" d may still mean there is some differentiation in cost structures between producers).

7 The second order condition ensuring maximization (equation 4), and the condition that producers require positive profits to produce correspond to the satisfaction of the two inequalities below:

$$(cd(a-c)/(bc-ad))y^{(bc-ad)/b} > -adK/bq(\theta/r)^{d/b}$$

$$(d(a-c)/(bc-ad))y^{(bc-ad)/b} > -K/q(\theta/r)^{d/b}$$

8 This assumption obviously downplays the importance of marketing research in production and pricing decisions within a stable market context. Much marketing research, however, is used for other purposes anyway, like exploring potential market areas or at least legitimating already made decisions to enter new areas. If some routine production and pricing decisions are based on marketing research, the error that might be introduced in ignoring this research (assuming its conclusions differ from those of the unaided producer) is small, we claim, relative to the error and intermediacy we would face in conceding that production and pricing decisions *are* based on marketing research.

9 Value can be viewed as measurable in dollar units. In discussing aggregate value and revenue later, we suggest the assumption that aggregate value equals aggregate revenue provides a convenient calibrating device. Thus if $240 million is spent on frozen pizzas annually, we assume that all the frozen pizzas purchased are "worth" $240 million to the aggregate consumer. The difficulties entailed in actually measuring this "worth" motivated the first author to design techniques for estimating market parameters without directly measuring value (see Leifer, 1985). The researcher, however, has to make an assumption about how much valuations differ across products (b) and, without data for multiple production periods, an assumption about the aggregate satiation (γ), a factor discussed later.

10 This imagery stands in sharp contrast to the fluidity of competitive markets in economics (aside from Chamberlain, 1933), where only the aggregates matter. The distinct reputations of producers are not "frictional" effects in the $W(y)$ model, but the basic building blocks of markets.

11 This potential is dependent upon a/c being greater than $1/\gamma$. The γ dimension, however, can be suppressed for present purposes.

12 The point (1,1) is a sort of "black hole" in the topology of market structures. It is the point where the lines of maximal inequality and equality intersect, and hence represents a most peculiar situation. Mathematically, a Gini index is not defined at the (1,1) point, and no stable market is possible there either. At the (1,1) point, spreads on cost and value between producer goods are identical for producers and consumers, respectively, as are sensitivities to shifts across production volumes.

Why this symmetry in spreads and shift sensitivities between producer and consumers precludes a stable market is a puzzle we must leave to the reader to solve. The solution to this riddle may give insight into the prerequisites for interfaces in general which tie together two distinct sides.

REFERENCES

Berkowitz, S. D., 1982. *An Introduction to Structural Analysis: The Network Approach to Social Research*. Toronto, Canada: Butterworths

Boorman, S. A., 1975. "A combinatorial optimization model for transmission of job information through contact networks." *Bell Journal of Economics*, 6 (Spring): 216–49

Breiger, Ronald, 1981. "Structures of economic interdependence among nations." in P. M. Blau and R. K. Merton (eds.), *Continuities in Structural Inquiry*. Beverly Hills: Sage, pp. 353–80

Burt, Ronald S., 1982. *Toward a Structural Theory of Action: Network Models of Social Structure, Perception, and Action*. New York: Academic Press

Chamberlain, Edward H., 1933. *The Theory of Monopolistic Competition*. Cambridge, Mass.: Harvard University Press

Granovetter, Mark, 1985. "Economic action and social structure: the problem of embeddedness." *American Journal of Sociology*, 91: 481–510

Intriligator, Michael D., 1978. *Econometric Models, Techniques, and Applications*. Englewood Cliffs, N.J.: Prentice-Hall

Kanter, Rosabeth Moss, 1977. *Men and Women of the Corporation*. New York: Basic Books

Leifer, Eric M., 1985. "Markets as mechanisms: using a role structure." *Social Forces*, 64 (2) (December): 442–72

Lorrain, F. P., and Harrison C. White, 1971. "Structural equivalence of individuals in social networks." *Journal of Mathematical Sociology*, 1 (January): 49–80

Love, Geoffrey, 1982. "An investigation of block-modeling techniques applied to international trade flows." Unpublished undergraduate thesis, Harvard University

Miller, Ross M., and Charles R. Plott, 1983. "Product quality signaling in experimental markets." Working Paper No. 40/82, School of Management, Boston University

Porter, Michael E., 1980. *Competitive Strategy*. New York: Academic Press

Riley, John G., 1975. "Competitive signalling." *Journal of Economic Theory*, 10: 174–86
    1979. "Information equilibrium." *Econometrica*, 47: 331–59

Shubik, Martin, 1982. *Game Theory in the Social Sciences*. Cambridge, Mass.: MIT Press

Smith, Alasdair, 1982. *A Mathematical Introduction to Economics*, Totowa, NJ: Barnes and Noble

Snyder, David, and Edward L. Kick, 1979. "Structural position in the world system and economic growth, 1955–1970: a multiple network analysis of transnational interactions." *American Journal of Sociology*, 84: 1096–126

White, Harrison C., 1963. *An Anatomy of Kinship*. Englewood Cliffs, NJ: Prentice-Hall

    1981a. "Production markets as induced role structures." In S. L. Leinhardt (ed.), *Sociological Methodology*. San Francisco: Jossey-Bass, pp. 1–57

    1981b. "Where do markets come from?" *American Journal of Sociology*, 87: 517–47

    1987. "Varieties of markets." In Barry Wellman and S. D. Berkowitz (eds.), *Structural Sociology*. Cambridge University Press (in press)

Williamson, Oliver E., 1975. *Markets and Hierarchies: Analysis and Antitrust Implications*. New York: The Free Press

Winship, Christopher, 1978. "Allocation of time among individuals." In Karl F. Schuessler (ed.), *Sociological Methodology*. San Francisco: Jossey-Bass, pp. 75–100

4

What is money? A social structural interpretation[1]

Wayne E. Baker

There is probably not more than one hundred dollars in actual cash in circulation today. That is, if you were to call in all the bills and silver and gold in the country at noon tomorrow and pile them up on the table, you would find that you had just about one hundred dollars, with perhaps several Canadian pennies and a few peppermint life-savers. All the rest of the money you hear about doesn't exist. It is conversation money. When you hear of a transaction involving $50,000,000 it means that one firm wrote "$50,000,000" on a piece of paper and gave it to another firm, and the other firm took it home and said, "Look, Momma, I got $50,000,000!" But when Momma asked for a dollar and a quarter to pay the man who washed the windows, the answer probably was that the firm hadn't got more than seventy cents in cash.

This is the principle of finance. So long as you can pronounce any number above a thousand, you have got that much money. You can't work this scheme with the shoe-store man or the restaurant owner, but it goes big on Wall St. or in international financial circles.

(Robert Benchley)

Two trends are revolutionizing the monetary system, and with it the definition of money: first, recent advances in telecommunications and electronic data processing have altered the transaction technology of the economy; second, a plethora of new financial assets that are close substitutes to money – NOW accounts, money market shares, overnight Eurodollar deposits, overnight repurchase agreements – have been developed at an increasing rate. While the question "What is money?" once was simple to answer, the revolution of the monetary system has made this question increasingly difficult. Yet more than ever the question must be answered, especially if monetary policy is to serve as a reliable means to guide the economy. The purpose of this chapter is to offer a sociological approach to the definition of money that may help to answer the question "What is money?"

The question of money has been the focus of the energies and talents of many economic theorists, policy-makers, and practitioners (e.g. see citations below). But the approach developed in this chapter differs substantially from conventional economic perspectives both theoretically and methodologically. It begins with a fundamentally different – and possibly incompatible – premise of social science inquiry, one outside the established paradigms of mainstream economic research. In this paradigm, the market is viewed as social structure (White, 1981a, 1981b; Baker, 1984a, 1984b) and, by extension, the market economy is also viewed as social structure (Baker, 1984c). The present analysis develops the implications of this social structural conceptualization of markets and market economies for the definition of money.

Money holds more attributes than those cited in the standard economic litany: a medium of exchange, a means of payment, a unit of account, and a standard of deferred payment. In addition to these, money performs two other fundamental social functions; as Parsons and Smelser (1956: 71) note, "money represents the *generalization* of purchasing power to *control decisions* to exchange goods . . . and it symbolizes attitudes" (i.e. prestige). The first of these social functions is particularly germane for defining money. To put it succinctly, money contains the ability to command goods, services, and people; it is power.

If money is power (if "money talks"), then what is used as money and how money is used are determined by those who control economic resources in a society. From a structural perspective, those actors in the core of the economy – those who control resources (including financial assets) – define money through their collective actions. In other words, money is related to the underlying social structure of the market economy.

The relationship between structure and money has long been recognized by economic anthropologists, since they have had to grapple with the perplexingly variegated money-stuff of diverse cultures that are neither capitalist nor integrated by markets (e.g. Dalton, 1967). Economists, who confront money only in a single economic context – the market economy – have lost sight of the fact that money, as well as markets, is socially constructed. Money seems to take on a life of its own, just as the market does – as if they were both independent of their societal integument (Barber, 1977; Polanyi, 1977). The definition of money, I suggest, even in a capitalist context, should be considered to be a social construction, and the question of money can be answered only by examining the social structure of the economy and the power relations contained therein.

In general, the question of money turns on a fundamental distinction: whether society is considered to be subordinate to the economy, or the economy is considered to be subordinate to society. The former position characterizes mainstream economics, especially monetary theory and policy. The latter position characterizes economic sociology (e.g. Baker 1984a, 1984c; Granovetter, 1985; Barber, 1977; Simmel, 1950) and is the position I take in this analysis of money.

The methodological approach developed in this chapter also differs fundamentally from that employed in conventional economics. Since monetary theory (and policy) is a field of macroeconomics, conventional definitions of money focus on monetary assets at an extremely high level of aggregation. While it is recognized that the economy is based on concrete exchanges, the money stock is measured as the sum total of these exchanges. In contrast, I argue that money should be analyzed at a relatively disaggregated level, one that captures the patterns of asset substitutability at the level of behavioral exchanges. Thus, the unit of analysis in the approach presented here differs from that typically used in the measurement of money.

This chapter is presented in five sections. In section I, I present a brief review of monetary policy and the increasingly intractable problem of defining money. In section II, I discuss alternative views of money, especially the economic anthropological view of money as a reflection of the socioeconomic organization of society. In this section, I extend this view to money in the market economy, and review the social structural conceptualization of the market economy (Baker, 1983, 1984c) on which the current analysis rests. In brief, the underlying structure of a financial market economy is hypothesized to be a core and periphery. The core is expected to be occupied by the powerful actors in the economy. If money reflects the socioeconomic structure of an economy, then the relative "moneyness" of the assets should reflect the core–periphery structure of the economy in which they are exchanged. The main hypothesis of this chapter is that the assets exchanged in the core position of this economy are the closest to money and the assets exchanged in the peripheral position are the furthest from money. This relationship, I argue, represents the power of the core actors, their control over resources in the economy.

In section III, I present the data and methods used to test this hypothesis. Section IV presents the findings. Concluding remarks are presented in section V. A primer on financial futures is presented in appendix A. An excursus on structural equivalence and portfolio composition and management is presented in appendix B.

I Monetary policy and the problem of defining money

Monetary policy and fiscal policy

It is well known that the federal government regulates the engines of the market economy in two basic ways: fiscal policy and monetary policy. Fiscal policy refers to the use of taxation and public expenditures to moderate swings in the business cycle and to foster an expanding economy with full employment and relatively stable prices. Monetary policy has the same objectives, but focusses on a different means to obtain them – regulating the supply of money in the economy.

The efficacy of fiscal and monetary approaches to economic action has long been a subject of debate. On the one hand, the chief advocates of the monetary approach, originating in the Chicago School and championed by Milton Friedman, assert that controlling the money supply is the *only* way to achieve growth, full employment, and relatively stable prices. On the other hand, during the later 1930s Keynes and other economists argued that money matters little, and instead stressed the importance of taxes and government expenditures. In the so-called post-Keynesian synthesis, both monetary and fiscal variables are considered to be important. While the emphasis of each administration varies by political ideology – proponents of fiscal policy tend to be politically liberal, while advocates of monetary policy tend to be politically conservative – every administration practices some mix of fiscal and monetary policies in the attempt to meet its objectives.

Rudiments of monetarism

The quantity theory of money

The theoretical basis of monetarism is a simple identity that describes the interrelationships of the money supply, velocity, price level, and real GNP:

$$MV = PQ$$

In this equation, M is the amount of money in the economy (such as cash plus demand deposits). V is a concept of money turnover, the velocity of money – the rate at which the money supply turns over per year as it is used in transactions. P is the average level of prices in the economy. And Q, for want of anything better, is measured as real GNP – the quantity of goods and services produced in the economy, adjusted for inflation (or deflation).

A simple example will serve to illuminate the dynamics implied by this identity. If a nation's central bank – in the US the Federal Reserve – decides to decrease the quantity of M by selling government bonds (and thereby drawing money out of the economy), then PQ should also fall, holding V constant. Monetarists contend that such a decrease in M would tend to result in a reduction in P (i.e. a reduction in prices or inflation).[2] In recent years, the practice of monetary policy has evolved into a set of operational procedures that includes setting targets for monetary aggregates, publicly announcing those targets, and then attempting to control the instruments of monetary policy to meet those targets.

Defining the money supply: trends and problems

If monetary theory is to be a reliable guide to economic action, then it is obvious that precise measurement of the amount of money in the economy is essential; without a good measure of the money supply, it is impossible to design monetary policy properly and carry it out. Up until the 1960s, defining the money supply was not a problem: M1 (cash, currency, and demand deposits) remained the principal means of payment (Cagan, 1979: 120). During the 1960s, the problem began.

Prior to the 1960s, cash, currency, and demand deposits (i.e. checks) were the primary means of payment, means used to effect transactions for the full spectrum of goods and services. But rising interest rates on short-term, highly liquid assets such as Treasury bills made these assets increasingly attractive as substitutes for money. Since no interest could be paid on checking accounts, businesses and households had an incentive to minimize the amount of money held in demand deposits and to place anything above the minimum needed for transactions into other financial instruments. Though such substitutions were increasingly made after World War II, they did not substantially affect cyclical fluctuations in the demand for M1 (Cagan, 1979: 120).

As Cagan (p. 121) summarizes, two developments fostered the invention of substitutable financial assets for demand deposits: "Interest rates on other assets rose to historically high levels, and the new computer technology reduced the costs of record keeping for high-turnover accounts." One of the well-known financial inventions spawned early on by this environment is the "negotiated order of withdrawal" (NOW) savings account. With the approval of NOW accounts, banks are granted the right to pay interest on checking accounts. NOW accounts precipitated the creation of innovative financial assets by banks, thrift institutions, and others. The proliferation of new instruments has also extended into the organized financial markets with the invention of various new financial contracts, such as stock options, stock index futures, other financial futures, and the like.

With the rise of financial innovations, the boundaries between what is money and what is not have become increasingly blurred. This became evident in economists' systematic overpredictions of the demand for money since 1973 (e.g. Goldfeld, 1976; Garcia and Park, 1979). As Cagan (1979: 128) puts it, "The public is apparently getting along with less M1 than these equations say the public wants." The plausible explanation for this phenomenon is that economic actors are increasingly using means other than cash or demand deposits to facilitate transactions. In other words, other financial assets, which were previously used as a store of value, have come to be used at least partially as vehicles for effecting transactions. From 1976 through 1977, for instance, alternative financial instruments (such as NOW accounts) displaced demand deposits by $8.4 billion (Paulus and Axilrod, 1976; reported in Cagan 1979: 131).

The use of alternative financial instruments has been and is facilitated by advances in transaction technology. It would be impossible, for example, to take advantage of a highly liquid alternative asset if a transfer could be made only by a personal visit to a financial institution's office or solely by mail.[3] There have been numerous improvements in transaction technology, and more are developed every day. For example, it is now possible to make an intercontinental cash withdrawal, receiving cash in the host country's currency and debiting the recipient's account in another country in that country's currency. In some supermarkets, point-of-sale (POS) terminals are used that accept a customer's debit cards at the check-out counter and automatically debit the customer's bank account; the POS system makes cash, credit cards, and checks obsolete. It is also possible to comparison shop for home mortgages via home computers. Generally, improvements in transaction technology are overcoming the "friction" of space. Once markets were always constrained by geography and distance; now, societies are experiencing what I call "markets without propinquity" (Baker, 1981; also Baker, 1984a, 1984b, 1984c; cf. Webber, 1961).

In response to these shifts in the use of financial assets, the Federal Reserve amended the traditional definitions of money, developing four new monetary aggregates to replace the older measures of M1 through M5 (for details see Simpson, 1980). Old M1, for example, has been replaced by M-1A and M-1B. M-1A includes currency and demand deposits (net of demand deposits held by foreign commercial banks and official institutions); M-1B is M-1A plus "other checkable deposits" – NOW accounts, ATS (automatic transfer from savings) accounts, credit union share draft balances, and thrift institution demand deposits (Simpson, 1980). Table 4.1 presents all the new measures of money along with their dollar amounts.

II Money and social structure: alternative views of money in society

In Western economies, money and markets are so intimately related that the terms "money economy" and "market economy" are often used synonymously. It is, in fact, difficult to speak of money without (at least implicitly) making reference to the use of money in market exchange; for, as Dalton (1967: 256) puts it, "In the economies for which the English monetary vocabulary was created, there is one dominant transactional mode, market exchange, to which *all* money uses relate."

Yet money is used in other types of economies, ones in which markets do not exist or exist only peripherally. The uses of money in these contexts, as I briefly discuss below, differs so strikingly from money and its uses in capitalist societies that the relationship between these nonmarket forms of money and social structure is obvious. The argument that I propose here is that money and its uses in capitalist contexts similarly reflect the structure of the economy, the social structure of the *market* economy.

Table 4.1 *New measures of money and liquid assets*[a]

Billions of dollars, not seasonally adjusted, November 1979

Aggregate and component	Amount
M-1A	372.2
Currency	106.6
Demand deposits[b]	265.6
M-1B	387.9
M-1A	372.2
Other checkable deposits[c]	15.7
M-2	1,510.0
M-1B	387.9
Overnight RPs issued by commercial banks	20.3
Overnight Eurodollar deposits held by US nonbank residents at Caribbean branches of US banks	3.2
Money market mutual fund shares	40.4
Savings deposits at all depository institutions	420.0
Small time deposits at all depository institutions[d]	640.8
M-2 consolidation component[e]	−2.7
M-3	1,759.1
M-2	1,510.0
Large time deposits at all depository institutions[f]	219.5
Term RPs issued by commercial banks	21.5
Term RPs issued by savings and loan associations	8.2
L	2,123.8
M-3	1,759.1
Other Eurodollar deposits of US residents other than banks	34.5
Bankers' acceptances	27.6
Commercial paper	97.1
Savings bonds	80.0
Liquid treasury obligations	125.4

[a] Components of M-2, M-3, and L measures generally exclude amounts held by domestic depository institutions, foreign commercial banks and official institutions, the US government (including the Federal Reserve), and money market mutual funds. Exceptions are bankers' acceptances and commercial paper for which data sources permit the removal only of amounts held by money market mutual funds and, in the case of bankers' acceptances, amounts held by accepting banks, the Federal Reserve, and the Federal Home Loan Bank System.

[b] Net of demand deposits due to foreign commercial banks and official institutions.

[c] Includes NOW, ATS, and credit union share draft balances and demand deposits at thrift institutions.

[d] Time deposits issued in denominations of less than $100,000.

[e] In order to avoid double counting of some deposits in M-2, those demand deposits owned by thrift institutions (a component of M-1B), which are estimated to be used for servicing their savings and small time deposit liabilities in M-2, are removed.

[f] Time deposits issued in denominations of $100,000 or more.

Source: Federal Reserve Bulletin, 5 (66), 1980.

Money and social structure in nonmarket contexts

In a classic essay on primitive money, economic anthropologist George Dalton (1967) analyzed money in noncapitalist, nonmarket economies, contrasting such primitive money with our Western view of money as dollars, marks, sterling, yen, etc. As he states, "if one asks what is 'primitive' about a particular money, one may come away with two answers: the money-*stuff* – woodpecker scalps, sea shells, goats, dogs' teeth – is primitive (i.e. different from our own); and the *uses* to which the money-stuff is sometimes put – mortuary payments, bloodwealth, bridewealth – are primitive (i.e. different from our own)" (Dalton, 1967: 254–5).

Confronted with such money-stuff and money uses, some field researchers have concluded (erroneously in Dalton's view) that primitive money is merely a precursor or forerunner of money as we know it (e.g. as Armstrong [1924; 1928] assumed). But this view misses the connection between socioeconomic structure and money. Money as we know it derives its peculiar characteristics from the socioeconomic organization of capitalist society: a society integrated by markets. Market integration determines all money uses: as a medium of exchange, a means of payment, a unit of account, and a standard for deferred payment (Dalton, 1967: 256–9). Sociologically, one may also add money as a symbol of prestige and as an instrument of potential and manifest power (Parsons and Smelser, 1956). Money in market contexts is "general purpose" money (Polanyi, 1957): the value of almost everything may be expressed in terms of "how much"; as Simmel (1950: 414) put it, "money becomes the most frightful leveler."

Unlike dollars and marks, primitive money is "limited-purpose" money and does not possess the peculiar bundle of traits conferred by market exchange. Instead, primitive monies reflect their own particular social structural context. While it is not necessary to delve into a detailed discussion of nonmarket contexts and money, two concrete examples help to make the point that money reflects socioeconomic structure.

In primitive nonmarket societies, redistribution and reciprocity are the transactional modes used to distribute and allocate resources (rather than market-mediated resource allocation). Transactions involving the exchange of money-stuff reflect obligatory payments to friends, kin, chiefs, priests, and so forth (Dalton, 1967). In the Trobriands, for example, two valuables – armshells and necklets of red shell-discs – are circulated through reciprocal exchange. Unlike American or European money, these two valuables cannot be used for any other purpose; they cannot be replaced with substitutes; they must travel in fixed, opposite directions; and they cannot be held for long periods of time in the same hands (Malinowski, 1921).[4] Similarly, in the New Guinea Highlands, pigs and shells are ceremonially exchanged among "big-men" who gain and lose prestige by their relative success in reciprocal exchange (e.g. Strathern, 1971). In both societies, families, groups, and tribes are integrated through such reciprocal exchange, and alliances and control of warfare are fostered by the big-men (both societies are "stateless" and lack market integration).

Money and social structure in the market economy

Throughout the social science literature on capitalist societies, any discussion of money is (implicitly) predicated on the assumption of a *market* economy. When economists speak of "monetary aggregates," for example, everyone knows that the concepts implicitly refer to general purpose money in a market integrated society. Most discussions of money in capitalist contexts also rest on another less often noted assumption about the socioeconomic context of money: the market economy is assumed to be a homogeneous, undifferentiated – indeed structureless – entity, as several sociologists have noted (White, 1981a, 1981b; Baker, 1984a, 1984b, 1984c; Leifer and White, this volume; Barber, 1977; Polanyi, 1977; Hodson and Kaufman, 1982).

Yet a clue that the assumption of structurelessness is unrealistic is the Federal Reserve's recent redefinition of the monetary aggregates, a redefinition of what is used as money in society (Simpson, 1980). If the economic anthropologists are right – if money and its uses reflect underlying socioeconomic structure – then the need to redefine the monetary aggregates indicates major shifts in the plates of the socioeconomic substratum. By understanding the structure of a market economy, one can better connect observations of how money is used and what is used as money to the underlying organization of the economy itself.

The economy as a network of interlocking markets

In contrast to the conventional economistic view of the market economy as an abstract and generalized market mechanism, I have proposed that the market economy may be conceptualized and modeled as a social network of interlocking markets (Baker, 1984c). As the market is a social structure (e.g. White, 1981a, 1981b; Baker, 1984a, 1984b; Faulkner, 1983), the market economy is an interconnected set of social structures (markets). In other words, a market economy is a "structure of social structures."

In that analysis (Baker, 1984c), I explored the conceptualization of the economy as a network of interlocking markets by applying the approach to two different market economies: an international financial economy and a local hospital economy. The approach worked equally well in these diverse cases. The international financial economy I modeled is the same as the one presented here, but the purpose of the present analysis is to draw out the relationship between the social structure of this economy and the definition of money.[5]

I hypothesized that the financial market economy would be comprised of a core and periphery. The core would be composed of the heavily used securities markets, and would be dominated by the main commercial actors in the system – banks, investment companies, institutional investors, and the like. The periphery of the economy would be composed of the foreign currency markets, and would be occupied by the amateur and noncommercial actors in the system – a host of persons such as students, clerks, retired persons, military and civilian personnel, and the like. The hypotheses about the membership of the various positions in the economy (i.e. its core and periphery) are supported by the nearly ubiquitous finding in social structural research of the importance, power, and centrality of banks and financial institutions in the economy (e.g. Mizruchi, 1982; Mintz and Schwartz, 1981a, 1981b; Galaskiewicz, 1979; Roy, 1983; Burt, 1978/9; Pennings, 1980). The hypotheses about the placement of markets in the structure of the economy (i.e. in the core or in the periphery) are based on two considerations. First, I hypothesized that the assets could be divided on the basis of type (security vs. currency); second, I hypothesized that the security markets would comprise the core because these assets (e.g. US Treasury bills and bonds) are more closely linked with American capital than are the currencies which, in the economy analyzed here, are all based on foreign monies.[6] (Findings are summarized in section IV.)

Structure, power, and control of money

An economy differentiated into a core and periphery structure indicates an unequal distribution of power. The core actors in an economy dominate other actors, control the flow of capital, and wield political power. In contrast, the peripheral actors are in a weak and powerless position.

The finance capital perspective argues that power is located in financial institutions, especially banks (e.g. Mintz and Schwartz, 1985; Fitch and Oppenheimer, 1970; Kotz, 1978; National Resources Committee, 1939). If this is true, then banks and other financial institutions should be located in the structural core of the economy (as I have hypothesized in the present case). Indeed much research has suggested that financial institutions do dominate in the economy. Mintz and Schwartz (1981a: 851), for example, have concluded that "the system is dominated by a handful of interconnected major New York banks and insurance companies which form the center of an integrated national network." Elsewhere they have suggested that bank centrality is a function of control of capital flows (Mintz and Schwartz, 1985). Others have argued that financial institutional control of lending patterns and institutional stockholding ties financial institutions and corporations together, with financial institutions as the dominant actors (e.g. Kotz, 1978; Fitch and Oppenheimer, 1970).

If the core actors, such as financial institutions, control important resources in the economy, then they certainly control the resource that is the lifeblood of a market economy – money. And by controlling money, core actors possess the means to control economic decisions (Parsons and Smelser, 1956: 71). This control, I argue, implies that core actors define money – what it is and how it is used.

This brings us to the critical hypothesis of the analysis. If core actors define and control money, then those financial assets exchanged in the core should be the closest to money (i.e. to cash). Put somewhat differently, the relative "moneyness" of financial assets declines as distance from the core increases. In this chapter, I test this hypothesis by (1) modeling the structure of a financial economy based on the exchange of financial assets, and locating the core and periphery of the economy; (2) independently assessing the relative moneyness of the assets; and (3) determining whether or not the assets exchanged in the core are the ones that are the closest to money.

III Data and methods

The social structural interpretation of money is illustrated by examining a set of financial futures markets (see appendix A for definition of financial futures). These markets were chosen for three methodological reasons: first, the approach I propose requires data at a very disaggregated level. Such data are generally unavailable, but they have been obtained through special surveys of participation in financial futures markets (e.g. Hobson, 1978). Second, the financial assets included in this analysis constitute a naturally complete set, which solves the boundary specification problem that plagues many analyses of asset substitutability. Third, the data include distinctions between fundamentally different uses of the same financial assets – hedging and speculation (see appendix A). The purposes of exchange are generally not known or are not measurable when other financial assets are studied.

Though financial futures are not typically included in studies of money, there is a compelling theoretical rationale for including them. Financial futures instruments possess both investment attributes and means of payment (transaction) attributes, as do many of the instruments included in the Fed's redefined monetary aggregates (see table 4.1). While financial futures cannot be used directly as a means of payment (as several other money substitutes cannot), they are quite liquid, and can be quickly converted into cash via the organized futures markets.

A reason that financial futures may have been ignored is that, as a store of wealth, they are relatively less important than other financial assets. However, this appearance belies the fact that financial futures are linked to underlying markets of enormous size and importance. For example, there is almost a half trillion dollars in outstanding marketable US Treasury debt, upon which several financial futures instruments are based (Powers, 1981: 675). Given the enormous bases of financial futures, they deserve study in their own right. Moreover, their close connection to major markets indicates that they reflect and represent underlying social structure and its relationship to major financial assets.[7]

Data

Most analyses of money utilize measures of the total quantity held of each particular asset of interest. That is, the volume of an asset is measured as the grand total of all positions held by all actors. For this analysis, I have used data at a much more disaggregated level. Specifically, the unit of analysis is the volume of an asset held by a specific type of economic actor (e.g. commercial banks). All holdings of a particular asset are represented by a vector v of length n in which each data point represents the quantity of the asset held by a specific type of actor (who is a member of a population with n types of actors). To compare with the conventional measure of an asset, the quantity of an asset at the aggregate level is simply the sum of vector v.

Given a set of m financial assets and a population of n actors, there would be m vectors of length n. Together, these vectors would form a $n \times m$ matrix, representing the position of n actors in m markets at one point in time. Each row in the matrix represents a specific actor's "portfolio." Each column represents the transactions of a specific asset that have been made. If different transaction purposes are considered (and can be measured), say k purposes, then the $n \times m$ matrix could be disaggregated to create $kn \times m$ matrices.

Figures 4.1 and 4.2 contain data in this format. The data come from the Commodity Futures Trading Commission's (CFTC) survey of financial futures markets, reported in Hobson (1978). These matrices represent the portfolios held by 34 groups of actors across nine different financial markets, broken out by four types of participation (hedging-long, hedging-short, speculative-short, and speculative-long), as of the day of the CFTC's survey (November 30, 1977). These 34 groups represent the entire universe of actors in this financial market economy.[8] (The nine assets, the locations at which they are traded, and the 34 groups of actors are listed in tables 4.2 and 4.3.)

Each row represents the portfolio of a specific *group* of actors. Ideally, the portfolio of each member of a single group should be included in a network analysis. However, individual-level data are considered confidential by the CFTC, and only semi-aggregated data are made public. Fortunately, even though the CFTC will not release the disaggregated data, it does report the number of actors in each group who traded as speculators and as hedgers. With this additional information, it is possible to move closer to the ideal of fully disaggregated data. By dividing the total volume held by a particular group by the number of actors in the group, it is possible to derive the portfolio held by the average member of a group. Since the numbers of speculators and hedgers within a single group are different, this calculation is made separately

Figure 4.1 *Blocked matrix of speculative positions*

	Long positions									Short positions								
	1	5	2	3	4	6	7	8	9	1	5	2	3	4	6	7	8	9
1	0	0	14	0	0	0	0	0	0	0	0	19	0	0	0	0	0	0
2	6	2	0	0	0	7	2	2	13	30	0	0	0	0	56	3	1	0
29	51	21	33	6	0	27	30	23	8	73	26	111	1	0	7	5	2	0
3	313	39	784	559	82	8	0	10	1	301	0	787	526	104	0	0	0	0
4	207	0	25	3	0	4	1	42	10	253	18	50	8	0	7	2	0	10
5	0	0	0	0	0	0	0	0	0	0	0	0	0	0	0	0	0	0
6	339	117	94	0	3	175	79	202	577	414	99	53	13	0	74	38	27	147
7	24	0	30	0	0	3	2	11	1	5	2	0	1	0	0	0	0	0
8	33	15	28	0	3	44	66	147	160	41	47	12	0	0	35	20	16	75
9	333	0	35	0	13	6	5	45	1	329	6	70	36	3	3	0	0	0
10	0	0	0	0	0	0	2	0	0	0	0	0	0	0	0	4	0	0
11	538	53	70	0	47	16	92	193	338	551	48	111	1	0	19	61	16	9
12	1072	24	545	21	10	154	142	201	119	1096	61	554	9	3	47	10	18	8
13	2472	329	7121	488	209	707	618	2248	749	2229	798	7233	300	168	535	233	1749	611
15	1122	55	652	15	39	133	217	152	202	883	98	523	18	13	71	40	7	12
14	87	1	15	2	4	51	16	12	22	80	6	10	2	0	15	17	0	0
16	396	62	238	3	39	173	141	156	80	732	58	291	14	0	84	9	11	64
17	1052	82	241	6	87	297	323	431	164	1170	145	361	20	27	102	69	46	10
18	4	1	8	0	1	2	0	6	0	8	0	9	0	0	0	0	0	3
19	145	9	16	2	3	12	12	18	14	168	7	44	2	0	1	10	6	2
20	39	8	12	2	1	23	5	31	8	47	6	19	0	0	17	0	1	0
21	3	0	2	0	0	1	1	0	4	3	1	3	0	0	0	0	0	0
22	77	20	32	0	17	75	16	85	14	97	23	39	2	0	6	6	2	0
23	187	7	27	4	2	10	7	77	24	169	6	26	2	1	1	2	10	1
24	202	24	70	2	0	107	63	58	40	171	14	114	6	1	17	5	11	3
25	74	7	16	2	0	18	17	50	20	89	24	22	0	0	0	5	1	3
26	902	8	138	25	4	40	40	83	25	857	8	143	31	2	19	3	1	1
27	455	46	122	6	5	83	55	101	30	461	51	145	7	10	56	5	4	5
28	163	7	207	5	13	54	51	150	56	134	17	153	12	1	5	3	51	13
30	152	43	116	0	29	115	30	38	23	170	45	122	3	0	52	1	8	2
31	349	64	208	156	12	109	139	91	97	415	54	218	133	4	44	3	7	0
32	11	6	4	0	0	2	15	1	1	14	0	8	2	0	0	0	0	0
33	73	7	67	2	0	20	25	23	11	64	22	52	2	0	4	2	4	1
34	81	4	45	1	1	24	52	26	9	83	5	42	3	0	0	0	3	2

NOTE: Column numbers correspond to numbers assigned to markets in table 4.2.
Row numbers correspond to numbers assigned to actors in table 4.3.

for the speculative and hedging portions of a portfolio. The portfolio of the average actor is a better basis for assessing structural equivalence than portfolios comprised of the raw volume data.

Most measures of money quantities are made over time. However, the CFTC has not fielded regular surveys of these financial futures markets, and the only other survey it has conducted (Jaffe and Hobson, 1979) was not designed to collect comparable data. The purpose of this chapter, however, is only to develop an approach for determining the empirical substitutability of financial assets, an approach for identifying each subset of assets that share the same degree of moneyness. The research agenda suggested by this analysis includes studying the behavior of such newly defined monetary aggregates over time.

Figure 4.2 *Blocked matrix of hedging positions*

	Long positions									Short positions								
	1	5	2	3	4	6	7	8	9	1	5	2	3	4	6	7	8	9
1	10	0	894	207	0	0	0	0	0	77	0	1470	100	0	0	0	0	0
2	290	0	99	1	0	0	30	42	71	325	5	427	197	0	0	0	0	0
29	0	1	0	10	0	0	0	0	0	0	0	1	10	0	0	0	0	0
3	963	38	1717	510	0	1	2	85	0	352	11	1356	628	105	13	49	166	137
4	1575	0	1490	513	41	0	0	0	0	1552	0	581	322	236	0	0	0	0
5	112	0	297	0	0	0	0	0	0	1	0	691	0	0	0	0	0	0
6	163	1	2446	214	0	134	.1	0	0	120	1	1828	244	0	17	0	1	0
7	0	0	110	30	0	0	0	0	0	14	0	789	30	0	0	0	0	0
8	91	0	80	0	5	3	7	6	0	166	2	100	2	10	11	6	0	0
9	592	0	5	0	7	1	0	0	0	610	0	14	0	0	0	0	0	0
10	0	567	0	0	0	315	237	197	200	0	133	0	0	0	1629	1650	1383	1662
11	71	257	1362	192	24	156	13	436	198	136	147	925	184	13	50	119	1767	253
12	29	0	65	0	0	0	1	0	0	29	0	32	0	0	0	0	0	0
13	242	62	111	27	0	222	97	1	82	587	3	241	139	0	337	269	163	378
15	0	0	120	0	0	2	0	0	2	0	0	8	4	0	0	0	0	0
14	0	0	0	0	0	0	0	0	0	0	0	0	1	0	0	0	0	0
16	0	0	0	0	0	0	0	0	0	0	2	0	0	0	0	0	0	0
17	0	0	0	0	0	0	0	0	0	0	0	0	0	0	0	0	1	0
18	0	0	0	0	0	0	0	0	0	0	0	0	0	0	0	0	0	0
19	0	0	0	0	0	0	0	0	0	0	0	0	0	0	0	0	0	0
20	0	0	0	0	0	0	0	0	0	0	0	0	0	0	0	0	0	0
21	0	0	0	0	0	0	0	0	0	0	0	0	0	0	0	0	0	0
22	0	0	0	0	0	0	0	0	0	0	0	0	0	0	0	0	0	0
23	0	0	0	0	0	0	0	0	0	0	0	0	0	0	0	0	0	0
24	0	0	0	0	0	0	0	0	0	0	0	0	0	0	0	0	0	0
25	0	0	0	0	0	0	0	0	0	0	0	0	0	0	0	0	0	0
26	0	0	0	0	0	0	0	0	0	0	0	0	0	0	0	0	0	0
27	0	0	0	0	0	0	0	0	0	0	0	0	0	0	0	0	0	0
28	0	0	0	0	0	0	0	0	0	0	0	0	0	0	0	0	0	0
30	0	0	0	0	0	0	0	0	0	0	0	0	0	0	0	0	0	0
31	0	0	0	0	0	0	0	0	0	0	0	0	0	0	0	0	0	0
32	0	0	0	0	0	0	0	0	0	0	0	0	0	0	0	0	0	0
33	0	0	0	0	0	0	0	0	0	0	0	0	0	0	0	0	0	0
34	0	0	0	0	0	0	0	0	0	0	0	0	0	0	0	0	0	0

NOTE: Column numbers correspond to numbers assigned to markets in table 4.2.
Row numbers correspond to numbers assigned to actors in table 4.3.

Table 4.2 *Financial futures markets surveyed in the CFTC study*

Market name	Exchange name
1. US Treasury bills 90 days futures	International Monetary Market (IMM) at the Chicago Mercantile Exchange (CME)
2. GNMA mortgages	Chicago Board of Trade (CBT)
3. US Treasury bonds	CBT
4. Commercial paper loans	CBT
5. Canadian dollar	IMM–CME
6. Swiss franc	IMM–CME
7. Deutsche mark	IMM–CME
8. Pound sterling	IMM–CME
9. Japanese yen	IMM–CME

Table 4.3 *Universe of actors in the financial futures markets*

1. Mortgage banks
2. Commercial banks
3. Securities dealers – FMC (futures commission merchants) (commodity brokers who are also securities dealers)
4. Securities dealers – non FMC
5. Savings and loans associations
6. Investment companies (includes mutual funds, closed-end investment companies, and unit investment trusts)
7. Institutional investors (includes other large-scale investing institutions such as life insurance companies and pension funds)
8. Other financial institutions
9. Real estate developers and builders
10. Foreign exchange dealers (only international monetary market arbitraters)
11. Other commercial interests
12. Employers and financial institutions
13. Futures industry (includes most commodity brokers, employees of such brokers, floor traders, and professional speculators, but commodity brokers who were also securities dealers at the time of the survey are classified as [3] above)
14. Investment and commodity advisors
15. Private investors and investment clubs
16. Retail proprietors and employees
17. Other managers, proprietors, and officials
18. Clerical and kindred workers
19. Sales workers and purchasing agents
20. Craftsmen, foremen, and kindred workers
21. Laborers and other primary workers
22. Insurance and real estate workers
23. Accountants and auditors
24. Engineers and others in physical sciences
25. School and college personnel
26. Lawyers and judges
27. Physicians and medical personnel
28. Other professional occupations
29. Farmers and farm managers
30. Housewives
31. Retired persons
32. Students
33. Military and civilian government workers
34. Miscellaneous

Source: Hobson (1978); definitions of actor groups, pp. 24–5.

Modeling the structure of the market economy

As I have discussed in detail elsewhere (esp. Baker, 1984c), the structure of a market economy can be modeled by applying the rule of "structural equivalence" to actor-by-market matrices. Structural equivalence is an algebraic concept that has been applied to a variety of network data and is the basis of blockmodeling (e.g. Lorrain and White, 1971; White, Boorman, and Breiger, 1976; Breiger, Boorman, and Arabie, 1975). Blockmodeling has been applied to a number of economic structures, including international trade (Breiger, 1981; Snyder and Kick, 1979; Steiber, 1979), music markets (Faulkner, 1983), and financial and hospital markets (Baker, 1981, 1983, 1984c, 1985, 1986).

The rule of structural equivalence identifies the subsets of structurally equivalent actors, markets, and types of participation. Structurally equivalent actors similarly participate in these markets; structurally equivalent markets are used in similar ways by the population of actors; structurally equivalent types of participation are similar uses of these markets. Once the structurally equivalent subsets are identified, the core and peripheral positions in the economy can be located, and inferences made about the specific structure of a market economy.

Three three-way data structure – types of participation by actors by markets – can be conceptualized as a "market box" (Baker, 1984c). The market box is analyzed using the three-dimensional blockmodel approach (Baker, 1986). Specifically, the market box is blocked by unfolding it along each dimension, applying CONCOR (Breiger, Boorman, and Arabie, 1975), and reorganizing the box according to the permutations derived for each dimension.

As described above, average portfolios instead of raw volume data were included in the market box. Average portfolios are closer to the ideal of individual-level portfolios, and thus are better for determining structural equivalence. To obtain the blockmodel image of the financial economy, the partitions derived from the market box (based on average portfolios) were imposed on the original raw data matrices (figures 4.1 and 4.2).[9] The density of each of the submatrices formed by the intersection of structurally equivalent subsets was calculated. Submatrices with densities below a certain cut-off were coded as "zeroblocks" (designated by a "0"), and all those above the cut-off were coded as "bonds" (designated by a "1"). The resulting matrix (the "blockmodel image") represents the structure of the economy at a higher level of aggregation. Finally, this image was interpreted to determine the specific structure (e.g. core–periphery) of the economy.

Analyzing the "moneyness" of financial assets

Currency is the standard means of payment. Substitutability is measured against this standard – the degree to which other financial assets share the same attributes as currency (i.e. their degree of moneyness). It is generally agreed that demand deposits (checking accounts) are very close substitutes to currency; as a means of payment, they are almost identical. The full array of money assets conventionally considered to be more or less substitutes of currency is presented in Table 4.1.

Several alternative analytical approaches have been used to measure the empirical "moneyness" of financial assets. For example, Barnett (1980) and Spindt (1984) applied standard index number procedures to produce monetary aggregates (though the theoretical bases of Barnett's and Spindt's approaches are somewhat different). Chetty (1969) developed a method for aggregating monetary assets by estimating the elasticities of substitution among various assets. In an interesting application of factor analysis to time-series data, Koot (1975) used factor analysis to extract the dimensions of moneyness from quarterly monetary data. He located two factors that explained about 81 per cent of the variance in currency: currency and demand deposits loaded most highly on one factor (which he called "money"), and time deposits, time deposits plus CDs, mutual saving bank shares, savings and loan association capital, and US savings bonds loaded most highly on a second factor (which he called "near-money").

In this analysis, I have employed the concept of structural equivalence to determine the subsets of substitutable assets. Because an actor's position in a market is represented by the number of contracts (volume) an actor holds of the asset exchanged in that market, the analysis of the structural equivalence of markets simultaneously determines the structural equivalence of the assets traded in these markets. Structurally equivalent assets are those that are used interchangeably by actors in the economy. Each subset of structurally equivalent assets is a "monetary aggregate" in the classic economic sense.

In general, structural equivalence may be thought of as a social structural operationalization of the economist's concept of "economic substitutability." Economists typically study substitutability relationships by examining cross-interest elasticities (e.g. see Chetty, 1969). However, in this sociological approach to the problem of economic substitutability, I have focussed on concrete relationships at the disaggregated behavioral level, based on empirical portfolios held by specific groups of actors. Instead of cross-interest elasticities, the rule of structural equivalence is used to measure substitutability (see appendix B for a theoretical discussion of structural equivalence and portfolio composition).

The rule of structural equivalence defies the composition of monetary aggregates (i.e. the membership of structurally equivalent asset groups. For this analysis, the relative moneyness of each subset of assets – how close each subset is to currency – must also be assessed. Theoretically, I expect that the subset of structurally equivalent assets with the greatest number of *bonds* in the economy will be the subset closest to money. Further, the fewer bonds a subset of assets has, the less money-like it is. To evaluate the validity of this theoretical expectation, I have used a combination of other quantitative and qualitative measures, such as the correlation of various subsets of assets with currency over time and the similarity of various qualitative attributes.

IV Findings and discussion

This section is divided into two main parts. First, the empirical structure of the financial market economy is presented. Second, the relative moneyness of the various subsets of structurally equivalent assets is evaluated, and compared to the underlying structure of the economy.

The structure of the financial market economy

Structurally equivalent actors

Hobson (1978) splits the 34 categories of actors into two main groups: "commercial traders" and "other traders" (in table 4.2, actors numbered 1–11 and 12–34, respectively). As a starting hypothesis, I expected that the 34 actors would be divided into these same groups. The application of CONCOR to the population of actors yielded the following two groups:

> *Subpopulation 1*: Mortgage banks, commercial banks, farmers and farm managers, securities dealers (FCM), securities dealers (not FCM), employees of financial institutions, private investors and investment clubs, savings and loan associations, investment companies, institutional investors, other financial institutions, other commercial interests, real estate developers and builders, futures industry, and foreign exchange dealers.
>
> *Subpopulation 2*: Investment and commodity advisors, retail proprietors and employees, other managers, proprietors and officials, clerical and kindred workers, sales workers and purchasing agents, craftsmen, foremen and kindred workers, laborers and other primary workers, insurance and real estate workers, accountants and auditors, engineers and others in physical sciences, lawyers and judges, physicians and medical personnel, other professional occupations, housewives, retired persons, students, military and civilian government workers, and miscellaneous.

The two subpopulations correspond roughly to Hobson's categories, except that several "other traders" are included with the commercial group (Subpopulation 1). They do, however, seem to fit well in the commercial category: *farmers and farm managers* – historically, these actors are the oldest and most experienced users of financial futures markets, and thus participate in these markets in ways similar to the commercial actors; *employees of financial institutions* – by virtue of employment with major commercial actors, these employees would likely benefit from the insider information they are privy to, trading in patterns similar to their employers; *private investors and investment clubs* – though this is a nebulous grouping, it may be assumed that these actors are more likely to trade like the commercial actors, since they identify their main occupation as investor; and *futures industry* – this grouping should be classified as commercial, since trading futures is a part of their business. Given the inclusion of these actors in Hobson's (1978) "commercial" category, this group is renamed "commercial/professional."

Subpopulation 1 contains an eclectic mix of commercial/professional actors that should be subdivided. Sociological research suggests that banks and large insurance companies ("Institutional investors" in the CFTC data) occupy different positions in the economy (e.g. Mintz and Schwartz, 1981b, 1985). Thus, I expected that an application of CONCOR to Subpopulation 1 would separate banks and nonbank institutions. CONCOR yielded the following divisions:

> *Subpopulation 1a*: mortgage banks, commercial banks, and farmers and farm managers.
> *Subpopulation 1b*: securities dealers (FCM), securities dealers (not FCM), employees of financial institutions, private investors and investment clubs, savings and loan associations, investment companies, institutional investors, other financial institutions, other commercial interests, real estate developers and builders, foreign exchange dealers, and futures industry.

These subgroups reveal important distinctions between members of the commercial/professional class that are consistent with other sociological research.

Structurally equivalent markets

Conventionally, the nine financial markets would be assigned to groups based on the predominant attributes of the assets traded in them. Hobson (1978), for example, classifies these assets into two main groups:

> *Fixed-income securities*: bonds, paper, GNMA, and bills.
> *Foreign currencies*: Canadian dollars, Swiss francs, Japanese yen, Deutsche marks, and British pounds.

This division on the basis of attributes may serve as a guiding hypothesis to expectations about the division of assets on the basis of structural equivalence.

The first application of CONCOR to the nine asset vectors (figures 4.1 and 4.2) yielded a bipartite split that corresponds fairly closely with the groups identified on the basis of attribute similarity:

Supermarket 1: bonds, paper, GNMA, bills, and Canadian dollars
Supermarket 2: Swiss francs, Deutsche marks, British pounds, and
Japanese yen

The term "supermarket" is used to denote that each subgroup is more than a single market; it is an aggregation of similarly used market institutions (see Baker, 1984c).

The only apparent anomaly in this split is the inclusion of Canadian dollars with the fixed-income securities. To better understand this division, it is useful to examine the zero-order correlations of the various assets. The correlation coefficients of each asset pair are presented in descending order in table 4.4.

Each subset of structurally equivalent assets should contain assets that are highly correlated with each other. In contrast, the correlations of assets from different structurally equivalent groups (i.e. one from Supermarket 1 and one from Supermarket 2) should not be highly correlated with one another. As can be seen in table 4.4, the correlations of all the possible pairs of currencies are quite high, with the exception of the pairs containing Canadian dollars. The correlation coefficients of the pairs of fixed-income securities are relatively high. The correlations of mixed pairs (one fixed-income security and one currency) are relatively low, but the Japanese yen/paper pair and the three Canadian dollar/fixed-income security pairs indicate fairly high association. Viewed overall, the basis of the split of Supermarket 1 and Supermarket 2 is evident in the pattern of the zero-order correlations.

To explore the possibility of internal structure, CONCOR was applied to Supermarket 1, yielding the following division:

Supermarket 1a: bills and Canadian dollars.
Supermarket 1b: bonds, paper, and GNMA.

Examining the pattern of correlation coefficients underlying these two subgroups (table 4.4) shows the basis for including bills and dollars in the same subset.

Despite the observed structural equivalence of T-bills and Canadian dollars, they form a puzzling subset because they are two different types of assets – a currency and a fixed-income security. The second subgroup, Supermarket 1b, makes sense because it contains only fixed-income securities; the third subgroup, Supermarket 2, makes sense because it contains only foreign currencies. The main question is, therefore, why are Canadian dollars and T-bills structurally equivalent?

T-bills are included with a currency because, compared to all the other fixed-income securities, bills are the closest to money: a highly liquid, short-term debt instrument, with low market risk and no credit risk. The investment behavior of corporations and financial institutions attests to this closeness to money: whenever these organizations have excess cash, they invest it in

Table 4.4 *Zero-order correlation coefficients of market pairs, descending order*

Market pair		Type	Correlation coefficient
Swiss	Germany	C	0.9137
German	Japan	C	0.9085
Swiss	Japan	C	0.7533
UK	Japan	C	0.7069
T-bills	GNMA	F	0.6464
GNMA	Bonds	F	0.6439
German	UK	C	0.6271
Bonds	Paper	F	0.6079
GNMA	Paper	F	0.5170
Swiss	UK	C	0.4875
GNMA	Canada	M	0.4303
Paper	Japan	M	0.4300
T-bills	Canada	M	0.3825
Bonds	Canada	M	0.3680
T-bills	Bonds	F	0.3658
GNMA	UK	M	0.3572
T-bills	Paper	F	0.3346
Canada	UK	C	0.3107
T-bills	Japan	M	0.3068
T-bills	UK	M	0.3050
GNMA	Japan	M	0.3022
Canada	Swiss	C	0.2977
Canada	Japan	C	0.2509
Canada	Germany	C	0.2477
T-bills	Germany	M	0.2472
T-bills	Swiss	M	0.2406
Paper	UK	M	0.2282
Paper	Germany	M	0.1938
Paper	Canada	M	0.1862
GNMA	Germany	M	0.1630
GNMA	Swiss	M	0.1353
Bonds	UK	M	0.1341
Bonds	Japan	M	0.1296
Bonds	Germany	M	0.0531
Bonds	Swiss	M	0.0387
Paper	Swiss	M	0.0277

Note: For type of market pair: C = currencies only; F = fixed-income securities only; M = mixed pair.

Treasury bills. It would make sense, therefore, that the futures markets in T-bills would be structurally equivalent with a currency. The question now becomes, why Canadian dollars?

Of the five foreign currencies, Canadian dollars are the closest to American dollars. That is, the relationship of Canadian dollars and American dollars varies far less than the relationship of American dollars to the other foreign

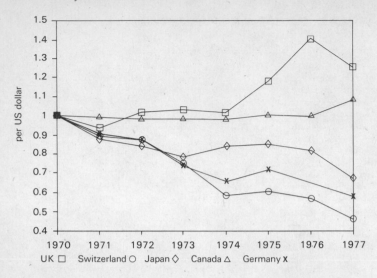

4.3   Comparison of exchange rate volatility. Source: Data from *International Financial Statistics*, Yearbook, 1984.

currencies. As shown in figure 4.3, in the 1970–7 period, the exchange rates of the British pound, Swiss franc, Japanese yen, and the Deutsche mark to the American dollar fluctuated drastically, while the exchange rate of Canadian dollars to American dollars showed much less variation. Since the value of the Canadian dollar historically is quite similar to the value of the American dollar, it seems reasonable that Canadian dollar futures would be structurally equivalent to futures instruments based on the American dollar's closest equivalent of money – US Treasury bills.

In sum, the rule of structural equivalence served to identify subsets of equivalent assets (supermarkets) based on participation patterns, revealing "hidden" equivalencies – interchangeable assets, most notably Canadian dollars futures and Treasury bills futures, that were not obvious from a comparison of attributes.

Structurally equivalent types of participation

As outlined above and defined in detail in appendix A, actors may take four different types of positions in these nine futures markets: speculative-long, speculative-short, hedging-long, and hedging-short. An interesting question concerns the structural equivalence of these types of participation: which types are similar and which are not?

The application of CONCOR to the types of participation revealed the following bipartite split:

Supertype 1: speculative-long and speculative-short.
Supertype 2: hedging-long and hedging-short.

At first, it seems surprising that the split did not occur along long/short lines: long and short positions are inherently contradictory. Instead, patterns of speculative trading, long and short, are structurally similar; patterns of trading for hedging purposes, long and short, are structurally similar. Examination of the data matrices reveals at least one reason for the separation of speculation and hedging: almost every actor uses these markets for speculation, but only commercial/professional actors use these markets for hedging.

Core–semiperiphery–periphery structure

Now that the subgroups of structurally equivalent actors, markets, and types of participation have been determined, the raw data matrices can be reordered to reveal the positions in the economy. Figures 4.1 and 4.2 show the blocked matrices at the two-dimensional level (i.e. the matrices are not collapsed by type of participation). The first part of the discussion below will focus on interpreting the two-dimensional models.

The intersection of a specific subgroup of actors and a specific subset of markets demarcates a "position" in the economy. To determine the blockmodel image of this economy, the density of each submatrix in figures 4.1 and 4.2 was calculated and each submatrix with a density of less than or equal to 49.25 contracts (half the average density) was coded as a "0" (zeroblock) and each submatrix with a density greater than 49.25 contracts was coded as a "1" (bond). The calculated submatrix densities and the corresponding image are shown in table 4.5 (top panel).

The two-dimensional blockmodel image indicates a core–semiperiphery–periphery structure (Baker, 1984c). The core supermarket (assets) is Supermarket 1a (Canadian dollars and T-bills), connected by eight bonds. The semiperipheral supermarket is 1b (fixed-income securities, except T-bills), connected by six bonds. And the peripheral supermarket is Supermarket 2 (foreign currencies, except Canadian dollars) connected by five bonds.

The core actors in this system are Subpopulation 1b (nonbank financial institutions and other commercial/professional actors), connected by twelve bonds. The semiperipheral actors are Subpopulation 1a, the banks, connected by four bonds. The peripheral actors, the large amateur/nonprofessional group, are linked by only three bonds.

The empirical structure of this system confirms the hypothesis that this system would be composed of a core and periphery, modified to include a semiperiphery. The actors who dominate in this system are the nonbank commercial/professional actors; they hold more bonds than any other subpopulation of actors. They are the only group to hold a bond in the core supermarket across every type of participation. They similarly dominate in

Table 4.5 *Matrices of submatrix densities and blockmodel images*

Two-dimensional blockmodel   Supermarket

		1a	1b	2			
Speculative-	Subpop. 1a	13.33	5.89	9.33	0	0	0
long	Subpop. 1b	295.21	302.11	164.23	1	1	1
	Subpop. 2	127.84	35.44	56.62	1	0	1
Speculative	Subpop. 1a	21.50	14.56	6.17	0	0	0
short	Subpop. 1b	303.29	294.33	81.33	1	1	1
	Subpop. 2	142.74	36.96	11.04	1	0	0
Hedging-	Subpop. 1a	50.17	134.56	11.92	1	1	0
long	Subpop. 1b	198.46	260.17	49.98	1	1	1
	Subpop. 2	0.00	0.00	0.05	0	0	0
Hedging-	Subpop. 1a	67.83	245.00	0.00	1	1	0
short	Subpop. 1b	160.17	235.86	208.75	1	1	1
	Subpop. 2	0.05	0.02	0.01	0	0	0

Three-dimensional blockmodel   Supermarket

		1a	1b	2			
Speculative	Subpop. 1a	17.42	10.22	7.75	0	0	0
long & short	Subpop. 1b	299.25	298.22	122.78	1	1	1
	Subpop. 2	135.29	36.20	33.83	1	0	0
Hedging	Subpop. 1a	59.00	189.78	5.96	1	1	0
long & short	Subpop. 1b	179.31	248.01	129.36	1	1	1
	Subpop. 2	0.03	0.01	0.03	0	0	0

the semiperipheral supermarket. These structural patterns, I suggest, indicate the power exercised by the core actors in this financial system.

Another indicator of the power held by the core actors involves the exposure that this group has in the markets. Exposure is the difference between long and short positions. For example, if an actor is long 100 contracts and short 50 contracts, the actor is exposed to a loss should prices fall. If an actor is long and short the same number of contracts, then he/she holds a risk-free position; no matter which way prices go, the net worth of the actor's portfolio will not change. Exposure in the present case can be assessed by examining the difference between long and short speculative positions and between long and short hedging positions. These differences are calculated using the matrices of subdensities and dividing the long matrices by the short matrices, yielding:

Long/short speculative positions

.620	.405	1.513
.973	1.026	2.019
.896	.959	5.129

Long/short hedging positions

.740	.549	—
1.239	1.103	.239
0	0	3.985

A perfectly risk-free position is indicated by a quotient of 1.0. As a class, the core actors hold the most balanced (risk-free) positions in the core supermarket; they also hold relatively balanced positions in the semiperipheral supermarket. The greatest disparities occur in the peripheral supermarket, but since this supermarket *is* peripheral, it may not be as important to consider. Thus, excluding the peripheral supermarket, the core actors tend to hold the portfolios with the least risk.

The structural patterns revealed by examining the two-dimensional blockmodel image are mirrored in the three-dimensional image, though the three-dimensional image is a more parsimonious representation of social structure (table 4.5, bottom panel). As in the two-dimensional model, the core supermarket contains the Canadian dollars and T-bills; the core actors are the nonbank commercial/professional actors; and the overall structure of the economy is a core–semiperiphery–periphery.

The moneyness of assets

The rule of structural equivalence identifies the subsets of assets that are used similarly in the financial economy. The structurally equivalent assets with the greatest number of bonds should be the closest to money, and the moneyness of assets decreases as the number of bonds connecting them decreases. By these criteria, the three subsets of structurally equivalent assets are ordered as:

(1) Canadian dollars and T-bills.
(2) Commercial paper, GNMA, and T-bonds.
(3) British pound, Deutsche mark, Japanese yen, and Swiss franc.

Other data offer corroboration of this ordering. It is generally accepted that T-bills are close money substitutes. Canadian dollars track more closely with American dollars than do any of the other foreign currencies (as expressed by historical exchange rates, illustrated in figure 4.3). Since T-bills and Canadian dollars are close money substitutes, it makes sense that the futures based on these assets are money substitutes; furthermore, these two assets were found to be structurally equivalent and to jointly occupy the core of the economy.

The assets exchanged in the semiperipheral position – futures on fixed-income securities – are based on assets included in the Fed's redefined monetary aggregates (e.g. the Fed's measure of "L" includes commercial paper and liquid Treasury obligations – see Table 4.1). Furthermore, the assets in this subset are derivatives of essentially American capital assets. Thus, it seems reasonable that the subset of futures based on these assets, though not as close to money as the first set, is closer to American money than the foreign currencies.

The placement of the foreign currency futures in the peripheral, least money-like position is corroborated by the highly volatile exchange rates of the foreign currencies (see figure 4.3) that indicate that foreign currencies are poor substitutes for American dollars.

V Conclusion

The analysis confirms the hypothesis that the definition of money is related to the underlying social structure of the economy. The economy was discovered to be constructed as a core, semiperiphery, and periphery. The core of the economy was occupied by the nonbank commercial/professional actors, who held dominant positions in the core supermarket where the assets closest to money are exchanged. This structural dominance indicates the control of core economic assets – the means to determine economic decision-making – enjoyed by the core actors.

If the core actors control and define money, then the policy implications are profound. It implies that the widely held opinion that the Federal Reserve controls the economy is too simplistic; those who privately control assets also control the economy. Most of the various assets used as money substitutes, including all those analyzed in this chapter and most of those included in the Fed's redefined monetary aggregates (table 4.1), are not inventions of the government – they are invented and controlled in the private sector. Trends such as improvements in transaction technology only *facilitate* the development and use of new financial instruments; they do not *cause* their creation.

This position is consistent with the finance capital perspective (discussed in section II), though it is the *nonbank* financial institutions, not the banks, that occupy the core. But it is also consistent with some strands of theory in the more conventional economic literature. Bryant (1980, 1983), for example, notes that money is not an actual instrument of monetary policy. The central bank cannot perfectly control the money stock. The money stock is influenced not only by the central bank but also by the other significant actors in the economy, such as financial intermediaries and the nonfinancial private sector (Bryant, 1980: 5). Due to the behaviors of nongovernmental actors, the money stock can never be perfectly controlled by monetary policy. Bryant labels these private influences as "nonpolicy disturbances" in controlling money. The source of "nonpolicy disturbances," I suggest, is the power exercised by the core actors in the economy.

At the very least, this chapter suggests an alternative approach for determining monetary aggregates. While all other approaches use highly aggregated data, this approach suggests that the substitutability of assets should be measured on a disaggregated level. This, however, presents logistical problems. One advantage of using highly aggregated data is that the analyst simply does not have to contend with a massive amount of information. With my approach, an analyst would have to mount a substantial data collection effort and analyze a fair amount of information. These logistical problems, I believe, are not insurmountable. One strategy would be to conduct a survey of financial assets (such as the CFTC's surveys [e.g. Hobson, 1978]) every quarter, and determine substitutabilities using the rule of structural equivalence. Once subsets of structurally equivalent assets are identified, the quantity measures of monetary aggregates can be determined by simply adding the total amounts of the monetary assets that jointly occupy the same subset.

Of course, this strategy might result in different mixes of monetary assets from time to time and from economy to economy (if it were applied across various capitalist societies). For some, this would be a problem; Yeager (1968: 46), for example, has argued that "it would be awkward if the definition of money . . . had to change from time to time and country to country." While such changes might pose thorny analytical problems, it is unrealistic to hope that the answer to "What is money?" will not change over time or across economies.[10] As the social structure of an economy changes, so does the social structural definition of money and its uses. The Fed's redefined monetary aggregates are evidence that shifts do occur, and that the monetary authorities recognize (albeit reluctantly) that the definition of money must be correspondingly amended.

To adopt this approach as a means to measure and define monetary aggregates, the following steps would be necessary. First, a full set of financial assets should be selected for consideration. This set would include all the assets currently included in the Fed's redefined monetary aggregates (table 4.1), major financial futures instruments, and possibly other assets. Second, the volume of these assets held by actors should be surveyed at equal intervals over time. A complete census could be attempted, but it would be more cost-effective to sample the population of actors. Third, the subsets of structurally equivalent assets should be determined, using the approach presented in this chapter. All actors surveyed should be included in this analysis, unless there is some reason to select a subset of actors. Fourth, once the subsets of structurally equivalent assets are identified, the aggregate quantity of each subset should be determined for enough time points (weekly, monthly, quarterly) to create reliable time-series data. Fifth, the time-series of these structurally defined subsets of assets should be analyzed to determine how they relate to the performance of the economy.[11]

As long as the structure of the economy changes, money and its uses will also change, and money will have to be redefined repeatedly. A valid answer to the question "What is money?" can only be found by relying on a behavioral analysis of the relationship between the underlying social structure of the economy and what is used as money and how money is actually used. But if the principal locus of control does not reside in the hands of the central bank, then any governmental effort to regulate money will remain a vain enterprise.

Appendix A: A primer on financial futures

Definition of futures contract

A futures market is a formally organized, centralized institution in which actors can buy and sell futures contracts. A futures contract is an obligation to make a transaction at a specified future time. Specifically, a futures contract may be defined as:

> an agreement to buy or sell a stated quantity of an asset (or service) of given quality for delivery (or rental) at a future date (or over a period of time) at a specified price (or with some provision for its specification). Most such contracts also name the delivery point (or points) where the future transaction will take place. (Burns, 1979: 31)

The earliest futures contracts were established in agricultural commodities – corn, wheat, oats, eggs, and others. Futures markets in financial instruments, such as the nine assets analyzed in this study, have been established only recently (the first in 1972).

The price of a futures contract on some commodity represents the present price of a future commodity (a commodity to be delivered at some future date), not the future price of a present commodity (Allen, 1983: 6).

Types of participation in futures markets

Long and short positions

A long position involves buying (owning) a commodity. If an investor thinks that the price of IBM stock will increase, for example, he/she may buy IBM stock (go long in IBM stock), hoping to sell it later at a higher price. Going long follows the maxim: "Buy low, sell high." A short position involves selling a commodity. If an investor thinks the price of IBM stock will fall, he/she may sell IBM stock (go short), hoping to buy IBM stock later at a lower price. Going short follows the maxim: "Sell high, buy low."

In the futures market, an actor who goes long buys a futures contract, assuming the obligation to accept delivery of a certain quantity of a commodity at a future date. Conversely, an actor who goes short sells a futures contract, and assumes the obligation to deliver a certain quantity of a commodity in the future.

Speculation and hedging

Actors participate in futures markets for two main reasons: speculation and hedging. Speculation involves taking a position in the market for the purpose of profiting from price changes. For example, a speculator who thinks that prices will rise in the future may buy a commodity now, hoping to sell it at a higher price at some point in the future.

Hedging is the opposite of speculation. Hedging is the process of using the futures market to offset or shift the risk of adverse price movements. Hedging is quite similar to acquiring price insurance. An example of hedging with financial futures should clarify using futures for price insurance. Suppose a corporate portfolio manager has a number of Treasury bonds in the portfolio and wishes to protect the portfolio against loss if the price of bonds should decline. To do this, the manager could sell futures on Treasury bonds. Should the price of the bonds fall in the future, the loss on the bonds would be offset by the gain realized through the futures transaction.

Appendix B: Economic excursus: Structural equivalence and portfolio composition

The purpose of this appendix is to relate the concept of structural equivalence to portfolio composition and management, linking the analysis presented in the body of the chapter with some of the more conventional concepts of financial theory. To expedite the discussion, I present hypothetical portfolios at the binary level only.

Behavioral postulates

Most financial and economic theories rest on the assumption of hyperrationality. However, market actors are more realistically described as subject to bounded rationality; though they attempt to make economically rational decisions, they are constrained by the inherent limitations of human cognitive powers and capacities (Baker, 1984a: 778; also, e.g., Williamson, 1981). In the present situation, the conventional economic assumption of hyperrationality is unnecessary; my analysis assumes only that the actors are intendedly rational.

The individual portfolio

The manager of a portfolio attempts to develop a portfolio that achieves some objectives (e.g. minimizes risk, obtains some stated return, maintains some liquidity level, etc.). By whatever criteria a manager uses to evaluate particular assets, the manager will attempt to assemble a portfolio that meets those objectives.

Assume that a manager's objective is to invest idle cash in assets that realize some return (e.g. interest, appreciation), while maintaining high liquidity and low risk; in other words, the manager's objective is to invest in assets close to money (e.g. Treasury bills). Assume that the manager has four assets to evaluate (A to D), and, by whatever evaluation criteria seem relevant, the manager rates two as close money substitutes (A, B) and two as unlike money (C, D). Given these ratings, there are three portfolios the manager could assemble:

	A	B	C	D
Portfolio 1:	1	0	0	0
Portfolio 2:	0	1	0	0
Portfolio 3:	1	1	0	0

Given that A and B are rated similarly, the manager should be indifferent as to the choice of Portfolio 1 or 2. However, since the relative moneyness of A and B cannot be known perfectly (i.e. the postulate of bounded rationality), the prudent choice is to select Portfolio 3. This course of action follows one of the basic principles of portfolio diversification: as the number of assets in a portfolio increases, the risk of the total portfolio decreases.

Multiple portfolios

Consider the addition of four more actors, each with the same objectives as the first actor. Assume two cases: (1) the four additional actors all agree with the original actor's evaluation of the four assets (the theoretically perfect case of homogeneous evaluations); (2) the four additional are only in partial agreement with the original actor's evaluation (the realistic case of heterogeneous evaluations). Consider the portfolios assembled in each case:

Case 1	A	B	C	D
Actor 1:	1	1	0	0
Actor 2:	1	1	0	0
Actor 3:	1	1	0	0
Actor 4:	1	1	0	0
Actor 5:	1	1	0	0

Case 2	A	B	C	D
Actor 1:	1	1	0	0
Actor 2:	1	1	0	1
Actor 3:	1	1	1	0
Actor 4:	0	0	1	1
Actor 5:	1	0	0	0

As shown in Case 1, all actors agree on the moneyness of the various assets and take identical positions in the four markets. In Case 2, there is considerable disagreement. Actor 2, for example, has assembled a portfolio in which assets A, B, and C, are treated as similar. Actor 5 holds a position only in A; this actor has not developed a diversified portfolio. Actor 4 disagrees completely with Actor 1.

The similarity/dissimilarity of portfolios can be assessed by applying the rule of structural equivalence to the rows. In Case 1, it is obvious that composition of all actors' portfolios is the same (they are all structurally equivalent). In Case 2, structurally equivalent portfolios are less obvious. CONCOR reveals two subsets of structurally equivalent portfolios: (1, 2, 3, 5) and (4).

The concatenated individual portfolios form the matrix of a financial system (as shown above). Each column-vector represents the holdings of a particular asset across a population of portfolios. In Case 1, it is obvious that assets A and B are structurally equivalent – they are used in identical ways by the population of actors. Assets C and D are structurally equivalent – they are not used by all actors. In Case 2, though there are diverse opinions about the relative moneyness of assets, A and B are structurally equivalent, and C and D are structurally equivalent.

Under the portfolio objectives assumed above, the subset of structurally equivalent assets that is closer to money is the one with more bonds in the system. The image associated with this hypothetical system is:

$$\begin{matrix} 1 & 0 \\ 1 & 1 \end{matrix}$$

which holds with any density cut-off $< .5$ and $> .25$. Therefore, assets A and B are used as money substitutes in this system.

NOTES

A version of this chapter was presented at the 1986 Sunbelt Social Network Conference, Santa Barbara, California (February 1986).

1 I gratefully acknowledge the helpful comments and suggestions made by Mitchel Abolafia, Ronald L. Breiger, Joseph M. Burns, Phillip Cagan, Thomas M. Dietz, Robert G. Eccles, James Ennis, Ronald B. Hobson, Eric Leifer, and Harrison C. White on earlier versions of this chapter. I also thank the editors of this volume for insights that helped to shape the final version.

2 Of course, some economists disagree fundamentally with this view. Many economists, particularly those in the Keynesian camp, argue that velocity is too unstable and too much the subject of random forces to make the money supply a good control variable.

3 Elsewhere I have discussed the effects of transaction technology (or, more generally, "contact technology") on the performance of financial markets (Baker, 1984a, 1984b) and on the role of spatial interaction in hospital utilization (Baker, 1985). In the securities markets, assets are exchanged in "crowds" via face-to-face interaction, a relatively primitive form of contact technology. With this form of

contact technology, I found that actors were unable to communicate efficiently in large crowds, exacerbating price volatility and impairing market performance. In hospital markets, where face-to-face interaction is required, I found that patients' utilization of hospitals was largely determined by the distance between communities and hospitals and a "hometown advantage" that hospitals benefit from in their own communities.

4 There are a number of divergent interpretations of reciprocal exchange in the Trobriands. Grofman and Landa (1983), for example, view the primitive money-stuff of the Trobriands as instruments close to modern money. They impute maximizing motives to the actors, and import rationalist economic theories to this context. In short, they view the Kula valuables as money in a market economy. Other views, such as Dalton's, contend that this is essentially a nonmarket economy, and the traits of money in market and nonmarket contexts are fundamentally different.

5 A major difference between the earlier analyses (Baker, 1983, 1984c) is that in the earlier papers I modeled the economy by using data on a sample of actors, while here I have expanded the analysis to include the entire universe of actors. The results, however, are strikingly similar – testimony to the robustness of the theoretical and methodological approach. Some comparisons of the results based on the sample and the universe are presented in later sections.

6 Most of the actors in this system are located in the US. More than 90 per cent of the actors in each of the security markets are located in the US. A lower percentage of actors in each of the currency markets is located in the US (from a high of 81 per cent in Japanese yen to a low of 65 per cent in Canadian dollars).

7 The importance of including financial futures in monetary studies is underscored by the tremendous increase in the volume of trading in these instruments over the past several years. For example, the volume of financial futures traded at the Chicago Board of Trade grew from 0.5 million contracts in 1977 to 23.7 million contracts in 1983. The 23.7 million contracts had a cash market value of more than $2 trillion (Chicago Board of Trade, 1984).

8 In the original analyses (Baker, 1983, 1984c), a subset ($n = 16$) of actors instead of the universe was analyzed. Specifically, all the commercial actors were included (actors nos. 1–11 in table 4.3), along with the subset of noncommercial actors (actors nos. 29–33 in table 4.3). The results of the analysis of the subset and the universe are almost identical. Most important, the same subgroups of structurally equivalent markets (assets) were identified. The actors in both analyses fit into almost the same structurally equivalent subgroups (see note 9). Compared to the present analysis, only 1 actor of the 16 jumped from one category to another. Based on $n = 16$, the real estate developers and builders were located in the amateur category; when based on $N = 34$, they are located in the commercial/professional category.

9 In the earlier analyses (Baker 1983, 1984c), the blockmodel image was formed directly from the blocked matrices of average portfolios. In the present case, I have formed the images from the blocked raw data matrices (figures 4.1 and 4.2). In both cases, however, the same image and interpretation result (though the image is more robust using the raw data matrices).

10 Definitions of money do vary from economy to economy. As Bryant (1980: 21–37) summarizes, the composition of national money stocks varies strikingly among Western economies.

11 A specific application of the approach developed here concerns *The Special Study of Futures and Related Markets* mandated by the US Congress (Public Law 97–444). In this special study, Congress expressed strong concern over the effect of the proliferation of new financial instruments on the economy, especially on the formation of real capital in the economy. For example, many critics of the proliferation of new financial markets fear that these new instruments would divert funds away from the underlying capital markets (so-called "diversionary effects"). As I described in an earlier paper (Baker, 1983), the social structure (network) approach to modeling the economy could be applied to operationalize and model such diversionary effects.

REFERENCES

Allen, Julius W., 1983. *Issues in the Regulation of Futures and Options Trading.* The Library of Congress, CRS Report No. 83–108 E (June)

Armstrong, W. E., 1924. "Rossel Island money: a unique monetary system." *Economic Journal*, 34: 243–9

1928. *Rossel Island.* Cambridge University Press

Baker, Wayne E. 1981. "Markets as networks: A multimethod study of trading networks in a securities market." Unpublished Ph.D. dissertation, Northwestern University, Evanston, Ill.

1983. "Intermarket structures: modeling the interrelationships of markets and traders." Paper presented at the annual meeting of the American Sociological Association, Detroit, Michigan (August)

1984a. "The social structure of a national securities market." *American Journal of Sociology*, 89: 775–811

1984b. "Floor trading and crowd dynamics." In Patricia Adler and Peter Adler (eds.), *The Social Dynamics of Financial Markets.* Greenwich, Conn.: JAI Press, pp. 107–28

1984c. "The economy as a network of interlocking networks." Paper presented at the annual meeting of the American Sociological Association, San Antonio, Texas (August)

1985. "Spatial interaction and the formation and structure of social networks: the case of a local hospital economy." Paper presented at the fifth annual meeting of the Sun Belt Social Network Conference, Palm Beach, Florida (February)

1986. "Three-dimensional blockmodels." *Journal of Mathematical Sociology*, 12 (2): 191–223

Barber, Bernard, 1977. "Absolutization of the market: some notes on how we got from there to here." In Gerald Dworkin, Gordon Bermant, and Peter G. Brown (eds.), *Markets and Morals.* Washington, DC: Hemisphere, pp. 15–31

Barnett, William A., 1980. "Economic monetary aggregates: an application of index number and aggregation theory." *Journal of Econometrics*, 14: 11–48

Breiger, Ronald L., 1981. "Structures of economic interdependence among nations." In Peter M. Blau and Robert K. Merton (eds.), *Continuities in Structural Inquiry*. Beverly Hills: Sage, pp. 353–80

Breiger, Ronald L., Scott A. Boorman, and Phipps Arabie, 1975. "An algorithm for clustering relational data with applications to social network analysis and multidimensional scaling." *Journal of Mathematical Psychology*, 12: 328–83

Bryant, Ralph C., 1980. *Money and Monetary Policy in Interdependent Nations*. Washington, DC: Brookings Institution

1983. *Controlling Money: The Federal Reserve and its Critics*. Washington, DC: Brookings Institution

Burns, Joseph, 1979. *A Treatise on Markets: Spot, Futures, and Options*. Washington, DC: American Enterprise Institute

Burt, Ronald S., 1978/9. "A structural theory of interlocking directorates." *Social Networks*, 1: 415–35

Cagan, Phillip, 1979. "Financial developments and the erosion of monetary controls." In William Fellner (ed.), *Contemporary Economic Problems*. Washington, DC: American Enterprise Institute, pp. 117–51

Chetty, V. Karuppan, 1969. "On measuring the nearness of near-moneys." *American Economic Review*, 59: 270–81

Chicago Board of Trade, 1984. *The Financial Futures Professional*. vol. 8, no. 1 (January 23). Chicago Board of Trade

Dalton, George, 1976. "Primitive money." In George Dalton (ed.), *Tribal and Peasant Economies*. Austin: Texas Press, pp. 254–81

Faulkner, Robert, 1983. *Music on Demand: Composers and Careers in the Hollywood Film Industry*. New Brunswick, NJ: Transaction

Fitch, Robert, and Mary Oppenheimer, 1970. "Who rules the corporations?" *Socialist Revolution*, 4: 73–108; 5: 61–114; 6: 33–94

Galaskiewicz, Joseph, 1979. *Exchange Networks and Community Politics*. Beverly Hills: Sage

Garcia, Gillian, and Simon Pak, 1979. "Some clues in the case of the missing money." *American Economic Review*, 69: 330–4

Goldfeld, Stephen M., 1976. "The case of the missing money." *Brookings Papers in Economic Activity*, 3: 683–730

Granovetter, Mark, 1985. "Economic action and social structure: the problem of embeddedness." *American Journal of Sociology*, 91: 481–510

Grofman, Bernard, and Janet Landa, 1983. "The development of trading networks among spatially separated traders as a process of proto-coalition formation: the Kula trade." *Social Networks*, 5 (December): 347–65

Hobson, Ronald B., 1978. "Futures trading in financial instruments." Division of Economics and Education, Commodity Futures Trading Commission, Washington, DC (October)

Hodson, Randy, and Robert L. Kaufman, 1982. "Economic dualism: a critical review." *American Sociological Review*, 47: 727–39

Jaffe, Naomi, and Ronald B. Hobson, 1979. "Survey of interest-rate futures markets." Division of Economics and Education, Commodity Futures Trading Commission, Washington, DC (December)

Koot, Ronald S., 1975. "A factor analytic approach to an empirical definition of money." *The Journal of Finance*, 30: 1081–9

Kotz, David, 1978. *Bank Control of Large Corporations in the United States*. Berkeley: University of California Press

Lorrain, F. P., and Harrison C. White, 1971. "Structural equivalence of individuals in social networks." *Journal of Mathematical Sociology*, 1: 49–80

Malinowski, Bronislaw, 1921. "The primitive economics of the Trobriand Islanders." *Economic Journal*, 31: 1–15

Mintz, Beth, and Michael Schwartz, 1981a. "Interlocking directorates and interest group formation." *American Sociological Review*, 46: 851–69

1981b. "The structure of intercorporate unity in American business." *Social Problems*, 29: 87–103

1985 *The Power Structure of American Business*. University of Chicago Press

Mizruchi, Mark, 1982. *The American Corporate Network: 1904–1974*. Beverly Hills: Sage

National Resources Committee, 1939. "The structure of the American economy." Washington, DC: Government Printing Office. Reprinted in Paul Sweezy, *The Present as History*. New York: Monthly Review Press, 1953

Parsons, Talcott, and Neil J. Smelser, 1956. *Economy and Society*. New York: Free Press

Paulus, John, and Stephen H. Axilrod, 1976. "Recent regulatory changes and financial innovations affecting growth of the monetary aggregates." *Federal Reserve Staff Memo*, November 2

Pennings, Johannes, 1980. *Interlocking Directorates*. San Francisco: Jossey-Bass

Polanyi, Karl, 1957. "The economy as instituted process." In Karl Polanyi, Conrad M. Arensberg, and Harry W. Pearson (eds.), *Trade and Market in the Early Empires*. Chicago: Henry Regnery, pp. 243–306

1977. *The Livelihood of Man*. New York: Academic Press

Powers, Mark J., 1981. "Financial instruments futures markets." In Frank J. Frabozzi and Frank G. Zarb (eds.), *Handbook of Financial Markets: Securities, Options, and Futures*. Homewood, Ill.: Dow Jones-Irwin, pp. 674–8

Roy, William G., 1983. "The unfolding of the interlocking directorate structure of the United States." *American Sociological Review*, 48: 248–57

Simmel, Georg, 1950. *The Sociology of Georg Simmel*, translated and edited by Kurt H. Wolff. New York: Free Press

Simpson, Thomas D., 1980. "The redefined monetary aggregates." *Federal Reserve Bulletin*, 66: 97–114

Snyder, David, and Edward L. Kick, 1979. "Structural position in the world economy and economic growth." *American Journal of Sociology*, 84: 1096–126

Spindt, Paul A. 1984. "Money is what money does: monetary aggregation and the equation of exchange." Typescript, Washington, DC: Board of Governors of the Federal Reserve Board

Steiber, Stephen, 1979. "The world system and world trade: an empirical exploration of conceptual conflicts." *Sociological Quarterly*, 20: 23–36

Strathern, Andrew, 1971. *The Rope of Moka*. Cambridge University Press

Sweezy, Paul, 1972. "The resurgence of finance capital: fact or fancy." *Socialist Revolution*, 8: 157–90

Webber, M. M., 1961. "Order in diversity: community without propinquity." In L. Wingo (ed.), *Cities and Space: The Future Use of Urban Land*. Baltimore: Johns Hopkins University Press

White, Harrison C., 1981a. "Production markets as induced role structures." In Samuel L. Leinhardt (ed.), *Sociological Methodology 1981*. San Francisco: Jossey-Bass, pp. 1–57

  1981b. "Where do markets come from?" *American Journal of Sociology*, 87: 517–47

White, Harrison C., Scott A. Boorman, and Ronald L. Breiger, 1976. "Social structure from multiple networks. I. Blockmodels of roles and positions." *American Journal of Sociology*, 81: 730–80

Williamson, Oliver E., 1981. "The economics of organization: the transaction cost approach." *American Journal of Sociology*, 87: 548–77

Yeager, Leland B., 1968. "Essential properties of the medium of exchange." *Kyklos*, 21: 45–69

5

Corporation, class and city system

Donald A. Palmer and Roger Friedland

In Ersilia, to establish the relationships that sustain the city's life, the inhabitants stretch strings from the corners of the houses, white or black or gray or black-and-white according to whether they mark a relationship of blood, of trade, authority, agency. When the strings become so numerous that you can no longer pass among them, the inhabitants leave: the houses are dismantled; only the strings and their supports remain.

Italo Valcino, *Invisible Cities*

Introduction

The composition and growth of territorial communities have been theorized to depend upon their position within larger systems of such communities. Thus analyses of cities and regions have increasingly moved from focussing on attributes of places toward the study of the relations among them. In this chapter, we review past conceptions of the city system in market economies – conceptions that we argue are not appropriate for advanced Western societies like the United States. We then present an alternative conception of the US city system, examine its determinants, and consider how a city's position in this system affects its growth.[1]

Activity without actors

Various mechanisms governing the relationships among places have been studied. Whether conceptualized as exchange, function or industry, these mechanisms are all based upon some form of *activity*.

In central place theory, places are linked to one another in spatially segregated, hierarchically ordered market areas. Higher-order, more central places produce for lower-order, less central places, each higher-order place exchanging its goods and services with hinterlands of ever larger extent. A city's size determines the size of its local market and the extent to which it can support specialized forms of production, and thus is an indicator of its centrality in the national system of cities (Berry, 1964, 1965, 1967, 1973).

In human ecological theory, places are linked to one another in a hierarchically organized territorial division of labor. Higher-order places dominate lower-order places by coordinating the specialized production in which the latter engage (Hawley, 1950, 1968, 1971; Duncan *et al.*, 1960; Duncan and Lieberson, 1970). Thus dominant places export capital and administration, while nondominant places export raw materials and production (Winsborough, 1960; Lincoln, 1978). Nonmetropolitan areas close to major metropolitan centers specialize more in manufacturing and have a higher proportion of production workers relative to those areas more distant from these centres (Lincoln and Friedland, 1977). Further, human ecology, along with export-base and growth-pole theories, assumes that what a place exports, based upon its comparative advantage, will determine its capacity for growth (Hawley, 1968; Perloff and Wingo, 1961; Milne, Glickman and Adams, 1980). This approach has been made dynamic by assuming that places go through stages of development, from export specialization, to import substitution, industrial diversification, and, finally, regional control (Thompson, 1965).

Economic geographers have further developed this perspective, arguing that industries, and not places, have a life cycle, and that shifts in the system of places can be derived from the geographic distribution of industries and their position in these life cycles. As industries age, scale of production increases, production becomes more routine, capital is substituted for labor, agglomeration economies decline in importance, and plants are decentralized in space (Hirsch, 1967; Norton and Rees, 1979; A. Scott, 1982). This leads to a slowing of growth in the original centers of once-new industries. The ability of a central place to grow thus depends upon its ability to nurture new industries (Duncan and Lieberson, 1970). Thus the phenomenal employment growth of the "sunbelt" has been attributed to its large share of new industries (Mollenkopf, 1983; Watkins and Perry, 1977).

In the understanding of any form of social organization there is a tension between functional and political theories. Functional theories tend to focus upon the way social activities are organized by a social system without regard to the actors or structures which control those activities. When functional theories do examine structures, these structures' attributes (including their location) are derived from the functions they perform for the system. Political theories tend to focus upon actors or structures whose interests and powers, and the conflicts between them, shape the organization of activity and hence the system (Alford and Friedland, 1985). All of the approaches summarized above assume that the system of places can be analyzed in terms of the locational requirements of economic activities that organize the relationships between places, without respect to the actors or structures which control that activity. Techniques of production and costs of communication change. Industries age. The comparative advantages of different places consequently change. In their wake, urban systems are reproduced or transformed.

More specifically, the above theories ignore organizational and class actors and the structures in which they are embedded.[2] When corporations, their managers and directors, and the relationships among them are analyzed, their locations are viewed as determined by the operation of the urban system. For example, human ecologists who analyze the geographical structure of the corporation use the locations of corporate headquarters as indicators of the kinds of activity characterizing a place, in this case coordination, which in turn is a function of the place's position in the national system of cities, in this instance its dominance (Hawley, 1971; Lincoln, 1978). More recently, economic geographers have argued that the divergent pattern of corporate interlocks between countries reflects their respective stages in the evolution of their urban systems (Semple and Phipps, 1982; Semple and Green, 1983). Thus, the above theories do not consider that organizational or class structures may determine a place's position in the urban system. The resulting conception of the urban system is highly deterministic. Policy options are tightly circumscribed by the constraints of comparative locational efficiency. Without actors, there can be no interests, no power, and hence no politics (Friedland and Palmer, 1984).[3]

We take the political approach in this chapter and focus on the organization and class actors in cities and the structures in which they are embedded. Aspects of the social structure of advanced Western societies – rather than city systems in general – leads us to believe that this approach is more appropriate than the functionalist one. The functionalist approach was more appropriate for a time in which relationships between organizational and class actors and thus exchanges between cities were more likely to be adjudicated by the market. Then, the system of places connected firms and the elites who controlled them. Fundamental changes in the organizational and class structure of the US (discussed in the next section), however, have occurred in the last century. Increasingly the economy is dominated by a handful of large corporations and their elites, and these actors have evolved nonmarket mechanisms for regulating the relationships between them and thus the cities in which they are located. Today, firms and the elites who control them are coming to connect places. Further, the pattern of these nonmarket relationships diverges from their market precursors. As a result, the process by which growth is transmitted between places has changed and the applicability of previous theories of the city system has been circumscribed. In the rest of this chapter we will elaborate the changes in the organizational and class structure of the US, the impact these changes have had on the nature and pattern of connections between cities, and the impact these connections have on city growth.[4]

Cities as nodes in organizational and class structures

Three developments in corporate and class structure accompanying the transition from competitive to monopoly capitalism have transformed the city system.

First, over the course of the twentieth century, large firms have adopted multidivisional structures. The multidivisional form is distinguished from the functional form in its hierarchical segregation of productive and even routine administrative functions from strategic functions. This facilitates long-term planning and entry into new and diverse geographical and product markets, both by direct plant investment and acquisition (Chandler, 1969, 1977). As a result, firms increasingly locate their headquarters, which are responsible for strategic decision-making, in places distant from their production facilities. Further, they increasingly locate their production facilities, which are run as semi-autonomous enterprises, distant from each other. These semi-autonomous enterprises often obtain their inputs from and dispense their outputs to other subunits of the corporation to which they belong (Hayter and Watts, 1983). In this way, transactions between different enterprises have come to be regulated by administrative chains of command, or *intraorganizational structures*, instead of the market for commodities.

Second, corporations have increasingly established long-term resource exchange contracts, joint ventures, and interfirm stockholding agreements with their competitors, buyers, and suppliers. These linkages reduce uncertainty associated with transactions between otherwise autonomous firms, which are operating in increasingly concentrated industries (Pfeffer and Salancik, 1978). As a result, resource exchanges between corporations are increasingly regulated by boundary spanning linkages, or *interorganizational structures*, instead of the market for commodities.

Third, the basis of relationships between corporate elites, or *intraclass structures*, has changed. In the past, corporate elites were both managers and members of an owning family and were bound to other corporate elites through kinship relations or ownership in the same firms (Rochester, 1936; Lundberg, 1938). But, increasingly, firm ownership has been separated from control, and institutional stockholders are becoming the dominant owners (J. Scott, 1979; Herman, 1981; but see Useem, 1980; Glasberg and Schwartz, 1983). This development has both forced and allowed corporations to recruit professional top management nationally rather than from local owning families. Today, corporate elites are bound to one another through common university attendance, and social club, corporate board, and public policy group memberships (Domhoff, 1967, 1975, 1983). As a result, the relationships between corporate elites are increasingly regulated by social networks instead of kinship and common stock ownership.[5]

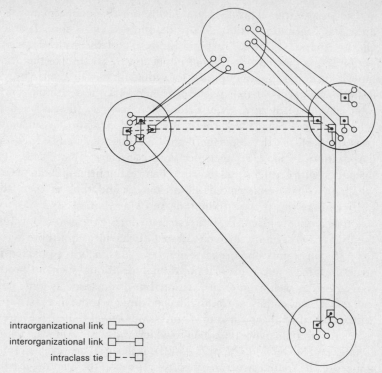

intraorganizational link □———○
interorganizational link □———□
intraclass tie □– – –□

5.1   Intraorganizational and interorganizational linkages and intraclass ties between four hypothetical cities.

These three developments, by reducing the impact of market constraints on firm behavior and location, have changed the nature and pattern of the relations which constitute the city system and thus the geographic distribution of economic activities. The urban system is still a spatial structure for production and exchange. But the connections in this structure are decreasingly simple market exchanges and increasingly composed of organizational linkages and class bonds. Capitalist elites, the corporations they command, and the plants and headquarters that compose them are situated in space. Thus the intraorganizational, interorganizational, and intraclass structures in which these actors are embedded have a spatial structure. More importantly, this spatial structure organizes the city system, in that places are differentially integrated into the organizational and class structures, and variably connected to each other through them (figure 5.1). The position a place occupies in these corporate and class structures will affect its growth. More specifically, the level and kinds of economic activity that take place in a city or region will be affected by how it is integrated into these corporate and class structures.

The organizational linkages and class bonds that connect cities, however, are not exogenous or functionally determined by a spatial structure of efficient markets. Rather, they are the result of the strategic decisions of corporations that have locational implications. Some, like the decision to move a headquarters, are explicitly locational (that is, motivated by the firm's desire to change its spatial structure). Others, like the decision to engage in a joint venture or merger, might be only implicitly so (that is, motivated by other concerns but change the firm's spatial structure as an unintended consequence). The developments in the US economy, discussed above, enable corporations to make strategic decisions considering more sites, at greater distances, with greater speed than ever before. But firms differ in the extent to which they have experienced these changes and thus in their ability to participate in this process (Bluestone and Harrison, 1982).

Further, once in place, the spatial structure of organizational links and class bonds may affect future corporate strategic behavior, acting both as resources for and constraints on corporate actions. Thus, a firm's position in these structures may affect explicit locational decisions such as headquarter movement, as well as implicit locational decisions such as joint venture or merger. Recent empirical research has documented the increased frequency with which firms engage in joint ventures and mergers, and has even explored the factors that influence the extent to which and manner in which firms do so (Pfeffer and Salancik, 1978; Burt, 1980a). It has not, however, examined the impact of the spatial structure of corporations on these strategic behaviors.

The rest of the chapter explores our alternate conception of the city system in greater detail. The spatial structure of interorganizational and intraorganizational linkages and intraclass bonds are attributes both of the corporation and its elites, as well as the city system. Our primary purpose is to examine the determinants of the spatial structure of organizational and class structures and the impact they have on the cities embedded in them. In the process we will consider the impact this structure has on corporate behavior as well.[6]

Determinants of the corporate and class structure of the city system

The intraorganizational structure

A city system has an intraorganizational structure based upon the geography of ownership and control of multiplant firms. This structure consists of the geographical distribution of headquarters and plants and the relationships of ownership and control between them. These interlocal connections of ownership and control are the product of decisions by corporate elites to locate their firms' headquarters and plants in specific places.

The *number* and *type* of corporate headquarters located in a place are important dimensions of its position in the city system. According to central place theory, the most central places, as indicated by population size, will contain the greatest volume of administrative activity and, by inference, the greatest number of large corporate headquarters. The number and size of corporations a place can support are thought to depend on its accessibility to labor, producer, and consumer markets. Central places both have larger such markets and are more accessible to markets in other places.

Numerous cross-sectional studies show that there is a strong positive association between city size, indexed by population, and administrative activity, measured by percentage employed in administrative occupations (Duncan *et al.*, 1960; Duncan and Lieberson, 1970). The relationship between the size of a place and the number of headquarters situated in it, though, is more ambiguous. Many studies report that there is a direct relationship between population size and the number of *Fortune* 500 corporations located in a city (see Lincoln, 1978; Eberstein and Frisbie, 1982). However, several studies that characterize the stability and change in the geographic distribution of headquarters location over the last few decades suggest that this relationship is far from perfect and may even vary over time and between urban systems (Semple, 1973; Semple and Phipps, 1982; Stephens and Holly, 1981; Burns and Pang, 1977). Aiken and Strickland, in one of the most innovative of these studies, used temporal rank order correlations to compare the changing distribution of population and corporate headquarters among cities in the United States and Germany, countries which are decentralized in terms of population and governmental structure (Aiken and Strickland, 1983a; Strickland and Aiken, 1983). They found that a city's population rank in the US was, on average, highly stable between 1917 and 1980. But its rank in terms of the number of headquarters situated in it varied considerably. In Germany, which was examined for only the most recent period (1950 to 1980), the stability of a city's rank was very high with respect to both population and the number of headquarters it possessed.

We have broken down the changing spatial distribution of the largest US industrial corporate headquarters into its component parts – birth, relocation, acquisition, and death – and charted each by type of place and region (Friedland, Palmer, and Dumont, 1986). Focussing on relocation (we discuss acquisition in the next section), we found that almost one-quarter of the approximately 650 firms listed as among the top 500 industrial corporations in either 1960 or 1975 moved their headquarters between these two years. There was a substantial reorganization of the distribution of headquarters by type of place. Contrary to central place theory but consistent with reports in the popular press, central cities were net losers of corporate headquarters, while the less central suburbs were net gainers. Many writers have noted that the "frost belt," or the northeast states, has lost industrial employment to the "sunbelt," the southern and western states, and some argue that this portends a major shift in economic and political power in the US (Watkins and Perry, 1977; Sale, 1975). Others have disputed this claim, pointing out that while employment has indeed shifted away from the north, most of the employment created in the south and west remains controlled by corporations headquartered in the north (Birch, 1979; Schmenner, 1982; Bluestone and Harrison, 1982). Our analysis supports the latter view. While the New York-centered Middle Atlantic region experienced a net loss of headquarters, the Boston-centered Northeast region reaped an equally large net gain. The other seven regions experienced little net change.

Research on the relationship between size of place and size of corporation is similarly equivocal. Westaway (1974) has shown that in Britain there is a strong positive association between the size of corporations and the size of the cities in which they are headquartered. Our examination of the headquarter locations of the largest 500 US industrial corporations in 1964, however, reveals a different picture. US locales can be crudely categorized into four types of places of differing centrality. Standard Metropolitan Statistical Areas (SMSAs) are areal units that contain: (1) a central county in which the largest city, called the "central city," has more than 50,000 inhabitants, and (2) a number of adjacent counties that are metropolitan in character and economically and socially integrated with the central county. The most central places are situated in large SMSAs – those SMSAs that have a central city with over 100,000 inhabitants. Within these areas, central cities are most central and their suburbs are somewhat less so. Still less central places are situated in small SMSAs – those SMSAs whose central cities have less than 100,000 inhabitants. Least central are small cities not situated in SMSAs. We found that the largest corporations (as measured by assets) were headquartered in the central cities of large SMSAs, smaller firms were headquartered in their suburbs and in the central cities of small SMSAs, and the smallest corporations were headquartered in small cities. However, the correlation between a corporation's size and the population size of the SMSA in which it was headquartered (90 per cent of all corporations were headquartered in SMSAs) was quite weak (Friedland, Palmer, and Stenbeck, 1986).

We think the evidence on the number and types of headquarters located in the largest US cities is not completely consistent with central place theory, because the large corporation has changed, in ways discussed in the last section, since that theory was first formulated. As a result, the characteristics of firms and places that influence headquarter location have changed. At the turn of the century, corporate headquarters were preoccupied with the administration of production and firms utilized the functional organizational structure. This constrained headquarters to locate proximate to their plants, which were their principal object of attention, and to locate their plants proximate to each other. Under these conditions, a firm's size was indicative of the market to which the place in which it was headquartered was accessible. The firm's plants depended on the same market, and organizational structure and headquarter function both dictated that the headquarter place be accessible to the market. But over the course of this century, corporate headquarters have become increasingly preoccupied with the acquisition and processing of information required for the formulation and implementation of strategic decisions and firms have increasingly adopted the multidivisional form. This both requires and allows corporate headquarters to locate at a distance from their plants, no longer their principal object of attention, to whatever place strategic information is most abundant. It also allows plants of the same firm to be situated distant from each other, wherever demand is sufficient or factor costs more optimal. Under this arrangement, a firm's size does not dictate the size of the place in which it is headquartered.[7] This may explain the apparently contradictory results reported above. We think major firm size and place size are correlated in Britain, but not in the US, because Britain is geographically much smaller than the US. As a result, British firms may have more spatially concentrated production structures than US firms.

Human ecology theory implicitly takes the separation of production and administration into account. According to human ecologists, as regions grow, the functions performed by cities within them become more specialized. Nondominant cities within the region, which tend to be small, specialize in production while dominant cities, which tend to be large, specialize in coordination – the administration of exchange between nondominant cities.[8] Thus human ecologists expect the relationships between a place's size and the number of corporate headquarters situated in it to be imperfect. Growth is the cause of a more proximate determinant of the size of a place's administrative sector – specialization in coordination. Consistent with this, Berry and Kasarda (1977) have shown that among SMSAs, the percentage of people employed in administrative occupations increases with population growth. Further, Lincoln (1978) has shown that the number of *Fortune* 1000 corporate headquarters located in an SMSA is a function of its size *and* occupational differentiation, an indicator of the extent to which it specializes in trade. And Eberstein and Frisbie (1982) have shown that an SMSA's position in the dominance hierarchy, measured partially by the number of *Fortune* 1000 corporations headquartered there, was a function of its size *and* the amount of different types of products that it shipped and received to a large number of other places. No one has examined the relationship between the characteristics of corporations and the extent to which their headquarter places are specialized in coordination.

The human ecology approach is an improvement upon central place theory, because it focusses more closely on the functions corporate headquarters actually perform. We think the human ecology approach itself can be improved upon by focussing on the structures corporate headquarters actually use to perform those functions. In order to coordinate production, corporate headquarters must acquire and process strategic information and thus must locate in cities that possess a plentiful supply of such information.

A corporation's demand for strategic information should depend on its organizational structure. Perhaps most important is the nature of a corporation's dependencies on other firms. The more industrially diverse and spatially dispersed a firm, the more different types of organizations on which it is dependent and the more uncertainty to which it is exposed. The more structurally constrained the markets in which a corporation produces (as measured by the extent to which establishments in those markets buy and sell from a small number of monopolized sectors), the more intense those dependencies and the uncertainty they engender will be (Burt, 1980a). The larger a firm, the more other organizations are dependent on it and the more likely that other organizations will try to influence it. Information exchange is one strategy for coping with uncertainty and influence attempts (Pfeffer and Salancik, 1978). The extent to which a firm is engaged in long-term contracts, acquisitions, and joint ventures with other firms should also increase a firm's demand for strategic information, because firms require information to implement such strategies. Finally, adoption of the multidivisional form may increase a firm's demand for strategic information in its headquarter city, because it centralizes strategic decision-making in the firm's headquarters (although it probably reduces a firm's demand for nonstrategic information and thus routine business services, because it decentralizes tactical decision-making to its operating units).

A corporation's class structure may also influence its demand for strategic information. Family-controlled firms may not have a smaller need for strategic information than management-controlled firms, but they may be less willing to recognize this need. The acquisition of strategic information requires establishing relationships with agents outside of the firm and these relationships inevitably threaten to dilute the control corporate decision-makers have over the day-to-day affairs of their firms. Family elites are believed to place a higher value on retaining such control than managerial elites (Pugh *et al.*, 1969). Further, corporations whose directors are well integrated into the national, as opposed to the local, interlock network may have a smaller demand for strategic information generated by local sources, because they have access to strategic information generated in other locales. Thus, geographically dispersed, industrially diverse, and structurally constrained corporations that engage in many long-term contracts, joint ventures, and acquisitions, and use the multidivisional form, will have the greatest demand for strategic information, as will management-controlled firms whose directors are not well integrated into the national interlock network. For the most part, these firms will also be the largest corporations.

The extent to which a city is a source of strategic information should depend on its organizational and class structure. A corporation can purchase strategic information from specialized business service firms and financial institutions situated in its headquarter city. Alternatively, its top managers and directors can acquire strategic information informally from the elites of other firms headquartered in its city by living in the same neighborhoods, sitting on the same corporate boards, and belonging to the same social clubs, cultural institutions and public policy-making groups as these elites do. Thus cities which have many business service firms, financial institutions, corporate headquarters, and capitalist class social institutions should be the best sites for the acquisition of strategic information. These will, of course, tend to be the largest, most occupationally differentiated cities.

Thus we expect that a city's size and the degree to which it specializes in coordination will be associated with the number and size of corporations headquartered there. This association, however, should be largely spurious – the result of the association between a range of other corporate and city characteristics, with which both are highly correlated. These characteristics pertain to the organization and class structures of corporations and cities, and the relationship between them is driven by the dynamics of the supply of and demand for strategic information.

We have begun to examine the relationship between the organizational and class structures of large corporations and the organization and class characteristics of the places in which they are headquartered. Our first study analyzes the determinants of the population size of the metropolitan area in which each of the largest 500 industrial corporations in 1964 was headquartered. The results of this analysis support our arguments above. The most important determinant of the centrality of a corporation's headquarter locale is the geographic dispersion of its production facilities – the more dispersed its production, the more central its headquarter locale. The structural autonomy of corporations also affects the centrality of their headquarters location, with autonomous firms situating their headquarters in peripheral locales. Finally, adoption of the multidivisional form has a positive effect on the centrality of a firm's headquarter place. Most important, controlling for these organizational structure effects, a corporation's size does not influence the centrality of its headquarter locale (Friedland, Palmer and Stenbeck, 1986).

This study is limited in several respects. First, we have not considered many dimensions of the organization and class structure of corporations that may influence the centrality of their headquarter locations (e.g. the extent to which their directors are integrated into the national interlock network). Second, we have not conceptualized the centrality of headquarter places in terms of the organization and class structure of those locales. Finally, any association between the organizational and class structures of firms and the cities in which they are headquartered may not be solely the result of the aggregation of past headquarter location decisions. Corporations may change and be changed by the organizational and class structures of the cities in which they locate. For example, the presence of many large corporate headquarters in a city may stimulate the co-location and growth of organizations with extralocal linkages, such as business service firms, which may stimulate the dispersion of its corporation's plants in space. This suggests that future studies should examine the relationship between firm and city characteristics in a dynamic design. In subsequent studies we plan to use the full range of organizational and class structures of corporations to predict the likelihood that firms will relocate their headquarters to more central or less central locations, as measured by a composite indicator of the number of organizational sources of strategic information they possess.

The number and types of headquarters located in a place are not the only determinants of its position in the intraorganizational structure of the city system. Also crucial are the linkages headquarters maintain with their plants in other places. According to central place theory, firms should locate their plants in the hinterland of the headquarter place or in nearby central places lower in the city system hierarchy. Preston (1971) presents evidence that this portrait is accurate for the Pacific Northwest. He ranks cities in five categories according to their centrality (indicated by a measure of the extent to which cities export goods) and shows that the pattern of headquarter and plant locations organizes these cities into two geographically segregated nested hierarchies. There are, however, two problems with this study. First, the author determined a city's position in one or the other of the hierarchies by designating it a hinterland place of the city in which the majority of its plant headquarters were situated. Second, he ignored all production facilities controlled by headquarters situated outside the region. Both procedures systematically ignore deviations from the hierarchical pattern predicted by central place theory.

An earlier study, which does not suffer from these weaknesses, paints a more complex picture. Pappenfort (1959), who studied plants located in Illinois but controlled by headquarters situated in and outside the state, demonstrated that while plant locations are influenced by central place forces, central place hierarchies overlap. Specifically, he showed that a firm's headquarter location tends to be more central than the locations in which its plants are situated. But the centrality of a location is influenced by its proximity to multiple dominant centers. Thus firms headquartered in the greater Chicago area, Illinois' central dominant, tended to locate their headquarters closer than their plants to the city's center. Firms headquartered in Illinois but outside of Chicago, however, tended to locate their head-quarters closer than their plants to places that were dominated by Chicago *and* St. Louis, the nearest competing central dominant. The extent to which a place was dominated by the two centers was measured by the sum of the distances between it and each metropolitan area, weighted by the number of manufacturing establishments in each area. Finally, the plant locations of firms headquartered outside of Illinois differed depending on their headquarter region. Firms headquartered in the Northeastern United States were more likely than firms headquartered elsewhere to situate their plants in places central to Chicago and St. Louis. Pappenfort implies that this reflects the dominant position of Northeastern cities and the subordinate position of cities in other regions with respect to Chicago.

Finally, the most recent and most comprehensive study to date suggests that the problems with central place theory's explanation of the spatial distribution of corporate plants in the United States go beyond the complex overlapping of hinterlands. Examining large corporations headquartered in six Far Western cities, Pred (1977) found that firms locate their plants not just outside the hinterland of their headquarters place (for example, at opposite ends of the country), but frequently in places more central than their headquarter place. Although the spatial structure of a firm's operations does appear to differ depending upon the region in which it is headquartered, the Far West does not contain the nation's most geographically dispersed firms (Friedland and Palmer, 1983).

These studies suggest that headquarter and plant locations are increasingly distant from one another and that the relationship between the two is decreasingly governed by central place dynamics. Thus, human ecologists, who attribute these developments to improvements in communication and transportation technologies, examine headquarter and plant location as independent phenomena. They argue that, as urban systems evolve, some places within them specialize in production while others specialize in administration. Further, they show that the place characteristics associated with the presence of manufacturing facilities are the opposite of those associated with the presence of office activity (Duncan *et al.*, 1960; Lincoln, 1978). We believe, however, that this approach overestimates the independence between the location of the headquarters and plants of the same firm. It also ignores the organization and class structures that affect specific firms, as opposed to the general technological developments that affect all firms – structures that mediate this interdependence between headquarter and plant location.

Our alternative explanation of plant location integrates central place theory and its critique. Specifically, we argue that a firm's decision to locate a plant in a particular place depends partly on the distance between that place and the corporation's headquarters (Taylor, 1975; Watts, 1980). The extent to which and manner in which this distance constraint operates, however, depends on the industries in which corporations produce and the organization and class structures they use. As industries develop, technologies become more routine, capital is substituted for labor, and profit rates fall. The routinization of technology and substitution of capital for labor allow firms producing in "old" industries to disperse their plants in space (Hirsch, 1967; A. Scott, 1982), and the decline in profitability encourages them to enter new industries. Further, as firms grow, they generate uncertainty for other organizations with which they are interdependent. These other organizations attempt to influence them in response to this increased uncertainty. And corporations, in turn, are compelled to avoid these control attempts by entering new product and geographic markets, becoming more diversified and spatially dispersed (Pfeffer and Salancik, 1978). Because places are not equally conducive to production in different industries, the more industrially diversified a firm becomes, the more spatially dispersed it is likely to be. However, structural inertia, which increases with age, may inhibit corporations from adapting to their environments in the ways described above.

Family-controlled firms, in which a group of individuals own a controlling block of stock, are less likely to diversify and spatially disperse their production. This is partly because diversification and spatial dispersion require the decentralization of control, which family interests avoid (Pugh *et al.*, 1969). Also family-controlled firms eschew interlocking directorates (Zeitlin, 1974; Burt, 1980b) and divisionalized administrative structures (Palmer, Friedland, Jennings and Powers, 1984, 1985).[9] They are also less likely to expand through acquisition. These strategies and structures facilitate spatial dispersion. Interlocking directorates with other corporations headquartered in distant places provide a firm with information about potential production sites in those distant locales. Divisionalized organizational structures are more appropriate than functional structures to manage spatially dispersed production (Chandler, 1969, 1977). And corporate acquisition is typically accomplished through nationally integrated financial institutions, which possess information about potential candidates for acquisition distant from the firm's headquarter locale.

An impressive and growing body of research on plant location decisions in New York State indicates that product life cycle processes play a significant but limited role in influencing firms to locate plants outside of their home region. While some plants appear to exit the state because they are late in the product life cycle, the high-technology sectors, which are early in the product life cycle, have higher-than-average employment gains *and* losses. This research also suggests that organization and class structures influence firms to situate their plants outside their home region. The plants of large corporations are more likely to exit the state than are those of small corporations, presumably because their parent firms pursue diversified strategies, adopt divisional structures, and have directors who are well integrated into the national business elite (Schwartz *et al.*, 1983, 1984, 1985, 1986; Yago *et al.*, 1984; Korman *et al.*, 1986).

In an attempt to evaluate the detailed model outlined above, we characterized the production structures of the largest 500 US industrial corporations in 1964 – measuring the number of cities and the number of states in which they produced. Our analyses partially confirm central place and ecological theory. Corporations headquartered in more central or dominant places, as indicated by their population size, are likely to be both more industrially diverse and geographically dispersed. The analyses also confirm the industrial aging argument. Corporations specializing in older industries are more geographically dispersed. Finally, the analyses support our integration of organization and class theory. Industrially diverse corporations are more geographically dispersed, while old firms, which were founded at a time when transportation technologies dictated that they construct large plants near their headquarter locale, are more geographically concentrated. Further, family-controlled firms are less geographically dispersed than those that are management-controlled. These results provide the first evidence that plant location decisions are not simply a function of industrial and urban system market constraints (Friedland, Palmer and Stenbeck, 1986).

This study, however, has several limitations. It does not assess the impact that the organizational and class structure of headquarter and plant locations may have on the distance at which firms situate their plants from their headquarters. As noted above, firms headquartered in cities with a plentiful supply of strategic information may find it easier to disperse their production in space. Further, the study, by implicitly viewing plant rather than headquarter locations as problematic, ignores the impact that a firm's plant location decisions may have on the location of its headquarters. As noted above, geographical dispersion may lead firms to situate their headquarters in central places. Thus, researchers should examine the plant location process over time and focus on the characteristics of and relationships between places as factors influencing this process. A few authors have described the change and stability of the interorganizational structure of the city system (Rees, 1978; Ross, 1982). In future studies, we plan to examine the organizational and class structure of corporations and cities that influence firms to close, relocate and open plants in cities distant from their headquarter locale (see also Jennings, 1986).[10]

Interorganizational structure

The interorganizational structure of the city system is composed of those connections that link the administrative structures of large firms headquartered in different places. These connections, which vary in extensiveness from long-term contracts to ownership relationships, link the decision-making apparatuses of two firms and thus give one firm some measure of control over another. We focus here on two types of long-term contracts: bank correspondent arrangements, in which one bank deposits capital in another bank in return for services (for example, check clearing) and lending agreements, in which a bank provides capital to a nonfinancial institution in return for interest. We also focus on the most extensive type of ownership relationship, corporate combination, in which the control of one firm's operations is transferred to another.

Both central place and human ecology theory view the geographical pattern of long-term contracts as an indicator of the volume of economic activity between places. Thus, both would predict that the most central/dominant places, as indicated by population size, would be the highest banking centers; that is, would have the most banks, most involved in extralocal loans and most often selected as correspondents by banks in other locales. Further, both would predict that the pattern of loans and correspondent selections between the various centers would be hierarchically organized, with the largest centers having the most extensive hinterlands. This seems to be the case. Only the largest US cities have sufficient banking activity to be granted federal reserve bank status. The largest of these have the highest percentage of extralocal loans and lend at the greatest distance. New York City, for example, has a national hinterland, while St. Louis only a regional one (Duncan *et al.*, 1960; Lieberson, 1961). Further, banks in the major metropolises (New York City, Chicago, etc.) are the ones most often selected as correspondents by other US banks. New York City receives the most selections, many of which are from the less central/dominant Chicago (as determined by population size). Chicago receives the next most selections, many of which are from the lesser centers, St. Louis, Minneapolis, Kansas City, and Dallas, but few of which are from the more central/dominant New York City (Duncan and Lieberson, 1970). Examining the correspondent selections of cities in Iowa, Lieberson and Schwirian (1962) found that city size is directly proportionate to the average distance at which banks located in them select correspondent banks and that the city size of selected banks tends to be larger than the size of cities in which their selecting bank is located.

While these results are consistent with central place and human ecology theory, they do not contradict the organizational and class theory of the city system that we offer. Most important, we would expect interorganizational linkages involving banks to correspond closely to the patterns predicted by central place and human ecology theory, because state and federal government regulation restricts the extent to which banks can participate in the three historical developments that increase locational flexibility (e.g. the prohibition of interlocks between commercial banks), and also circumscribes the use of the flexibility banks do possess (e.g. the prohibition of interstate banking). Further, this evidence does not show that the organizational and class structures of banks have no effect on the geographical structure of the relationships in which they are embedded. In fact, Lieberson and Schwirian

(1962) also found that a bank's size was directly related to both the distance at which it selected correspondents as well as the size of the locales in which banks selecting them as correspondents were located. Lieberson (1961) also found that large banks were most involved in extralocal loans. And Ratcliff (1980), who studied the involvement of St. Louis banks in lending relationships, found that, controlling for size, banks whose directors had many intraclass bonds with national corporate elites allocated a larger percentage of their loans to extralocal corporations as opposed to local mortgages.

There have been no central place or ecological explanations of the spatial structure of corporate combination, which, since the turn of the century, has been less subject to state and federal regulation (Fligstein, 1985). We may infer an explanation from these theories, however, because they implicitly assume that headquarter relocation and corporate acquisition are analogous processes. Both are major determinants of the spatial distribution of corporate headquarters, which urban geographers and sociologists theorize and typically study cross-sectionally. When a firm is acquired, its headquarter activities are transferred to the headquarters of the acquiring firm. And when the two are headquartered in different places, one place actually loses a headquarter and the other effectively gains one. Thus central place and human ecology theory would predict that corporations headquartered in large cities that are specialized in trade will be the most acquisitive, and will target firms headquartered in their hinterland.

In a recent study, Green and Cromley (1984) tested and found support for a gravity model of corporate mergers that is not derived from but is consistent with central place and human ecology theory. This model is predicted on the assumption that the likelihood that two firms will merge depends on the amount of information they have about each other, and that the amount of information they have about each other will be greater, the larger and closer headquarter cities are to one another. Consequently, it predicts that the extent to which firms in two cities merge with one another will be positively affected by the combined size of the cities and negatively affected by the local distance between them. This study is, however, limited in two respects. First, it focusses only on firms headquartered in the three most central cities in the US – New York, Chicago, and Los Angeles. Second, it does not distinguish between acquiring and acquired firms, and thus between gaining and losing cities. As a result, the evidence it reports may not be generalizable, and, even to the extent that it is, may, contrary to central place theory, be consistent with the conclusion that places lose, rather than gain, headquarter activities in proportion to their size.

We are just now beginning a more comprehensive analysis of the spatial pattern of the 123 corporate combinations that involved the top 500 US corporations in 1960 and that took place between 1960 and 1975 (Friedland, Palmer, and Dumont, 1986). The results suggest, contrary to central place and human ecology theory, that relocation and acquisition have somewhat different geographies. The pattern of combination did not differ from that of relocation with respect to region. Once again, our research suggests that there have been no major shifts in the distribution of corporate control from frost belt to sunbelt.[11] The pattern of combination, however, did differ from that of relocation, with respect to type of place. Further, the type of place pattern for acquisition does not completely conform to central place or human ecology theory. The most central/dominant places (large central cities and their suburbs) were *net* gainers and the less central/dominant places (small central cities and small cities) were *net* losers. Further, the bulk of firms lost by the suburbs of large central cities, small central cities, and small cities were acquired by firms headquartered in large central cities. Large central cities, however, experienced the largest *proportionate* loss of firms due to acquisition. They lost about one-quarter of their 1960 headquarter base while small cities lost only one-twentieth. Almost all of this loss was due to the acquisition of large central city corporations by firms in the same or other large central cities. Central place and human ecology theory cannot predict the pattern of intralocal acquisition; that is, they cannot predict why large central cities will lose a greater percentage of their firms to intralocal acquisitions than other types of places, or why some large central cities will lose more firms to intralocal acquisitions than other large central cities. These theories are concerned with the volume of administrative activity in a place, and intracity acquisitions do not alter the volume of administrative activity in a city – only the organizational form this activity takes. Central place and human ecology theory could explain the pattern of inter-central city acquisitions if the gains and losses correspond to the city size hierarchy among central cities. An impressionistic examination of the evidence, however, suggests that this is not the case.

To fill the gap between urban theory and the empirical evidence, we again turn to organization and class theories of the corporation. According to the resource dependence perspective, firms that are competitively interdependent (that is, that produce in the same industry) or symbiotically interdependent (that is, that produce in industries which supply one another with resources necessary for production) combine to eliminate the uncertainty associated with these interdependencies (Pfeffer and Salancik, 1978). Burt (1980a) has developed this approach both theoretically and methodologically at the industry level of analysis. If industries are not randomly distributed in space, it is possible that these organizational level processes influence any systematic changes observed at the geographical level. Corporate control may migrate between two types of places or two regions because the dominant industry in one is interdependent with the dominant industry in the other.[12]

This approach is limited, however, by its assumption, which it shares with Green and Cromley (1984), that corporate combination is cooperative rather than conflictive. Specifically, it does not distinguish between acquired and acquiring firms. Thus, this approach can potentially explain why one type of place or region possesses firms that tend to combine with firms headquartered in another. But it cannot explain why one type of place or region *gains* control over another. Further, it analyzes combination without respect to the power structure within which large firms are positioned. These power relations, which derive from other dimensions of the interorganizational structure as well as the intraclass structure, are patterned systematically in space. Thus, the spatial pattern of corporate combination may be influenced by the spatial structure of interorganizational linkages and intraclass bonds.

We think that corporate combination is the result of a contest for economic dominance between firms. The outcome of this struggle for dominance is determined by the economic resources that firms possess. A firm's resources are, in turn, substantially determined by the position it occupies in the network of interorganizational linkages, the most important of which involve debt to and ownership by financial institutions, and the position its elites occupy in the network of intraclass bonds. Specifically, we expect to find that large corporations that are well integrated into organizational and class structures will tend to acquire firms that are smaller and less integrated into these structures than themselves.

We also think that the repeated operation of this process fosters the development of a normative framework among corporate elites that legitimizes its persistence. Thus corporate combination often appears to be as conflict-free as proponents of the resource dependence perspective assume. When a firm violates this normative order, however, conflict becomes overt. Thus, when the bidder is smaller than the target, overtures for combination are more likely to take the form of a surprise tender offer by the bidder and to be labelled "unfriendly" by the target (Steiner, 1975). The crucial factors regulating the resolution of such open battles, however, remain the organizational and class structures that produce the normative order the contests violate. Thus preliminary evidence indicates that bidders tend to be more successful in unfriendly takeover attempts if they are more integrated than their targets in the intraclass network (as indicated by interlocking directorates), even controlling for the relative size of bidder and target (Palmer, Friedland, Ross, and Murray, 1986).

Taken together, these results suggest that the volume of acquisitions involving firms headquartered in the same locale or in two different locales will depend on the extent to which firms headquartered in those places are interdependent with each other. The organizational and class resources possessed by firms in a locale will determine whether the place is a winner or loser in interregional contests. In general, we expect that locales that provide a home for large, well-integrated firms will gain headquarters, because these firms will most often be the dominant partner in mergers and the bidder rather than target (and victorious regardless of their role) in acquisitions. Since the actors that control resources required for the acquisition of a firm are likely to be concentrated in that firm's locale (for example, the families or banks who own the firm's stock), extralocal linkages and bonds are likely to be most important for the out-of-city bidder, while local connections are likely to be most important for the target. Thus, cities whose firms are primarily connected with each other (rather than extralocal firms) are likely to lose few firms to and gain few firms from acquisition, while cities whose firms are primarily connected to firms in other locales will experience the exact reverse.

Finally, we expect that acquisitions involving firms headquartered in the same locale will be friendly more often than acquisitions involving firms in different locales. And acquisitions involving firms in the same locale will have a greater tendency to be friendly when firms in that locale maintain extensive connections with one another. The elites of firms headquartered in the same locale are more likely to share a common normative framework, and the extent to which this is the case will depend on the extent to which they and their firms are connected to one another.

Intraclass structure

The intraclass structure of the city system consists of the geographical structure of social relationships among corporate elites. Intraclass bonds between the directors of two firms may be forged through indirect mechanisms, such as residence in the same neighborhood, membership in the same social club, and participation in the same public policy-making group. Or they may be forged through the direct mechanism we focus on here, overlapping corporate board memberships – interlocking directorates.[13] Neither central place or human ecology theory has been used to explain the geographical pattern of these social relationships. We might, however, expect these theories to predict that elites in large cities specializing in trade will maintain the most bonds, and that these bonds will connect them with elites in smaller places specializing in narrow branches of production in their hinterland.

Green (1984) has presented evidence consistent with this portrait. He tested and found support for a gravity model of interlocking, which stipulated that the number of interlock ties connecting firms in two locales would be directly related to the size of the locales, the presence of large commercial banks (which play a crucial role in trade) in at least one of them, and the distance between them. In the absence of evidence on the balance of power between the firms these interlock ties join (as measured perhaps by interlock direction), however, it is unclear whether or not the largest trading centers dominate the smaller production-oriented places. Further, in the absence of a spatial mapping of the ties, it is unclear whether or not the pattern of ties actually delineates segregated regions as central place and, to a lesser extent, human ecology theory would predict. The cluster analyses of several political sociologists help to fill this gap. They show that interlocking tends to occur among firms headquartered in the same geographical region (Allen, 1978; Bearden *et al.*, 1975; Sonquist and Koenig, 1975; Mintz and Schwartz, 1981a, 1981b, 1985) although Mizruchi's (1982) analysis shows that such regionalization has been declining over the twentieth century.

While these empirical results conform fairly well to central place and human ecology theory, we think the fit obscures more than it reveals. Specifically, we expect that the population of and distance between cities, which have been the center of attention in past studies, are related to more fundamental properties of the city system – the number and types of organizations located in places and the intraorganizational, interorganizational, and intraclass relations between them. Population size is associated with the number of corporations headquartered in a place. More important, proximity between two places is associated with the extent to which firms in them produce in interdependent industries and the elites of these firms are members of the same social circle. It is the characteristics of and relations between corporations and their elites, not the size and distances between places, which *explain* the volume of interlocking within and between places.

According to the resource dependence perspective, intraclass bonds are a device for reducing uncertainty associated with competitive and symbiotic interdependence. Consistent with this view, corporate interlocks are found to connect firms that are interdependent with one another (Allen, 1974; Burt, 1980b, 1983; Burt, Christman, and Kilburn, 1980; Pennings, 1980: Pfeffer and Salancik, 1978). Further, firms that produce in interdependent industries tend to locate their headquarters near one another (see Quante, 1976: 5) Economists argue that this allows firms to take advantage of agglomeration economies or to reduce transportation costs associated with their production activities. We think it also allows firms to acquire information about each other's behavior. As noted above, we found that corporations producing in structurally constrained markets tend to locate their headquarters in central places, presumably because such locales are rich in strategic information. By locating in the same place, the elites of interdependent firms can establish intraclass bonds with one another, both indirectly, through common neighborhood residence, social club membership, and public policy-making group participation, and directly, through overlapping corporate board memberships. In fact, we think this latter factor is replacing the former as the principal cause of the co-location of the headquarters of interdependent firms, because the growing spatial separation of productive and strategic functions in large corporations cuts the link between plant and headquarter location. Increasingly, the production facilities of two firms in the same industry can be located in the same place, while the corporate headquarters controlling these facilities may be situated in different and distant locales. Such is the case with Houston's externally controlled oil industry (Feagin, 1983). Thus, places that are close to one another are likely to be connected by many interlocking directorates, because the headquarters in them are likely to coordinate corporations that are interdependent with one another.

According to many class theorists, firms become interlocked because their directors know and trust one another as the result of indirect intraclass bonds they have forged through common neighborhood residence, social club membership, and public policy-making group participation (Domhoff, 1967; Bonacich and Domhoff, 1981; Koenig and Gogel, 1981). These indirect intraclass bonds, like the interlocks they give rise to, are structured according to the interests and capacities of corporate elites – both of which are partially determined by their location in space. Elites whose corporations are headquartered near one another share an interest in influencing local state developmental and redistributive policies that affect the growth of their locale, because the success of their firms depends, to varying extents, on this growth. Intraclass bonds of all kinds may be used to organize such elite political participation (Molotch, 1976, 1979; Friedland and Palmer, 1984).[14] Further, elites who reside near one another find it easier than elites residing in distant locales to become active in the same organization and thus to establish such social relationships (cf. Shaw, 1976). This implies that the intraclass structure has a spatial structure not only because its elements (that is, people) are situated in space, but because the spatial distribution of its elements is an important determinant of its existence.[15] Thus, places that are close to one another are also likely to be connected by many interlocks, because the elites in them are likely to have an interest in and the capacity to establish intraclass bonds, of which interlocking directorates are the most direct form. In addition, any indirect intraclass bonds, such as common social club membership, that arise between elites in two nearby places may further propel these elites to establish direct intraclass bonds, such as interlocking directorates, with one another.

Together these points suggest that headquarter proximity will increase the likelihood that two corporations will become interlocked, but that much of this proximity effect will be mediated by the effects of the level of interdependences between corporations and the level of social interaction between their elites. There are no studies that address this question directly, but we have conducted one that bears on it (Palmer, Friedland, and Singh, 1986). Data were collected on 234 pairs of firms that were joined by an interlock tie in 1962 and accidentally lost one of the interlocks that composed their tie between 1962 and 1964. We wished to identify the factors that cause firms to reconstitute their accidentally disrupted tie (by creating a new interlock between them). We found that proximity, but not interdependence, increased the likelihood that two industrial corporations would reconstitute their tie. The impact of indirect intraclass bonds on reconstitution could not be examined, because we did not include a measure of the extent to which the corporation elites in our study maintained such bonds with one another.

At first glance, this result seems to partly contradict our discussion above. Its interpretation is not straightforward, though, because the study focussed on the reconstitution rather than the initiation or presence of ties. One possible explanation of this result is that interdependence, as much past research suggests, leads firms to initiate ties with firms in industries that pose uncertainty for them. But these ties help reduce uncertainty by facilitating easily replaceable information channels, rather than more extensive and thus more costly to abandon formal linkages (such as long-term contracts). It is also possible that interdependence leads firms to initiate ties with firms in industries that pose uncertainty for them, but this is not because such ties reduce uncertainty. It is rather because interdependence between firms, like proximity, increases social interaction between their elites (for example, through day-to-day business dealings) and social interaction increases the likelihood of interlocking. Both of these explanations imply that when a tie is accidentally disrupted, the firms involved need not replace the departed director with another person from their previous tie partner's board, but rather could replace him with a director of another firm that produces in the same industry as their previous tie partner. Further, both explanations are consistent with the anomalous finding that interlocks that are patterned as if to reduce uncertainty caused by interdependence do not substantially increase industry profitability (Burt, Christman, and Kilburn 1980; Burt, 1983).[16]

We also found, apparently in contradiction to our discussion above, that there was no bivariate association between proximity and interdependence among the sample of firms tied in 1962. But again interpretation of this result is complicated by the fact that we examined only tied firms. One possible explanation is that indirect intraclass bonds, the presence of which is not measured but is likely to be highly correlated with proximity, may serve as a substitute for interlocks as mechanisms for reducing intercorporate uncertainty. That is, interdependent firms that are headquartered in the same city do not need to be interlocked and vice versa. This is consistent with another of our results. We found that corporations engaged in interorganizational linkages (such as long-term contracts, joint ventures and interfirm stockholding) were more likely to reconstitute their ties – which are presumed to facilitate these relationships – when they were headquartered in *different* cities as opposed to the same city. This last point suggests that past analyses of the relationship between interdependence and interlocking, which ignore headquarter location, are misspecified. The association between interdependence and interlocking should be weak or nonexistent when firms are located in the same city, as Galaskiewicz *et al.* (1985) have found, and strong when firms are located in different cities. Further, this entire discussion underscores a point that is implicit in most of what has come before, that location behavior should be considered as one of a panoply of interorganizational mechanisms corporations can use to manage their environment.

We have not yet begun to examine the geographical structure of corporate interlocks. We expect, however, that the volume of interlocks between two locales will depend primarily on the extent to which firms headquartered in them are interdependent with each other. We expect that the density of interlocks within a locale will depend on the extent to which the success of firms headquartered there depends on local growth, because this determines their elites' interest in establishing local intraclass bonds with one another. Firms with spatially concentrated production structures (that is, that locate a high percentage of their plants in their headquarter locale) are more dependent on their locale than firms with dispersed production structures, because a larger percentage of their operations is influenced by the growth of their headquarter locale. As noted above, small, industrially specialized, family-controlled firms that use the functional form administrative structure should be most likely to exhibit such concentrated production structures. We also expect the density of interlocks within a locale to depend on the ownership structure of the firms headquartered within it, because this determines the capacity of their elites to establish extralocal bonds. Management-controlled firms will be better able than family-controlled firms to establish extralocal bonds, because their elites are more likely to have been recruited from other locales, in which they belonged to elite institutions where such bonds are forged. Managerial elites should attempt to preserve their membership in extralocal elite institutions and the intraclass bonds they give rise to, because the security of their present corporate leadership position (as well as their opportunity to obtain future such positions) hinges more on the support of the corporate community in general (that is, the national assemblage of corporate directors – especially multiple, inner-group directors) than on the ownership of stock in a specific firm. We do not, however, expect the density of interlocks within a locale to be influenced by the level of interdependence between firms headquartered in it, because indirect intraclass bonds facilitated by proximity serve as the substitute for such direct intraclass bonds.

The intraorganizational, interorganizational and class determinants of urban growth

We believe that urban growth is increasingly determined by the location of dominant organizations, such as corporate headquarters and plants. The number of these organizations situated in a place and the nature of the relationships they and their elites maintain with organizations and elites in other locales determine the number of dependent organizations, such as business service firms, that will be attracted to the place.[17] Further, the number and relationship of dominant and dependent organizations situated in a place will, in turn, influence its employment and population expansion.[18]

This approach differs from past theory and research in several ways. First, central place and human ecology do not theorize the cause of population size, but instead consider it the determinant of the number and character of jobs, as well as dependent and even dominant organizations in a locale. We argue that these theories, and the primacy they place on size, are more appropriate to economies where markets are highly competitive and firms have not internalized market dependencies. In such urban systems, the growth of jobs and organizations in a place depends on its centrality or dominance as indexed by its size. But today, markets are less competitive and firms have internalized many of their market dependencies. Increasingly, the growth of places depends on the number, character, and relations of the organizations and elites located there.

Second, while most theorists of urban phenomena consider cities to occupy positions in a larger urban system, researchers seldom take interurban connections explicitly (that is, empirically) into account. Central place theorists consider cities to occupy positions in a system of hierarchically ordered market centers. Typically, however, they measure a place's position in that hierarchy by its size, or the extent to which it exports goods to other places (Wilson, 1984; Preston, 1971). Human ecologists consider cities to occupy positions in a national interurban division of labor. Typically, however, they measure a place's position in that division of labor by its industrial or occupational specialization (Duncan *et al.*, 1960; Galle, 1963; Lincoln and Friedland, 1978). Thus researchers who study urban growth, including those who study population growth, consider it to be a function of exogenous factors, such as population size and age, or indicators of urban linkages, such as economic specialization. For example, in their analysis of metropolitan population and employment growth in 39 SMSAs, Kain and Niedercorn (1975) take changes in manufacturing employment, considered as the export base of the economy, as a function of three factors: metropolitan population size; metropolitan age; and the difference between the equilibrium level of metropolitan manufacturing employment, defined as an average percentage of metropolitan population for all areas, and its existent level in the metropolitan area. The model assumes that as technological changes overcome the friction of space and value-added becomes more important than access to raw materials, manufacturing will tend to disperse evenly across the country, leading to an equalization of the manufacturing employment to population ratio (see also Crowley, 1978).

Finally, those analysts of urban systems who do examine the relationships between places tend to conflate the corporate and class structures of places with the spatial distribution of economic activity. They do not search for the relationship between them because they assume that the spatial distribution of corporate and class structures is simply a result of the same market processes that distribute all economic activity. Thus, as noted above, several human ecologists have examined the spatial distribution of lending agreements (McKenzie, 1933; Duncan *et al.*, 1960; Lieberson, 1961) and bank correspondent arrangements (Lieberson and Schwirian, 1962; Duncan and Lieberson, 1970). But in each case, these interorganizational linkages have been considered indicators rather than determinants of the magnitude of economic activity between places.

Population and employment

The only study to examine the impact of dominant organizations on population growth in the locales in which they are situated was conducted by Aiken and Strickland (1983b). This path-breaking analysis examines the impact of large corporate headquarter location on metropolitan population growth in four European countries: France, the United Kingdom, Germany, and Italy. They find that the impact of headquarter location varies by country and by time. Those metropolitan areas in which corporate headquarters were concentrated in the 1950s grew more rapidly over the subsequent decade, controlling for the size of the region, in all four countries. However, this impact declined in the subsequent decade, remaining significant only in Italy. Further, the impact varied cross-nationally, with population impacts lowest in France and the United Kingdom, and greatest in Germany and, to a lesser extent, Italy.

These overtime and cross-national variations in impact may be due to differences in the organizational and class structures of the corporations headquartered in these countries. The authors suggest that the between-decade difference in population impact of corporate headquarter location may be due to the increasing importance of nonlocal linkages, presumably fostered by the adoption of multidivisional organizational structures in postindustrial societies. These nonlocal linkages, because they disperse economic activity to distant places, reduce the impact of corporate headquarters on population growth. They speculate that cross-national differences may be due to the earlier adoption of the multidivisional structures in Germany and possibly Italy when compared to the later and less pervasive penetration of such managerial hierarchies in France and the United Kingdom. These structures, because they take the place of the market as the coordinating mechanism in the economy, increase the impact of corporate headquarters on population growth.

While fascinating, these explanations appear to embrace two contradictory arguments. Aiken and Strickland seem to argue, as we do, that the multidivisional form allows firms to disperse their productive activity in space. Thus, cities possessing the headquarters of corporations with such structures should grow more slowly than cities with functionally organized corporations. This is consistent with the decline in headquarter impact on population growth over time, but not with their cross-national comparisons. If the multidivisional structure fosters extralocal production linkages and firms in Germany were the first to adopt this structure, corporate headquarter location should impact local population growth less, not more, in Germany than in the other countries, whose firms divisionalized later. On the other hand, Aiken and Strickland also seem to argue that the multidivisional form allows firms to become centers of coordination and thus tertiary and quarternary employment growth in the economy. Thus cities in which the headquarters of corporations with such structures are located should grow more rapidly than cities with functionally organized corporations. This is consistent with the greater impact of headquarter location on population in Germany relative to other countries, but not with the over-time variation they report. If the multidivisional structure stimulates local tertiary and quarternary growth and this structure is becoming increasingly widespread over time, the impact of headquarters on population growth should be increasing, not decreasing over time. The resolution of this apparent paradox requires further study.[19]

Researchers should directly investigate the ways in which a corporation's organizational and class structure influences specific forms of employment and hence population growth of the place in which it is headquartered, perhaps by examining the growth effect of the interaction between *number* and *type* of corporate headquarters in a locale. Large size, industrial diversity, and geographical dispersion of production facilities should increase the effect headquarters have on the tertiary and quarternary employment growth of the cities in which they are situated. Each, because it exacerbates a firm's need for information, especially specialized information used in strategic decision making, increases a firm's demand for commodities produced by the tertiary and quarternary sectors. Further, as suggested above, a corporation's administrative form should also influence the effect its headquarter has on this type of local employment growth, because administrative form affects the extent to which its demand for different types of information is centralized in the headquarter locale. Multidivisional form firms should demand more strategic information but less nonstrategic information from the locales in which they are headquartered, because the multidivisional form centralizes strategic decision-making but decentralizes tactical decision-making. Thus they should stimulate growth in those components of the tertiary and quarternary sectors that supply strategic information (for example, specialized business services) while depressing growth in those components of these sectors which supply nonstrategic information (for example, routine business services). Controlling for the effects of these variables, the geographic dispersion of production facilities, interorganizational links, and intraclass bonds may decrease the effect headquarters have on population growth. Each increases the volume of extralocal contracts for labor or capital (inputs and outputs) in which a firm engages.

Studies of employment have concentrated on production facilities. These also indicate that the manner in which a corporate subunit is integrated into the spatial structure of organization linkages and class bonds, in particular, whether it is locally or absentee controlled, influences its impact on local employment. Production that is locally controlled is likely to have a greater impact on local employment because corporations tend to locate their most innovative industrial plants (especially those housing their research and development operations) near their headquarters (Malecki, 1981). Such plants have higher growth rates and are more dependent on local agglomerative conditions. Absentee corporate production tends to be concentrated in industries later in the product cycle, more routine, and integrated into multi-regional production structures. Less dependent upon local agglomerative conditions, it is likely to be more footloose, slower growing, and less likely to facilitate spinoffs. Numerous studies suggest that whether plants are locally or absentee controlled influences the nature of their growth generation (Stern and Aldrich, 1980). Compared to locally owned production facilities, branch plants of corporations headquartered elsewhere have lower closure rates (Erickson, 1980, 1981) but they are more likely to exist (Barkley, 1978). Further, the growth of branch plants is less stable than locally controlled firms (Erickson, 1980, 1981). Absentee branch plant production retards certain kinds of local employment growth, especially in the business service sector (Brue, 1975; Birch and MacCracken, 1981).

In addition, local integration into national corporate production is likely to lead to high levels of acquisition of local, smaller firms producing in non-routine areas (Schmenner, 1982). Such acquisition may slow the rate of growth of agglomerative industries early in the product cycle. The division of large multilocational corporations have much lower rates of spinoff of new firms than do smaller, independent firms (Cooper, 1973; Storey, 1981; Cross, 1981; Fothergill and Gudgin, 1979). All of this research indicates that the nature of a plant's linkage to its corporate headquarters influences its impact on local growth. In the future, researchers should examine how the organizational and class characteristics of the corporations to which they are linked influence the nature of this impact.

Dependent organizations

Among dependent organizations, business service firms are increasingly an important source of urban employment and thus population growth

(Mollenkopf, 1983; Kasarda, 1982). Central place and human ecology theory view a city's position in the urban system as a determinant of business service activity. Large cities have high business service sector activity (Duncan *et al.*, 1960). Berry and Kasarda (1977) have shown that population growth in the periphery, as opposed to the core, of metropolitan areas is associated with the expansion of the business service sector. We do not take issue with these findings but dispute the implicit assumption that population size is a cause rather than effect of a place's organizational structure. Eberstein and Frisbie (1982) have shown that a place's centrality in the interurban trade network is associated with a combined indicator, of which business service activity is one constituent, of the degree to which it performs metropolitan functions. This research gets closer to the process by which business service sector activity is stimulated. We propose that business service sector activity is a function of the number and types of corporate headquarters in a place and the linkages they and their elites maintain with dominant organizations in other places.

Large firms require increasing amounts of information, especially information used in formulating and implementing strategic decisions, to insure their success. Business service firms are increasingly important sources of this information (Cohen, 1981; Friedland, 1983). Business service firms tend to locate near their corporate clients for several reasons. Most important, servicing a client is at the same time production, research and development for business service firms. To be effective, the representatives of a business service firm must gain access to extensive information about a client's operations. This information subsequently becomes part of the business service firm's knowledge base, which it uses to serve other firms. Corporate elites must trust the representatives of business service firms before they will release strategic information because its indiscrete dissemination could harm their corporations. By locating in the same place as potential corporate clients, business service firms increase the likelihood that their representatives will socially interact with corporate elites. Such social interaction facilitates the development of trust upon which these exchanges between corporate elites and business service firms are based.

Large corporations, however, will differ with respect to the amount of strategic information they need, the places from which they obtain it, and the organizational subunits in which they process it. As noted earlier, the largest, most diversified and dispersed corporations may require the most strategic information, because they are interdependent with a large number of other organizations. Old firms should require less strategic information because they produce in industries that are late in the product life-cycle and their ability to engage in strategic activity is inhibited by structural inertia. Family-controlled corporations may use in-house staffs to acquire strategic information, rather than contract with business service firms, because doing so preserves their sole control of the decision-making process. Corporations whose directors are well integrated into the national interlock network may contract with nonlocal, as opposed to local, business service firms, because they have contacts with the elites of such firms. Finally, corporations using the multidivisional structure may contract with local, as opposed to nonlocal, business service firms, because they centralize the most important strategic decisions in the headquarter unit.

We have begun to examine the relationship between the number and types of corporations headquartered in a place and the level of business service activity there. Our first study analyzes the determinants of the number and receipts of management consulting establishments situated in US cities that had at least one top 500 industrial corporation in 1964. We found that the number of headquarters in a city has a strong positive effect on its level of business service activity. This effect is greater among cities with large geographically dispersed corporations that use the multidivisional form and smaller among cities with old corporations whose elites are integrated into the national interlock network. Further, the impact that the number and types of corporations headquartered in a city has on its business service activity far outweighs the impact of the city's metropolitan area population size (Palmer, Friedland, and Roussel, 1986). In a future study we plan to explore these relationships as they develop over time.[20]

Conclusion

To understand a place's potential for growth, one must examine not just the number of dominant businesses located there, but also the organizational and class structures in which these businesses are embedded. These organizational links and class bonds are the consequence of corporate strategic behaviors. And once in place, they shape corporate behavior as well. Much work remains before this corporate geography can be adequately theorized and estimated empirically. Such work will require not only the modification of existent theories of place, but of organization and class structure as well.[21]

NOTES

This chapter has been influenced by our many discussions with P. Devereaux Jennings. We are also grateful to Beverly Duncan, Otis Dudley Duncan, Mark Granovetter, Mark Mizruchi, Harvey Molotch, and Maggie McLoughlin for comments on a previous version of this chapter and Mommy Fortuna's for the stool at the end of the counter.

1 This chapter elaborates the determinants of the organizational and class structures that connect cities and the effects these structures have on the growth of the locales connected by them. We have discussed the political implications these organizational and class structures have for urban politics elsewhere (Friedland and Palmer, 1984).

2 Two other structures – states and families – also deserve more careful attention as mechanisms of interurban growth transmission. As states have become more centralized and more intrusive in the workings of the economy, and as family forms and sexual divisions of labor have changed, these structures too might be expected to affect the workings of the urban system.

3 This argument parallels one made at the level of the world system. Most theorists derive a nation's position in the world system from the functions it performs for that system (Wallerstein, 1976). Recently, however, other theorists have argued that a nation's position in the world system is significantly influenced by class conflict, particularly conflict between segments of the capitalist class within nations (Zeitlin, 1984).

4 There are, of course, some sectors and places where the competitive market still determines the relationships between firms and their elites, and there are some firms that have not experienced the transformations we describe below. In these instances, market relations still tightly constrain the activities of firms, their location, and indeed their very survival. This, for example, remains the case with small, young firms whose birth and death rates follow closely the urban hierarchy (Pennings, 1982). Autonomy from the market and from space are intimately related (Friedland and Palmer, 1985).

5 We do not argue, as some do (Galbraith, 1967), that these developments have erased the capitalist class character of advanced Western societies. Corporate elites are, by virtue of their relation to the means of production, members of the capitalist class. The pattern of bonds among members of the capitalist class reflects the division of labor within this class; the most central elites being finance capitalists (Soref, 1980). Further, *interclass structures* link the capitalist class to the working class. These structures, which may be economic (for example, union agreements) or political (for example, corporatist policy making groups), determine the level and nature of class conflict and cooperation (for example, strike activity). While we will not deal in this chapter with the geography of interclass relations, the corporate locational problem is clearly in part an attempted solution to class conflict and labor control (Bluestone and Harrison, 1982; Storper and Walker, 1983; Massey and Meegan, 1978; Gordon, 1977; Clark, 1981).

6 Our analysis, at this juncture, is intranational. This focus, necessitated by the lack of theory and data in the terrain we are exploring, is clearly inadequate given that organizational and class structures are increasingly international in scope. In the future, we intend to expand our analysis to include these relationships. In such studies, the role of the nation state will be even more central.

7 Of course, where firms have little control over the market and are primarily concerned with efficient production, their plants will be located near their headquarters and their size will be more closely related to the size of the city in which they are headquartered.

8 There is some confusion in past theory and research regarding the significance of place size. Some view it as an indicator of dominance, while others view it as a cause of dominance (Frisbie, 1982).

9 The strength of the relationship between family control and use of the multidivisional form depends on the manner in which these aspects of a corporation's organizational and class structure are operationalized.

10 We also plan to examine the differential impact changes in communication and transportation technologies may have on plant locations by identifying the industries in which corporations produce, indexing the extent to which these industries are sensitive to such changes, and coding firms accordingly.

11 The frost belt and sunbelt states were not the big losers and gainers of corporate control respectively. While the Deep South region experienced a net gain in control functions due to acquisition, it was relatively minor (5 per cent of its 1960 headquarter base). On the other hand, the East Border region, which includes Virginia, West Virginia, Kentucky and Tennessee, experienced a net loss (15 per cent of its 1960 base). Further, the Northeast and Mid-Atlantic regions experienced a net gain of control functions, again less than 5 per cent. The states that experienced the largest net gain were the Mountain (10 per cent), West Border (10 per cent) and Far West (7 per cent). Those regions experiencing the largest net loss, next to the Deep South, were in the West and East North Central regions. These results are not consistent with other studies, which report that central regions in the US and the UK are gaining control through acquisition (Dicken, 1976; Watts, 1981; Smith, 1979).

12 Actually, this issue is complicated by the different impacts interindustry dynamics have on plant and headquarter location. We discuss this in the next section.

13 Some researchers consider interlocking directorates to be interorganizational linkages, rather than intraclass bonds. For a discussion of this issue, see Palmer (1983).

14 In his seminal work, Molotch argued that those economic actors who depended on the growth of the place in which they were located constituted a "growth machine" dedicated to the expansion of activity and intensification of land use in that place (Molotch, 1976). It is the agglomerative nature of urban growth that lays the basis for a coalition structure between banks, developers, newspapers, and retail stores. In this perspective, growth is not simply a technical result of locational advantages. It is also politically determined (see also Mollenkopf, 1983). We have argued elsewhere that industrial corporate elites are not as uniformly passive as the growth machine theory might expect (Friedland and Palmer, 1984). Locally headquartered corporations, family-controlled corporations, corporations with regionally concentrated production structures, and corporations that bank their profits in land are all more likely to participate in the politics that generate local or regional growth because their profitability is more likely to depend on local growth.

15 The interdependence between spatial and social structure is clear when one examines the emergence of capitalism. Under conditions of initial urbanization, guild organization was based upon occupational differentiation *within a locality*, business organization was based upon occupational solidarity, membership in guilds was heritable, and business was executed in a relatively traditional and anti-competitive manner. The rise of cross-local business organization depended upon the predominance of formal contract between free individuals, solidarities based upon class, and business executed in a rational and highly competitive manner. Just as guild organization depended upon local structure, class organization depended upon translocal structure (Poggi, 1983).

16 Burt argues that interlocks that are patterned as if to reduce uncertainty associated with interdependence do not substantively increase industry profitability, because

there is little variance in the extent to which industries engage in such interlocking (Burt *et al.*, 1980; Burt, 1983).

17 We also expect, but do not discuss here, that the nature of the relationships among dominant organizations in the same, as opposed to different, locale(s) will affect a city's growth. This is because the nature of these relationships will affect the capacity of dominant organizations to coordinate political influence over the economic policies of the local state (Friedland and Palmer, 1984) as well as their capacity to coordinate economic development directly.

18 Our description is intended to capture only the most important causal paths in the urban growth process. It is, of course, also the case that the population growth generated by these dominant organizations will have its own independent effect on a place's economic growth (Greenwood, 1981).

19 The timing and extensiveness of the adoption of the multidivisional form may not only be a cause of the distribution of population in a country, but also its consequence. France and England, which adopted complex corporate forms later and much less extensively than Germany or Italy, also have more geographically centralized distributions of population and corporate headquarters. In these countries the agglomeration of population and headquarters may provide less of an incentive to internalize the market (Friedland and Palmer, 1985).

20 The relationship between corporate size and demand for specialized business services may not be linear. Specifically, the largest corporations may be able to substitute power for information or achieve the economies of scale necessary to internalize specialized business services. For example, the largest firms have increasingly moved to develop their own legal departments rather than relying on the services of the major law firms.

21 We have not, for the most part, discussed how the characteristics of places, such as local public policies, a principal focus of past research on the geographical distribution of growth, impacts the growth of firms and places. But these policies are not exogenous to the organizational and class structures we consider here. Specifically, local policies are partially a function of the intraorganizational, interorganizational, and intraclass structures described in this chapter (Friedland and Palmer, 1984).

REFERENCES

Aiken, Michael, and Donald Strickland, 1983a. "Corporate influence and the German urban system: headquarter location of German industrial corporations, 1950–1982." Unpublished typescript, Sociology Department, University of Pennsylvania

1983b. "Corporate control and metropolitan growth: a four-nation comparison." Unpublished typescript, University of Pennsylvania, February

Alford, R., and R. Friedland, 1985. *Powers of Theory: Capitalism, the State and Democracy.* Cambridge University Press

Allen, Michael Patrick, 1974. "The structure of interorganizational elite cooptation: interlocking corporate directorates." *American Sociological Review*, 39 (June): 393–406

1978. "Economic interest groups and the corporate elite structure." *Social Science Quarterly*, 58 (4): 597–615

Barkley, David, 1978. "Plant ownership characteristics and the locational stability of rural Iowa manufacturing." *Land Economics*, 54: 92–9

Bearden, James, William Atwood, Peter Freitag, Carol Hendricks, Beth Mintz, and Michael Schwartz, 1975. "The nature and extent of bank centrality in corporate networks." Paper presented at the annual meetings of the American Sociological Association, San Francisco

Berry, Brian, 1964. "Cities as systems within systems of cities." In John Friedman and William Alonso (eds.), *Regional Development and Planning*. Cambridge, Mass.: MIT Press, pp. 116–37

    1965. "Research frontiers in urban geography." In Philip Hauser and Leo Schnore (eds.), *The Study of Urbanization*. New York: John Wiley

    1967. *The Geography of Market Centers and Retail Distribution*. Englewood Cliffs: Prentice-Hall

    1973. *The Human Consequences of Urbanization*. New York: Macmillan

Berry, Brian, and John D. Kasarda, 1977. *Contemporary Urban Ecology*. New York: Macmillan

Birch, David L., 1979 *The Job Generation Process*, M.I.T. Program on Neighborhood and Regional Change

Birch, David L., and Susan MacCracken, 1981. "Corporate evolution: a micro-based analysis." Technical report, MIT Program on Neighborhood and Regional Change

Bluestone, Barry, and Bennett Harrison, 1982. *The Deindustrialization of America*. New York: Basic Books

Bonacich, Philip, and G. William Domhoff, 1981. "Latent classes and group membership." *Social Networks*, 3 (3): 175–96

Brue, Stanley, 1975. "Local employment and payroll impacts of corporate mergers." *Growth and Change*, 6 (4): 8–13

Burns, Leland S., and Wing Wing Pang, 1977. "Big business in the big city: corporate headquarters in the CBD." *Urban Affairs Quarterly*, 12 (4): 533–44

Burt, Ronald, 1980a. "Autonomy in a social topology". *American Journal of Sociology*, 85 (4): 892–925

    1980b. "Cooptive corporate actor networks: a reconsideration of interlocking directorates involving American manufacturing." *Administrative Science Quarterly*, 25: 557–82

    1983. *Corporate Profits and Cooptation*. New York: Academic Press

Burt, Ronald, Kenneth P. Christman, and Harold C. Kilburn, 1980. "Testing a structural theory of corporate cooptation." *American Sociological Review*, 45: 821–41

Chandler, Alfred, 1969. *Strategy and Structure*. Cambridge, Mass.: MIT Press

    1977. *The Visible Hand*. Cambridge, Mass.: Harvard University Press

Clark, G. L., 1981. "The employment relation and the spatial division of labor: a hypothesis." *Annals of the Association of American Geographers*, 77: 412–24

Cohen, Robert, 1981. *The Corporation and the Metropolis*. New York: Conservation of Human Resources Project, Columbia University

Cooper, Arnold C., 1973. "Technical entrepreneurship: what do we know?" *R & D Management*, 3: 59–64

Cross, M., 1981. *New Firm Formation and Regional Development*. Farnborough: Gower Press

Crowley, Ron, 1978. "Labor force growth and specialization in Canadian cities." In L. S. Bourne and J. W. Simmons (eds.), *Systems of Cities*. New York: Oxford, pp. 207–19

Dicken, P., 1976. "The multiplant business enterprise and geographical space: some issues in the study of external control and regional development." *Regional Studies*, 10: 401–12

Domhoff, G. William, 1967. *Who Rules America?* Englewood Cliffs, NJ: Prentice-Hall

 1975. "Social clubs, policy-planning groups and corporations: a network study of ruling class cohesiveness." *Insurgent Sociologist*, 5 (3): 173–84

 1983. *Who Rules America Now? A View for the 80s*. Englewood Cliffs, NJ: Prentice-Hall

Duncan, Beverly, and Stanley Lieberson, 1970. *Metropolis and Region Revisited*. Beverly Hills: Sage

Duncan, Otis Dudley, W. R. Scott, Stanley Lieberson, Beverly Duncan, and Hal Winsborough, 1960. *Metropolis and Region*. Baltimore: Johns Hopkins University Press

Eberstein, J. W., and W. P. Frisbie, 1982. "Metropolitan function and interdependence in the US urban system." *Social Forces*, 60: 676–700

Erickson, Rodney, 1980. "Corporate organization and manufacturing branch plant closures in nonmetropolitan areas." *Regional Studies*, 14 (6): 491–502

 1981. "Corporations, branch plants, and employment stability in nonmetropolitan areas." In John Rees, Geoffrey Hewings, and Howard Stafford (eds.), *Industrial Location and Regional Systems*. New York: Bergin, pp. 135–53

Feagin, Joe R., 1983. "The capital of the sunbelt: Houston's growth and the oil industry." Unpublished typescript, Department of Sociology, University of Texas, Austin

Fligstein, Neil, 1985. "Growth of the large firm in the American economy: 1880–1985." Unpublished typescript, University of Arizona Department of Sociology, ch. 3

Fothergill, S., and G. Gudgin, 1979. *The Job Generation Process in Britain*. London: Centre for Environmental Studies, Research Series No. 32

Friedland, Roger, 1983. *Power and Crisis in the City: Corporations, Unions and Urban Policy*. New York: Schocken

Friedland, Roger, and Donald Palmer, 1983. "The geographical structure of corporate production: a descriptive analysis." Unpublished typescript, Department of Sociology, University of California, Santa Barbara

 1984. "Park Place and Main Street: business and the urban power structure." In Ralph Turner (ed.), *Annual Review of Sociology*, 10: 393–416

 1985. "Space in organizational and class theory." Paper presented at the NIMH Research Training Program Seminar, Stanford University

Friedland, Roger, Donald Palmer, and Mary Dumont, 1986. "Corporations and the urban hierarchy in the United States." Unpublished typescript, Department of Sociology, University of California, Santa Barbara

Friedland, Roger, Donald Palmer, and Magnus Stenbeck, 1986. "The determinants of corporate spatial structure: urban, industrial and

organizational systems." Unpublished typescript, Department of Sociology,
University of California, Santa Barbara

Frisbie, W. P., 1982. "Theory and research in urban ecology: persistent problems
and current progress." In H. M. Blalock (ed.), *Sociological Theory and
Research: A Critical Appraisal*. New York: Free Press, pp. 203–19

Galaskiewicz, Joseph, Stanley Wasserman, Barbara Rauschenbach, Wolfgang
Bielefeld, and Patti Mullaney, 1985. "The influence of corporate power,
social status, and market position on corporate interlocks in a regional
network." *Social Forces*, 64 (2), 403–31

Galbraith, J. K., 1967. *The New Industrial State*. Boston: Houghton Mifflin

Galle, Omer R., 1963. "Occupational composition and the metropolitan
hierarchy: the inter- and intra-metropolitan division of labor." *American
Journal of Sociology* (November): 260–9

Glasberg, Davita Silfen, and Michael Schwartz, 1983. "Ownership and control of
corporations." *Annual Review of Sociology*, 9: 311–32

Gordon, David, 1977. "Class struggle and the stages of urban development." In
David Perry and Alfred Watkins (eds.), *The Rise of the Sunbelt Cities*.
Beverly Hills: Sage, pp. 55–82

Green, Milford B., 1984. "The importance of spatial structure in the interurban
interlocking directorate networks of Canada and the United States."
Unpublished typescript, Department of Geography, University of Western
Ontario

Green, Milford B., and Robert Cromley, 1984. "Merger and acquisition fields for
large United States cities: 1955–1970." *Regional Studies*, 184: 291–301

Greenwood, M. J., 1981. *Migration and Economic Growth in the US*. New York:
Academic Press

Hawley, Amos H., 1950. *Human Ecology: A Theory of Community Structure*.
New York: Ronald
  1968. "Human ecology." In D. Sills (ed.), *International Encyclopedia of the
Social Sciences*. New York: Crowell, Collier & Macmillan, pp. 328–37
  1971. *Urban Society*. New York: Ronald

Hayter, Roger, and H. D. Watts, 1983. "The geography of enterprise: a
reappraisal." *Progress in Human Geography*, 7 (2): 157–81

Herman, Edward S., 1981. *Corporate Control, Corporate Power*. Cambridge
University Press

Hirsch, S., 1967. *Location of Industry and International Competitiveness*. Oxford:
Clarendon Press

Jennings, P. Devereaux, 1986. "A dynamic analysis of corporate plant location in
the US: 1970–75." Unpublished PhD dissertation proposal, Department of
Sociology, Stanford University

Kain, John F., and John H. Niedercorn, 1975. "An economic model of
metropolitan development." In John F. Kain (ed.), *Essays on Urban Spatial
Structure*. Cambridge. Mass.: Ballinger, pp. 115–30

Kasarda, John D., 1982. "Urban prospects and policies for the nineties." Paper
presented at the annual meetings of the American Sociological Association,
San Francisco, September

Koenig, Thomas, and Robert Gogel, 1981. "Interlocking directorates as a social
network." *American Journal of Economics and Sociology*, 40 (1): 17–30

Korman, Hyman, Sen-Yuan Wu, Peter Brantley, Frank Romo, and Michael Schwartz, 1986. "The causes of plant closings: an assessment of competing hypotheses." Unpublished typescript, Department of Sociology, State University of New York, Stony Brook

Lieberson, Stanley, 1961. "The division of labor in banking." *American Journal of Sociology*, 66 (5): 491–6

Lieberson, Stanley, and K. P. Schwirian, 1962. "Banking functions as an index of intercity relations." *Journal of Regional Science*, 4: 69–81

Lincoln, James R., 1978. "The urban distribution of headquarters and branch plants in manufacturing: mechanisms of metropolitan dominance." *Demography*, 15 (2): 213–22

Lincoln, James R., and Roger Friedland, 1978. "Metropolitan accessibility and socioeconomic differentiation in non-metropolitan areas." *Social Forces*, 57 (2): 688–96

Lundberg, Ferdinand, 1938. *America's Sixty Families.* New York: Citadel Press

Malecki, E. J., 1981. "Recent trends in the location of industrial research and development: regional development implications for the US." In John Rees *et al.* (eds.), *Industrial Location and Regional Systems.* New York: Bergin Publishers, pp. 217–37

Massey, D., and R. Meegan, 1978 "Industrial restructuring versus the cities". *Urban Studies*, 15: 273–8

McKenzie, W. H., 1933. *The Metropolitan Community.* New York: McGraw-Hill

Milne, William, Norman Glickman, and F. Gerard Adams, 1980. "A framework for analyzing regional growth and decline: a multiregion econometric model of the United States." *Journal of Regional Science*, 20: 173–89

Mintz, Beth, and Michael Schwartz, 1981a. "Interlocking directorates and interest group formation." *American Sociological Review*, 46 (6): 851–69

1981b. "The structure of intercorporate unity in American business." *Social Problems*, 29 (2): 87–103

1985. *The Power Structure of American Business.* University of Chicago Press

Mizruchi, Mark, 1982. *The American Corporate Network: 1904–1974.* Beverly Hills: Sage

Mollenkopf, John, 1983. *The Contested City.* Princeton University Press

Molotch, Harvey, 1976. "The city as a growth machine: toward a political economy of place." *American Journal of Sociology*, 82 (2): 309–31

1979. "Capital and neighborhood." *Urban Affairs Quarterly*, 14 (3): 289–312

Norton, R.D., and J. H. Rees, 1979. "The product cycle and the spatial decentralization of American manufacturing." *Regional Studies*, 13: 141–51

Palmer, Donald, 1983. "Broken ties: interlocking directorates and intercorporate coordination." *Administrative Science Quarterly*, 28: 40–55

Palmer, Donald, Roger Friedland, P. Devereaux Jennings, and Melanie Powers, 1984. "Testing a political economy model of divisionalization in large US corporations." Paper presented at the annual meeting of the Academy of Management, Boston

1985. "Mode of control and devisionalization in large US corporations." Paper presented at the annual meeting of the American Sociological Association, Washington, DC

Palmer, Donald, Roger Friedland, Jerry Ross, and Alan Murray, 1986. "Mergers and acquisitions among the largest US Corporations between 1962 and 1968." Unpublished typescript, Stanford University Graduate School of Business

Palmer, Donald, Roger Friedland, and Amy Roussell, 1986. "Corporate headquarters and business service activity." Paper presented at the annual meeting of the American Sociological Association, New York

Palmer, Donald, Roger Friedland, and Jitendra Singh, 1986. "The ties that bind: organizational and class bases of stability in a corporate interlock network." *American Sociological Review*, 51: 781–96

Pappenfort, Donnell M., 1959. "The ecological field and the metropolitan community: manufacturing and management." *American Journal of Sociology*, 64: 380–5

Pennings, Johannes M., 1980. *Interlocking Directorates.* San Francisco: Jossey-Bass
  1982. "Organizational birth frequencies: an empirical investigation." *Administrative Science Quarterly*, 27: 120–44

Perloff, Harvey, and Lowdon Wingo, Jr., 1961. "Natural resource endowment and regional economic growth." In J. J. Spengler (ed.), *Natural Resources and Economic Growth*. Washington, DC: Resources for the Future, pp. 192–212

Pfeffer, Jeffrey, and Gerald R. Salencik, 1978. *The External Control of Organizations*. New York: Harper and Row

Poggi, Gianfranco, 1983. *Calvinism and the Capitalist Spirit*. Amherst: University of Massachusetts Press

Pred, Alan, 1977. *City Systems in Advanced Economies*. London: Hutchinson

Preston, Richard E., 1971. "The structure of central place systems." *Economic Geography*, 47 (2): 136–55

Pugh, D. S., D. J. Hickson, C. R. Hinings, and C. Turner, 1969. "The context of organizational structures." *Administrative Science Quarterly*, 14 (March): 115–26

Quante, Wolfgang, 1976. *The Exodus of Corporate Headquarters from New York City*. New York: Praeger

Ratcliff, Richard, 1980. "Banks and corporate lending: an analysis of the impact of the internal structure of the capitalist class on the lending behavior of banks." *American Sociological Review*, 45 (4): 553–70

Rees, John, 1978. "Manufacturing headquarters in a post-industrial urban context." *Economic Geography*, 54 (4): 337–54

Rochester, Anna, 1936. *Rulers of America*. New York: International Publishers

Ross, Christopher, 1982. "Regional patterns of organizational dominance: 1955–1975." *Sociological Quarterly*, 23: 207–19

Sale, Kirkpatrick, 1975. *Power Shift*. New York: Random House

Schmenner, Roger W., 1982. *Making Business Location Decisions*. Englewood Cliffs, NJ: Prentice-Hall

Schwartz, Michael, Peter Brantley, Hyman Korman, Sen-Yuan Wu, and Frank Romo, 1986. "Corporate networks and plant closings in New York State."

Paper presented at Conference on Work and Production in the United States and France, Paris, April

Schwartz, Michael, Gail Lerner, Hyman Korman, and Glenn Yago, 1983. "Deindustrialization in New York State metropolitan areas." Paper delivered to Thematic Session on Problems of Urban Growth and Decay, Society for the Study of Social Problems, Detroit, August

Schwartz, Michael, Sen-Yuan Wu, and Hyman Korman, 1984. "Corporate and governmental decision-making in deindustrialization." Paper presented at 6th Annual North American Labor History Conference, Detroit, October 1984, to be published in Robert Liebman and Michael Schwartz (eds.), *Deindustrialization: Causes and Consequences* (forthcoming)

Schwartz, Michael, Sen-Yuan Wu, Hyman Korman, and Peter Brantley, 1985. "Capital flows, disinvestment and plant closings: the structural foundations of local fiscal crisis." Paper presented at invited colloquium, Department of Sociology, Syracuse University, under revision for Richard G. Braungart (ed.), *Research in Political Sociology*. Greenwich, Conn.: JAI Press

Scott, Allen J., 1982. "Location patterns and dynamics of industrial activity in the modern metropolis." *Urban Studies*, 19: 111–42

Scott, J. 1979. *Corporations, Classes and Capitalism*, New York: St. Martins

Semple, R. Keith, 1973. "Recent trends in the spatial concentration of corporate headquarters." *Economic Geography*, 49 (4): 309–18

Semple, R. Keith, and Milford B. Green, 1983. "Interurban corporate headquarters relocation in Canada." *Cahiers de Géographie de Quebec*, 27 (72): 389–406

Semple, R. Keith, and Alan G. Phipps, 1982. "The spatial evolution of corporate headquarters within an urban system." *Urban Geography*, 3: 258–79

Shaw, Marvin, 1976. "An overview of small group behavior." In Marvin Shaw, *Contemporary Topics in Social Psychology*. Morristown, NJ: General Learning Press, pp. 335–68

Smith, I. J., 1979. "The effect of external takeovers on manufacturing employment change in the Northern Region between 1963 and 1973." *Regional Studies*, 13: 421–37

Sonquist, John, and Thomas Koenig, 1975. "Interlocking directorates in the top US corporations: a graph theory approach." *Insurgent Sociologist*, 5 (Spring): 196–229

Soref, Michael, 1980. "The finance capitalists." In Maurice Zeitlin (ed.), *Classes, Class Conflict, and the State*. Cambridge, Mass.: Winthrop Publishers, pp. 62–82

Steiner, P. O., 1975. *Mergers: Motives, Effects, Policies*. Ann Arbor: University of Michigan Press

Stephens, J. D., and B. P. Holly, 1981. "City system behavior and corporate influence: the headquarters location of US industrial firms: 1955–1975." *Urban Studies*, 18: 285–300

Stern, Robert, and Howard Aldrich, 1980. "The effect of absentee firm control on local community welfare: a survey." In John J. Siegfried (ed.), *The Economics of Firm Size, Market Structure and Social Performance*. Washington, DC: USGPO

Storey, D. J., 1981. "New firm formation, employment change and the small firm: the case of Cleveland County." *Urban Studies*, 18: 335–45

Storper, Michael, and Richard Walker, 1983. "The theory of labor and the theory of location." *International Journal of Urban and Regional Research*, 7 (1): 1–41

Strickland, Donald, and Michael Aiken, 1983. "Historical trends in the distribution of corporate control in the American urban system: the concentration of industrial headquarters and capital, 1917–1980." Unpublished typescript, Sociology Department, Washington University, St. Louis

Taylor, M. J., 1975. "Organizational growth, spatial interaction, and locational decision making." *Regional Studies*, 9: 313–23

Thompson, Wilbur R., 1965. *A Preface to Urban Economics*. Baltimore: Johns Hopkins Press

Useem, Michael, 1980. "Corporations and the corporate elite." *Annual Review of Sociology*, 6: 41–77

Wallerstein, Immanuel, 1976. *The Modern World System: Capitalist Agriculture and the Origins of the European World Economy in the Sixteenth Century*. New York: Academic Press

Watkins, Alfred J., and David C. Perry, 1977. "Regional change and the impact of uneven urban development." In D.C. Perry and A. J. Watkins (eds.), *The Rise of the Sunbelt Cities*. Beverly Hills: Sage, pp. 19–54

Watts, H. D., 1980. *The Large Industrial Enterprise: Some Spatial Perspectives*. London: Croom Helm
    1981. *The Branch Plant Economy: A Study of External Control*. London: Longman

Westaway, John, 1974. "The spatial hierarchy of business organizations and its implications for the British urban system." *Regional Studies*, 8: 145–55

Wilson, Franklin, 1984. "Urban ecology: urbanization and system of cities." *Annual Review of Sociology*, 10: 283–330

Winsborough, Hal H., 1960. "Occupational composition and the urban hierarchy." *American Sociological Review*, 25: 894–7

Yago, Glen, Hyman Korman, Sen-Yuan Wu, and Michael Schwartz, 1984. "Investment and disinvestment in New York, 1960–1980." *Annals of the American Academy of Political and Social Science*, 475 (September): 28–38

Zeitlin, Maurice, 1974. "Corporate ownership and control: the large corporation and the capitalist class." *American Journal of Sociology*, 79 (March): 1073–119
    1984. *The Civil Wars in Chile*. Princeton University Press

Part II
National and international business structures: a comparative perspective

6

The structure of class cohesion: the corporate network and its dual

James Bearden and Beth Mintz

Introduction

The techniques of structural analysis have been applied to the business community in various ways and a particularly popular application has been in the study of interlocking directorates. Assuming that intercorporate relations can be traced through an investigation of structural ties, recent work in the area has mapped corporate interaction patterns in an attempt to address the question of cohesion within the business community. A consistent finding of such network analyses has been the identification of commercial banks as important actors in the world of big business (Bearden *et al.*, 1975; Mariolis, 1975; Sonquist and Koenig, 1975; Norich, 1980; Mintz and Schwarz, 1981; Mizruchi, 1982, 1983; see also Allen, 1974; Burt, 1979, 1980, 1983). Many investigators have concluded from this and similar evidence that bank boards are the primary location for collective decision-making within the corporate world (Bearden, 1982; Glasberg, 1981; Mintz and Schwartz, 1985).

At the same time, a second set of studies has focussed on identifying sources of cohesion within the capitalist *class*, concentrating on the role of individuals in unity formation. Research in this realm has identified shared background, friendship networks, and membership on policy planning bodies as mechanisms of cohesion. Domhoff's (1967, 1970, 1975, 1979, 1983) work has been particularly good in identifying institutions dominated by the capitalist class and documenting their usefulness in cohesion formation. Useem (1978, 1979, 1984) has investigated class fractions, arguing that members of the inner group of the capitalist class – including, among others, business people with ties to multiple companies – are in a position to transcend individual interests and formulate general class policy. He and others have found that individuals who sit on the boards of directors of two or more major corporations are more likely than single directors to belong to exclusive social clubs and hence more likely to share the friendship networks and social class backgrounds attributed to members of the upper class (Zeitlin, 1974; Domhoff, 1975; Soref, 1976; Useem, 1978, 1979, 1984, Bonacich and Domhoff, 1981; Gogel and Koenig, 1981; see also Galaskiewicz and Rauschenbach, 1979; Ratcliff,

Gallagher and Ratcliff, 1979; Ratcliff, 1980; Burch, 1981; and Whitt, 1981).

Thus, two approaches have been popular in the study of cohesion formation in advanced capitalist society; while one approach uses the corporation as the unit of analysis, the second method emphasizes capitalists as the major unit of interest. And while investigations of the corporate system have used structural analyses to identify mechanisms of cohesion, studies of the capitalist class have concentrated on the attributes of corporate directors. In addition to different units of analysis, then, the two approaches have used different methodologies to address the question of conflict resolution in modern capitalism.

We argue two points. First, we find the results of studies of both corporate behavior and of capitalist behavior compelling. Certain members of the capitalist class occupy positions which distinguish them from their counterparts, while certain corporations occupy distinctive positions as well. While each approach has identified potentially mediating mechanisms for the resolution of conflict within the corporate world, the relationship between these units is unclear. Although recent studies suggest that these systems are mutually interacting (Koenig, Gogel, and Sonquist, 1979; Ornstein, 1982; Palmer, 1983a, 1983b) the details of this relationship remain undeveloped.[1]

We believe that the next step in research on corporate cohesion formation is an investigation of the relationship between class and corporations in modern American capitalism. We ask under what circumstances institutional position is important; under what circumstances class background is important, and what the different role structures of each are. The ultimate question, however, is whether one or the other – corporate organization or class organization – is determining. And without this final piece, we argue, both approaches remain unfinished.

Second, we argue that a structural analysis is a good starting point for unraveling this relationship; that we have much to learn from applying the types of methods typically used in studies of the corporate network to investigations of the capitalist class; and that each network looks at a different aspect of class organization. The present study addresses this issue in two ways. First, it investigates the function of different types of directors in uniting the corporate network. Thus, using the corporation as the unit of analysis, it asks what types of individuals are most crucial in organizing the business world. Second, by changing the unit of analysis, it studies the network of directors and investigates the role of different individuals in system unity. Hence, it uses a network analysis of the relations among corporate *directors* to identify sources of cohesion within the capitalist class. This method produces information about the organization of class relations in a form comparable to the information we have on American corporations. Combining findings from both networks, we begin to address the question of the relationship between institutional position and class structure in modern capitalism.

Data collection

The data used in this chapter were first collected as part of a joint project of the Research Group on Intercorporate Structure of the European Consortium for Political Research. Results of the first analysis appear in a joint publication of the group: *Networks of Corporate Power*, edited by Frans N. Stokman, Rolf Ziegler, and John Scott.

Data were collected for the year 1976 on the 200 largest nonfinancial firms (defined by sales) and the 50 largest financial institutions (defined by assets) in the United States. The 200 largest nonfinancials contained two firms which were subsidiaries of other companies in the sample. Since our data set was designed for comparability with nine European countries, we included the subsidiaries but selected two additional nonfinancial firms. Exxon Corporation was the largest nonfinancial with sales of approximately $49 billion. Associated Dry Goods was ranked 200 with sales of $1.5 billion. Sales were used to rank nonfinancial corporations because it is a dynamic measure reflecting yearly output levels. The list of corporations was compiled from the various listings published by *Fortune* magazine in 1977 and compared to the "*Forbes* Sales 500." Corporations of relevant size which were omitted by *Fortune* were identified and included in the data set.

Since financial institutions do not have sales in the traditional sense, assets are a better measure of the relative size of these companies. Again, using the *Fortune* list, supplemented by *Forbes*, we selected the 50 largest financial corporations of 1976. BankAmerica was the largest with assets of $74 billion, while Harris Bankcorp was the smallest with a $5 billion asset total. This list included 27 commercial banks, 13 insurance companies, and 10 diversified financials.

The names and executive positions, if any, of the directors on the boards of the 252 firms in the sample were taken from the 1977 *Standard and Poor's Register of Corporations, Directors and Executives*. This source was also used to identify the principal affiliation of directors who were not executives of one of the sample corporations.

Data analysis

The data were analyzed with a package of computer programs developed for social networks called *Graph Definition and Analysis Package* (GRADAP). GRADAP, a powerful and versatile tool for social network analysis and SPSS compatible, was developed in the Netherlands by an interuniversity group from the Universities of Amsterdam, Groningen, and Nijmegen.[2]

The first analysis presented below considers the corporate network and asks which types of individuals are most important in system unity. With this aim, we collected data on the backgrounds of all directors who sat on more than one corporation in our sample; that is, of all interlockers. The 252 corporations under investigation included 3,976 positions occupied by 3,108 people. Thus, 564 (18 per cent) of the directors held multiple positions. For these interlockers we collected information on principal affiliation as defined by place of full-time employment, as well as data on social elite status.[3]

Using GRADAP we identified what types of interlocks – ties created by bankers, by executives of nonfinancial corporations in our sample, or by outsiders – were overrepresented; what types of interlocks occurred more frequently than we would expect given the proportion of different types of directors available. We emphasize that this procedure uses the corporation network to investigate the role of directors in forming the system. While the unit of analysis is the corporation, we ask about the role played by different types of directors in system unity.

Our second analysis concentrates on the structure of the person-by-person network. While the corporation network is defined by ties between corporations created by shared individuals, the person or director network looks at ties among directors created by shared board memberships. It is the dual of the corporation network (Breiger, 1974).

Given a graph composed of two sets of objects, points and relations, the dual is the graph in which the role of these two sets of objects is reversed (Breiger, 1974; Berkowitz, 1982). In our data the points were first defined as corporations and the relations defined as interlocking directorates. The dual, the person graph, has individual directors as points related by common membership on a corporate board.

While the person network is generated from the corporation network, it has different properties and the two systems are related in a complex, little-understood manner. In the general case, different structural levels may be analyzed as hypernetworks producing maps of relationships distinct from the original network (Mariolis and Jones, 1982). With the present problem, the level of analysis has turned from organizations to individuals. The dimensions of the matrix representation are much larger for the person network and the cell entries are different (Breiger, 1974). Since there are many possible duals associated with a given graph (Berkowitz, 1982), the analysis of the person network can be expected to yield results nontrivially different from those of the corporation graph (see Breiger, 1974).

In our analysis of the person network, two directors are tied if and only if they are members of two or more of the same boards. Since our sample was defined by board membership, every director automatically shares a board with at least several other people. This is in contrast to the corporate graph where interlocks do not necessarily occur; in fact, there were 24 isolates in the corporate network.

Thus, although corporations must act in order to interlock, directors are tied to other directors simply by their board membership. For this reason, we restricted the definition of a tie within the person graph to shared membership on two or more boards.

We note that in the network of corporate interlocks double ties have been used to produce a graph in which structure is more easily visible. Sonquist and Koenig (1975), for example, found that the subgroup structure of a corporation graph was difficult to discern when ties were defined as single interlocks, but that interpretable cliques were generated when only double interlocks were considered. Although not our primary motive in defining the person network, we expect that the stringent criterion for director ties will help highlight the structure of the person network in a similar way. By restricting ties in the person graph to shared membership on two boards, we reduced the number of relevant directors from 564 to 260. We assume that this will make it easier to discern network structure.

To investigate what types of directors interact in particular ways, we applied GRADAP's procedure "subgraph" to the person network in order to detect components. A component of an undirected graph is a maximal connected subgraph. This procedure generated 13 components with four or more members; these groupings will be analyzed below.

Results: the corporate network

The corporate network is sparse: the total number of interlocks within the system is 1,086, while only 3 per cent of ties between all possible pairs of corporations are maintained. Nevertheless, 228 (90 per cent) of the companies under investigation are directly tied to at least one other firm.

Although some corporations are united by more than one director, 84 per cent of the tied companies share just one director; 13 per cent share two directors, 2 per cent share three, and only 1 per cent share four or more. Similarly, a majority (64 per cent) of interlocked directors sit on only two boards, while 24 per cent hold three positions, 8 per cent hold four and 4 per cent hold four or more positions. A small proportion of all directors creates the ties in the network and duplication of intercorporate links is not commonplace.

The 1976 US corporate network is a loosely integrated uncentralized system. As in previous studies, financial firms were the most central in the whole network and in regional group formation (Dooley, 1969; Levine, 1972; Allen, 1974; Bearden *et al.*, 1975; Mariolis, 1975; Sonquist and Koenig, 1975; Bunting, 1976; Mintz and Schwartz, 1981, 1985; Mizruchi, 1982; Roy, 1983). For a detailed explication of these results, see Bearden and Mintz (1984).

Although commercial banks in particular are the organizing units of the

Table 6.1 *Types of interlocks within the network*

Type	Interlocks	
	Number	Per cent
Executive financial	133	10.5
Executive production	445	35.1
Secondary	691	54.5
Business[a]	(360)	(28.4)
Nonbusiness	(100)	(7.9)
Other[a]	(231)	(18.2)
Totals	1,269	100.1

[a] Secondary interlocks in the business and nonbusiness categories are created by directors with three or more positions. Other secondary interlocks are created by unidentified directors and those with fewer than three positions.

interlock network, bankers themselves do not play a corresponding role. Table 6.1 shows that bankers create only 10.5 per cent of the ties formed by different types of directors. Instead, as previous research has suggested, outsiders, i.e. board members without executive positions in the corporations under investigation, are responsible for the cohesion of the system: they form 54.4 per cent of the interlocks in the 1976 network (Bearden and Mintz, 1984).

In particular, businessmen and women without full-time affiliations with corporations in our sample are the most crucial actors in terms of system unity. As table 6.1 demonstrates, outside business people with three or more directorships create 28.4 per cent of the interlocks under investigation. These six women and 89 men – 16.8 per cent of the directors who interlock – are disproportionately important in uniting the corporate world. When we divide the interlock network into regional groupings, these directors are disproportionately responsible for interregional linkages; they are crucial in tying together each region, as well. They are as important in the densely connected portions of the network (the center) as in the sparser areas and they serve to tie the dense subsets to peripheral corporations.[4]

These findings do not suggest that the largest corporations in the United States depend on representatives from the small business community to solidify their relationships. Rather, these directors come from two sources. Those directors with three or more positions with business affiliations outside of our population are drawn from companies of substantial size: the mean total sales of their home firms was just over one billion dollars in 1976, or two-thirds the size of Associated Dry Goods, the smallest company under investigation.

Executives retired from the largest corporations in the United States comprise the second subset: they make up 36 per cent (34) of the directors with

Table 6.2 *Number of positions by principal affiliation, outside directors
with three or more positions*

| Principal | Number of positions | | |
affiliation	Three	Four	Five or more
Retired executive	33%	38%	46%
Other business	50%	38%	31%
Nonbusiness	17%	23%	23%
Number	(54)	(26)	(13)

three or more board positions without inside affiliations. As table 6.2
illustrates, these individuals become more dominant as the number of board
positions increases. These findings suggest that the individuals most
important in solidifying the network of corporate interlocks come from two
different segments of the business world. The first group – the numerically
dominant category – is composed of individuals affiliated to very large, but
not the largest, corporations. Although they come from a sector which is far
from trivial in terms of total sales and assets, they do not represent the
corporations which we would expect to mediate among the different interests
within the business world.

The retired executives, on the other hand, are in some ways the heart of the
corporate elite. Virtually all have been CEOs and have long experience at the
top of the corporate hierarchy. Their high number of positions indicates the
breadth of their experience. Such directors, relatively free from ties to
particular corporations, are in a position to develop a generalized class point
of view (Fennema, 1982).

Thus, analysis of the corporate network has identified two types of
directors important in system unity. Retired executives, we suggest, are
recruited because of institutional position as a result of years of active
leadership in the largest corporations in the United States. Directors from
smaller firms, on the other hand, are more likely to be members of the social
upper class and, hence, their role in cohesion formation seems to be a result of
class position.

This interpretation is based on data presented in Table 6.3. When we
compare elite status as defined in the usual way – by membership in one of a
selected set of social clubs or policy groups – we see that directors drawn from
smaller corporations are more likely to have elite connections. They are 16.8
percentage points more likely than insiders and 10.6 percentage points more
likely than retired executives to be members of the social elite. This
relationship holds when we control for number of positions. Previous
research has demonstrated that social elite status is correlated with the
number of directorships held (Soref, 1976). As a group, interlockers drawn

Table 6.3 *Principal affiliation by elite status*

Principal Affiliation	Elite status	Bank board member (outsider)
Insider	59.1%	54.5%
	(143)	(114)
Outside retired	65.3%	45.3%
	(49)	(34)
Smaller business	75.9%	68.4%
	(60)	(54)
Other	47.6%	29.8%
	(80)	(50)

from the smaller business community have fewer directorships than the other groups of interest. They are about 10 percentage points more likely than insiders and retired executives to occupy only two positions. Thus, they are more elite in spite of fewer boardships.

At the same time, the elite status of the group is primarily a result of membership in social clubs. When we compare insiders, retired executives, and outside business people in regard to membership on important policy planning associations, we find little difference. Their club activity, then, seems to be the major distinguishing characteristic and their inclusion in the interlock network, we suggest, derives from their social status.

Moreover, directors from the smaller business sector are more likely to sit, as outsiders, on the boards of major commercial banks than other categories of board members (table 6.3). This difference is striking, since earlier research has identified bank boards as major conflict-reducing mechanisms within the corporate world (Mintz and Schwartz, 1985). Our findings emphasize that bankers are not crucial actors in system unity. Those directors who tie the system together, however, do sit on bank boards. Those individuals who are recruited because of their class position, we argue, help shape bank strategy. This underscores the importance of the bank boards and suggests this as the location at which class relations and corporate organization are most intertwined.

Our analysis of the role of directors in unifying the corporate network suggests that the boardrooms of the largest firms in the United States are major locations for the intersection of class and institutional interests. While executives of these very large corporations participate in this process, the system is held together by outsiders representing these two components of corporate America. This suggests that there are two mechanisms for participation in general policy formation at the very highest levels of American business; that institutional position *or* elite social background serves as a vehicle for decision-making participation. Major commercial banks are particularly relevant in this regard. They seem to be a primary

Table 6.4 *The thirteen largest components in the person network*

	Number of	Mean number of
Region	members	positions per member
1. National	38	3.4
2. Semi-national	21	3.0
3. New York	18	3.2
4. Detroit	10	3.1
5. New York	10	3.2
6. Pittsburgh	8	2.6
7. Boston	8	2.3
8. West Coast	7	2.7
9. Minneapolis	6	2.7
10. New York	5	3.6
11. Chicago	5	2.8
12. New York	4	3.5
13. National	4	3.0
Total	144	Average 3.1

meeting place for these groups, and because of this, we suspect that the decisions made in the board rooms of these banks serve different functions than those worked out in the most important policy planning groups; that it is on bank boards where institutional and class interests are most crucially mediated.

Components

Turning from the corporate network to the network of relations among directors, we emphasize the structure of the components generated in the 1976 network of corporate directors. The most striking characteristic is the regional character of the groupings (table 6.4). Of the 13 components identified, most have a regional base. The major exceptions are the two largest. Although the first ($n = 38$) has a strong New York City orientation, we have labelled it a national grouping because it draws members from a number of states.[5]

The second largest component ($n = 21$) contains a tight-knit Chicago group ($n = 14$) and a small Minneapolis–St. Paul contingent ($n = 4$), as well as representatives from the West Coast ($n = 2$) and New York ($n = 1$). Although at first glance this looks like a smaller, less extensive version of the national component, the dominance of Chicago members – both numerically and positionally – emphasizes its regional base. For this reason we classify this a seminational, rather than a national, grouping.

The third component contains 18 members: 14 directors from the New

York area and 4 from Chicago. Because of the New York dominance, we consider this a local component. The remainder of the groupings reflects the same types of regionality. In all, the following locales are characterized by the type of internal interlocking which generates components: New York, Detroit, Pittsburgh, Boston, the West Coast, Minneapolis, and Chicago.

The components of the person network, then, contain a national grouping, a seminational grouping and a number of geographically defined subsets. This structure echoes the subgroups found in the corporation network, and it is important to remember that this similarity is not a result of calculating the dual of the corporation network. Instead, these findings point to the existence of a social map closely corresponding to the corporate map.

Previous studies of corporate interlocks have identified regional groupings of densely interlocked companies tied into the national system by bridging firms. The Chicago area in particular has been identified as a regional center with national ties. Organization of the director network parallels this structure: it reveals regionally organized directors maintaining extensive ties within their locale. Ties among directors headquartered in Chicago parallel the position of the area in the corporate network: straddling national and regional status.

At the same time, members of the national component – along with directors in the seminational grouping – unite the regions. Together, the national and seminational components contain representatives from six of the seven locales identified in the component analysis. Members of these components, then, play a bridging role among regions. The national component in particular, the seminational component less crucially, but certainly with importance, function in the capacity of unifying the locales. Individuals included in these groupings are major actors in this process.

The existence of a national system, coupled with a set of dense regional linkages, suggests, if not a consonance of interest among individuals in each group, at least a vehicle for achieving consensus. This suggests a two-stage process of cohesion formation and a division of labor – a local consensus-forming process tied into a national network of class relations. Given this structure, two questions are raised: (1) in what ways are component members distinguished from their noncomponent counterparts? and (2) do regional component members differ from national and seminational members? We explore these points below.

Component versus noncomponent members

Of the 260 individuals included in the network of director relations, 144 (55.2 per cent) maintained the types of ties which generated the component structure discussed above. When we compare the characteristics of directors in and out of components we find differences between the groups which are summarized in table 6.5.

Table 6.5 Kramer's V for component membership by various characteristics

	Component membership			
	All positions	2 positions	3 positions	≥4 positions
Elite status	.009 (elite > nonelite)	.039 (elite > nonelite)	.010 (elite > nonelite)	.178 (nonelite > elite)
Social club	.006 (nonclub > club)	.128 (nonclub > club)	.066 (club > nonclub)	.019 (nonclub > club)
Policy association	.028 (nonpolicy > policy)	.151 (policy > nonpolicy)	.173 (nonpolicy > policy)	.365 (nonpolicy > policy)
Principal affiliation[a]	.063 (insiders > . . . > other)	.182 (smaller bus. > . . . > other)	.154 (other > . . . > smaller bus.)	.182 (other > . . . > sm. bus.)
Bank board	.168 (bank > nonbank)	.193 (bank > nonbank)	.038 (nonbank > bank)	.075 (bank > nonbank bus.)

[a]The table summarized in this row has 8 cells; all others have 4 cells and, thus, Vs for this variable cannot be compared to other Vs presented.

When we define elite status by membership in an elite social club or an important policy planning group, attendance at an elite prep school, or listing in the *Social Register*, although a majority of directors in the person components are elite, members of elite groups are no more likely to be in components than their nonelite counterparts ($V = .009$). When we control for number of positions, the relationship remains very weak (table 6.5) except in the case of directors with four or more boardships: 92 per cent of nonelite directors in this category are component members compared to 75 per cent of elite individuals ($V = .170$). While big linkers – directors with four or more positions – are routinely both component members (78.9 per cent maintain interlock patterns which generate component structure as opposed to 54.5 per cent of individuals with three positions and 45 per cent of two position directors) and socially elite (77.2 per cent), elite status and component membership are negatively related in this case. The very individuals most typically associated with elite status, then, are those less likely to generate component structure.

Looking at elite status more carefully, we find differences between the social elite and the political segment of the group in terms of component membership.[6] Neither social club nor policy planning membership is strongly associated with component inclusion: 54.9 per cent of members of elite social clubs are included in components as compared to 55.5 per cent of nonclub members ($V = .006$); 52.8 per cent of directors who belong to policy groups are in components versus 56 per cent of nonpolicy group directors ($V = .028$). When we control for number of positions, however, we find that directors who are members of important policy planning organizations and sit on two corporate boards are more likely to maintain the types of interlock patterns which generate components than their nonpolicy group colleagues (58.1 per cent vs. 40.6 per cent; $V = .151$). At the same time, individuals with policy group affiliations and three boardships are less likely to be included in components than their nonpolicy group counterparts ($V = .173$); while directors with four or more positions with these affiliations are less likely still ($V = .365$).

Social club membership works in a different way: the only relationship of interest is the case of directors with two positions who do not have club affiliations: they are more likely than two position individuals who belong to these elite establishments to be component members (50.7 per cent vs. 37.9 per cent). Although the association is still relatively weak ($V = .128$; see table 6.5), when we compare it to the relationship when we do not control for number of positions, the difference is striking. Moreover, we note that a majority (74.2 per cent) of these directors are either active or retired executives of corporations in our sample, suggesting that institutional affiliation is important in component membership.

In terms of elite status, then, although component membership is not strongly related to either social club activity or policy planning participation on the general level, directors with two positions who belong to elite clubs are less likely to maintain the type of interlock relationships which produce component structure. This suggests that component membership may produce the same type of well-defined network that club membership reflects and that tight-knit corporate interlocking may be an alternative mechanism which seems so necessary for cohesion formation. This interpretation is supported by the relationship between elite status and component membership for directors with four or more positions reported above. Although big linkers are typically elite, the nonelite are more likely to be grouped in components.

At the same time, the fact that directors with two board positions who belong to important policy groups are more likely than nongroup members to maintain the types of interlocks which produce components suggests that component structure reflects more than an informal social network; it implies that political and social functions overlap among component members. And the underrepresentation of policy group members with three or more positions indicates that the dense patterns of interlocking are not a replication of traditional networks but reinforce the notion of an alternative mechanism for the establishment of channels of interaction.

This process is clarified by an investigation of the principal affiliation of component members. Earlier, in our analysis of the corporate network, we emphasized the role of class background and institutional position in the formation of the interlock network, noting that socially elite directors from businesses slightly smaller than those in our sample, together with retired executives from the very largest corporations, were most important in terms of system unity. When we examine the role of different types of directors in component formation (table 6.5), we find that although the relationship between principal affiliation and component membership is weak ($V = .063$), insiders are slightly more likely to be component members than other types of directors: 58 per cent of insiders, 54.3 per cent of retired executives, 52.9 per cent of smaller business representatives, and 50 per cent of other directors maintain the type of interlock patterns which form components. When we control for number of positions, however, directors with two boardships are again distinct: smaller business representatives are more likely to be in components than other types of individuals ($V = .179$), and these directors tend to have elite social club affiliations.

Although a moderate relationship is maintained as number of positions increases, the order is reversed (table 6.5). In the case of three board seats, for example, 40 per cent of small business executives, 53.8 per cent of retired inside directors, 54.5 per cent of current insiders, and 70 per cent of other directors are component members. While these figures support the argument that component membership may serve as an alternative to social elite status in the creation of tight interaction networks, as the number of positions increases the total number of individuals in each cell decreases, suggesting caution in interpreting this relationship. Hence, we emphasize that insiders and retired executives – two groups we consider to represent the institutional elite – are slightly more likely to be component members than outside directors. We also emphasize the tendency of directors with two board seats to be from the smaller business community – a group we consider to represent the social elite – and we note in passing that directors in the "Other" category become important in this regard as number of positions increases.

Taken together, these results suggest that the structure of relations among directors of the very largest corporations in the United States produces interaction networks containing a broader membership than social clubs or other traditionally elite groups of that type. Composition of the components indicates that directors group together along diverse lines and include individuals who are less likely to maintain the types of contacts most often researched by power structure investigators. Individuals with two positions, for example, who participate in the generation of component structure, are either policy group members, social club members from the smaller business community, or nonclub members who are active or retired executives of one of the firms in our sample. Independent of number of positions, board members with past or present employment in the largest corporations are also likely to participate in the types of interlock relationships which produce components. The merging of these categories – and differences between the social and institutional base of each – suggests the network of interlocks uniting directors as a location for the intersection of class and organizational interests. And due to this intersection, we believe that ties created by shared boardships produce a network of relationships among directors which helps bridge the differences between class and institutional interests; that the director network functions as a mechanism for uniting the diverse interests within the business world.

Moreover, our data suggest an institutional location for the mediation process. A seat on the board of directors of a major commercial bank is associated with component membership: 61.6 per cent of bank directors and 44 per cent of nonbank directors are included in components ($V = .168$). As table 6.5 indicates, this pattern is again strongest in the case of individuals with two positions: 53 per cent of bank directors and 35.8 per cent of nonbank members are component members ($V = .193$). When we control for principal affiliation, we find that bank directors are consistently more likely to maintain interlock patterning which creates components than their nonbank counterparts, indicating that a bank directorship is more important than institutional affiliation in generating component structure. From this we conclude that it is on the boards of major commercial banks that class and corporation most often meet.

Table 6.6 *Percentage of component members with various characteristics*

Component	Bank board	Policy group	Social club	No. of positions		N
				Two	⩾ Three	
National	74	50	58	26	74	(38)
Seminational	86	14	57	48	52	(21)
regional	65	17	47	43	57	(85)

Finally, we repeat that directors with multiple positions and/or bank board members are the most likely candidates for component membership. When we interpret the tight interlock patterns which create components as mechanisms facilitating cohesion formation, our results parallel the structure of the corporate network. Previous research has documented both the role of big linkers in forming the interlock network (Soref, 1976; Koenig, Gogel, and Sonquist, 1979) and the position of bank boards in mediating among the different interests within the corporate world (Mintz and Schwartz, 1981); a parallel role is performed in the network of director relations. Our analysis of the corporation network (above) has emphasized the same intersection of institutional and class interests and has identified bank boards as the location in which these relations are most intertwined. Again we have a parallel process on the level of the director network.

National, seminational, and regional components

We have interpreted the existence of a national, a seminational and regional groupings as indicative of a dual process of cohesion formation and an implicit assumption of this interpretation is that regional component members differ from their national and seminational counterparts. As table 6.6 demonstrates, there are clear differences between the national and regional cases. Members of the national component tend to be bank directors, members of elite social clubs, affiliated with policy planning groups, holders of several directorships, and insiders in one of the sample companies (table 6.7). Members of regional components are less likely to be bank directors, less likely to be in a social club or a policy planning group, less likely to hold several directorships, and slightly more likely to be executives of a sample company. In general these results suggest that members of the national component are members of a national ruling class while the members of the regional components are important local elites. The strongest evidence for this interpretation is the percentage of component members who belong to elite groups. There is a 33 percentage point difference in policy planning group membership between the national and regional groupings and an 11

Table 6.7 *Percentage of component members with principal affiliations as identified*

Component	Smaller[a]		Business	Other	N
	Insiders[b]	Retired[c]			
National	50	18	11	21	(38)
Seminational	43	24	19	14	(21)
Regional	56	15	12	16	(85)

[a]Refers to directors who are executives in corporations ranking between the 253rd and 500th largest companies in the USA.
[b]Refers to directors who are executives in the corporation under investigation.
[c]Refers to retired directors who were executives in one of the sample corporations.

percentage point difference in terms of social club membership. Since our sample is drawn from the corporate elite, this is strong evidence that the national component members have power elite characteristics (Domhoff, 1983).

In addition, national component members are 9 percentage points more likely than their regional counterparts to be bank directors and 12 percentage points more likely to have three or more directorships. It is clear that, among corporate directors, national component members are the most elite.

With regard to principal affiliation, the differences are less clear (table 6.7). A slightly larger percentage of regional component members are inside directors of a sample corporation and a slightly smaller percentage are in the residual category labeled "Others." This suggests that the national component draws members slightly more often from law firms, universities, and other nonbusiness sources, indicating that cosmopolitan status is not solely the result of an executive position within one of the very largest corporations, but that national prominence derives from a variety of sources.

In general, however, there is little variation in principal affiliation between national and regional components. Instead, the important differences between the groups are in terms of social club membership, bank director-ships and, most strikingly, policy group affiliation. These differences point to two coordinating layers within the network of director relations. On the national level, directors with elite credentials meet on the boards of very large corporations. They are distinguished from regionally organized directors most importantly by participation in the types of political decision-making typically attributed to policy group members. When we use institutional affiliation as indicative of corporate, rather than class, interests, we do not find the national component to be more institutionally based. Instead, it is on the national level where the social and political segments of corporate directors most closely overlap and it is on this level that bank boards are most important in this process.

The seminational component does not fit clearly into this division. Eighty-six per cent of its members are bank directors, a proportion even greater than the national component; 57 per cent belong to elite social clubs, a figure close to national status. Yet, only 14 per cent of its directors have policy group membership. We interpret these findings as reflective of Chicago's position in corporate America: neither truly regional nor truly national. Bank boards are fundamental to organizing the national elite of the Chicago area – national by virtue of directorships on the boards of the very largest firms in the United States, but, at the same time, seeming to serve as a location for regional decision-making.

Conclusion

Our investigation of the relationship between corporations and class in modern American business has considered both the corporate network and the director network, each of which addresses a different aspect of capitalist organization. In the corporate network, we found the individuals most important in solidifying the network of interlocks to be socially elite directors, from the smaller business community as well as retired executives of companies in our sample. Given the class base of the former and the institutional histories of the latter, we interpret these findings as suggesting that the interlock network is held together by two segments: those representing class interests and those representing institutional interests. The frequency of outside directorships on major commercial banks for both groups points to the role of banks as a meeting point in this process.

Our analysis of the network of relations among directors found that the individuals most important in solidifying that system are more diverse than in the corporate case, yet still maintain strong class and institutional bases. We interpret these findings as indicative of an alternative to, rather than a duplication of, the networks formed on the basis of elite social status, suggesting that the ties maintained by directors of the largest companies in the United States produce a structure of relations through which class and institutional interests meet. And, as in the corporate network, bank boards are where this overlap most often occurs.

Taken together, these findings suggest that there are two routes – obviously mixed together – to participation in the organization of relations at the highest levels of American capitalism: either leadership of one of the largest corporations in the business world or social elite credentials combined with leadership of a somewhat smaller firm.

In addition, we have found a regional base to the director network, as well as a hierarchical arrangement of ties in which national and seminational component members are drawn from many of the locales characterized by regional component structure. The national and seminational groups thus serve as mechanisms for unification. The national component is more class-based than its regional counterparts, while at the same time maintaining strong institutional representation. From this structure, we conclude that it is within the national component that the two most important segments of capitalist organization meet and it is on this level that differences most certainly emerge.

Finally, we emphasize the parallels in structure between the corporate and director networks. Regional organization, the role of big linkers in unifying the system, the merger of institutional and class interests, all occur on both levels and describe different parts of class organization. The final overlap between the corporate network and its dual, however, is bank board membership, and it is at this point that the analyses of the networks most strongly converge.

Analyses of the corporate and director networks have provided complementary information in addressing the question of the relationship between class and organization in the modern business world. Our findings suggest that both networks are important to this question, although the diversity found in the investigation of the component structure of the director network indicates that it is on this level that the issue should be pursued. Hence, we conclude that it is within the network of relations of directors where we see the overlap between institutional and class interests most clearly and where we must look for an understanding of the relationship between these two defining segments of American business structure.

NOTES

An earlier version of this chapter was presented at the annual meeting of the American Sociological Association, Detroit, 1983. The authors would like to express their appreciation to Frans Stokman, Frans Wasseur, and the Institute of Sociology at Groningen University for generating the computer runs for this analysis. They also thank S. D. Berkowitz, Phillip Bonacich, Nick Danegelis, G. William Domhoff, Meindert Fennema, H. Gilman McCann, Joris Nobel, Michael Schwartz, and J. Allen Whitt for comments on previous drafts.

1 See Useem (1980) for a discussion of this literature.
2 For information on the availability of GRADAP contact: Professor Dr. Frans N. Stokman, Sociologisch Instituut, Rijksuniverssiteit, Oude Boteringestraat 23, 9712 GC Groningen, The Netherlands.
3 Social elite status was defined by membership in a small list of policy planning groups identified by Domhoff (1970) and Bonacich and Domhoff (1981) including the Brookings Institute, the Business Council, the Business Roundtable, the Conference Board and the Advertising Council. Similarly, elite social clubs were identified by Domhoff (1970) and supplemented by the following from Bonacich and Domhoff (1981): the Metropolitan Club (Washington, DC) and the Union League. Additionally, anyone who was either listed in the *Social Register* or who attended one of the elite prep schools identified by Domhoff (1970) was included.

4 The only portion of the interlock network in which these directors were not important was within bank-centered 2-cliques. See Bearden and Mintz (1984) for a description of these 2-cliques and for a discussion of the role of these directors in solidifying regional subsets.
5 One of the smallest components generated ($n=4$) also has a national base uniting directors from California, New York, and St. Louis. We are less interested in this grouping because of its small size.
6 "If exclusive social clubs are a source of social cohesion, major business policy associations are the crucible of political cohesion" (Useem, 1980: 56).

REFERENCES

Allen, Michael, 1974. "The structure of interorganizational elite cooptation." *American Sociological Review*, 39: 393–406

Bearden, James, 1982. "The board of directors in Large US Companies." Unpublished PhD dissertation, Department of Sociology, State University of New York at Stony Brook

Bearden, James, William Atwood, Peter Freitag, Carol Hendricks, Beth Mintz, and Michael Schwartz, 1975. "The nature and extent of bank centrality in corporate networks." Paper presented at the meetings of the American Sociological Association

Bearden, James, and Beth Mintz, 1984. "Regionality and integration in the United States interlock network." In F. Stokmen, R. Zeigler and J. Scott (eds.), *Networks of Corporate Power: An Analysis of Ten Countries*. Oxford: Polity Press, pp. 234–49

Berkowitz, S. D., 1982. *An Introduction to Structural Analysis: The Network Approach to Social Research*. Toronto: Butterworths

Bonacich, Phillip, and G. William Domhoff, 1981. "Latent classes and group membership." *Social Networks*, 3: 175–96

Breiger, Ronald, 1974. "The duality of persons and groups." *Social Forces*, 53: 181–90

Bunting, David, 1976. "Corporate interlocking." *Directors and Boards*, 1: 6–15

Burch, Philip, Jr., 1981. "The business roundtable: Its make-up and external ties." *Research in Political Economy*, 4: 101–27

Burt, Ronald, 1979. "A structural theory of interlocking corporate directorates." *Social Networks*, 1: 415–35

1980. "Cooptive corporate actor networks: a reconsideration of interlocking directorates involving American manufacturing." *Administrative Science Quarterly*, 25: 557–82

1983. *Corporate Profits and Cooptation*. New York: Academic Press

Domhoff, G. William, 1967. *Who Rules America?* Englewood Cliffs, NJ: Prentice-Hall

1970. *The Higher Circles*. New York: Random House

1975. "Social clubs, policy planning groups, and corporations: a network study of ruling class cohesiveness." *Insurgent Sociologist*, 5: 173–84

1979. *The Powers That Be*. New York: Random House

1983. *Who Rules America Now?* Englewood Cliffs, NJ: Prentice-Hall

Dooley, Peter, 1969. "The interlocking directorate." *American Economic Review*, 59: 314–23

Fennema, Meindert, 1982. *International Networks of Banks and Industry.* Boston: Martinus Nijhoff

Forbes, weekly. New York: Forbes, Inc.

Fortune, bi-weekly. Chicago: Time, Inc.

Galaskiewicz, Joseph, and Barbara Rauschenbach, 1979. "Patterns of interinstitutional exchanges: An examination of linkages between cultural and business organizations." Paper presented at meetings of the American Sociological Association

Glasberg, Davita, 1981. "Corporate power and control: the case of Leasco Corporation versus Chemical Bank." *Social Problems*, 29: 104–16

Gogel, Robert, and Thomas Koenig, 1981. "Commercial banks, interlocking directorates and economic power: an analysis of the primary metals industry." *Social Problems*, 29: 117–28

Koenig, Thomas, Robert Gogel, and John Sonquist, 1979. "Models of the significance of interlocking corporate directorates." *American Journal of Economics and Sociology*, 38: 173–83

Levine, Joel, 1972. "The sphere of influence." *American Sociological Review*, 37: 14–27

Mariolis, Peter, 1975. "Interlocking directorates and the control of corporations." *Social Science Quarterly*, 56: 425–39

Mariolis, Peter, and Maria Jones, 1982. "Centrality in corporate interlock networks: reliability and stability." *Administrative Science Quarterly*, 24: 571–84

Mintz, Beth, and Michael Schwartz, 1981. "The structure of intercorporate unity in American business." *Social Problems*, 29: 87–103

1985. *The Power Structure of American Business.* University of Chicago Press

Mizruchi, Mark, 1982. *The American Corporate Network: 1904–1974.* Beverly Hills: Sage

1983. "Relations among large American corporations, 1904–1974." *Social Science History*, 7: 165–82

Norich, Samuel, 1980. "Interlocking directorates, the control of large corporations and patterns of accumulation in the capitalist class." In M. Zeitlin (ed.), *Classes, Class Conflict, and the State.* Cambridge, Mass.: Winthrop

Ornstein, Michael, 1982. "Interlocking directorates in Canada: evidence from replacement patterns." *Social Networks*, 4: 3–25

Palmer, Donald, 1983a. "Broken ties: interlocking directorates and intercorporate coordination." *Administration Science Quarterly*, 28: 40–55

1983b. "On the significance of interlocking directorates." *Social Science History*, 7: 217–31

Ratcliff, Richard, 1980. "Banks and corporate lending: an analysis of the impact of the internal structure of the capitalist class on the lending behavior of banks." *American Sociological Review*, 45: 553–70

Ratcliff, Richard, Mary Elizabeth Gallagher, and Kathryn Strother Ratcliff, 1979. "The civic involvement of bankers: an analysis of the influence of economic power and social prominence in the command of civic policy positions." *Social Problems*, 26: 298–313

Roy William, 1983. "The unfolding of the interlocking directorate structure of the United States." *American Sociological Review*, 48: 248–57

Sonquist, John, and Thomas Koenig, 1975. "Interlocking directorates in the top US corporations: a graph theory approach." *Insurgent Sociologist*, 5: 196–230

Soref, Michael, 1976. "Social class and division of labor within the corporate elite." *Sociological Quarterly*, 17: 360–8

Standard and Poor's Register of Corporations, Directors, and Executives, annual. New York: Standard and Poor's Corp.

Stokman, Frans, Rolf Zeigler, and John Scott, 1984. *Networks of Corporate Power: An Analysis of Ten Countries*. Oxford: Polity Press

Useem, Michael, 1978. "The inner group of the American capitalist class." *Social Problems*, 25: 225–40

　1979. "The social organization of the American business elite." *American Sociological Review*, 44: 553–71

　1980. "Corporations and the corporate elite." *Annual Review of Sociology*, 6: 41–78

　1984. *The Inner Circle*. New York: Oxford University Press

Whitt, J. Allen, 1981. "Is oil different? A comparison of the social background and organizational affiliations of oil and non-oil directors." *Social Problems*, 29: 142–55

Who's Who in Finance and Industry, annual. Chicago: Marquis Who's Who, Inc.

Zeitlin, Maurice, 1974. "Corporate ownership and control: the large corporation and the capitalist class." *American Journal of Sociology*, 79: 1073–119

7

Intercorporate structures in Western Europe: a comparative historical analysis

John Scott

The aim of this chapter is to discuss the structural features of big business in the major West European countries. The countries chosen for study are not intended as the basis of a comprehensive survey of West European economies. Rather, they are drawn from the work of a research group which has carried out the first truly comparative investigation of intercorporate structure. The countries selected do, however, constitute all the major economic powers and their trading partners and associations. The countries to which most reference is made are Britain, France, Germany, Italy, the Netherlands, Austria, and Switzerland. The obvious omissions from this list are the countries of the Iberian peninsula and Scandinavia, both of which areas have peculiar and distinct features which set them apart from the major industrial economies.

The research group on intercorporate structure, referred to in the text as the "Bad Homburg Group" after the town in which many of the group meetings took place, brought together researchers from a number of countries to collaborate on an investigation into interlocking directorships in ten countries.[1] In addition to the countries mentioned above, there were participants from the USA (see the chapter by Bearden and Mintz in this book) and Finland, together with a "transnational" team (see the chapter by Fennema and van der Pijl in this book). The study involved the collection of comparable data in each of the countries and the use of the same set of computer programs, computer analysis being carried out centrally at Groningen University. Although some results from the national studies have been presented in various sources, the first major compilation of the comparative studies has only recently become available in the book *Networks of Corporate Power* (Stokman, Ziegler and Scott, 1985). The present chapter draws upon some of the results presented in that book and attempts to place these results in the context of an interpretation of the development of the European economy over the last 150 years.

The central focus of the Bad Homburg Group has been on the structure of relations between enterprises which is created when one person is a member of two or more boards of directors. This structure was conceptualized as a social network and was studied through the mathematical techniques of graph theory. In this theoretical framework an interlocking directorship or simply an interlock, is the unit from which complex structures are built up, and the resulting structure can be analyzed in terms of the density, its degree of centralization, and so forth. Network analysis has proved a very powerful way of studying business structure, and has generated a number of insights into national variations in intercorporate structure.

This chapter will draw on historical evidence in order to outline the main trajectories of industrial development which can be discovered in Western Europe. The various national trajectories will be related to the current structure of business organization in each of the countries. On this basis it will be possible to use a model of intercorporate relations to illuminate some of the generic features of the advanced capitalist economies as well as the main foci of national variation in business structure.

A model for late capitalism

In this section a model for the interpretation of the West European economies will be presented, the aim of this model being to depict the main structural mechanisms at work in these economies. The model will bring out those features which can be regarded as generic to the societal type as well as pointing to the major foci of national variation. It may perhaps be contentious to describe the contemporary economies of Western Europe as exemplifying "late capitalism," and so certain caveats are in order. The term "late capitalism" does not imply acceptance of a particular variant of Marxian theory (see Habermas, 1976). The term is used simply as a descriptive label for the current stage of capitalist development; a convenient way of indicating the major transformations which capitalist economies have experienced since the early years of the epoch of capitalist industrialism. Equally, the term is not to be taken as implying a belief in a monolithic model to be imposed on all countries. The recognition of national variations must go hand in hand with a recognition of certain general, underlying trends. Various countries have perhaps followed different routes and have moved at varying paces, but these variations are constrained by the generic features of capitalist development. The structuring mechanisms depicted in the general model of late capitalism constitute a crucial touchstone for understanding the specific mechanisms in operation in the various countries.

The concept of late capitalism implies, as its necessary complement, a notion of the "early capitalism" from which it has developed. The latter is understood here to refer to a society in which atomistic markets operate within an economy with a significantly, or predominantly, agrarian and mercantile character.[2] In such an economy, the characteristic form of business enterprise is the individual or family-owned firm in which managerial power is the prerogative of the owner. The exemplar for this stage of industrial capitalism is Britain in the first half of the nineteenth century and, as will be shown in a later part of this chapter, other countries have approximated to this model to varying degrees and in historically unique ways. In the stage of late capitalism, high levels of overall economic concentration have resulted in the emergence of a big business sector in which atomistic markets have increasingly given way to greater and greater degrees of monopolization. Concentration within industry, commerce, and banking results from a growth in the size of the business enterprise and an increased level of interconnection between these enterprises. The form taken by the business enterprise involves a transition from personal possession to impersonal possession, and many aspects of this transition can be grasped through the concept of "financial capital."

The legal form of business and changing patterns of ownership have resulted in the gradual replacement of individual and family shareholders by the "institutional" holdings of financial intermediaries such as insurance companies, pension funds, and bank trust departments (Scott, 1979). Individual shareholders do not disappear – there is a constant rise and fall of entrepreneurial firms – but in the majority of companies individual shareholdings fall to the level of insignificance for purposes of corporate control. The small personal shareholders, like the financial intermediaries, have a legal right to participate in the benefits of company operations, but they are effectively excluded from participation in strategic control. These trends are not limited to the industrial and commercial sectors, and the financial intermediaries are themselves owned and controlled in exactly the same way. While family and individual shareholders may vary in importance from one country to another, and while the main types of shareholding intermediary may also vary, the general trend is for the big business sector to become increasingly characterized by depersonalized patterns of property ownership. A complex system of intercorporate shareholdings and credit relations emerges, with particular enterprises being controlled by those who are recruited from and through the specific constellations of interests which constitute their dominant shareholders. Thus the control of an enterprise has to be analyzed in relation to "the concrete situation within the corporation and the constellations of intercorporate relations in which it is involved" (Zeitlin, 1974: 1091). In this structure of relations banking and industrial capital come closer to form "finance capital" (Hilferding, 1910). The major enterprises combine both of these forms of capital within themselves, or they form parts of larger groupings in which both are combined. "Interest groups," "empires," "combines", and the diversified multidivisional enterprise are possible forms of fusion which form units of finance capital. Relations within and between these units are cemented through what Hilferding called the "personal union," and which are now termed "interlocks."

The structural forms of organizational fusion which constitute finance capital can be analyzed in terms of the capital relations, commercial relations, and personal relations from which they are constructed (Scott, 1982a). The main concern of this chapter is the interlocking directorship, so it is necessary to try to classify the various types of interlock and their association with capital and commercial relations. The most important distinction to make is that between "primary interlocks" and "loose interlocks." A primary interlock exists where an inside (or executive) director in company A holds an outside (or non-executive) directorship in company B. Such a director may be seen as representing his or her base company on the board of another and this relationship may involve the imposition of a director of A on B's board, the cooptation of A by B, or a combination of these two relations. Thus, the primary interlock is a particularly strong relationship, though imputing directionality to the relation is no straightforward matter. Primary interlocks typically express, reinforce, or effect some form of institutional link between the companies – financial participations, credit relations, trading relations, etc. – and it is for this reason that the structures generated by such interlocks can be presumed to have some primacy in the analysis of intercorporate relations. By contrast, "looser" forms of interlocking find their main significance alongside these primary relations. One such type of loose interlock is that "induced" by the existence of two primary interlocks. If an insider from A holds outside positions in both B and C, then a loose interlock is induced between B and C. The interlock between B and C is consequential upon the common relationship of both B and C to A; it is not itself primary, as it involves a relation between two outside positions. Induced interlocks are consequences, intended or unintended, of the structure of primary interlocks. If the primary interlocks in the network are carried by a small number of people, then there will be a large number of induced interlocks. If, on the other hand, many separate executives carry the primary interlocks, then proportionally fewer induced interlocks will be created.

The other main form of loose interlock is analytically quite independent of primary interlocks. These "secondary" interlocks are those personal relations which involve two outside positions and which are not consequential upon the existence of primary interlocks: the presence of a politician, a retired civil servant, or a retired businessman on two company boards creates a secondary interlock between the companies. It must be emphasized that the relations of induction, consequentiality, and independence referred to above are analytical concepts. In concrete situations it is always necessary to discover through empirical analysis the connections of cause and effect which subsist between the various types of interlock and any possible notions of "directionality" that they might involve.

In terms of the general model proposed here, the structure of primary interlocks should be expected to give an indication of the major institutional links which exist between enterprises. Secondary and induced interlocks may be regarded as bonds which reinforce and cement the primary links by opening up additional channels of communication between the enterprises. But their significance goes beyond this. In so far as the structure of the network of secondary interlocks diverges from the structure of the network of primary lines, the former no longer simply reinforces the latter. Rather, secondary interlocks may generate a structure of relations between enterprises which is relatively unconnected with the institutional links which constitute the substructure of the intercorporate system. Secondary interlocks can be regarded as channels through which business information is able to flow and which therefore create opportunities for cohesion and coordination at the level of the system as a whole. That is, they relate to system integration rather than to the dyadic relations between particular enterprises.

The many discussions of the concept of finance capital have often revolved around the interpretation which is to be placed upon the position of banks in the intercorporate systems of late capitalism. The concepts which have been presented above permit a clarification of this problem. Banks are central to the flow of capital between enterprises and will therefore be involved in a number of institutional links, from the provision of short-term working capital to underwriting and participation in share capital. As such, an important way of analyzing the role of banks in various national economies is to examine the pattern of primary interlocks in which banks are involved. It is here that a major point of differentiation in national economies might be expected to occur: a differentiation between segmented and centralized networks.

Preferential lending and other mechanisms through which particular banks enter into relatively enduring relationships with particular industrial and commercial companies tend to create loosely structured communities of interest centered around each of the banks. The bank boards constitute forums in which major capitalist interests allied to that bank come together and are able to establish a limited degree of coordination in the behavior of their base companies and, perhaps more importantly, to exercise a degree of influence over subordinate enterprises. This pattern has been described as one of bank-centered spheres of influence and may be regarded as one of the major variant forms of late capitalism. Banks, however, are important not only in terms of primary interests, but also in terms of secondary interlocks. The centrality of banks in intercorporate networks is, therefore, a pointer to a function over and above that described. In addition to the role in the mobilization of capital which they exercise as financial intermediaries, banks accumulate and mobilize business information. Through the numerous induced and secondary interlocks which they carry, the boards of banks are points at which the information possessed by participants in big business is centralized and from which it can be disseminated. Banks are, literally, information banks. To the extent that loose interlocks are confined within spheres of influence, so the segmentation of the network is reinforced; but to the extent that loose interlocks transcend any such spheres and bridge the gap between them, they extend the community of interest to the system as a whole. In the latter case, loose interlocks create a network which permits a degree of system coordination and cohesion. If one pole of intercorporate structure is the division of the economy into relatively distinct spheres of influence, the other pole is the formation of a unified structure with little internal segmentation. This polarization has been analyzed by the Bad Homburg Group through the concept of structural centralization, understood as a measure of the extent to which a network possesses a structural "center." The center of a network is an attribute of the network as a whole and not of particular agents and is formally defined as the largest 2-clique of locally central enterprises which are mutually reachable at distance two or less. That is to say, a center comprises a group of enterprises which are individually central in the network and which either interlock directly or have their directors meeting on the board of a third company. The members of a center have a high degree of cohesion because of the numerous meetings of their board members. A high level of interlocking, resulting in a high density, is likely to be associated with the existence of a structural center and with the consequent absence of major lines of structural cleavage between spheres of influence.

In this section some of the general mechanisms operating in late capitalist economies have been discussed, and some of the points at which different national economies might be expected to show alternative ways of expressing these mechanisms have been indicated. It has been assumed that there is a tendency for all late capitalist societies to move closer to the picture presented in this model, but that this tendency is countered by the legacies bequeathed by the particular patterns of historical development which specific societies have undergone.

Routes to late capitalism

In studies of economic development, no less than in other areas of sociology, unilinear evolutionary theories have been roundly rejected. The one-time orthodoxy of the Rostow model (Rostow, 1960) has been rejected in favor of a world system model based on the work of Wallerstein (1974). The latter stresses the interdependence of countries and their historical location within an overarching world system. The model does not rule out any idea of general social transformations – far from it; instead it directs the researcher to a study of the various "routes" which different societies have taken in making such transformations.

Capitalist industrialization is perhaps the major transformation of the world system in the last two hundred years. Britain, as the "first industrial nation," underwent a pattern of industrialization made possible by its position within the European political and economic system. Later European industrializers, in radically different political and economic environments, had the British experience available to them as a model to be followed or, more typically, avoided. Their industrialization occurred in a world economic system in which Britain had achieved a position of dominance with respect to technology, markets, and political power. But the British lead was only relative and not absolute. Other societies were well on the way to securing the necessary preconditions, so British dominance inevitably came under challenge. A number of the circumstances favorable to industry in Britain were emerging later and more slowly in some parts of Continental Europe. But, even if such endogenous changes might have generated a takeoff in these areas, the threat to their industries posed by the increasingly powerful British economy meant that their response to these circumstances was fundamentally altered. Traditional domestic industries collapsed under the impact of cheap British goods, and Britain gradually squeezed others out of international trade. Only after the Napoleonic Wars could an effective response be made, though by then the increased gap between Britain and the other European countries meant that the task of emulation was that much greater than before. At mid-century Britain was still the only industrial country, though there were small pockets in Belgium, France, and Germany; by the last quarter of the century Britain was rapidly being challenged by other industrializers.

The United States of America became the main challenger to British dominance, and Japan soon began state-sponsored economic growth. Within Europe Germany was, from the 1870s, the most notable industrializer, with France rapidly following the German example. Each country "took off" from its own unique location within the European system, yet certain common patterns can be discerned. In all the late industrializers the state and financial intermediaries played a far more active role than was the case in British industrialization, and the newer technologies were employed in the more advanced industries. Within this common pattern, certain important variations exist: a number of different "routes" to late capitalism were followed. By the beginning of the twentieth century the world was beginning to be divided among a number of industrial powers (see Kemp, 1978; Gershenkron, 1962).

These later routes of capitalist industrialization can be differentiated according to the differing role of the banking system. Two polar types of bank can be defined: the "mobilier" type of bank, where long-term credit is mobilized for use in industrial development: and the commercial type of bank, where credit is short-term only and is distributed on a "retail" basis. The mobilier bank was first introduced in Belgium and France and such banks generally remained separate from commercial banking, but in Germany the banking system involved a powerful fusion of mobilier and commercial banks, forming the so-called "universal" or general banks. The universal type of investment bank was important because of its ability to mobilize capital from a wide variety of sources and to put it to work as productive capital. This created a "circle of mutual assistance and reinforcement" (Landes, 1969: 205) as the clients of the banks generated the capital which the banks could mobilize in other areas to encourage other clients (see also Gille, 1970). This discussion makes it possible to identify three main routes of industrial development. These three routes can be termed the *entrepreneurial system*, the *holding system*, and the *hegemonic system*. They structured the industrial transformation of the capitalist world system, and the major countries of Western Europe can, with few exceptions, be understood in terms of one or other of these patterns. Those which offer contrasting patterns prove useful in understanding the general mechanisms involved. The entrepreneurial system characteristic of Britain involved the dominance of commercial banking and a pattern of industrialization in which the primary agents of economic growth were the family-controlled firms financed mainly by the ploughback of internally generated funds. The hegenomic system, characteristic of Germany, was the situation in which the large universal banks and the large industrial and commercial enterprises were allied through the credit mechanism, through shareholdings, and through personal interlocks. The hegemonic system is one in which one particular type of enterprise holds sway over all others, though the hegemonic type of enterprise may constitute a meeting place for capitalist interests rather than acting simply in terms of its own self-interest. Central to the relation of hegemony is the fact that the behavior of the dominant enterprise(s) alters the conditions in the environment of other enterprises, the altered environmental circumstances ensuring the production of a complementary response on the part of the subordinate enterprise(s). The latter are constrained by their objective circumstances and not necessarily by any intent to dominate. The hegemonic enterprise is simply involved in significant, regular, and direct influence over other enterprises (Mintz and Schwartz, 1985). Between these two routes is the holding system, which was characteristic of France and also of Belgium. The mobilier banks were important factors in industrialization, but were not fused into universal banks and were, in consequence, less powerful in these countries, and the characteristic form of business became the interest group in which a "holding company" stood at the focal point of a system of enterprises operating in both the financial and the industrial sectors. The mutual exchange of shares and directors among various companies in the group ensures a common coordination and control in a group that falls short of a single, unified enterprise. If these relations were to become tight and close, the group would constitute a "combine," where a number of the separate enterprises within the group set up joint ventures, cartels, and other common organizations. But typically the holding system comprises groups with a looser structure than the combine, though the system may involve some functional links which create a certain degree of vertical or horizontal integration.

Of the three routes to late capitalism which have been identified, the entrepreneurial pattern was historically the earliest. The history of British industrialization is well known and needs only brief discussion here. Much has been made of the "uniqueness" of the British experience, though it is true to say that all patterns of social transformation are historically unique. Nevertheless, the claim does point to a number of particularly distinctive features of its Industrial Revolution. Britain was not only the first industrial society, it was also the first capitalist society – and this early development of capitalism was one of the key factors underpinning British industrialization. Furthermore, and unlike later industrializers, the British takeoff was in almost complete isolation from large national banks. At the local level, the manufacturing firms of the eighteenth century had close relations with the small country banks, which often provided short-term capital on a "rolling" basis and so formed an important element in long-term industrial funding. The major factor in capital accumulation, however, was self-financing by the entrepreneurial family firm. By drawing on the resources of their extended family networks and entering into partnerships with other families, industrial capitalists could extend the scope of their businesses without resorting to banking capital or to the Stock Exchange. The Industrial Revolution of the late eighteenth century, therefore, was based upon an entrepreneurial system of capital accumulation (Mathias, 1969; Deane, 1967).

From the 1870s a transformation of the banking system led to the breaking of the links between industrial firms and country banks, as the latter were incorporated into a banking system based in the City of London. This separation of banking and industry persisted until well into the twentieth century and took the form of a split between metropolitan and provincial economies. The "City" was at the heart of the metropolitan economy and held its position as the pivot of the world economic system. City dominance in international trade was the basis of British imperial power. But in the provinces the entrepreneurial family firm prevailed. Economic concentration in the late nineteenth century occurred through the amalgamation of family enterprises, with family control persisting in the enlarged enterprises. When this resulted in a struggle for dominance between those families whose firms had been amalgamated, the adoption of more efficient forms of management was often inhibited (Hannah, 1976). Families wanted to maintain control over their firms and operated in well-tried ways in secure niches rather than expanding and thereby risking loss of control. This feature of British industry in the years leading up to World War I, which has often been characterized as "entrepreneurial failure," was an important factor in allowing the late industrializers to challenge and then to overtake Britain.

The political and economic circumstances of Germany in the early nineteenth century militated against rapid industrialization. Although the dominance of Prussia had led to the formation of the Zollverein (Customs Union) over most of Germany, capital accumulation was greatly inhibited by the unwillingness of landowners to invest in industry and by the small size of the bourgeoisie, which meant that there was insufficient profit to plough back into production. The heavy industry of the Rhine and Ruhr generally drew on foreign capital, especially French and Belgian, though the Prussian state ensured that control remained in German hands. The German banks were of crucial importance in mobilizing capital and in providing short-term credit, and legal limitations on block voting in corporate affairs ensured that company boards were filled with bankers (Kitchen, 1978). During the 1860s the banks were active in replacing foreign with domestic capital. The depression of the 1870s forced greater cooperation between banks and industry and led to increased concentration in both banking and in industry. In the banking sector this movement of concentration enhanced the position of the "Four Ds" – the Diskontogesselschaft, and the Darmstadter, Dresdner, and Deutsche banks. Following the example set by the early French and Belgian mobilier banks, a number of credit banks were formed in the second half of the century. Austria, the western part of the Habsburg Empire, was also dependent on banking capital for its industrialization. The Credit Anstalt was formed by the Rothschilds and rapidly adopted the practices of universal banking. By the turn of the century the large Berlin banks were all-pervasive in Germany. With their affiliates and associates they formed massive national banking chains and, as "universal" banks, they combined mobilier and commercial banking functions: they were involved in industrial credit, share issues, underwriting, and participations, and they sought board level representation. Specializing in the heavy industries of coal, iron, steel, engineering, and chemicals, the big banks were especially close to the major cartels which regulated these industries (Henderson, 1961: 62ff).

Thus, German industrialization was based around big banks and big joint stock companies organized into combines and cartels. Most of the larger German firms – Krupp, Thyssen, Siemens, Mannesmann, and later mergers such as Vereinigte Stahlwerke, Daimler-Benz, and I. G. Farben – were allied with the banks through capital and personal relations. The banks took shareholdings in the big firms, but the main base of the relationship was the voting rights which they held in their massive trust holdings – the so-called Depotstimmrecht. These close capital relations became the crucial mechanism in generating the capital required by big business. But the relationship was not one way. Industrialists accommodated their interests with those of the banks by becoming directors of banks, the largest industrials being allied in this way with several banks (Tilly, 1974; Kocka, 1980: 90; Gille, 1970: 285–7). If the banks colonized industry, then it is just as true to say that industry colonized the banks. In Austria too there was a close relationship between banking and industry, but Austrian industry remained dependent on foreign capital until the 1930s, and the big banks maintained their position as mobilizers of foreign capital.

German enterprises, therefore, operated in an economy dominated by bank-controlled and bank-allied companies, and it is this situation which can be described as hegemonic. Enterprises remained distinct from one another or were formed into tight combines, but the holding system was of little import. Enterprises and combines were controlled by varying coalitions of family shareholders and major bankers, but the major structural feature of the business system was the capital and personal union which existed between the banks and industry. This situation did not involve the dominance of "bankers" over "industrialists"; it involved the institutional dominance of the banking enterprises. Bank boards brought together bank executives and industrialists, and these interests jointly determined the banks' policies in relation to their clients and associates. The banks, both collectively and individually, were an all-pervasive force determining the conditions under which other enterprises were forced to act. Whether as a matter of deliberate intent or as an unintended consequence of banking practices, such bank hegemony was the characteristic feature of the German economy in its formative period.

Through the seventeenth century the French state grew in size and power and at the end of the eighteenth century it was the most powerful nation in Europe. Its political dominance (Smith, 1978) was matched by its position as Britain's closest economic challenger in the capitalist world system. Unlike Britain, however, the breakthrough to an industrial economy did not occur. The political upheavals of the late eighteenth and early nineteenth centuries – revolution and European wars – held the country back from further economic advance. Only when peace was established in 1815 was the state both willing and able to turn its attention to economic development (Fohlen, 1970). When industrialization did begin to take off – from the 1860s – the state and the banking system became crucial supplements to the earlier family enterprises.

The Parisian "haute banques" – Rothschild together with Mallet, Vernes, Marabaud – were primarily orientated toward state finance and foreign trade, and as there were few banks outside Paris there were virtually no credit facilities available for domestic business in the first half of the nineteenth century. During this period industrial activity was confined largely to family enterprises dependent on self-financing. Only from the 1860s did mobilier banks such as the Crédit Lyonnais and the Société Générale become involved in industrial credit and come to challenge the old banking establishment, which was increasingly forced to adopt the same practices of industrial investment and participation. The old banks' role as "banques d'affaires" was recast as they became major participants in the share capital of large industrial enterprises, in a number of cases taking substantial minority stakes and in many more holding blocks of 1 or 2 per cent.

In order to survive in a period of big business in which banking groups were playing an increasingly important role, the old family firms had either to ally themselves with existing bank groups or form rival groups. Although both strategies were pursued, most family enterprises did not wish to take up the funds which were available through the mobilier banks. These families regarded the maintenance of the integrity of the family firm as an end in itself (Gille, 1970: 280–1; Palmade, 1961). In Britain this "entrepreneurial failure" had its main impact in the period after the industrial takeoff. Those family enterprises which chose to follow the route of independence had to amalgamate into larger groupings and adopted decentralized forms of management as a way of maximizing their family control within the enlarged groupings. Thus, loose holding systems emerged as the dominant characteristic of the French economy.

Similar processes produced the holding system in Belgium, which was until 1830 a part of the Kingdom of the Netherlands (itself only recently independent of the French Empire). Despite some growth in the wool and cotton industries in the late eighteenth and early nineteenth centuries during the period of French imperial control, heavy industry was slow to develop. Landed capital was not easily mobilized for industrial development, owing to the poorly developed banking system, so industry could not advance significantly until the formation of the Société Générale. Formed by the king of the Netherlands specifically to finance industrial development in the south (the area that is now Belgium), this company became heavily involved in coal, iron, and steel. After the separation from the Netherlands, and under its new name of Société Générale de Belgique, a number of vertically integrated combines were established in the heavy industrial sector. The SGB, with the Banque de Belgique and support from the state, ensured that by 1840 Belgium was second only to Britain in level of industrial development (Dhondt and Bruwier, 1970). Industrialization was, however, relatively slow, and much was occurring outside the sphere of the SGB. Family enterprises were forced to adopt similar methods to the SGB if they were not to become subordinate to it, and industrialists such as Solvay began to form rival investment banks in the 1860s (Gille, 1970: 285). The economy showed a marked differentiation between the SGB sector and the family sector, though each was structured through the holding system. Throughout the economy, therefore, industrial development took place in the context of interest groups in which industry, trade, and finance were combined and which used cross-shareholdings and interlocking directorships to cement control. Diversified and tightly controlled groups tended to be centered around trust or holding companies, and this was reinforced during the 1930s when banking legislation forced a legal separation between banking and nonbanking activities. The shareholding functions of the banks and family groups were organized into the modern "holding companies," understood as enterprises which manage a portfolio of participations for the purpose of control rather than simply as an investment (Daems, 1978: 2, 11–16; Cuyvers and Meeusen, 1976).

Those countries which diverge from the patterns identified above are important in providing a deeper understanding of the circumstances leading to the adoption of a particular pattern of industrial development. In both Switzerland and the Netherlands the prevailing feature of the economy was an international orientation. The Swiss economy in the first half of the nineteenth century was dominated by its many powerful private bankers, who formed three mobilier banks in the 1850s – the Schweizerische Bankgessellschaft (Swiss Bank Corporation, or SBG), the Schweizerische Kreditanstalt (Credit Suisse, or SKA), and the Schweizerischer Bankverein (Union Bank of Switzerland, or SBV). Both banking and industry were strongly oriented overseas, and such capital and personal relations as did occur were in relation to the exploitation of overseas markets. In the Netherlands a fairly well-developed banking system based in Amsterdam was associated with the important area of colonial trade and colonial produce. In the years before World War I, some of the larger banks became involved in the kind of capital and personal union characteristic of the German universal banks, but this had its focus in colonial enterprises. Industrial companies such as Van den Berghs, Jürgens, and Philips arose outside the bank-dominated sector – even the important Royal Dutch oil company had little association with the major banks. Clearly in both of these countries the relative unimportance of heavy industry and the considerable importance of overseas activity structured the emerging relationships within the business sector.

Undoubtedly the most important of the divergent patterns for the analysis presented here is that found in Italy, where a rather "mixed" route was followed. Italian industrialization was later than Belgian or French, and when industrialization began it was slow and protracted. State protectionist policies of the 1880s and 1890s, policies of customs tariffs and industrial support, coincided with a banking crisis which prevented the big national banks from participating in industrial development. Only in the period from the 1890s to 1914 was there any significant spurt in the rate of development. The key "agents of the spurt" (Cafagna, 1971: 317; Gershenkron, 1962: Ch. 4) were the state, banks, and entrepreneurs. The role of the state was limited to protecting heavy industry, textiles and food, and there was no direct involvement in production. The entrepreneurial families were most active in small and medium-sized businesses and thus the central agents in the big business sector were the banks. In the wake of the banking crisis two new banks were formed with German capital, and these banks adopted the universal bank practices prevalent in Germany. The banks were mainly active in the newer industries rather than the traditional sectors, but a legacy of the banking crisis was that the banks were less actively involved in corporate affairs than their German counterparts. Thus in Italy the hegemonic system failed to emerge, and various features of the holding system were to be found alongside the enterprises in which the banks were involved.

Structural features of late capitalism

Having identified the three main routes to late capitalism – the entrepreneurial, the hegemonic, and the holding system – it is now possible to turn to the contemporary structure of the late capitalist societies themselves. This section will explore the extent to which the historical route followed is associated with variations in present-day business structure.

The results of the research of the Bad Homburg Group show that there is a significant division between those countries in which the business system is relatively centralized. In the segmented category are Britain, France, and Italy, and in the centralized category are Germany, Austria, Switzerland, the Netherlands, and Belgium. Important questions are raised not only by the differences between these two categories but also by variations within them. Britain, France, and Italy, for example, are each segmented in significantly different ways, and the nature of structural centralization varies between Germany, Belgium, and Austria. The discussion which follows begins with Britain, goes on to consider Germany and similarly structured networks, and finally examines the remaining patterns. The results of the Bad Homburg Group relate, with minor variations (see Stokman, Ziegler and Scott, 1985), to the top 200 nonfinancial and top 50 financial enterprises for 1976 in each of the countries studied. Wherever possible, these results have been placed in the broader context of the contemporary business systems.

Family enterprise remained an important feature of the British economy until the 1960s, and a large number of big firms today remain subject to family control. Nevertheless, the central trend has been for the growth in concentration to be associated with a growth in "institutional" share ownership. The proportion of shares held by individuals has fallen over the postwar period and the main shareholding groups today are insurance companies, pension funds, investment companies, and bank trust departments. These financial intermediaries now own about two-thirds of the shares of British companies. The separation of the City and industry which developed at the end of the nineteenth century has gradually been abolished. The separation persisted until the interwar years, but the economic problems of the twenties and thirties forced commercial banks into a closer relationship with many of the major enterprises: in order to prevent the complete loss of the short-term capital which they had lent to the firms which were in trouble, the banks were compelled to provide additional capital on a long-term basis.

The insurance companies were brought into these arrangements by the banks, and the boardrooms of companies in coal, steel, engineering, shipping, and numerous other industries were filled with the representatives of the financial intermediaries. As the health of the companies improved, so the relationship with the banks was loosened. But, at the same time, the amount of money garnered by the insurance companies and, later, the pension funds made them major purchasers of company shares. This transformation in the relations between the financial and industrial sectors was a particularly marked feature of the postwar period.

The outcome of this restructuring of British capital has been a shift in the prevailing forms of strategic control. In the majority of the large enterprises the 20 or so largest shareholders collectively hold a majority or substantial minority of the shares, and these same intermediaries are important as providers of loan capital and short-term credit. While the group is too diverse to act in concert and so exercise one of the traditional forms of owner control, they are too important to be ignored by the internal executives and so will tend to be active participants in strategic control. The board reflects the constellation of interests which comprise the major shareholders (Scott, 1979, 1982a). Ownership is vested in interweaving shareholding and investing interests, and the resulting network of intercorporate capital relations is associated with the existence of interlocking directorships between the enterprises.

The Bad Homburg Group discovered that the British interlock network of 1976 was structured into loose spheres of influence centered around the major commercial banks and tied into a national community of interest (Scott and Griff, 1984). Each of the "Big Four" banks – Barclays, Lloyds, Midland, and National Westminster – had primary interlocks with distinct groupings of enterprises operating in finance, manufacturing, retailing, and other industries. The bank boards brought together executives from the major clients and associates of the banks and allowed a degree of coordination to emerge. These spheres of interest were loosely structured and cannot be seen as tight interest groups. It might be remarked parenthetically that the same situation seems to hold in the United States of America, despite the claim of Mintz and Schwartz (1985). The position of the banks can best be understood as a modified form of hegemony. This hegemony is not on the scale of that characterictic of the German banks before World War I, as the primary interlocks of the banks were not generally associated with large participations, but it is nevertheless an important feature of the intercorporate network. This is reflected in the fact that a number of primary interlocks and many secondary interlocks ran between spheres of influence to create a national community of interest, though the network showed a low level of centralization. The distinction between primary and secondary interlocks seems to be very much a career phenomenon: the executives who carried the primary interlocks became the "elder statesmen" of the business community on their retirement.

The German business system was, of course, severely disrupted by World War II and its aftermath. However, war damage, denazification, the breakup of firms, and partition all proved far less disruptive than might have been assumed. Indeed, the split between East and West led to American support for industrial reconstruction in the Federal Republic and so contributed to economic recovery. In West Germany, the concern of this chapter, many prewar firms were able to reestablish themselves on a "business as usual" basis. Families such as Krupp, Thyssen, Flick, and Quandt, together with newer entrepreneurs such as Schleiker, Grundig, and Springer, remained a potent force in the German economy of the sixties and seventies (Granick, 1962; Dyas and Thanheiser, 1976; Krejci, 1976).

The banks, too were able to recover much of their prewar position. Despite the growing importance of the regional and cooperative banks, which have adopted the practices of universal banking, the "Big Three" – Deutsche, Commerz, and Dresdner – have all maintained their dominance within the banking system. All three banks still have substantial participations and retain the right to vote trust holdings, but the scale of their direct participations has been reduced. Directly or in association with families the three banks were minority shareholders in almost half of the top 115 industrial companies of the late sixties (Krejci, 1976). The work of the Bad Homburg Group has confirmed this picture of continuing bank hegemony. The banks were important in determining the overall structure of the network, but they did not form specific combines or interest groups. The banks, the Allianz insurance, and the major industrials formed a dense core of 15 companies at the heart of a 34-member center which was particularly strong in heavy industry, mining, and utilities and which stretched across all German regions. This center was tied together through the primary interlocks carried by executives of financial companies, and such interlocks also allied smaller companies to particular banks. Primary financial interlocks tended to be associated with financial participations and other institutional links, so the German network formed a strongly hierarchical system. The banks held generalized, hegemonic dominance rather than exercising power in specific interest groups, but this hegemony was far looser than in the prewar economy.

This loosely structured form of centralized bank hegemony was also found in Switzerland and the Netherlands. The Big Three Swiss universal banks – SKA, SBV, and SBG – have gradually extended their control over the private banks, which are unable to engage in commercial banking, and they have forced the cantonal and savings banks into decline. In 1976 the banks, insurance companies, and major industrials formed a core of 12 very large multinational enterprises within a center of 28 companies. The core was especially dense, and this cohesion was reinforced by the Central Bank's recruitment policy of coopting the leaders of all the major enterprises to its board. Primary financial interlocks played a major role in structuring this center. As was the case with the German researchers, the hierarchy observed in the network was seen as reflecting the interdependence of the banks and major industrials. That is to say, the banks were forums for hegemonic domination rather than being agencies of "bank power." The Dutch banking system is also highly concentrated, though none of the Big Four – ABN, AMRO, RABO, and NMB – can be described as universal banks. Together with insurance companies and large industrials, the Big Four were part of a core of 15 within a structural center of 38 companies. As in Germany and Switzerland, primary financial interlocks were most important in structuring the network, with secondary interlocks generating more diffuse links. But the structure was rather less hierarchical, and important multinationals such as Unilever and Royal Dutch held relatively peripheral positions in the network.

Switzerland and the Netherlands, both of which followed the practice of the German two-board system of business administration, showed the pattern of loose, centralized bank hegemony found in Germany, though the Dutch network in particular was less hierarchical and showed some tendency for its major multinationals to have their main points of reference outside of the Netherlands. The centralized structure was also discovered in Austria, though this country shows an important divergence from the pattern described so far.

Following the collapse of the Creditanstalt in 1931, the bank came into state ownership. But the growth of a state sector was largely a postwar phenomenon. The German takeover of many Austrian firms in 1938 meant that at the end of the war these firms were, in effect, ownerless, though legally they were German property. The Austrian government therefore nationalized 70 enterprises in 1946 to prevent the Soviet Union from taking control of them as surrendered German property. This brought all of mining, steel, and oil, much of chemicals, metals and engineering, and another bank into public ownership. Although the two big banks were partly denationalized in the fifties – the state retained 60 per cent – these enterprises comprise a tightly coordinated group. The state banks, there being no other significant banks, retain many industrial participations, and all the nationalized industries except electricity are grouped under the public corporation ÖIAG. The network was found to have a center of 34 companies and, although it was superficially similar to the German network, the position of the state meant that a strong hierarchical interpretation could be given to the structure. The state determined the overall features of the network through the primary interlocks of ÖIAG and the two banks, each of which was associated with a distinct group of enterprises. Bankhaus Schoeller, the largest private bank, also constituted the coordinating point of a group, but was allied to the public enterprises. These four companies were the basis of the structural center of the network, and the particular pattern of alliance between public and private enterprises can best be described as "corporatist." The central structuring principle of the Austrian economy had changed from bank hegemony to corporatism.

So far one segmented and four centralized networks have been described. In all except the Austrian it has been argued that bank hegemony is the central structuring principle, though the form taken by this hegemony varies according to the route taken to late capitalism. In Austria, development along German lines was halted by the 1938 annexation and its postwar consequences. State acquisition of major parts of the banking and industrial sectors resulted in subsequent development in a corporatist direction. The contemporary patterns found in the remaining countries – Belgium, France, and Italy – show that corporatism is also becoming an important feature of those countries which have little history of bank hegemony. In the case of Belgium, however, the old holding system seems to have survived almost intact.

The power of "les holdings" in Belgium has been a common topic of popular politics and a considerable amount of academic research has gone into documenting the structure and extent of this power. The overwhelming position of the Société Générale de Belgique is scarcely questioned in debates on the economy. In 1969 the SGB controlled 25 of the 115 largest Belgian companies and was joint controller in a further eight. Among even larger companies, the top 41 of 1972, the SGB controlled eight, families controlled seven, and foreign companies controlled 16 (De Vroey, 1973; Rowley, 1974b). The Bad Homburg Group has confirmed this fact, if confirmation were needed. The Belgian intercorporate network of 1976 contained a very large structural center of 47 companies, far larger than any other European country. But the size of this center was almost entirely a consequence of the inclusion in the data set of the various holding and subholding companies in addition to parent and major operating companies. Many of the interlocks, that is to say, were within holdings and so resulted in the appearance of a large, dense center. The network center was dominated by the SGB and its affiliates, the main family holdings falling outside the large component – the center was virtually the SGB octopus itself. Virtually, though not exclusively: when the structure of the center itself was examined a number of distinct groupings could be discerned, each varying in its degree of overlap or affiliation with the SGB. Prominent amongst these were such groups as the Cobepa subsidiary of the French Paribas group and Electrobal, in which a number of groups participated. The most important group outside the large component was the Lambert family-controlled Bruxelles-Lambert, associated with the French Rothschilds.

Family control was the major factor in such groups as Coppée (Baron Coppée) and Electrorail (Baron Empain, a Belgian whose business was based in Paris until the late seventies), and other wealthy business families included

Böel, Solvay, Jansen, and de Launoit. The all-pervasive influence of the SGB was to be found mainly in coal, steel, and transport, though it invested in between 70 and 100 companies. Subholdings of the SGB included Sofina, Cockerill, Traction, eg. Electricité, Union Minière, Finoutremer, Sibeka, and many others. In addition to a significant number of foreign-controlled companies, there were participations by foreign interests in corporate ownership: Paribas and Lazard from France, Mediobanca (part of the IRI group) from Italy, and Imperial Continental Gas from Britain.

Belgium has an economic structure shaped by the activities of more or less tight groups of enterprises organized around focal enterprises. The major such group, the SGB, comprises a system of cross-shareholdings and a pattern of interlocking directorships which create a circle of control. The group is managed by a mix of financiers from the holding company itself, family shareholders, and "technocratic" executives.

The key factor in the recent development of Italy has been the increasingly active role of the state. State involvement in the economy was significantly increased under Mussolini and then again after the war. The state holding company Istituto per la Ricostruzione Industriale (IRI) was formed in 1929 and rescued three banks which had run into difficulties. In this way, the industrial participations of the universal banks were acquired by the state. Following later extensions of the public sector, the Italian state owned all of the electricity supply industry, and much of banking, communications, mining, metals, shipbuilding, and transport, and had important interests in mechanical engineering, chemicals, and cars. The Italian economy comprises a mixture of state and private holding companies, the dominant partner being the state. IRI owns three of the big four banks (Banca Commerciale Italiana, Credito Italiano, and Banca Roma), and directly or through subholding companies it participates in more than 150 other companies including Finsider, Finmeccanica, Italsider, Alfa Romeo, Aeritalia, and Alitalia. A second important state holding company, ENI, was formed in 1953 around the fascist oil company AGIP and is now a major force in the energy sector. Family wealth remains important and a number of private combines exist. The Agnelli family owns Fiat and has other industrial interests stretching from Cinzano to cement; the Pirellis are a major force in car tires and electrical cables; and the Pesenti family are involved in Italcementi, Bastogi, and in banks, newspapers, steel, and engineering (Earle, 1974). State and private capital jointly participate in the control of enterprises such as Zanussi, Olivetti, and Montedison. While showing some similarity to Belgium and France in the private sector, the Italian economy has no dominant private holding company such as Paribas, Suez, or SGB. Instead, there is a large public sector in which the former participations of the banking sector have been internalized.

The research of the Bad Homburg Group discovered that although there was a structural center of 21 enterprises, its core was extremely small. Further examination showed that two distinct structural centers could be identified, each with a higher density than the nominal center. One of these centers was based around state enterprises and included 21 heavily interlocked companies, tied together through various holding and subholding companies controlled by the state. The other structural center was composed of 14 private companies. Because the state used the device of a state holding company rather than monopoly public corporations, a distinct structure emerged. State and private enterprises rarely interlocked with one another, so the overall center was a purely nominal outcome of their infrequent connections (Chiesi, 1982).

The Italian network has moved from its prewar pattern to one in which the growth of the state sector has resulted in a certain degree of corporatism. But, unlike Austria, a powerful private sector has led to a division between the state and private industry. The case of France is useful for comparison here. Until the 1930s its economy was structurally similar to that of Belgium – the holding system prevailed – but a large state sector was built up after then. At the time of the researches of the Bad Homberg Group the French economy had a strong state sector within a predominantly private economy. The nationalization measures of 1981 have resulted in a state sector comparable to that found in Austria, but it is too early to assess the impact of this on network structure.

A number of banks and industrials were taken into public ownership during the 1930s, and the public sector was expanded during the fifties. The formation of a national plan required the state to take a highly interventionist role in which its numerous industrial participations were used as instruments in achieving the goals of the plan. Within the state sector and in the enterprises in which share ownership had become more dispersed, the role of those termed "technocrats" was strengthened. Educational credentials, especially a degree from one of the prestigious "grandes ecoles," became a crucial prerequisite for entry into many top executive positions (Granick, 1962: 38ff; Whitley, Thomas and Marceau, 1981). The largest firms which had some autonomy from the participating banks increasingly recruited such men to their top positions, and in these enterprises the overweening dominance of the bankers has waned somewhat. The enterprises were less likely to be tied to one particular holding (many were themselves major combines) and there were likely to be a number of banks and wealthy families participating in the share capital. The participating shareholders became coalitions of interests, and as the size of their holdings was reduced yet further they became looser constellations of shareholding interests (Morin, 1974).

The 1960s were an important period of transition in French business. An increasing number of firms adopted a strategy of diversification, and the "technocratic" enterprises increasingly adopted the multidivisional form of management. But the holding system remained of importance, often adopting more "conservative" strategies. Although they arose as a response to the massive capital requirements of late industrialization, the holdings have also been seen as a cultural response to the management of diversity – their form of administration allowed large diversified enterprises to be run without challenging the persistence of personal, family control (Dyas and Thanheiser, 1976: chs. 13 and 15; see also Caron, 1974, and Levy-Leboyer, 1980). France entered the 1970s with a significant state sector, but with the bulk of its economy being organized into more or less diverse groupings, some being family-controlled, some being bank-controlled, and an increasing number being controlled by loose constellations of interests.

In 1976 the state owned a number of major enterprises. It was a significant force in banking and insurance, it owned all utility, radio, television, coal, tobacco, rail and road transport companies, and it had considerable interests in vehicles, shipping, aerospace, oil, and chemicals. Outside the state sector a number of families remained important: Michelin, Dassault, De Wendel, Gillet, Empain, and Rothschild being amongst the leaders. The various groups at the head of French industry have been documented in *Dictionnaire* (Allard *et al*, 1978) and a great debate has taken place over the precise outlines and significance of the groups (see Sellier, 1974; Bleton, 1974; Chevalier, 1974; Simonnot, 1974; Bleton, 1976a and 1976b; Morin, 1974, 1976, 1977).

The work of the Bad Homburg Group has shown that the French network of interlocking directorships in 1976 had a clear structure but had no identifiable "center." The network was, instead, structured around the two largest private holding companies, Suez and Paribas. Each of these holding companies was at the center of a vast web of influence which encompassed a number of smaller groups and holding companies as well as some of the major "technocratic" enterprises. The Suez and Paribas webs overlapped with one another, often through their joint participation in the capital of the larger enterprises. Family holdings tended to remain outside these webs of influence, suggesting that the "personal" sector was separated from a sector dominated by more impersonal forms of ownership. Although the state was an important agent in the economy, there was little indication that this was associated with the formation of a distinct state web of influence: the intercorporate network was essentially a network dominated by private propertied interests.

The election of a Socialist government in 1981 has disrupted this pattern and there is little indication of what the emerging forms of intercorporate structure might look like. The state has taken over the rest of the banking system, major industrial companies, and both of the leading holding companies. Despite political wranglings and attempts to undermine the Socialist strategy, the acquisition of Suez and Paribas gave the state a large number of industrial participations to add to its portfolio of investments. The implications of this massive shift in ownership and control are still being worked through in practice, let alone in theory, and a clear picture has not yet emerged. The two large engineering firms owned by the state have engaged in an exchange of assets to create a single dominant state enterprise in each of the telecommunications and electrical engineering industries. To the extent that other state enterprises and participations are used in the same way, the structure of the intercorporate network will be radically transformed. This might involve a shift towards the formation of a unified state sector, as in Italy, or even Austria, or it might eventuate in a number of structurally isolated public monopolies as in Britain. The former is perhaps the most likely possibility, as the state has control of virtually the whole financial sector and this might be expected to form the basis of some kind of corporatist strategy.

Conclusion

The discussion in this chapter has tried to show the ways in which contemporary business structures are shaped by the patterns of industrialization and routes to late capitalism followed by the various countries. But these variations have taken place within the common framework of the structuring mechanisms of late capitalism. A major conclusion is that behind all the diversity is a common move towards bank hegemony of a loosely structured kind. The units of finance capital may be diversified enterprises, combines, or spheres of influence, but these typically operate within a corporate environment which is structured by the hegemonic position of banks. While the universal banks have tended to become less overweening, the commercial or retail banks have tended to take on a greater role in the provision of long-term capital. As a result the loosening of the German system has been matched by the tightening of the British system. Only in Belgium has the historical legacy of the holding system survived intact, and this may perhaps be ascribed to the uniquely powerful position held by the SGB in the Belgian economy.

The major factor countering this move toward bank hegemony is a factor which was deliberately excluded from the model presented earlier: the state. Although the state played an important role in the economic development of the late industrializers, and it was by no means unimportant in Britain, the state has become of particular significance only in the postwar period. Austria, Italy, and France all have substantial state sectors and in each case the emerging corporatist structures are centered around state control over the major banks. In Germany and Britain, the only other countries to have a significant number of state enterprises, state-controlled banking is conspicuous by its absence. In Germany VEBA and RWE are important state enterprises in chemicals, oil, mining, and electricity, and there is a state holding in Volkswagen, but in none of these does the federal state have complete ownership. Apart from the regional banks in which the Lander states have holdings, there is no real state participation in the financial sector. In Britain the central bank is in public hands, but no commercial banks or insurance companies have been nationalized. Nevertheless, Britain does have a large state sector. The British state enterprises typically take the form of monopoly corporations operating in single industries and there is little basis for any coordination of their activities. In those countries where the state has not made inroads into the banking sector, bank hegemony remains the norm.

A final word must be said about the role of foreign ownership in the European economies, although this is discussed more fully in the chapter by Fennema. Foreign subsidiaries within a national business network tend to be isolated or peripheral, and the presence of a high level of foreign penetration in an economy tends to lower the density and connectedness of the network. As more enterprises cross national boundaries and become major forces in foreign markets, it must be expected that both bank hegemony and corporatism will come under challenge. Much work has been carried out on the relative power of multinationals and the state, though virtually nothing has been written on the relative power of multinationals and the banks. Such issues must become of increasing importance as European multinationals become more active within Europe and as the already high degree of American penetration is matched by higher levels of Japanese involvement.

NOTES

1 The Bad Homburg Group was supported by the European Consortium for Political Research, the Wernher Reimers Stiftung, and various national research councils as well as the host universities and institutes. The results which will be discussed here are drawn from the national chapters published in Stokman, Ziegler, and Scott (1985), the participants having agreed to an embargo on publication until after the production of that volume. The colleagues upon whose work I draw are: Austria and Germany (Rolf Ziegler, Donald Bender, Herman Biehler, Gerhard Reissner), Belgium (Ludo Cuyvers and Wim Meeusen), France (David Swartz), Great Britain (myself and Catherine Griff), Italy (Antonio Chiesi), the Netherlands (Frans Stokman, Donald Elsas, Frans Wasseur), Switzerland (Peter Rusterholz).

2 As argued in Scott (1982b), Britain was a capitalist society well before it was an industrial society, so the term "early capitalism" is strictly a misnomer if applied to early industrial capitalism. With this caveat, the term is retained as a useful shorthand.

REFERENCES

Beaud, M., Bellon, B., Levy, A.-M., and Lienart, S. Allard, P., 1978. *Dictionnaire des groupes industriels et financiers en France.* Paris: Editions du Seuil

Bleton, P., 1974. "L'argent: pouvoir ambigu." *Economie et Humanisme*, 220: 18–31

1976a. "Le capitalisme français à l'ombre de l'université." *Economie et Humanisme*, 229: 6–20

1976b. "Bons concepts et méchantes realités." *Economie et Humanisme*, 229: 33–4

Cafagna, L., 1971. "Italy, 1830–1914." In Cipolla (1973b), pp. 279–328

Caron, F., 1974. "Investment strategy in France." In Daems and van der Wee (1974), pp. 96–144

Chandler, A. D., and Daems, H., 1980. *Managerial Hierarchies*. Cambridge, Mass.: Harvard University Press

Chevalier, J.-M., 1974. "La domination des firmes industrielles par les banques." *Economie et Humanisme*, 220, 32–7

Chiesi, A. M., 1982. "L'elite finanziaria Italiana." *Rassegna Italiana di Sociologia*, 23: 571–95

Cipolla, C., 1973a. *The Fontana Economic History of Europe*, Vol. 3. London: Fontana

1973b. *The Fontana Economic History of Europe*, Vol. 4, Part 1. London: Fontana

Cornwall, R., 1974. "France: the mask of modernity." In Rowley (1974a), pp. 5–22

Cuyvers, L., and Meeusen, W., 1976. "The structure of personal influence in the Belgian holding companies." *European Economic Review*, 8: 51–69

Daems, H., 1978. *The Holding Company and Corporate Control*. Leiden: Martinus Nijhof

Daems, H., and van der Wee, H. (eds.), 1974. *The Rise of Managerial Capitalism*. The Hague: Martinus Nijhof

De Vroey, M., 1973. *Propriété et pouvoir dans les grandes entreprises*. Brussels: CRISP

Deane, P., 1967. *The First Industrial Revolution*. Cambridge University Press

Dhondt, J., and Bruwier, M., 1970. "The Low Countries, 1700–1914." In Cipolla (1973b), pp. 329–66

Dyas, G. P., and Thanheiser, H. T., 1976. *The Emerging European Enterprise*. London: George Allen and Unwin

Earle, J., 1974. "Italy: the dominance of state corporations." In Rowley (1974a), pp. 47–65

Fohlen, C., 1970. "France, 1700–1914." In Cipolla (1973b), pp. 7–75

Gershenkron, A., 1962. *Economic Backwardness in Historical Perspective*. Cambridge, Mass.: Belknap Press

Gille, B., 1970. "Banking and industrialisation in Europe, 1730–1914." In Cipolla (1973a), pp. 255–300

Granick, D., 1962. *The European Executive*. New York: Doubleday

Habermas, J., 1976. *Legitimation Crisis*. London: Heinemann

Hannah, L., 1976. *The Rise of the Corporate Economy*. London: Methuen

Henderson, W. O., 1961. *The Industrial Revolution in Europe*. Chicago: Quadrangle

Hilferding, R., 1910. *Finance Capital*. London: Routledge and Kegan Paul, 1980

Kemp, T., 1978. *Historical Patterns of Industrialisation*. London: Longman

Kitchen, M., 1978. *The Political Economy of Germany, 1815–1914*. London: Croom Helm

Kocka, J., 1980. "The rise of the modern industrial enterprise in Germany." In Chandler and Daems (1980), pp. 77–116

Krejci, J., 1976. *Social Structure in Divided Germany*. London: Croom Helm

Landes, D. S., 1969. *The Unbound Prometheus*. Cambridge University Press

Levy-Leboyer, M., 1980. "The large corporation in modern France." In Chandler and Daems (1980), pp. 117–60

Mathias, P., 1969. *The First Industrial Nation*. London: Methuen

Mintz, B., and Schwartz, M., 1985. *The Power Structure of American Business*. University of Chicago Press

Mizruchi, M. S., 1982. *The American Corporate Network, 1904–1974*. Beverly Hills: Sage

Morin, F., 1974. "Qui détient le pouvoir financier en France." *Economie et Humanisme*, 220: 5–10

  1976. "Ombres et lumières du capitalisme français." *Economie et Humanisme*, 229: 21–32

  1977. *La banque et les groupes industriele à l'heure des nationalisations*. Paris: Calmann-Levy

Palmade, G. P., 1961. *French Capitalism in the Nineteenth Century*. Newton Abbot: David and Charles, 1972

Rostow, W., 1960. *The Stages of Economic Growth*. Cambridge University Press

Rowley, R. (ed.), 1974. *The Barons of European Industry*. London; Croom Helm

  1974b. "Belgium and Luxembourg: the power of les Holdings." In Rowley (1974a), pp. 104–24

Rutherford, M., 1974. "West Germany: people before profits." In Rowley (1974a), pp. 23–46

Scott, J. P., 1979. *Corporations, Classes and Capitalism*. London: Hutchinson, rev. edn, 1985

  1982a. "Property and control." In A. Giddens and G. Mackenzie (eds.), *Social class and the Division of Labour*. Cambridge University Press, pp. 228–47

  1982b. *The Upper Classes*. London: Macmillan

Scott, J. P., and Griff, C., 1984. *Directors of Industry*. Cambridge: Polity Press

Sellier, F., 1974. "Les banques et l'industrie américaine." *Economie et Humanisme*, 220: 11–17

Simonnot, P., 1974. "Du pouvoir bancaire en France." *Economie et Humanisme*, 220: 38–43

Smith, D., 1978. "Domination and containment." *Comparative Studies in Society and History*, 20: 177–213

Stokman, F., Ziegler, R., and Scott, J. P. (eds.), 1985. *Networks of Corporate Power: An Analysis of Ten Countries*. Cambridge, England: Polity Press

Tilly, R., 1974. "The growth of large scale enterprise in Germany since the middle of the nineteenth century." In Daems and van der Wee (1974), pp. 145–69

Wallerstein, I., 1974. *The Modern World System*. New York: Academic Press

Whitley, R., Thomas, A. B., and Marceau, J., 1981. *Masters of Business?* London: Tavistock

Zeitlin, M., 1974. "Corporate ownership and control: the large corporation and the capitalist class." *American Journal of Sociology*, 79: 1073–119

8

The articulation of power and business structures: a study of Colombia

Enrique Ogliastri and Carlos Dávila

Introduction[1]

By approaching business structure as a component of social structure, the present chapter analyzes the hegemony of business in the local and regional development of a Latin American nation (Colombia), as well as the relationships between public and private (business) elites. In the authors' view these are critical issues for the structural analysis of business, in particular in developing nations, and represent a needed complement to approaches centered upon economic concentration and market structure, the role of foreign investment, and internationalization of capital or corporate structure.

This chapter is part of a research project on power structure, class and economic development in the mid-seventies, carried out by the authors in urban Colombia. It covers eleven Colombian cities in the 100,000–500,000 population range. We begin by sketching the outlines of Colombian political economy. We then discuss the background of the study of business and power structures in Latin America, and in Colombia in particular, and the conceptual and theoretical orientations of the present research.

Empirical results are then examined in four parts: the class basis for the composition of the power structure; the fractions within business; the concentration of power in terms of interlocking directorates; and the cleavage of public and business sectors. The final section presents our general conclusions.

Some features of Colombian politics and economy

Located in the northwest corner of South America, Colombia is the third most populous country in Latin America, ranking behind Brazil and Mexico. In 1983 it had a population of 28 million. Its 1,141,748 sq. km. area exhibits important regional variations which reflect geographical, economic, and historical differences (Fajardo, 1978; Jaramillo, 1983: 191–4).

Most significantly, Colombia has an urban network different from the primate-city model characteristic of most Latin American countries. "Country of cities" – 3 of them over 1 million, 2 between 500,000 and 1 million, and 17 between 100,000 and 500,000 – an "urbanization of the economy" that reversed the rural–urban composition of the population has taken place in the last thirty years. By 1983, urban areas accounted for 66 per cent of the population in contrast to 39 per cent in 1951 (Flórez and Gonzáles, 1983: 45–6, 53–7).

The eleven cities covered in this study are part of the 15 *ciudades intermedias*, (middle-size cities of 100,000–500,000 population) that are at the same time *capitales de departamento* (state capitals or capital towns). The political and administrative structure in which the several states, their capitals and the rest of municipalities are embedded is one of a centralized state with a dominant executive branch. The constitutional principle of "political centralization and administrative decentralization" has in reality evolved towards centralization in both spheres.

The increasing centralism in the national level, or centralism in the country's capital, has taken place at the expense of the *departamentos* (states) and the municipalities, which have lost functions they held in the past (for example local police, education, and health). At the same time, the need for infrastructure and public works, growing state intervention in the economy, and the increase in social services expenditure have been conducive to the proliferation of central government agencies (paradoxically called "decentralized" institutes), in whose hands rest most development projects (Tirado, 1983: 63–4). Concurrent with this centralization of functions and loss of regional and local autonomy has been a progressive concentration of public revenues at the *gobierno nacional* (national government) level: municipal and state revenues amounted to 18 per cent of national tax revenues in 1978 in comparison to 36 per cent in 1967 and 50 per cent in 1945 (Ocampo, 1982: 56–7). At the same time policies have evolved in the past fifteen years which are oriented towards decentralization of some activities, particularly in middle-size cities where regional disparities in development are most pronounced. However, these have lacked continuity and have shown a short-run and pendular character (Reveiz and Montenegro, 1983: 151–3; Kruijt, Maiguashca, and Vellinga, 1983: ch. 2). In the early 1980s several proposals for decentralization were presented by various political sectors as well as by the administration, but were not enacted into law (Botero, 1983).

This reference to some features of the political structure is relevant for the analysis of the role of business structure in the development of the cities under consideration. The formal institutional context in which business operates suggests the need to provide an account of the ways business actors (individuals, firms, groups, and associations) have developed arrangements to cope with centralism, to obtain leverage in the national structure of power, and to strive to impose their interests in local and regional development.

These arrangements constitute important aspects of business structures that require empirical examination.

We now turn to an overview of the relevant features of the Colombian economy. Like other Latin American countries, Colombia is a backward, dependent capitalist society. The economy is predominantly based on the primary sector; coffee has played a leading role since the last decade of the nineteenth century. In 1979 it still represented about 60 per cent of Colombian exports, despite increasing industrialization which in 1980 amounted to 18 per cent of gross domestic product (Banco de la República, 1982: 40). Large *Cafeteros* (coffee growers and exporters) have enjoyed a noted influence in economic policy, channeled through their associational interest group, Fedecafé, founded in 1927. Although Fedecafé has been the subject of scholarly works (e.g. Koffman, 1969; Urrutia, 1983) and a matter of public controversy, its relationship to local business and politics has not been studied. Of particular interest is a comparison of these issues among coffee towns (three of the cities of our sample) and between these and non-coffee centers of similar size.

Although industry is concentrated in the three largest cities of the country, regional industrialization has taken place in the middle-size cities, which now contribute about 30 per cent of value-added and industrial employment (Flórez and Gonzalés, 1983: tables, 9, 10, and 11a) and play a critical role in regional and low-income markets. Colombian industrial structure, which has remained stable for the 1965–80 period in terms of concentration and specialization, is clearly related to urban structure as the pattern of the concentration of population (or hierarchical pattern of urban structure) reveals it (Reveiz and Montenegro, 1983: 125–33). The comparison between the industrial and non-industrial cities of our sample allows us to examine changes in the role of business in local life as urban centers grow and industrialize, and to explore the intermingling of the interests of merchants, landowners, cattle-ranchers and incipient industrialists. A notable feature of Colombian industrialization has been the coalescence of these classes into a power bloc (Misas, 1983: 26).

Foreign investment in industry, which increased rapidly after 1960, has been directed towards high-technology and capital-intensive sectors (Corchuelo and Misas, 1977: Ayala *et al.*, 1978), for the most part located in the three largest cities of the country. The eleven cities of our study therefore have little foreign investment with two notable exceptions (Cartagena and Pereira). The inclusion of these cities allows us to assess the influence of foreign capital in local affairs and its relationship to the national and international centers of power as a component of local business structure.

Perhaps the most important evolution in the Colombian economy during the last decade has been the rapid growth of the financial sector and the increase in the exports of marijuana and cocaine. The expansion of the financial sector (banks, investment funds, insurance companies, specialized financial intermediaries, etc.) during the 1970–9 period was 12 per cent, well above the 6 per cent growth of the economy as a whole (Caicedo, 1982; Reveiz and Montenegro, 1983). Trade in marijuana and cocaine has led to an important, even if illegal, economic activity whose effects have not been assessed. An estimate indicates that these exports amounted to $3,200 million in 1979, slightly below the total of the country's registered exports (Kline, 1983: 100). At the same time, as a result of capital accumulated in industry and commerce, financial conglomerates emerged and became the most powerful fraction of the bourgeoisie. A "financial oligarchy" resulted from this process of centralization of capital (Camacho, 1977; Silva, 1983: 188). Since none of the cities of the sample was a financial center of national importance, this centralization of development projects was conducive to their articulation into national and international financial centers. The nature of these relationships is another factor in local business structure.

In sum, the dominant role of coffee, industrial concentration, the minor role of foreign investment in regional industry, and the increasing importance of the financial sector constitute the critical characteristics of the Colombian economy germane to the analysis of regional and local business structures.

The study of power and business structure

The study of the relationships between power and business structures has not constituted a distinct field in Latin American social science. It is part of at least two different areas of scholarly endeavor: the sociology of power and elites and the analysis of industrialization. Power studies have examined the configuration of power structures either at the national or local level, mostly focussing upon the top of the structure – i.e. the elite. For the most part, they have evidenced the individualistic bias and neglect of social structure present in the field of power in American sociology and political science (Walton, 1971; 1977: 78).

In either of these fields the diversity of competing theoretical orientations – most notably "modernization" approaches, dependency, and varieties of Marxism – has not led to convergent interpretations but rather disparate and scattered findings. This is evident not only in the early, more general interpretations of Latin American underdevelopment (e.g. Lipset, 1967; Frank, 1967) but also in more recent literature on specific countries. The recent studies of Smith (1979) on Mexico's "power elite," McDonough (1981) on the role of Brazil's power structure and elite ideologies in undermining the authoritarian regime, and Becker (1983) on connections among Peru's mining transnationals, class and power in the 1968–80 period illustrate this problem. Although all three are rigorous scholarly works, as a whole they do not elaborate a coherent set of propositions on power and business structures which are useful in understanding diverse Latin American countries on a general level.

Under these circumstances, we restrict our review of relevant research to Colombia. For the most part, power analyses have been devoted to general characterizations of the country's political system. The continuity of electoral democracy, the absence of military dictatorships, the centralization yet relative weakness of the state (as compared to countries like Mexico or Brazil), and the endurance of the two-party system are characteristics stressed by authors with a variety of viewpoints. Despite this agreement, however, these patterns are interpreted in quite different ways: as an expression of elite-dominated economic development (Dix, 1967; Kline, 1983), elitist pluralism (Bailey, 1977), bourgeois democracy (Therborn, 1979), oligarchic democracy (Wilde, 1978), and elitist democracy (Cardoso and Faletto, 1979). The general level of discourse has prevented an empirical confrontation and resolution of the theoretical differences among these authors.

Studies on local and regional power are scarce; and most of them have been analyzed in Walton's systematic review of 20 community power studies carried out in Latin America. Walton concluded that though "the evidence is equivocal, larger, urbanizing cities tended to have more competitive structures of power" (1976: 160). In contrast to cities whose economic base is commercial and industrial, rural towns, whose wealth is mainly agricultural, are characterized by centralized, closed elites. This is one of the hypotheses that is being examined in the present study.

A second issue of study is the class composition at the top of the power structure. Typically, urban power and elite studies ignore class structure (Walton, 1976: 134; Dávila, 1976: 41–8; Whitt, 1979). On the other hand, the analysis of Colombian business structure via capital concentration (Camacho, 1977; Silva, 1977), monopoly capital (Misas, 1975, 1983), and the internationalization of capital in industry (Corchuelo and Misas, 1977) have not dealt with these phenomena at the regional and local level. The present study began the exploration of class interests represented by local elites and top organizations and groups and their linkages to the national structure of power.

Finally, a third unresolved issue concerns the relationship between economic and public elites. Rather than conceiving this as "cooperation" in the manner of Dent's (1973) study of two Colombian cities, we seek to ascertain whether power is fragmented between the public (state) and the private (business) sector.

In this intranation comparative study, the same research design and methodology were followed in each of the eleven cities studied. A study of the city of Bucaramanga established and tested the methodology (Dávila and Ogliastri, 1972; Ogliastri, 1973). Under the direction of the authors, the city of

Villavicencio was studied by Salazar (1974); Cartagena by Mogollón (1974); Pereira by Saldarriaga (1974); Cúcuta by García (1975); Pasto by Viveros (1975); Manizales by Vélez (1975); Armenia by Alvarez (1975); Popayán by De Angulo (1975); Barranquilla by Abello (1975); and Neiva by Muñoz (1976). A comparative analysis of eight of these cities was carried out by Dávila (1976).

We use the concept *power* in the Weberian sense as the capacity of social agents to impose their interests, if necessary in opposition to other agents (Weber, 1947: 180). It is a capacity for social control, and we specify that it derives from a variety of sources: property, position, and access to decisions, as well as the reputation for access to these sources of power. We focus here on power in the realm of economic development.

The *power structure* is composed of a number of elements and the patterns of relationships among them. The elements we consider are: stratification of power (focussed upon top agents of power at the organizational, personal, group, and class level); power concentration; alliances or cleavages among them; underlying class interests and the process of change in the power situation.

Local and regional power structures are articulated into the national power structure, through linkages of a varied nature – economic, organizational, and governmental. For this study, individuals, families, groups and organizations are all considered as agents of power and therefore subjects for empirical investigation.

In each city we first consulted knowledgeable "judges" for a list of the largest and most prominent organizations involved in economic development. We conducted personal interviews with the heads of these organizations and, using a structured questionnaire, we obtained detailed information on the power structure, inquired about their appraisal of the prospects for the development of the city, and about their own personal background. One of the questions about power asked each subject to identify "the most influential persons, groups, and organizations concerned with the development of the city." In this way it was possible to identify those having personal, albeit not necessarily positional, power. The interviews also revealed those who had participated in projects familiar to the respondents. Finally, we investigated in detail the decision-making history for the five largest and most important projects in the city during the decade. Through a combination of these four criteria we selected the 515 interviewees and obtained, for each city, rank order stratifications of powerful organizations, persons, groups, and extralocal organizations. To facilitate a comparison among the cities, we labelled the most powerful 19 persons of each city as the "top elite," and the rest of the persons interviewed we termed "intermediate elite."

This method combined the standard methodologies of position (Schulze and Blumberg, 1957) and interlocking positions (Walton, 1971), reputation (Hunter, 1953), decision-making, and participation (Dahl, 1961), to provide a comprehensive portrait of power among individuals, groups, organizations, and extra-local agents of power.

The findings are organized as follows. The composition of the power structure is initially analyzed, focussing on the social classes represented in the top elite as well as the existence of industrial, commercial, agribusiness, etc. fractions of capital. Concentration of power is then measured, using interlocking directorates, and elite mobility is assessed. Finally, the degree of cleavage between public and private (business) sectors of the elite is assessed.

Empirical findings

The assertion has recently been made, in an analysis of power in a Latin American country, that the object of power studies "is not to discover the power structure, as if there were serious doubts about its existence or even much mystery about its composition" (McDonough, 1981: 17). We have found, on the contrary, that it is indeed relevant, and that it provides a matter for controversy.

To analyze the power structure we identified top local organizations on the basis of their power. For that purpose we used four power indicators: position (or power bestowed by influential directors), reputation participation, and decision-making in development projects. For each indicator a rank-ordered list of organizations was prepared. Then the four indexes were combined into an overall power index, which permitted a ranking of the top local organizations; a cutoff point of 10 was used. This power stratification list (table 8.1) is a summary of the final lists of the ten top organizations for the cities under investigation, in which the computational details are omitted. To facilitate the analysis, the results of table 8.1 were then tabulated according to their public/private nature (table 8.2).

Table 8.1 indicates the total absence of local organizations representing working-class interests among the 110 top organizations (ten organizations for each of eleven cities). Labor unions are not present (a finding consistent with labor union weakness in the country as a whole, e.g. Ayala and Fonseca, 1981), nor are cooperatives, committees of community action in the poor areas of these cities, or popular associations of small and "micro" business that coexist with the modern capitalist economy. Even petty bourgeois groups and their organizations (small merchants, associations of professionals, teachers and the like) are excluded from the top ranks of power. All this points out the domination of the organizations of the big and middle bourgeoisie.

This finding is consistent with the class position of the members of the top elite, as shown in table 8.3, which includes the power stratification for the top ten individuals. This was determined by a procedure analogous to that followed in the case of organizations. The power indicators used were

Table 8.1 *Top organizations by combined power rank in eleven cities*

Rank	Barranquilla	Bucaramanga	Cartagena	Manizales	Pereira	Armenia	Cúcuta	Pasto	Neiva	Popayán	Villavicencio
1	Chamber of commerce	Industrialists' association (ANDI)	Chamber of commerce	Local financial corporation	Local finance corporation	Coffee growers' association	Local financial corporation	Chamber of commerce	State government	Local bank	Municipal services public corporation
2	Local financial corporation	Chamber of commerce	Industrialists' association (ANDI)	Local bank	City Council	Municipal valorization office	Chamber of commerce	Merchants' association (FENALCO)	Municipal government	Industrial firm	State government
3	National service corporation	Local financial corporation	Municipal services public corporation	Industrial firm (textiles)	Industrialists' association (ANDI)	State government	Civic action association	State government	"The banks" (unspecified)	State government	Cattlemen's association
4	Industrialists' association (ANDI)	State industry	Municipal government	Coffee growers' association	Chamber of commerce	Regional development corporation	Merchants association (FENALCO)	Municipal government	State university	Municipal council	City council
5	Electrification company	State government	City council	Industrialists' association (ANDI)	Municipal government	Industrial and agricultural	State university	State university	Municipal service corporation	State university	State valorization office
6	Free trade zone	Merchants' association (FENALCO)	Regional development corporation	Industrialists' group ("Azucenos")	Municipal services public corporation	Municipal service corporation	State government	Junior chamber	National housing institute (ICT)	Industrial firm	Chamber of commerce
7	Industrial firm	Populist party (ANAPO)	Electrification company	National coffee bank	State university	Municipal government	Coffee growers' association	Lions' club	National education service (SENA)	Chamber of commerce	Lions' club
8	Private university	Municipal government	Merchants' association (FENALCO)	Municipal valorization office	Public works association	National housing institute	Sugar producers' association	Refinery promotion committee	Electrification company	Electrification company	Municipal government
9	Merchants' association (FENALCO)	Local bank	State university	Municipal government	Municipal valorization office	State lottery	Municipal services public corporation	National government	Sports committee	City council	Merchants' association (ASCILLANOS)
10	Financial group	Local liberal newspaper	Construction industry association (CAMACOL)	Chamber of commerce	Regional development corporation	State planning office	National Agricultural Credit Bank	"The banks" (unspecified)	National Agricultural Credit Bank	National education service (SENA)	"The banks" (unspecified)

Table 8.2 *Ten top organizations by combined power rank in eleven cities*

Organization	Barranquila	Bucaramanga	Cartagena	Manizales	Pereira	Cúcuta	Subtotal largest cities	Armenia	Pasto	Neiva	Popayán	Villavicencio	Subtotal smallest cities	Total
Private														
Systemic, business association	4	3	5	4	4	5	25	2	2	—	1	3	8	33
Bank & finance	2	2	—	3	1	1	9	—	1	1	1	1	4	13
Manufacturing firm	1	—	—	1	—	—	2	—	—	—	2	—	2	4
Private university	1	—	—	—	—	—	1	—	1	—	—	1	1	2
Other	—	1	—	—	—	—	1	—	2	—	—	1	3	4
Total	8	6	5	8	5	6	38 (63.3%)	2	6	1	4	5	18 (36.0%)	56 (50.9%)
Public														
National government agency	—	—	—	—	—	—	—	1	1	2	1	—	5	5
Bank and finance	—	—	—	—	—	1	1	—	—	1	—	—	1	2
Public service enterprises (local, regional)	2	—	2	—	1	1	6	2	—	2	1	1	6	12
State, local government agency	—	2	1	2	2	1	8	5	2	3	2	3	15	23
City council	—	1	1	—	—	—	2	—	—	—	1	1	2	4
Political party	—	—	—	—	1	—	1	—	—	—	—	—	—	1
State university	—	1	1	—	1	1	4	—	1	1	1	—	3	7
Total	2	4	5	2	5	4	22 (36.7%)	8	4	9	6	5	32 (64.0%)	54 (49.1%)
							60 (100.0%)						50 (100.0%)	110 (100.0%)

Table 8.3 *Top individuals by combined power rank in eleven cities*

Rank	Barranquilla	Bucaramanga	Cartagena	Manizales	Pereira	Armenia	Cúcuta	Pasto	Neiva	Popayán	Villavicencio
1	Governor, conservative politician	Financier, industrialists	Industrialist, ex-mayor, ex-vice-minister	Industrialist, merchant, "Cafetero", "Azuceno"	Industrial promoter, agriculturalist	Mayor, lawyer	President, financial corp.	Civic promoter, bank official (Bogota)	Liberal senator, lawyer	Director, federal electrification agency	engineer, ex-mayor
2	Financier, industrialist	Construction industrialist	Governor, ex-mayor, industrialist	Industrialist, president financial corp.	Liberal senator, ex-governor	Governor	Manager, agribusiness, cattleman	Deputy, chamber of commerce	Conservative politician, MD	President, local bank, ex-governor	Minister, liberal senator
3	President, financial corporation	Industrialist, promoter	Liberal congressman, president public co.	Mayor, coffee exporter	Mayor, merchant	President, coffee growers', ex-mayor, MD	National minister, ex-governor	ex-national minister, MD	Liberal congressman, MD	Mayor, engineer	President, cattlemen's association
4	Industrialist	Industrialist, merchant	Industrialist, ANDI's president	Industrialist	President, financial corp	Liberal, senator, ex-governor, agriculturalist	ex-national minister, financier	Liberal politician	Mayor, architect	Engineer, ex-vice-minister, ex-governor	Government official, ex-governor, cattleman
5	Liberal politician, industrialist	Newspaper owner, liberal politician	Mayor, MD	President, Insurance co., "cafetero"	Industrial promoter	Vice-minister	President, civic action association, engineer	Manager, commercial firm	Conservative congressman, lawyer	Industrialist, promoter	Conservative politician
6	Conservative politician, industrialist	Director, waterworks, MD	President, chamber of commerce	Director, municipal valorization	Governor, engineer	Director, industrial and agricultural development corp.	Liberal senator, lawyer	Congressman, ex-mayor	Engineer, agriculturalist	Official national coffee association, ex-mayor	Cattleman, economist
7	Liberal politician, industrialist	Governor, conservative politician	Minister's deputy, ex-manager	President, local bank	ANDI's president, engineer	Merchant, cattleman	President, chamber of commerce, industrialist	Conservative senator	Governor, engineer	Governor, lawyer	Engineer, ex-governor
8	Urbanist	Liberal congressman	Conservative congressman	Conservative congressman, newspaper owner	Industrialist, merchant	Ex-governor, agriculturalist, architect	FENALCO's president, merchant	manager, commercial firm	Industrialist	Director, electrification company	Director, health service, ex-governor
9	Director, free trade zone	Liberal politician	Industrialist, merchant	Industrialist, merchant, "Cafetero", "Azuceno"	Dir. national development corp., engineer	Ex-governor, lawyer	Conservative senator, ex-minister	Merchant, industrialist	Liberal congressman, lawyer	Communist politician, university prof.	Lawyer, ex-governor
10	Liberal politician, merchant	ANAPO, alderman, MD	Director municipal services corporation	Industrialist, merchant, agriculturalist, "Azuceno"	Official financial corp., lawyer	Deputy, chamber of commerce	Industrialist, ex-governor	Conservative congressman	Industrialist, engineer	Liberal senator, ex-governor, cattleman	Agriculturalist, merchant, ex-conservative politician

Table 8.4 *Power and social class position*
(per cent)

| | Power rank | |
Social class	Middle elite	Top elite
Upper bourgeoisie	30	50
Middle bourgeoisie	48	41
Petty bourgeoisie	22	9
Total	100	100

Source: Ogliastri, 1983b: table 1, p. 5.

positions – occupying either chief executive jobs or being a member of the board of directors of local organizations ranked according to their reputation for power – participation in projects, key decision-making roles in the five most important local development projects, and an individual's reputation for power.

Table 8.4 demonstrates that half of the "top elite" (see p. 238) are made up of the "big bourgeoisie" and 41 per cent belong to the middle bourgeoisie.[2] In other words, 90 per cent of the top elite belong to the capitalist class: only 9 per cent are petty bourgeois and none is a worker: urban labor leaders are excluded from the top ranks of local power. Even the middle elite (78 per cent) is dominated by capitalists.

The predominance of organizations representing upper bourgeoisie interests is more marked in larger cities than smaller ones. Chambers of commerce, large industrialists' associations, merchants' associations, the large coffee-growers' association, industrial promotion foundations, and banks and financial corporations are the top organizations in the six larger cities. They represent 38 (or 63 per cent) of the top local organizations, markedly outweighing public ones (table 8.2).

In the smaller commerce and agriculture-based cities the public sector, rather than business organizations, tends to predominate. This includes municipal and state government, planning, valorization and public services enterprises, and state universities as well as regional offices of the national government "decentralized institutes." In all they add up to 22 (or 37 per cent) of top-rank local organizations. The exception is the old city of Pasto, a traditional agricultural and commercial center near the border with Ecuador.

These findings indicate that the coalition of big business and private interests strengthens as cities become industrialized, whereas the power of the state and public sector is the leading force in smaller cities. We believe that this pattern reflects the fact that economic growth and urban development force intercity competition for centralized public funds. This creates business activism in large cities, while business interests in backward cities are unmotivated and insufficiently developed to overcome traditional patterns of class rule rooted in the ownership of large estates, extensive cattle-raising, traditional technology and, in general, precapitalist social relations of production. This pattern is particularly clear in two of the cities of our study, which were important colonial centers and today remain stagnant.

Cities with an agricultural-based growth (Neiva and Villavicencio) exhibit a different pattern. As capitalist relations generalize to the surrounding area through the development of modern, commercial agriculture, commerce also enlarges its scale. Despite the articulation of agricultural interests into associations of cattlemen and producers of particular crops (e.g. rice, cotton, cocoa), their political role remains restricted on city-wide issues. Politicians and public officials as well as public sector organizations retain the major power. It seems that neither major urban development problems nor prospects for industrialization arise yet as critical issues to congregate private sector interests. In fact, industrialists' associations or industrial promotion institutions do not exist in these cities.

Class fractions, particularly finance capital, were important in delineating the patterns of classical capitalist development. We find little evidence of a distinct financial fraction among the members of the top power structure in these cities (see tables 8.1 and 8.2). Though there are financiers in the top echelons, their number is not large enough to constitute a group: they sum eleven (or 10 per cent) among the total 110 individuals constituting the top power ranks. For the most part (nine out of eleven) they are active on the larger cities (table 8.3). In terms of organizations the picture is the same: banks and financial corporations amount to 13, or 12 per cent of the total (table 8.2). In any case, it should be recalled that the financial sector is highly centralized in the country as a whole, and there exists a process of internal colonialism in which capital accumulation in intermediate cities is transferred to Bogotá, Medellín and Cali.

We found industrial, commercial, agricultural, and livestock economic interests in the power structure of the cities. How distinctive are these class fractions? Contrary to the classical pattern of capital development in Europe (Huberman, 1975; Prieto, 1980), a sequential development of these social classes did not occur in Colombia. Original capital made in gold mining, farming and commerce was invested in a wide range of other enterprises by families and individuals in some regions during the nineteenth century. When coffee became the most important export, import–export merchants, smaller bankers, mining firms, and organizers of land colonization enterprises were all attracted by this successful product (Brew, 1977). In addition, since the origins of industrialization and economic development these highly diversified *negociantes* (complete businessmen) have been very active in politics and public issues, representing a feature of the Colombian political economy (Dávila, 1985).

Table 8.5 *Interrelationships of investments among business fractions (per cent)*

Fraction	Investment in			
	Industry	Commerce	Agriculture	Cattle-ranching
Industrialists	—	42	30	31
Merchants	46	—	30	42
Agriculturalists	30	28	—	51
Cattlemen	30	38	45	—

Note: This table refers to 171 top individuals – i.e. the top 19 for nine cities; data for Manizales and Pasto are missing. Because of diversification of investments among these individuals, the total number of investments amount to 394: 100 in industry, 92 in commerce, 98 in agriculture and 104 in livestock.

On the basis of its principal investment, each person was classified in one of the fractions, e.g. industrialist; 42% of the industrialists also have investments in commerce; 30% in agriculture; and 31% in cattle-ranching.

Taken from Ogliastri and Guerra, 1980: table IV-I, p. 1644.

Our findings show the continuity of this pattern in the contemporary scene, at least in these middle-size cities (table 8.5).

Table 8.5 indicates, for example, that 51 per cent of farmers also have investments in cattle businesses, 42 per cent of industrialists have an investment in commerce, and 42 per cent of merchants have investments in cattle. The data suggest that the economic linking pins are commerce and cattle, probably because these were the activities where capital was originally accumulated (Ogliastri and Guerra, 1980).

An analysis of these four groups on the basis of their social background, career, ideology, and preferred development strategy indicates that the differences among them are not statistically significant. They are not distinct class fractions in sociological and ideological terms, but a diversified single class (Ogliastri and Guerra, 1980: table III-1, 1636–43). This appears to imply that the analysis of power in Colombia requires treating capitalists as a totality rather than as a set of fractions, but we feel it is not so simple. Two distinctive alliances seem to be operating here. There are correlations between the power of industrialists and merchants, and between the power of farmers and ranchers (table 8.6);[3] that is, in those cities where industrialists enjoy top power, merchants are also members of the top elite. Conversely, in the cities in which agriculturalists are found in the top ranks of power, so are cattlemen (Ogliastri and Guerra, 1980: 1650). The eleven cities under investigation are dominated either by one of these coalitions or the other.

Since concentration of power is a multidimensional concept, we focus on two of its facets: the network of linkages among top organizations and individuals created by interlocking directorates, and the permeability

Table 8.6[a] *Power of business fractions*

	Spearman's rank-order correlation			
	Industrialists	Merchants	Agriculturalists	Cattlemen
Industrialists	×	.633	− .51[a]	− .41
Merchants		×	− .325	− .275
Agriculturalists			×	.625
Cattlemen				×

[a]Negative values of Spearman's coefficient indicate negative relationship, i.e. in cities where industrialists are powerful, agriculturalists are not, and vice versa.
Source: Ogliastri and Guerra, 1980: table V-3, p. 1650.

(openness) of the elite to the influx of individuals of varied class positions and social status.

Interlocks can serve several purposes. The most obvious is the exchange of information and expertise among organizations, that is, the establishment of a stable means of communication and linkage (Allen, 1974: 395); but board overlaps may also be a mechanism of interorganizational coordination and control or elite cooptation of the environment (Allen, 1974; Pfeffer and Salancik, 1978).

For this analysis we took the list of power stratification for both organizations (table 8.1) and persons (table 8.3) as well as the information on the composition of the boards of directors of those organizations, in order to determine the number of interlocks among the top ten organizations and individuals. For each of these top individuals, membership on the board of a top organization or being its chief officer counted as one linkage. The sum of the number of linkages for the ten top elite members was taken as an indicator of the degree of power concentration. We assumed that power was more concentrated in cities where the set of linkages was denser, indicating the extent to which top individuals exert control over top organizations. Conversely, there is a broader distribution (lower concentration) of power in those cities where other people head the most important local organizations.

The set of linkages between top persons and top organizations was denser in the larger cities. These larger cities also exhibited higher levels of development, both in terms of economic growth and social development indicators (Ogliastri and Dávila, 1983). The total number of linkages ranged from 5 to 24, while the number of key officer linkages ranged from 1 to 6. Three of the cities had over 20 linkages – i.e. 2.0 linkages per person; five cities varied between 16 and 19; and two ranged between 5 and 13 linkages (table 8.7). The second dimension of concentration was concerned with indicators of social mobility (Ogliastri, 1976). The percentage of members of the top elite who were born into a wealthy family, who were rich themselves, and/or who

Table 8.7 *Power concentration: interlocking directorates among ten top organizations and individuals*

City	Type of linkage Board of directors	Chief executive officer	Total	Power concentration Rank	Category[a]
Barranquilla	12	5	17	4	B
Bucaramanga	14	2	16	7	B
Cartagena	20	4	24	1	A
Manizales	12	5	17	4	B
Pereira	20	3	23	2	A
Armenia	13	3	16	7	B
Cúcuta	9	4	13	9	C
Pasto	17	3	20	3	A
Neiva	ND	ND	ND	ND	ND
Popayán	10	6	16	7	B
Villavicencio	4	1	5	10	C

[a] A: High power concentration
B: Medium power concentration
C: Low power concentration

belonged to the high society of the town were taken as indicators of "elite openness." We found a pattern (with two exceptions) in which cities with an "open" elite, i.e. the top elite was not characterized by social status, inherited wealth and/or present wealth, tended to be those with lower development levels, the backward urban centers.

In general, the results on interlocking directorates indicate that concentration of power increases as cities grow and develop. This finding is contrary to the widely accepted hypothesis that fragmentation of power and pluralism are associated with the process of urban growth and development in Latin America (Walton, 1977).

How can we account for this pattern? In our view, it is closely related to the highly centralized nature of the Colombian state. With the prevailing political and administrative centralism, the capacity of local government to attract development funds from the national government (especially social welfare programs) is critical to continued growth. This political clout requires mechanisms for local coordination and organization: interlocking directorates and tightly knit elites are symptoms of such a structure.

A second, related indicator of this same pattern is the creation of associations to promote industrialization and local development. "Systemic organizations" (Lehman, 1969), whose membership is made up of other organizations (e.g. chambers of commerce, associations of industrialists, associations of merchants, foundations for development), occupy the top ranks in those cities with an industrial base and a closed, concentrated elite structure. In fact, 25 (or 42 per cent) of the top ten organizations in the six largest industrial cities are systemic organizations; even more remarkable, the chamber of commerce and industrialists' association are among the top three organizations in five of six cities. In the remaining case (the city of Manizales), although the highest rank corresponds to a financial corporation (not strictly a systemic organization), such an organization was created in the early 1960s to promote local industry.

In the smaller nonindustrialized cities (five of the urban centers studied), economic activity is centered around artisans, small industry, commercial agriculture and commerce. Businesses are mostly individual or family-run, and large, capitalist corporations and systemic organizations are relatively rare. The latter amount only to 8 (or 16 per cent) among the five smallest cities. The exercise of power seems to be more personalized and top private organizations are scarce. In contrast to the largest cities, where they made up 38 (or 63 per cent) of the top list, in the case of nonindustrial towns they represent only 36 per cent; public organizations total 64 per cent. Boards are not generalized as a mechanism for directing business and promoting or coordinating local endeavors. Concurrently, foundations to promote local development are scarce, with one exception (Armenia); chambers of commerce do not occupy ranks as high as in the industrial cities, except in the case of Pasto (table 8.2).

It appears that when these cities reach a threshold of about 200,000 inhabitants, developmental dynamics reach a standard mass. Nourished by an influx of rural immigrants who participate in an increasingly capitalist economy, the rhythm of capital accumulation accelerates. The larger market appears to attract additional private and public investment and the industrial prospects of the cities begin to exceed those of artisan businesses or small local manufacture. At that point, the needs for a physical infrastructure (energy, transportation, etc.) to develop local industry and the problems of urban development (stemming principally from accelerated rural migration, which aggravates problems of rural housing, basic services such as sewage, running water, electricity, education, health, and so on) become the crux of local public endeavor.

Our findings reveal that none of the intermediate cities can carry out their most important developmental activities without outside resources. In those projects which local elites consider to be the five most important, the dependence on Bogotá, the capital of Colombia, was paramount. In our survey half of these projects depended upon approval from Bogotá. Moreover, an overwhelming majority (80 per cent) of the key decisions in these projects were made in the public sector. In these circumstances the need for lobbying resources to put pressure on the ministries, national planning offices, and the headquarters of paradoxically called "decentralized" institutes became evident. The process of shaping the projects, promoting them at the local level, and preparing technical and economic studies to support demands for attention from the national locus of power required at least some local consensus, technical capability, and coordination for which systemic organizations as well as interlocking directorates seem to have been instrumental. Typically, depending upon the nature of the project, either the industrialists' association, the chamber of commerce, or the industrial promotion foundation plays a leading role in organizing a group or ad hoc committee composed of representatives of top organizations. They promote the idea, generate local support and enthusiasm, obtain funds for contracting feasibility studies, and travel to the country's capital for lobbying. Congressmen, politicians and eventually ministers and top government officials who represent the "regional quota" in the administration accompany the regional delegation and are instrumental as gatekeepers. A good example of this pattern was seen in the 1970s, when several cities competed for the allocation of car manufacturing plants by the central government. We would postulate that this local capacity to influence the central locus of power is made possible by the concentration of power in a few hands. That capacity is greater in the larger cities – those in which power is more concentrated. We would also postulate that such concentration was a necessary condition for successful expansion beyond the 200,000-person threshold.

Considering the context of the national structure, it could be asked to what extent the concentration of power in intermediate cities, as they become larger and more developed, took place at the expense of the capital city, and thus led to a dispersion of power in the national scene. Lack of local and regional autonomy, however, has produced a paradoxical strengthening of national centralization, because concentration of local power has been accompanied by a major articulation of these cities into the national power structure. This has increased their dependence on the center rather than confronting it.

The development projects already mentioned are not the only evidence of this dependence. Interviews with members of local elites demonstrated their common perception of extralocal control of the city's development in both the public and private sectors. An overriding majority (78 per cent) referred to a centralized public sector, out of the reach of local control. Three out of four elite members (76 per cent) pointed to the occurrence of the same phenomenon in the private sector.

These results are consistent with the out-of-town organizations they mention as the most influential in these cities (table 8.8). Specific Bogotá-based government agencies dealing with housing, industry, agriculture, education, public services, and the like, as well as the "national government" and government agencies in general (*institutos descentralizados*), are the most frequently mentioned organizations in six of the cities. Taken as a whole, they account for 40 (or 38 per cent) of a total of 106 citations in the eleven cities.

The banks and financial institutions, most of them private, commercial

Table 8.8 *Extralocal power: ten top out-of-town organizations*

Organization	Barranquila	Bucaramanga	Cartagena	Manizales	Pereira	Cúcuta	Subtotal largest cities	Armenia	Pasto	Neiva	Popayán	Villavicencio	Subtotal smallest cities	Total
Agency of national government	8	6	5	1	1	5	26	3	—	2	5	4	14	40 (37.8%)
Bank/financial institution	1	2	3	5	2	2	15	3	1	1	—	2	7	22 (20.6%)
Private association	1	1	—	2	3	—	7	3	—	2	1	2	8	15 (14.1%)
Multinational corporation	—	—	2	1	4	—	7	—	—	—	—	—	—	7 (6.7%)
Private company, private business group	—	—	—	1	—	3	4	1	4	5	3	2	15	19 (17.9%)
Other	—	—	—	—	—	—	—	—	3	—	—	—	3	3 (2.8%)
Total							59						47	106
Location of headquarters														
Bogotá							39						33	72 (67.9%)
Medellín							8						6	14 (13.2%)
Other Columbian cities							1						5	6 (5.7%)
Local							—						3	3 (2.8%)
Abroad							11						—	11 (10.4%)
							59						47	106

banks, whose headquarters are located in the capital and Medellín (Columbia's second-largest city) rank second with 21 per cent of nominations. They happen to be the most frequently mentioned in two coffee-based cities (Manizales and Armenia); they are absent only in the list of one of the smallest cities of the sample (Popayán). The banks act as mechanisms to transfer local and regional funds from the middle-sized cities of the study to the two major financial centers of the country, not the reverse, as can be seen from an analysis of local deposits *vis-à-vis* loans.

Dependence on private firms (for the most part manufacturing and retail trades business) with headquarters in Medellín and Bogotá, as well as small private business groups that are not yet finance capital groups, is another instance of extra-local control in the development of these cities. They have the highest number of citations in two of the smallest cities (Pasto and Neiva), totalling 19 (or 18 per cent) of influential out-of-town organizations mentioned, and rank third below national government and the banks. Their role as sources of economic activity and employment is particularly important in the commerce- and agriculture-based cities. Frequently they represent the few manufacturing plants (generally beer and beverages) existing in these localities.

It is noticeable that private business associations of industrialists (ANDI), coffee-growers (Fedecafé), and merchants (Fenalco) are repeatedly mentioned. They amount to 15 (or 14 per cent) of the total of 106 organizations for all cities, and are named in all but three of the eleven cities; they are mentioned with particular frequency in coffee-based cities. It should be recalled that these associations occupy the top echelons of local power in the cities of the study (cf. table 8.1). Their dual mention as both local and nonlocal organizations illustrates their dependence on headquarters in Bogotá and Medellín.

Thus the picture of dependence and centralism in the public sector that has been reiterated in this section is complemented by the same characteristic in finance and private business associations. The latter, principally through their central offices and staff (not their regional offices), have a much greater capacity to influence policy-making, penetrate the state and provide it with important assistance in moments of crisis (Hartlyn, 1983). At the regional level they are key actors whose power is not limited to their particular economic activity, but includes participation in development projects and activities, and a leading part in organizing local interests in their role of systemic organizations. All this political action is generally portrayed under the name of "civic action"; private business associations and chambers of commerce are self-named "civic forces," a label which obscures the economic interests they represent and the noticeable close, nonparticipative nature of the power structure in all the cities of the study.

Turning to dependence upon international centers of power, the elite perceive such linkages in only three cities. In two of them there exists significant foreign investment in manufacturing industry (a petrochemical complex in the case of Cartagena; three affiliates of consumer goods MNCs in Pereira). Out of the 106 nonlocal organizations mentioned by elite members, only eleven (or 10 per cent) of them are foreign. Eight apply to Cartagena and Pereira, and three to Manizales, where reference is made to foreign banks and insurance companies.

More striking are the results that in the eleven cities of the study international credit institutions are rarely mentioned. Though they provide the funds and are in the last analysis key decision-makers on many of the infrastructural programs (sewage, electricity, aqueducts, etc.) carried out by the central government in these cities, they are not visible to local elites. Similarly, the local elites do not seem to perceive the interdependence with the economy of nearby countries (Venezuela and Ecuador). In the case of Cúcuta and Pasto this reality became evident: the economic recession in Venezuela and Ecuador deeply hampered the commercial activity of these two border cities.

The separation between the public and private sectors is one of the cornerstones of democracy, whereas one of the basic assertions of Marxism has been that the rich rule, i.e. this separation is denied. The classic work of Miliband (1969) compared state and economic elites in European and American countries and found that they shared social origins, career patterns, and ideology, casting doubt on the pluralist contention of the fragmentation of power and empirically arguing for the class basis of the capitalist state. A review of recent research by Panitch (1981) concluded that the distinction between the public and the private sector has blurred in industrial countries. These results are, however, widely disputed and, even if validated, would not necessarily extend to dependent developing countries, even those on a capitalist trajectory.

To examine this issue, we looked at the top elite in terms of its public/private sector composition. In essence, a member of the top elite was classified in either the public or private sector according to the organizations in which he has made his career (Ogliastri, 1982, 1984). Our major finding is that only 85 per cent (36 per cent public and 49 per cent private) could be placed in these categories. There is a key 15 per cent subset of *polyvalents* who could not be placed in either group because they have careers in both sectors; and there is an equally important subgroup of organizations with a similar "mixed" character.

The comparison of public, private, and polyvalent elites along a number of background, career and ideology variables indicated a few statistically significant differences among them, which point out the unique role that polyvalents play and the fact that public and private elites do not exist as two distinct groups.

Table 8.9 *Socioeconomic characteristics and the careers of public, private, and polyvalent elites*

$N = 209$; i.e. the top 19 individuals in 11 cities

	Public elite (%)	Economic elite (%)	Polyvalent elite (%)
Status			
Belongs to "high" society (high social status family ($s = 0.014$; $c = 0.27$)	37.0	53.0	73.0
Social class			
Presently belongs to upper bourgeoise ($s = 0.03$; $c = 0.24$)	41.0	63.0	44.0
Income			
Had monthly income over Col. $30,000 (in 1975) ($s = 0.017$; $c = 0.35$)	36.0	53.0	32.0
Sources of income			
Public administration ($s = 0.00$; $c = 0.37$)	59.0	26.0	77.0
Politics (elected bodies or ministries) ($s = 0.00$; $c = 0.31$)	31.0	4.0	18.0
Management ($s = 0.01$; $c = 0.22$)	43.0	68.0	59.0
Industry ($s = 0.01$; $c = 0.23$)	18.0	41.0	23.0
Commerce ($s = 0.02$; $c = 0.21$	20.0	39.0	18.0

This table has been rearranged from a number of tables included in Ogliastri (1982, 1984).

It is a summary table. For each variable, *only one* of the values of the variable is included, e.g. that of most interest; one exception is "source of income," where 5 values are included – even in that case the information is not complete: the original contingency table has 12 values or different sources of income; s = probability; c = contingency coefficient.

Polyvalents are like public elites on some dimensions and like private elites on other dimensions, as shown in table 8.9. As in the case of the private elite, they typically (73 per cent) come from old prestigious families, usually ones which are no longer wealthy.

Family name or ancestry seems to be an important and visible factor in these cities, as evidenced by the high consensus on the part of the three high society judges that in each city classified the elite according to their social status (Ogliastri, 1984). Polyvalents rank very high in this regard; inherited social prestige implies for them moving in high society circles, belonging to exclusive social clubs, and attending private schools together with the private sector elite. All this happens even if their money is exhausted; their links and contacts with their old chums can be reactivated. Doors have been open since childhood that permit them to keep moving back and forth between the private and public sector.

In terms of their income level polyvalents are not like private sector leaders, but appear more like those of the public sector. Due to the careers they follow, both polyvalent and public sector elites do not stand out for their wealth: 44 per cent and 41 per cent respectively belong to the upper bourgeoisie, in contrast to 63 per cent of the economic elite; these social class results, however, do not make the group as distinct as the values of $s = 0.03$ and $c = 0.24$ indicate. Polyvalents' economic behavior is as diversified as that of the public servants and the percentage of both who had income derived from commerce, industry, and public administration is alike (table 8.9).

In brief, polyvalents do not have social background and career characteristics which would constitute a social group distinct from public and private elites. Rather, they are social hybrids: in their inherited social prestige they are similar to private sector elites; on the other hand, their income level, accumulated wealth, and economic diversification resemble those of public sector elites. It is precisely this dual role that accounts for their unique capacity for action in uniting the two sectors. As such, they constitute another mechanism for cohesion and organization of local elites.

The most notable feature of social homogeneity among these regional elites – whether they are public, private, or polyvalents – is that they all belong to the capitalist class: either the upper bourgeoisie, the middle bourgeoisie, or the petty bourgeoisie. None of them are part of the working class (Ogliastri, 1984).

Regarding ideology, data on a large number of issues were collected (diagnosis of city development, actual development strategies, the role of the state in development, social, economic, and political egalitarianism, foreign investment, centralism, and religion). The ideological profile of the three groups shows some interesting features (see table 8.10). However, when a comparison among them was made, most of the differences – e.g. those on diagnosis of city development and actual strategies among polyvalents and the public and private elites – were not statistically significant. Thus, the emerging picture is one of great similarity of ideology.

It should be recalled that public and private sectors are organizationally linked by interlocking directorates. These, as discussed in a previous section, are more important and larger in number as cities grow and industrialize. This fact seems to be clear for the top leaders of these cities. As a matter of fact, the majority of those in the private sector (67 per cent) consider a specific board in the public sector as the most important one. Conversely, for the majority of the public leaders (59 per cent) and the polyvalents (63 per cent), a board of directors in the private sector was considered their most important one. Corporatist forms of relating public and private sectors are not dominant in

Table 8.10 *Elite ideology*[a]

N = 209; i.e. the top 19 individuals in 11 cities

	Public elite (%)	Economic elite (%)	Polyvalent elite (%)
Diagnosis of city development			
Obstacles to city's development:			
Social (poverty: health, housing, education, etc.)	25	22	71
Political (lack of participation, partisan politics, institutional, etc.)	29	36	12
Economic (growth, geographical, technological, etc.)	17	23	6
Most important local projects[b]			
Industry	25	25	14
Electrification	8	10	25
Aqueduct, sewage, telephone	10	9	13
Role of state in development			
Favors limited state interventionism ($s = 0.003$; $c = 0.29$)	45	62	63
Egalitarian attitudes			
Social egalitarianism	63	54	84
Importance of directorates the elite belongs to:			
Most important:			
One in private sector	59	27	63
One in public sector	35	67	22

Notes: [a] This is a summary table that has been rearranged from a number of tables included in Ogliastri (1982, 1984).

[b] For some of the variables (e.g. most important local project) not all the values of the variable are included.

Colombia, but a good deal of interlocking representation is in the charters of many public organizations (Bailey, 1977).

The characteristics of the linkages between these middle-size cities and the nation's capital, i.e. those indicative of a high and increasing centralism, have been conducive to mechanisms in the way local power becomes organized. Coordination through networks of organizations linked at the top (boards) by elite members has evolved into a common pattern as cities grow and develop. This results in more ties to central government as well as to the central business structure of the society as a whole.

Local public and private sectors thus become integrated in the process of striving for attention and resources. And polyvalents, those who have a "mixed" career and hybrid social roles, are pivotal in linking them.

Summary and conclusions

This study has attempted to examine the articulation of power and business structure in the context of local and regional development. The setting is eleven middle-sized cities (100,000–500,000 pop.) in Colombia, a developing nation in Latin America. The five larger and more developed cities have industrial bases; the remainder are agricultural and commercial. The research relied upon the identification and interviewing of 515 top elite members in these cities and the analysis of secondary sources on local development.

One major finding of this study is that power is more concentrated in the larger, more developed cities than in smaller, backward urban centers. Using interlocking directorates among top local organizations as our indicator, we found that these linkages are increasingly pervasive and larger in number in the larger, industrial cities. In these interlock networks, moreover, there is a centrality of private business associations and other systemic organizations (Lehman, 1969) such as chambers of commerce and industrial promotion foundations. This finding runs counter to the hypothesis of recent reviews of power in urban Latin America (e.g. Walton, 1976), according to which pluralistic, fragmented, decentralized power structures arise with economic development.

Another symptom of power concentration can be found in the class composition of the top echelons of local power structures. The evidence points out the hegemony of the bourgeoisie in the historical power bloc. The absence of working-class participation in the structure of power is striking; the big bourgeoisie and the middle bourgeoisie dominate the petty bourgeoisie. This pattern holds for organizations and individuals as well. Power is therefore concentrated in the hands of one class to the exclusion of others. Though this configuration is found in all the cities studied, it is more pronounced in the larger ones.

The absence of cleavage between economic (business) and public elites in terms of their socioeconomic characteristics, career or ideology, together with the existence of a group of polyvalents whose careers are made in both sectors, is another significant finding. The polyvalents act as a link between the public and private sectors and tend to undermine postulated conflict between the sectors (e.g. Urrutia, 1983: ch. 6).

These findings should be interpreted in the context of the larger national power structure, both in terms of political dependence on central government and in connection with the centralized business structure of society. As the scale of cities begins to increase, the need for infrastructural investment becomes critical for urban and industrial development. The national government, which makes the decisions and controls the credit and other resources for urban development projects, therefore becomes a major factor for continued city growth. In an attempt to get access to these resources and to obtain some leverage at the national level, local elites become increasingly organized through the mechanisms detected in this study – i.e. interlocking networks, systemic organizations, and polyvalent leaders. Cities which fail to develop and successfully utilize these mechanisms are unlikely to prosper.

The increasing centralization in the private sector occurs through three mechanisms. First, banks and financial corporations are either filials or partially owned by Bogotá- and Medellín-based finance capital. Seeking the best return on investment, they transfer capital accumulated locally to money centers in Bogotá- and Medellín, a phenomenon closely related to the centralization of capital examined in Marxist analyses (Camacho, 1977).

Second, business associations (of industrialists, merchants, agriculturalists, etc.), which have been preoccupied with lobbying and protesting against growing government centralism and interventionism, must also centralize in their headquarters.

Third, the commercial sectors of the smaller cities are closely tied to wholesale suppliers, particularly those distributing the consumer goods of Medellín's industry. At the same time, to a large extent, the few manufacturing plants of the smaller cities are filials of firms based in Bogotá, Medellín, and Cali (the third largest Colombian city), creating a modicum of centralization even in these localities.

As a consequence of all these factors, the larger and more industrialized cities are intimately connected to the national power and business structure, and local elites begin to be integrated into the national political and business elite. The concentration of local power therefore does not create autonomy for the local areas, but makes them more intimately articulated (dependent) into the center. The process of development in these cities is also conducive to a change in the composition of local power structures. In the small cities agriculturalists and cattlemen dominate, while the larger cities tend to be dominated by industrialists and merchants. Because the latter exercise their power in a less personalized way, one of their roles in "civic" endeavors is the formation of organizational structures (Hirschman, 1958) for economic development tasks.

These results suggest the need to explore the relationship of city growth to the increasing unrest in several of these local areas and their surroundings. The escalation of problems of delivery and rising costs in public services in the late 1970s resulted in local, violent *paros cívicos* – civic movements that paralyzed local activities for as long as several days. As an example, in the short period of eight months (September 1977 to May 1978) 50 *paros cívicos* took place across the country – none of them in the four largest cities of the country (Bedoya, 1981: 6). The organizational leadership of these movements was located in community organizations representing the poor, ad hoc civic committees elected in popular meetings, and trade unions; traditional liberal and conservative influences were not significant (Fonseca, 1982; Bedoya, 1981: ch. 4). Not only working-class interests but also middle sectors (small merchants, teachers, artisans, etc.) were active in these protest movements, which almost inevitably included a petition to the central government for funds and programs for a reduction of tariffs on public services (e.g. electricity, telephones, aqueducts, etc.). It would appear that the exclusionary structure of power condemned important sectors of the population to a marginal existence, desperation, and violent forms of protest (Escobar, 1984: 91), the guerrilla movement included.

NOTES

1 This chapter is part of a research project supported in its initial phase by Universidad de los Andes (Colombia) and the Colombian Science Foundation (Colciencias). It is currently being sponsored in part by the Graduate Program in Economics, School of Interdisciplinary Studies, Universidad Javeriana (Colombia). The other support has been provided by the association of one of the authors with the Committee on Latin American and Iberian Studies of the Center for International Affairs, and the Graduate School of Education at Harvard University during the 1981–4 period. The authors are indebted to the group of students who helped in conducting the field work (see p. 238). The comments and suggestions of the editors of this volume, Michael Schwartz and Mark Mizruchi, on an earlier draft of this chapter are greatly appreciated. The authors remain solely responsible for its content.

2 Social class is understood in terms of social relations of production: groups which share the same relationship regarding the ownership of means of production. A scheme of four classes was used (big bourgeoisie, middle bourgeoisie, petty bourgeoisie, and proletariat). To determine the class position of the members of the elite, four indicators were utilized: property, sources of income, control and type of resources, and income level. The *big bourgeoisie* were classified as those who own, get income from and control large-scale enterprises and economic units (in manufacturing, agriculture, services) of the city. The *middle bourgeoisie* included those who earn high income as independent professionals who render their services to the big bourgeoisie (e.g. lawyers), or occupy managerial positions that permit them control over the productive system and the market even if they are not big owners. The *petty bourgeoisie* is made up of small business proprietors, professionals who do not occupy dominating positions, and/or employers. The *proletariat* are those who live as salaried workers in manufacturing or agriculture (Ogliastri, 1976: 234).

3 In each city, the power rank among fractions is based on the number of top elite members who have investments in a particular activity (e.g. industry, commerce, agriculture, cattle, ranching). The correspondence between paired ranks (e.g. industrialists and merchants, etc.) was calculated by using Spearman's rank-order correlation coefficent.

REFERENCES

Abello, M., 1975. "El desarrollo economico de Barranquilla: actitudes e ideologias de la elite del poder." B. S. Thesis (management), Universidad de los Andes, Bogotá

Allen, M., 1974. "The structure of interorganizational elite cooptation: interlocking corporate directorates." *American Sociological Review*, 39, 393–406

Alvarez, M. C., 1975. "Ideologías grupos y estructura de poder en Armenia." BS thesis (industrial engineering). Universidad de los Andes, Bogotá

Ayala, H., *et al*, 1978. "Gestión tecnológica en la industria de alimentos de Colombia." Universidad de los Andes – Universidad Eafit – Universidad del Valle, Cali (Colombia). Research report submitted to the International Development Research Center (IDRC, Canada)

Ayala, Ulpiano, and Fonseca, Luz A., 1981. "El movimiento huelguístico 1974–1981." *Desarrollo y Sociedad, Separata Estudios Laborales*, 1: 25–49

Ayala de Rey, M. V., 1976. "Modelo de regionalizacion nodal." *Placeación y Desarrollo*, 8: 33–55

Bailey, J., 1977. "Pluralist and corporate dimensions of interest representation in Colombia." In M. Malloy (ed.), *Authoritarianism and Corporatism in Latin America*. University of Pittsburgh Press

Banco de la República, 1982. *Colombian Economic Indicators*. Bogotá

Banco Mundial, 1974. *El Desarrollo Económico de Colombia: Problemas y Perspectivas, Informe de una Misión Enviada a Colombia en 1970 por el Banco Mundial*. Bogotá: Banco Popular

Becker, D., 1983. *The New Bourgeoisie and the Limits of Dependency: Mining, Class and Power in "Revolutionary" Peru*. Princeton University Press

Bedoya, Jaime Carrillo, 1981. *Los Paros Cívicos en Colombia*. Bogotá: Oveja Negra – Editográficas (translated from the French)

Botero, C., 1983. *Propuestas sobre Descentralización en Colombia*. Bogotá: Universidad de los Andes (Cider)

Brew, R., 1977. *El Desarrollo Económico de Antioquia desde la Independencia hasta 1920*. Archivo de la Economía Nacional, 38 Banco de la República, Bogotá

Caicedo, E., 1982. *Historia de las Luchas Sindicales en Colombia*, 4th rev. edn. Bogotá: Ceis

Camacho, A., 1977. *La Organización Social de la Centralización del Capital en Colombia*. Cali: Universidad del Valle

Cardoso, F., and Faletto, E., 1979. *Dependency and Development in Latin America*, rev. and expanded edn. Berkeley: University of California Press

Chaves, J., 1981. "Líderes, Informe sobre la conversión de la cinta ingind. Líderes y unificación de archivos." Working Paper, Universidad de los Andes, Bogotá

Corchuelo, A., and Misas, G., 1977. "Internacionalización del capital y ampliación del mercado interno: el sector industrial Colombiano." *Uno en Dos*, 8

Dahl, R., 1961. *Who Governs? Democracy and Power in an American City*. New Haven, Conn.: Yale University Press

Dávila, C., 1973. "A systematic review of power studies in Latin America." Working Paper, Northwestern University, Evanston, Ill.

1976. "Dominant classes and elites in economic development: a comparative study of eight urban centers in Colombia." PhD dissertation, Northwestern University

1985. "Diversificación económica y actividad política del empresariado en Colombia. Los negociantes de Bogotá y del Valle del Cauca, 1886–1930." Paper presented to the XII International Congress, Latin American Studies Association (LASA), Albuquerque, New Mexico, April 18–20

Dávila, C., and Ogliastri, E., 1972. "Elite y desarrollo. Un estudio en Bucaramanga." Research Report to the Colombian Science Foundation. Evanston, Ill.

De Angulo, D., 1975. "Liderazgo y organización social del desarrollo económico de Popayán," BS thesis (management), Universidad de los Andes, Bogotá

Dent, D. W., 1973. "Community cooperation in Colombia: a comparative study of public–private sector relationships in two urban areas." PhD dissertation, University of Minnesota

Dix, R., 1967. *Colombia: The Political Dimensions of Change.* New Haven, Conn.: Yale University Press

Drake, F. G., 1970. "Elites and voluntary associations: a study of community power in Manizales, Colombia." PhD dissertation, University of Wisconsin

Escobar, R., 1984. "Esquema de un Desarrollo Político para la Colombia de los Años Ochentas." *Revista Javeriana,* 507: 87–95

Fajardo, D., 1978. "Primer informe del proyecto para la síntesis y evaluación de algunos estudios sobre el sector rural Colombiano." Working paper, Ford Foundation, Bogotá

Flórez, L. B., and González, C., 1983. *Industria, Regiones y Urbanización en Colombia.* Bogota: Fines–Oveja Negra

Fonseca, L., 1982. "Los paros cívicos en Colombia." *Dessarrollo y Sociedad– Cuadernos Laborales,* Separata 3: 17–30

Frank, A. G., 1967. *Capitalism and Underdevelopment in Latin America: Historical Studies of Chile and Brazil.* New York: Monthly Review Press

García, M., 1975. "Elite y desarrollo: un estudio en Cúcuta. BS thesis (industrial engineering), Universidad de los Andes, Bogotá

Guerra, E., 1976a. "Estudio de las fracciones de clase en la burguesía Colombiana." MBA thesis, Universidad de los Andes, Bogotá

1976b. "Elite y desarrollo regional. Selección, depuración y ordenamiento de los datos y entrevistas. Metodología y recomendaciones para el menajo del banco de datos consignado en la cinta ingid/líderes." Working paper, Universidad de los Andes, Bogotá

Hartlyn, J., 1983. "Producer associations, the political regime and policy processes in contemporary Colombia." Paper presented to the XI International Congress of LASA, Mexico City, September 29–October 1

Herrera, G., 1979. "Análisis estadístico comparativo entre dirigentes empresariales y políticos." BS thesis (industrial engineering), Universidad Javeriana, Bogotá

Hirschman, A., 1958. *The Strategy of Economic Development.* New Haven, Conn.: Yale University Press

Huberman, L., 1975. *Los Bienes Terrenales del Hombre.* Medellín: Oveja Negra

Hunter, F., 1953. *Community Power Structure: A Study of Decision Makers.* Chapel Hill: University of North Carolina Press

Jaramillo, J., 1983. "Regiones y nación en el siglo XIX." In *Aspectos Polémicos de la Historia Colombiana del Siglo XIX. Memorias de un Seminario.* Bogotá: Fondo Cultural Cafetero

Kline, H., 1981. *Colombia: Portrait of Unity and Diversity*. Boulder, Colo.: Westview

Koffman, B., 1969. "The National Federation of Coffee-Growers of Colombia." PhD dissertation, University of Virginia

Kruijt, D., Maiguashca, F., and Vellinga, M., 1982. *Industrialización y Desarrollo Regional en Colombia*. Universidad Nacional de Utrecht

Lehman, E., 1969. "Toward a macro-sociology of power." *American Sociological Review*, 34: 453–65

Lipset, S., 1967. "Values, education and entrepreneurship." In S. Lipset and A. Solari (eds.), *Elites in Latin America*. New York: Oxford University Press

López, A., 1976. "Mensaje al Congreso Nacional." In Botero (1982), p. 35

López, H., y Otros, 1980. "El monopolio en Colombia." *Revista Universidad EAFIT*. No. Extra, Medellín

McDonough, P., 1981. *Power and Ideology in Brazil*. Princeton University Press

Merton, R., 1981. "Foreword: Remarks on theoretical pluralism." In P. Blau and R. Merton (eds.), *Continuities in Structural Inquiry*. London: Sage, pp. i–vii

Miliband, R., 1969. *The State in Capitalist Society. An Analysis of the Western System of Power*. New York: Basic Books

Misas, G., 1975. *Contribución al Estudio del Grado de Concentracion en la Industria Colombiana*. Bogotá: Tiempo Presente

   1983. *Empresas Multinacionales y Pacto Andino*. Bogotá: Fines-Oveja Negra

Mogollón, A., 1974. "El desarrollo económico de Cartagena: organización, liderazgo e ideologías." BS thesis (industrial engineering), Universidad de los Andes, Bogotá

Muñoz, D., 1976. "Grupos empresarialies en la Ciudad de Neiva." MBA thesis, Universidad de los Andes, Bogotá

Ocampo, A., 1982. "Centralismo, descentralización y federalismo en la historia Colombiana." *Revista Antioqueña de Economía*, 5: 56–7. Quoted in Tirado (1983), p. 66, n.10

Ogliastri, E., 1973. "Elite, class, power and social consciousness in the economic development of a Colombian city: Bucaramanga." PhD dissertation, Northwestern University

   1976. "Estudio comparativo sobre la movilidad intergeneracional en las elites regionales de nueve centros urbanos en Colombia." *Revista de Planeación y Desarrollo*, 8: 234–43

   1982. "Sector público y sector privado: análises de un mito." Working Paper, Harvard Center for International Affairs, Cambridge, Mass.

   1983a. "Liberales conservadores versus conservadores liberales: faccionalismos trenzados en la estructura de poder en Colombia." Paper presented to the XI International Congress of LASA, Mexico City, September 29–October 1

   1983b. "Estructura de poder y clases sociales: la democracia oligárquica en Colombia." Paper presented to the XI International Congress of LASA, Mexico City, September 29–October 1

   1983c. "Class fractions, power structure, and hegemony: a study in Colombia." Unpublished manuscript, Harvard University, Cambridge, Mass.

   1984. "Sector público y sector privado: un estudio sobre dingentes regionales Colombianos." Paper presented to the IV Colombian Congress of Research in Management, Barranquilla, Colombia, April 10–14

Ogliastri, E., and Dávila, C., 1983. "Estructura de poder y desarrollo en once ciudades intermedias de Colombia." *Desarrollo y Sociedad*, 12: 149–88

Ogliastri, E., and Guerra, E., 1980. "Fracciones de clase en la burguesía de cuidades intermedias de Colombia: un estudio sociológico." *Revista Mexicana de Sociología*, 4: 1631–61

Panitch, L., 1981. "Trade unions and the capitalist state." *New Left Review*, 125: 21–43

Pfeffer, J., and Salancik, G., 1978. *The External Control of Organizations*. New York: Harper and Row

Prieto, A., 1980. "La burguesía contemporánea en América Latina." *Advances de Investigación*, 4, Centro de Estudios sobre América, La Habana

Rabinovitz, F., 1968. "Sound and fury signifying nothing: a review of community power research in Latin America." *Urban Affairs Quarterly*, 3: 111–22

Reveiz, E., and Montenegro, S., 1983. "Modelos de desarrollo, recomposición industrial y evolución de la concentración industrial en las ciudades de Colombia, 1965–1980." *Desarrollo y Sociedad*, 11: 93–153

Salazar, M. C., 1974. "Organización social del desarrollo económico de Villavicencio." BS thesis (industrial engineering), Universidad de los Andes, Bogotá

Saldarriaga, J. B., 1974. "Poder y desarrollo. Una investigación en Pereira, Colombia." BS thesis (industrial engineering), Universidad de los Andes, Bogotá

Schulze, Robert, and Blumberg, Leonard, 1957. "The determination of local power elites." *American Journal of Sociology*, 63: 290–6

Silva, J., 1977. *Los Verdaderos Dueños del País. Oligarquía y Monopolios en Colombia*. Bogotá: Suramérica
    1983. *Tras la Máscara del Subdesarrollo: Dependencia y Monopolio*. Bogotá: Carlos Valencia

Smith, Peter, 1979. *Labyrinths of Power: Political Recruitment in Twentieth Century Mexico*. Princeton University Press

Therborn, G., 1979. "The travail of Latin American democracy." *New Left Review*, 113–14: 71–109

Tirado, A., 1981. *Descentralización y Centralismo en Colombia*. Bogotá: Fundación Friedrich Nauman – Oveja Negra

Urrutia, Miguel, 1983. *Gremios, Política Económica y Democracia*. Bogotá: Fondo Cultural Cafetero

Vaisman, I., 1976. "Liberales y conservadores: son diferentes? Un análisis estadístico." BS thesis (industrial engineering), Universidad de los Andes, Bogotá

Vélez, R., 1975. "Poder y desarrollo en Manizales." BS thesis (industrial engineering), Universidad de los Andes, Bogotá

Viveros, G., 1975. "Estructura de poder y desarrollo socio-económico en Pasto." BS thesis (industrial engineering), Universidad de los Andes, Bogotá

Walton, John, 1971. "A methodology for the comparative study of power: some conceptual and procedural applications." *Social Science Quarterly*, 52 (June): 39–60
    1976. "Structures of power in Latin American cities: toward a summary and

interpretation." In A. Portes and J. Walton (eds.), *Urban Latin America, The Political Condition from Above and Below.* Austin: University of Texas Press, pp. 136–78

1977. *Elites and Economic Development: Comparative Studies on the Political Economy of Latin American Cities.* Austin: University of Texas Press

Weber, Max, 1947. *The Theory of Social and Economic Organization.* Glencoe, Ill.: The Free Press, 1947

Whitt, J., Allen, 1979. "Toward a class-dialectical model of power: an empirical assessment of three competing models of political power." *American Sociological Review* (February): 81–100

Wilde, A., 1978. "Conversations among gentlemen: oligarchical democracy in Colombia." In J. Linz and A. Stepan (eds.), *The Breakdown of Democratic Regimes: Latin America.* Baltimore: Johns Hopkins University Press

9

Business–Government relations in modern Japan: a Tōdai–Yakkai–Zaikai complex?

Koji Taira and Teiichi Wada

Analysis of Japanese business–government relations is facilitated if we accept a working hypothesis at the outset: that business and government in Japan are like two major divisions of a well-run organization – Japan itself. Although some versions of "Japan, Inc." are generally considered extreme by many Japan specialists, there is no doubt that the Japanese have long accepted the concept of a "corporatist unity of government and business." (*kanmin ittai*) for the attainment of national goals.[1]

In this chapter, we intend to show how the personal networks and contacts of public officials and private business leaders render the formal structural distinction of government and business almost meaningless in Japan.

A simple model of the TYZ complex

In order to facilitate the interpretation and appreciation of detailed data presented in this chapter, we first offer a simple model showing how individuals with business leadership qualities go through life cycles and interact with one another in the management of Japan as a close-knit business-oriented society. Executive positions of leading corporations (the Japanese counterpart of "*Fortune* 500") are occupied predominantly by graduates of Tokyo University (Tōdai) and four other prestigious universities (Kyōto, Hitotsubashi, Keiō, and Waseda). The graduates of these universities also dominate leading bureaucratic positions in national government. Bureaucrats retire early, and many join leading corporations. A great majority of these bureaucratic and business leaders originate in middle- and upper-class families. Although recruitment from lower classes and elite turn-over take place on scales appropriate for the net expansion of the elite business sector over time, there is a roughly stable intergenerational elite reproduction mechanism which can be seen as a Tōdai–government–business complex, or Tōdai–Yakkai–Zaikai complex (TYZ complex hereafter).[2]

Every year, young men of 22 to 25 years old, upon graduation from Tōdai, fan out into the state bureaucracy, big business, and other areas of life. Those who have entered the civil service serve out their term and become ready to move to private business in their forties or fifties. By this time, their former classmates in giant corporations have also risen through the ranks and have become seasoned middle-level managers, some already contenders for leading positions. At this point the two streams of Tōdai graduates join forces in private business. The former bureaucrats among them occasionally return to government to participate in policy-making through consultative councils. There they encounter high-level civil servants who many years earlier were junior civil servants running errands for them when they were in leading positions. In this way, business also runs government. By this time, business leaders' and ex-bureaucrats' sons have graduated from Tōdai and have begun their ascent by the fast-track escalators in bureaucracy and business. The elites have also exchanged one another's sons and daughters through marital ties to further consolidate the privileges of leadership. Through occupational inheritance and dynastic alliance, the TYZ complex constantly renews its life cycle.

The TYZ complex protects itself against attacks on its exclusiveness by absorbing compatible non-Tōdai men into its fold from time to time in numbers just enough to ensure the climate of openness and fairness. All told, a few hundred interrelated families of the TYZ complex (with the imperial family at its apex) form an extended government of Japan. TYZ as a ruling class has also learned a princely art of "symbolic democracy" and endeavors to preempt the general public's potential dissatisfaction by benevolent concessions wrapped in the appropriate rhetoric of equitable distribution. The much touted Japanese planning and industrial policy based on a semblance of popular participation is an example of the TYZ art of governance. Throughout this chapter, we rarely encounter more familiar classes of Japan such as workers, clerks, salesman, shopkeepers, farm hands, etc. These are the subjects of Japan whom the TYZ complex rules. As a *raison d'être* of its rule, TYZ promotes a philosophy of national community called *schicksalverbundenheit* ("bound together for common destiny," a German expression well entrenched in Japanese vocabulary). The TYZ complex then obtains a large philosophical share in the definition of national interest which translates into laws and programs at politically opportune moments as the occasion demands.

More specifically, the Japanese economy is clearly subject to manipulation and leadership by the ruling class, although it is disguised as a market system. The masses of common folk are elements of the competitive market system. Their large numbers and limited individual means satisfy the analytical requirements of a competitive market – numerous sellers and buyers, none powerful enough to influence the forces of supply and demand, but all acting as obedient "price-takers." The market system they constitute works well, as if guided by a most efficient Invisible Hand. Upon a moment's reflection,

Table 9.1 *The occupation of the fathers of business leaders, 1960 and 1970, and high-level civil servants, 1977*

Occupation	% of fathers of business leaders	
	1960	1970
Government officials	11.5	14.4
Owners or managers of large or medium enterprises	22.0	27.9
Professional men	9.7	10.6
Small business owners	21.6	21.8
White collar workers (teachers, clerks, and sales workers)	9.0	6.9
Laborers	1.3	1.5
Farmers	24.0	16.9
(of whom, landlords)	(17.3)	(12.1)
Others	0.9	0.0
Total	100	100
Number of persons in the sample	974	1,062

Occupation	% of fathers of civil servants, 1977		
	All high-level civil servants	Top-class civil servants	Managing-class civil servants
Administrative, managerial	40.2	41.8	39.8
Professional	23.5	29.0	21.9
Clerical	10.0	10.9	9.7
Sales	10.4	5.4	11.7
Skilled and semi-skilled	1.2	0	1.5
Agricultural (including landlords)	7.2	1.8	8.7
No response, don't know	7.6	10.9	6.6
Total	100	100	100
Number of persons in the sample	251	55	196

Sources: For 1960 and 1970 business leaders, Mannari, 1974: 213; for 1977 civil servants, Muramatsu, 1981: 49.

however, anyone will see that the Invisible Hand is that of the TYZ complex. Most economists tend to limit their research to the study of the mass markets which do appear to be competitive, efficient, and rational by economists' standards.

The TYZ complex is a remarkable system of national economic management. But obviously it is not well understood.

The setting: similar social and educational backgrounds of TYZ members

Statistical data support the proposition that leading businessmen and civil servants who constitute the TYZ complex share common social and educational backgrounds. Social backgrounds are correlated with the occupational statuses of the subjects' fathers. Table 9.1 summarizes findings on the social backgrounds of business leaders and high-level civil servants. The data come from Hiroshi Mannari's study (1974) of business leaders of 1960 and 1970 and Michio Muramatsu's study (1981) of high-level civil servants of 1977. Although dates and terms are not the same between the two sources, roughly comparable social backgrounds of businessmen and civil servants are indicated by table 9.1.

By "business leaders" Mannari means chairmen, presidents, vice-presidents, and the two highest ranks of managing directors (*senmu* and *jōmu*). His 1960 study covers 400 of the largest firms with 1,525 business leaders, of whom 985 (65 per cent) responded to the questionnaire. The 1970 study covers 500 of the largest firms with 3,310 business leaders, of whom 1,080 (33 per cent) responded. Because of the poorer response rate in 1970, Mannari considers the 1970 study less reliable than the 1960 one. But the median age of business leaders is roughly the same for both years: 59 years with the difference of only a fraction of a year more for 1970 than for 1960. In view of great economic expansion during the 1960s and the larger sample of firms for 1970, Mannari expected the 1970 business leaders to be younger than the 1960 ones. This expectation is not borne out by the data. For both years, chairmen are on the whole eleven years older than the second-level managing directors (*jōmu*), 67 against 56, the ages of the other ranks in between. Many second-level managing directors of 1960 must have attained chairmanships by 1970 under the observed age differential between the two ranks. Table 9.1 shows that about 43 per cent of the 1960 and about 53 per cent of the 1970 business leaders originated in the families of government officials, owners or managers of large or medium firms, or professional men. (Although longitudinal observations on these changing ratios of social origins are interesting, we minimize them for the moment in the interest of a quick comparative overview.)

The Muramatsu study is based on a smaller sample of high-level civil servants in eight ministries. The sample includes all the administrative vice-ministers (the highest rank a career civil servant can reach in Japanese government) and bureau chiefs, as well as selected counselors (*shingikan*) and section chiefs. Their ages range from 45 to 55. According to table 9.1, more than 60 per cent of these high-level civil servants came from the families of men in professional, administrative, or managerial occupations. Allowing for different definitions of terms and different stages of Japanese economic development that apply to different groups of "fathers," one may say that the social backgrounds of Mannari's business leaders and Muramatsu's civil servants are generally similar.

It is not surprising that a greater proportion of business leaders than high-level civil servants appear to have originated in less prestigious families. The occupational structure of the 1920s and 1930s included smaller proportions of the working population in professional, administrative, and managerial classes than today. These classes have expanded over time in the course of economic growth and generated net upward social mobility from lower classes. The somewhat greater heterogeneity of business leaders' social origin compared to elite civil servants implies greater upward social mobility through business than through the state bureaucracy. More than a fifth of the 1960 business leaders originated in the class of small business owners and about a quarter in agricultural families. Proportionately fewer civil servants originated in these classes. Civil servants can also be expected to show greater homogeneity than business leaders. Admissions to state civil service are subject to the civil service examination and promotions in it are rigorously controlled by formal criteria. In the business world, entrance is easier and achievement counts more for promotion than in the civil service.

Table 9.2 summarizes the educational background of business and civil service leaders obtained by three studies: the aforementioned research by Mannari and Muramatsu and Takashi Kakuma's journalistic reports (1981) on business leaders of 1981. Kakuma's business leaders are chairmen, presidents, and vice-presidents, without Mannari's managing directors. His sample consists of 251 business leaders of some 60 major firms which are said to be popular among graduating college seniors as desirable employers to work for and which Kakuma himself considers significant contributors to Japanese economic growth. The number of Kakuma's business leaders is exactly the same as Muramatsu's civil service leaders, but this must have been purely fortuitous. The median age of Kakuma's business leaders calculated from their years of birth is 66 in 1981 (born in 1915). This is four years older than the average age of Mannari's business leaders of comparable rank. Age is an important factor for structuring Japanese organization, a point that is useful for understanding the rest of this chapter.

It is not surprising that all the civil servants are college graduates. What is

Table 9.2 *The distribution of business leaders and high-level civil servants by alma mater*

Institutions	Percentage of business leaders who were graduates of these institutions			Percentage of leading servants who were graduates of these institutions, 1977
	1960	1970	1980	
Tōdai	33.0	30.5	43.4	79.3
Prestigious Four[a]	30.3	25.7	26.5	8.8
Other universities	28.3	39.2	30.4	11.9
No college education	8.4	4.6	[b]	0.0
Total	100.0	100.0	100.0	100.0
Number (persons) [c]	1,062	1,076	251	251

[a] The four prestigious universities next to Tōdai are Kyōto, Hitotsubashi, Keiō, and Waseda.
[b] Not mentioned in the source.
[c] For the sample coverage, see text.

Sources: For 1960 and 1970 business leaders, Mannari, 1974: 73, 222–3; for 1980 business leaders, Kakuma, 1981: 27; for 1977 civil servants, Muramatsu, 1981: 56.

impressive in table 9.2 is that, even in 1960, 90 per cent of business leaders were college graduates. The proportion of college graduates among Kakuma's 1981 business leaders should have exceeded 90 per cent easily. (Japan had a multitrack educational system before the war, when all the 1960 and 1981 business leaders went to college. Here "college graduates" include not only graduates of institutions specifically called universities or colleges, but also those of institutions which were called higher (i.e. post-secondary) specialist schools. These institutions were promoted to university status after the war, when a unitrack educational system was introduced.)

With broader homogeneity due to the commonality of college education there also develops a finer differentiation among business leaders and higher-level civil servants due to variations in prestige among colleges and universities attended. Among all colleges and universities in Japan, one institution has contributed a disproportionate share of business and civil service leadership. That is Tokyo University (Tōdai). Graduation from the same institution should be a more powerful homogenizer than the same degrees from different institutions. The great majority of civil servants and most business leaders are Tōdai graduates. This at least implies that between civil service and a large segment of business leadership there exists an informal bond of camaraderie ("old boy" networks) because of a shared background in the same alma mater, Tōdai. Furthermore, taking the common grouping of five universities (Tōdai, Kyōto, Hitotsubashi, Keiō, and Waseda) as the most prestigious universities of Japan, and assuming that graduates of these universities tend to develop a greater degree of intimacy and cooperation among them than between them and graduates of other universities, we find nearly 90 per cent of high-level civil servants and nearly 70 per cent of business leaders belonging to this group. These figures leave no doubt that Japanese civil service and business are dominated by graduates of five universities and that, among them, Tōdai graduates constitute the core of leadership.

Zaikai: government of organized business

Japanese firms compete vigorously in the marketplace inside and outside of Japan. But, socially and politically, they strive to safeguard and promote collective business interests through four nationwide organizations. These organizations overlap in membership, but the role differentiation among them makes them complementary rather than competitive. The informal unity of leaders of these organizations reflects the existence of Zaikai, which is by itself invisible, informal, and indefinable (Yanaga, 1968; Tanaka, 1979). An unkind, but not entirely incorrect translation of the term would be "Brotherhood of Money." In this section we describe each of the four organizations of Zaikai, paying special attention to the characteristics of their leaders.

Keidanren

The most powerful, comprehensive, and unabashedly political organization is Keizai Dantai Rengōkai, or Keidanren for short (Federation of Economic Organizations), headed since 1980 by Mr. Yoshihiro Inayama, former president and chairman of Nippon Steel. Inayama also presides over the Industrial Structure Council. Keidanren's primary objective is to maintain Japan as a nation committed to a basically capitalist economic system with all that it implies for the honor and privileges of business. Toward this end, Keidanren actively seeks influence over the political, legislative, and administrative processes of Japan through political donations and legislative lobbying. The Liberal Democratic Party (LDP) is its political ally. The standing political program of Keidanren is to keep LDP in power. Keidanren's membership consists of 806 major firms, 110 trade associations, and 70 specially admitted individual persons.

Nisshō

Chambers of commerce and industry date from 1878, when the Japanese government began to encourage their formation. The current Chambers of Commerce and Industry Law was enacted in 1953. The law defines a chamber of commerce and industry as a regional industrial and commercial association organized for the improvement of commerce and industry as well as for the promotion of public welfare. The law explicitly forbids activities in support of political parties. But this does not prevent the Nihon Shōkō Kaigisho, or Nisshō for short (Japan Chamber of Commerce and Industry), the peak organization aggregating regional associations of chambers of commerce and industry, from advocating its views on public policy in the general interest of economy, industry, and commerce. Nisshō is dominated by Tokyo and other big-city chambers. Traditionally, the president of the Tokyo Chamber doubles as Nisshō president. Mr. Shigeo Nagano (1900–84), former president of Fuji Steel and former chairman of Nippon Steel and Nisshō president from 1970 till his death in 1984, is generally believed to have raised Nisshō to a status rivalling Keidanren.

The personal relationships of Keidanren's Inayama and Nissho's Nagano indicate the importance of personal networks as a factor in the concentration of leadership in the hands of a few selected individuals in Zaikai. Nagano (1900–84; Tōdai 1924) and Inayama (1904–; Tōdai 1927) were close friends who together lived the extraordinary history of Japan's steel industry. Nagano started his business career with Fuji Steel, a private concern, while Inayama started his with Yawata Iron and Steel, a government enterprise. In 1935, Yawata, Fuji, and a few other iron and steel producers merged to form (old) Nippon Steel. In 1937, at the Tokyo headquarters of the merged concern, Nagano was a section manager in the Purchasing Division, while Inayama was in the same capacity in the Sales Division. In 1950, General MacArthur broke up Nippon Steel into Yawata and Fuji as a part of his trust-busting program. Nagano became president of Fuji and Inayama managing director of Yawata (he was later to become president). In 1963, Nagano was elected president of the Iron and Steel Federation, one of the most powerful member federations of Keidanren. Two years later, he vacated it for Inayama, who remained in it until 1979. In 1970, Nagano and Inayama merged their firms to form new Nippon Steel, with Nagano as chairman and Inayama as president. In the same year, Nagano was invited into the presidency of Nisshō, which he held until his death in 1984. In 1980, after Nagano's desire to stay with Nisshō was confirmed, Inayama was elected president of Keidanren. In this way, having built the world's greatest steel company and having completed a major cycle of Japanese industrialization, the two close friends ruled Japan's business community and indirectly governed Japan itself.

Nikkeiren

Nihon Kei'eisha Dantai Renmei (Nikkeiren for short, Japan Federation of Employers' Associations) consists of 47 regional (largely prefectural) associations and 54 industrial associations. Since 1979 its president has been Mr. Bunpei Ōtsuke (1903–; Tōdai 1928), chairman of Mitsubishi Mining and Cement. The member employers of Nikkeiren are nearly 30,000 firms, employing about a third of Japan's wage and salary earners, roughly corresponding to the extent of unionization of these workers. The *raison d'être* of Nikkeiren is the existence of the employers' class enemy: militant labor unions. In recent years, labor militancy has collapsed to the point of extinction. With this, many employers are beginning to doubt the need for maintaining Nikkeiren. Nikkeiren has been a part of Japan's postwar violent labor history. While Keidanren was working at the most elevated and elegant level of Japan's ruling power, Nikkeiren was bloodying its nose in the slugging matches with labor unions in order to safeguard employer prerogatives within a capitalist system. Today, one of the most important services of Nikkeiren to its members is the provision of strategies and guidelines for coping with labor unions during collective bargaining. In the course of struggles with labor, Nikkeiren has captured the relevant unit of the Japanese government, the Ministry of Labor. Nikkeiren's dominance over the labor policy of this ministry has been such that Nikkeiren is often referred to as the alternative Ministry of Labor. Its directorate and secretariat provide an ideal environment for the second career of retired Labor Ministry officials.[3]

Dōyūkai

Popularly called "Committee for Economic Development" in English, which is not a translation of its name, Dōyūkai is a committee of ideologues for a dynamic and responsible capitalism. It was organized in 1946 by younger businessmen then in their forties, who were perhaps prematurely thrust into reponsible business positions by the postwar purge of older leaders who had collaborated with the Japanese military during the war. Dōyūkai had a long period of stable leadership from 1960 to 1975 under the late Mr. Kazutaka Kikawada of Tokyo Electric Power Company (1899–1977; Tōdai 1926). During this period of consolidation and growth, the Dōyūkai philosophy of new capitalism was called "Kikawada-ism." It emphasized the autonomy of the private sector and orderly economic growth as prerequisites for a harmonious society. Thus, on the one hand, the private business sector declared independence from government controls, and on the other hand promised to deliver prosperity which would do away with class war between labor and capital. Kikawada's successor as Dōyūkai chairman is the incumbent Mr. Tadashi Sasaki (1907–; Tōdai 1930), former president of the Bank of Japan and current member of the Economic Council. Dōyūkai formulates and promulgates a business philosophy to ensure respectability for business in Japanese society. Now that liberalization and internationalization of the Japanese economy have been realized to a large extent and prosperity has extinguished class war, Dōyūkai has run into an identity crisis and a loss of direction. The young energetic ideologues of new capitalism have also aged. Some have passed away. Humorists twist "Dōyūkai" into "Dōyū kai?" ("How do you say?" or "What's the name of the group?"). Cynics call it "Rōyūkai" (Committee of Senile Friends).

Characteristics of Zaikai leaders

In light of the pattern of human resource allocation of Japan reviewed above, it is certainly not a coincidence that the presidents of all four Zaikai organizations were Tōdai graduates. Kakuma's reports afford some more observations on the educational backgrounds of a larger number of Zaikai leaders. Especially useful is the information on the educational backgrounds and ages of the presidents of regional chambers of commerce and industry, and of the presidents of regional employers' associations.

In connection with column A of table 9.3, we can note some unique organizational characteristics of Dōyūkai. Unlike other more formal interest associations, Dōyūkai retains considerable informality on the basis of individual membership. It is a self-governing group of nearly 1,000 individual members. Day-to-day services are run by one chairman (Tadashi Sasaki), five or fewer vice-chairman, and a full-time secretary. There are some 130 members of the operating committee for a term of two years and 20 senior advisors with a long history of personal involvement in Dōyūkai. Those elected to the Diet are given leave of absence from Dōyūkai membership. Kakuma lists all these individuals together with their years of birth and educational backgrounds. All are active executives of major corporations and banks (chairmen, presidents, vice-presidents, managing directors). Several of them are former high-level civil servants (vice-ministers and bureau chiefs). Educationally, they are unusually homogenous: four-fifths of them are graduates of the Prestigious Five, led by Tōdai. This might suggest the possible existence of a selection mechanism which Dōyūkai as a club of individuals can enforce to ensure commonality and compatibility of personal characteristics.

Although Dōyūkai once enjoyed a reputation as "young Turks of Japanese business," one has to note that the median age of its leading group was 66 years in 1980, by no means "young." Their age distribution suggests something about intergenerational shifts of weights among age groups. Based on Kakuma's report, the distribution looks as follows:

Born in 1909 or before	36 persons (24 per cent)
Born in 1910–19	75 persons (50 per cent)
Born in or after 1920	38 persons (26 per cent)

The mainstay of Dōyūkai leadership is the generation of the 1910s. This can be compared with Mannari's 1960 business leaders whose mainstay was the generation of the 1900s. In the late 1940s and 1950s, there was a rejuvenation of business leadership due to the purge of wartime business leaders. By 1980, the earlier distortions had been corrected and the age structure of business leadership stabilized. In due course, therefore, the mainstay of Dōyūkai leadership would shift to the generation of the 1920s. One may well imagine that younger members are constantly recruited and screened by the imperative of degrees from the Prestigious Five. Behind the stability of age structure

Table 9.3 *The distribution of four groups of business leaders by alma mater (per cent)*

Institutions	(A) Dōyūkai leaders	(B) Presidents of national affiliates of Nikkeiren	(C) Presidents of regional chambers of commerce	(D) Presidents of regional affiliates of Nikkeiren
Tōdai	48.3	54.7	21.6	26.9
Prestigious Four	34.2	32.1	29.4	23.1
Other universities	17.4	7.5	17.7	40.4
No college education	0.0	5.7	31.3	9.6
Total number (in persons)	149	53	51	52
Median year of birth	1914	1913	1910	1906

Sources: Kakuma, 1981: (A), pp. 195–203; (B), pp. 245–8; (C), pp. 273–6; (D), pp. 239–45.

among business leaders based on the intergenerational uniformity of leadership qualifications, one inevitably suspects the existence of a powerful force or institution that ensures the intertemporal continuity of values and preferences. This force or institution is the family, as discussed on pp. 288–93 below.

Since local-scale enterprises do not need first-class talent for their management, Tōdai graduates can be expected to be either fewer in number or not present at all among the officials of regional business associations. Table 9.3, columns C and D, bears this out. In these associations, even people without a college degree are as numerous as Tōdai graduates. At the regional level of business, there has obviously been opporunity for success without first going to college. Regional leaders are also somewhat older than national leaders, as may be seen from the median ages of the two groups of business leaders. Since the national Zaikai leadership is dominated by younger Tōdai graduates, the center–regional hierarchy of leaders appears to be a colonial regime in which Tōdai-educated national leaders lord it over less educated and humbler regional businessmen.

Enterprise groups

Zaikai leaders are extraordinary individuals. But purely individual qualifications for Zaikai leadership are not observable, because Zaikai leaders first have had to prove their worth by successful careers in major corporations before they become involved in Zaikai and because in the scheme of things it is the corporations rather than individuals that are represented at Zaikai and advisory councils for the state. Japan's industrial structure is just as oligopolistic as any other major industrial society. It is already taken as a point of departure that the "business leaders" worth our attention are those occupying top managerial and executive positions in Japan's "*Fortune* 500." Zaikai leaders are drawn from an even more restricted circle of giant corporations.

The major corporations fall into several "enterprise groups" (*kigyō shūdan*) (Henderson, 1973; Okumura, 1982; Miyazaki, 1983). An enterprise group coheres through regular "social" gatherings of presidents or chairmen of the affiliated companies. The most extensive and powerful enterprise groups, which are household names in Japan, are Mitsubishi, Mitsui, Sumitomo, Fuyō, Daiichi-Kangin, and Sanwa (Henderson, 1973, appendix 7). The "social" groupings of major corporations is a product of a legal ban on outright mergers or extensive interlocking ownerships. A prewar enterprise group then called "Zaibatsu" (plutocratic clique) was held together by a peak holding company through chains of vertical and horizontal interlocking share holdings as well as fully owned subsidiaries in diverse industries. Major Zaibatsu groups were dissolved by General MacArthur, but their member firms "socially" regrouped themselves after the end of America's occupation of Japan in 1952. These are the enterprise groups of today.

Utilizing the nature of Japan's power structure, which can be seen to consist of the state bureaucracy and Zaikai, Miyazaki (1983) offers an ingenious "index of power" for various corporations and enterprise groups. The unit of power in this case is a sort of "man-council" (as man-hour, passenger-mile, etc.). When a corporation has one of its men sitting on an advisory council for the state, or serving as a member of a Zaikai organization or the Japan Productivity Center, one unit of power is assigned to that corporation. If the same man is a member of two or more advisory councils, two or more units of power accrue to that corporation. Miyazaki computes these "power units" for each of the relevant corporations engaged in defined power-wielding activities and then classifies the corporations by enterprise group. He produces 14 enterprise groups as a consequence. Among them, the direct heirs to the four major Zaibatsu of prewar days – Mitsubishi, Mitsui, Sumitomo, and Fuyō – are seen to have acquired the largest number of power units. Thus, the powerful organs which manage the Japanese economy, like the advisory councils for the state, Zaikai, and the Japan Productivity Center, are under the sway of four major enterprise groups that have descended from prewar Zaibatsu. Zaikai can be said to be essentially Zaibatsu.

Business–government cohesion in economic policy-making

Since the end of World War II, Japan has been practicing economic planning which is more than "indicative" but far less than "binding," "commanding," or *"dirigiste"* (Taira, 1970). An economic plan is a statement of economic policy found useful by the prime minister. A new prime minister invariably orders a new economic plan or the revision of the existing one to suit his political objectives. Since all prime ministers but one since 1945 have been conservatives, and since they have been elected to office with the support of the business community, their political objectives coincide with business interests to a large extent.

Within the perimeter of choices set by the prime minister's political promises, the Economic Planning Agency (EPA), a subunit of the Prime Minister's Office, prepares the plan in collaboration with the Economic Council (Keizai Shingikai). The EPA officials ensure the technical consistency of all parts of a plan, and interplan consistency of ideals, logic, and analysis to maintain the integrity of government. However politically strong, no prime minister can extract from the EPA a purely politically motivated plan which makes little sense in terms of analytical soundness and technical feasibility. On the other hand the EPA planners work with the Economic Council, whose principal members are the prime minister's friends. The Economic Council is a hierarchical organization of committees, subcommittees, and project groups topped by 30 titular members of the Council who oversee the planning process and approve the plan, when formulated. The plan approved by the Council is forwarded to the prime minister, who in turn presents it to the Cabinet of the Ministers of State for discussion and adoption. The Cabinet's adoption of the plan makes it official as an instrument of economic policy.

There are therefore many cross-currents of different views and interests affecting the economic plan. If the economic plan has predictable biases and if overall stability of policy is maintained over time, these qualities of the plan may be inferred from the interest configurations within the Economic Council. Although nearly three hundred people are involved in the planning process, the titular members number only 30 and can be individually examined. Table 9.4 lists the 1983 members by interest configurations noticeable among them. (The EPA officials who sit on the Council *ex officio* are not included in the list.)

These members of the Economic Council are all prominent persons whose biographical details are available in *Who's Who*-type publications like *Jinji Kōshinroku*, whose 1981 edition contains such information on about 110,000 persons, starting with the reigning emperor and his household. Since the Economic Council advises the prime minister, it can be expected that its members are appointed from among the most esteemed Japanese nationals. By their current organizational or professional affiliation, the largest group is composed of private business leaders (table 9.4, nos. 1–9). We would consider this a minimal indicator of business influence over Japanese economic planning. To this, we would add Mr. Gotō Noboru (no. 17), who runs the *Tōkyū* business conglomcrate, but who on the Council carries the pedigree of a Tokyo Chamber of Commerce official. There are also men associated with public and quasi-public enterprises (nos. 10–16). All told, 17 out of 27 counselors appointed from outside the government can be considered representatives of the business community of Japan.

With the exception of three labor leaders on the Council, other counselors can be considered friends of business, if occasionally critical of business behavior or business conditions. For example, two counselors from the academic world (nos. 25 and 27) are leading economists who generally accept "modern" analytical approaches. They are not known for anti-business or pro-labor views. They are analytical guardians of the market–rational efficiency of resource allocation. Further, a counselor counted on the public interest side, Mr. Enjōji Jirō (no. 22), is the chairman of the Economic Council and comes from Japan's foremost commercial press on business and economics, which publishes the *Nihon Keizai Shinbun* (Japan Economic Journal), nicknamed Japan's *Wall Street Journal*. He is in a position to exercise leadership over the agenda and activities of the Economic Council and to give publicity to economic planning through his newspaper.

Table 9.4 *Members of the Economic Council and their socioeconomic backgrounds, 1983*

No.[a] Name	Current position	Year of birth	Education	Primary career	Zaikai connections[b]
A. Private corporations					
1. Ishihara, Kaneo	Comptroller, Japan Industrial Bank	1911	Tōdai (1934)	Ministry of Finance	None
2. Ibe, Kyōnosuke	Chairman, Sumitomo Bank	1908	Tōdai (1933)	Sumitomo Bank	*Keidanren* Board member; *Dōyūkai* Board member
3. Matsuzawa, Takuji	Chairman, Fuji Bank	1913	Tōdai (1938)	Fuji Bank	*Nikkeiren* Board member
4. Hiraiwa, Gaishi	President, Tokyo Electric Power	1914	Tōdai (1939)	Tokyo Electric Power	Vice-president *Keidanren*
5. Segawa, Minoru	Counselor, Nomura Securities	1906	Ōsaka Com. Univ. (1929)	Nomura Securities	Chairman, *Keidanren* Price Committee
6. Nakada, Otokazu	President, Mitsubishi Estate	1910	Otaru Com. Univ. (1932)	Ministry of Finance	Member, *Dōyūkai* Operating Committee
7. Nakayama, Yoshihiro	Counselor, Niigata Engineering	1914	Tōdai (1938)	Ministry of Foreign Affairs	None (Member, Industrial Structure Council)
8. Hasegawa, Norishige	Chairman, Sumitomo Chemical	1907	Tōdai (1931)	Sumitomo group	Vice-president *Keidanren*
9. Yamamoto, Shigenobu	Vice-chairman, Toyota Motor	1916	Tōdai (1939)	MITI	Council member *Keidanren*
B. Public and quasi-public organizations					
10. Sumita, Satoshi	Vice-president, Bank of Japan	1916	Tōdai (1940)	Ministry of Finance	None
11. Sasaki, Tadashi	President, National Institute for Research Advancement	1907	Tōdai (1930)	Bank of Japan	President, *Dōyūkai*
12. Tokunaga, Hisatsugu	Counselor, National Oil Corporation	1909	Tōdai (1938)	MITI	None

	Name	Position		Education	Prior affiliation	Other affiliations
13.	Murata, Hisashi	President, JETRO	1910	Tōdai (1936)	MITI	None
14.	Ōkita, Saburo	President, Institute for Domestic and International Policy Studies	1914	Tōdai (1937)	EPA; former Foreign Minister	None
15.	Takeda, Seizō	President, Japan Grain Inspection Association	1915	Tōdai (1939)	Ministry of Agriculture; EPA	None
16.	Tanimura, Hiroshi	(former) President, Tokyo Stock Exchange	1916	Tōdai (1938)	Ministry of Finance	None
C. Business interest						
17.	Gotō, Noboru	Vice-president, Tokyo Chamber of Commerce and Industry	1916	Tōdai (1940)	Tokyo Electric Express Railway	Board member in all of *Keidanren, Nikkeiren,* and *Doyukai*
D. Consumer interest						
18.	Nakabayashi, Sadao	President, Federation of Consumer Cooperatives	1907	Waseda (1932)	*Hochi* Newspaper	None
E. Labor interest						
19.	Usami, Tadanobu	President, *Dōmei*	1925	Takachiho Com. College (1945)	Fuji Textiles	None
20.	Tateyama, Toshifumi	President, *Chūritsu Roren*	1923	Kyushu Univ. (not completed)	Electric industry worker	None
21.	Makieda, Motofumi	President, *Sōhyō*	1921	Teachers' training school (1940)	Secondary school teacher	None
F. Public interest						
22.	Enjōji, Jirō	Counselor, Nihon Keizai Shinbun, *Japan Economic Journal*	1907	Waseda (1933)	*Japan Economic Journal*	None

Table 9.4 (cont.)

No.[a]	Name	Current position	Year of birth	Education	Primary career	Zaikai connections[b]
23.	Saigusa, Saeko	Social critic	1920	Tokyo Women's College (1941)	Editor-in-chief, *Fujin Kōron*	None
24.	Kawano, Shigetō	Professor emeritus, Tōdai	1911	Tōdai (1936)	Tōdai	None
25.	Kumagai, Hisao	Professor of Economics, Kansai University	1914	Tōdai (1937)	Osaka Univ.; former Director, EPA Research Inst.	None
26.	Mukaibō, Takashi	Professor emeritus, Tōdai	1917	Tōdai (1939)	Tōdai; former president	None
27.	Shinohara, Miyohei	Professor of Economics, Seikei University	1919	Hitotsubashi (1942)	Hitotsubashi; former Director, EPA Research Inst.	None (Member of Industrial Structure Council)

[a]These numbers are for identification only. In no way do they represent the ranking of the Counselors or the seating order at the Council meetings.
[b]For Zaikai etc., see text.

Sources: *Shūkan Tōyō Keizai* (Weekly Oriental Economist) (August 20, 1983), p. 170; *Jinji kōshinroku*, 1981.

One unusual person on the Council is Saigusa Saeko, lady counselor, who has distinguished herself as the editor-in-chief of a highbrow women's journal, *Fujin Kōron*, of the prestigious Chūō Kōronsha, which publishes a number of public affairs journals and books, including the well-known *Chūō Kōron*. She now operates as an independent social critic.

Looking over the list of Council members, the three labor leaders are the only people who stand out with distinctive professional and personal characteristics. They are younger and less formally educated. In contrast, two-thirds of the Council members are Tōdai graduates, though the Tōdai domination of the Council is somewhat eclipsed by its chairmanship going to a Waseda graduate, Mr. Enjōji Jirō. It is nevertheless remarkable that Tōdai obtains such a concentration of the Council membership, while Waseda has two and other universities one each.

Another important characteristic of the members of the Economic Council is that, even among the nine counselors from private business corporations, only five of them can be considered purely private businessmen. The other four are former civil servants who took up a second career in private business after retiring from the civil service. In addition, all the counselors but one from the public or quasi-public enterprises are former civil servants. The singular exception is Mr. Sasaki Tadashi (no. 11), whose primary lifelong career was with the Bank of Japan. Dr. Saburo Ōkita (no. 14), who appears as president of a research society here, has had an illustrious career in the EPA and a number of public and quasi-public organizations. Recently he also served as Minister of Foreign Affairs. Among the "public interest" members of the Council, Professors Kumagai and Shinohara (nos. 25 and 27) have served as directors of the EPA Institute of Economic Research. Professor Kawano (no. 24) presided over the Institute of Developing Economies, controlled by MITI, for a long time. Thus, all told, 13 counselors out of a total of 27 are either former civil servants or have had personal experience in the EPA bureaucracy. To this one might add Mr. Sasaki, former president of the Bank of Japan, and Professor Mukaibō, former president of Tōdai (no. 26), as public officials indistinguishable from civil servants proper. From all this, it appears that the mainstream of interests involved in Japanese economic planning is a confluence of business, bureaucracy, and Tōdai; i.e. the Tōdai–Yakkai–Zaikai complex.

The significant presence of former civil servants on the Economic Council should be a facilitating factor in the relationship between it and the EPA bureaucracy. (In fact, it is often heard that the private corporations' need for people to handle government relations is the stimulus for retiring high-level officials to move to private business, as noted in the next section of this chapter.) Furthermore, most of the counselors who are ex-officials are now septuagenarians, while the EPA officials in responsible managerial positions, who direct the secretarial services for the Council, are in their mid-forties. The counselors in effect belong to the age groups of the EPA officials' fathers. In a society like Japan where, other things being equal, the worth of a person is age-graded, one can well imagine how respectfully the younger Tōdai graduates on active duty must behave toward the parent-level Tōdai graduates who are also former high-level officials. Dr. Ōkita, former EPA Planning Division Director and former Minister of Foreign Affairs, is a graphic illustration of this kind of counselor–official relationship. In his younger days, Dr. Ōkita played a prominent role on the bureaucratic side of the economic planning process. He now sits on the Council side and examines the planning papers presented by EPA officials. Dr. Ōkita also single-handedly created a new professional group known as "government econo-mists" (*kanchō ekonomisuto* – no adequate Japanese word exists for "economists").[4] Once the brilliant civil servants with Tōdai-compatible intelligence learned the art of economic analysis and applied it to the abundant economic data that they monopolized, they could easily make the EPA a most powerful think-tank that no private research organization, let alone individual economist, could challenge.

A look at the column labeled "Zaikai connections" in table 9.4 reveals that many private business leaders who are not former civil servants are involved in the sociopolitical activities of the business community, Zaikai, described earlier. An apt example from table 9.4 is Mr. Gotō Noboru (no. 17), vice-president of the Tokyo Chamber of Commerce and Industry at the time of appointment to the Council, who currently serves as a member of the board in all other Zaikai organizations. Multiple office holdings of this kind are by no means unusual. Miyazaki (1983) found that there were 127 Zaikai leaders, who, in addition to their main positions as presidents, chairmen, or counselors of their corporations, held four to ten positions in Zaikai organizations and advisory councils of the government in 1980.

The Japanese law for the organization of state administration, Article 8, encourages the establishment of advisory councils for various kinds and levels of administration. Over the years, councils based on this legal stipulation have mushroomed to an apparent excess, giving rise to reform attempts on several occasions. Sato (1978) shows that when the recent law for the liquidation and consolidation of advisory councils was passed in 1978, there were already 246 councils.[5] In addition, the prime minister, ministers of state, and chiefs of units in various ministries have been using extralegal, private advisory groups. A full picture of these private groups is not available, however. Advisory councils and groups may be a way of maximizing citizen partici-pation in the administrative processes. But inquiries into the members of these organs and the interests that they apparently represent tend to show lopsided interest configurations which can hardly be called a fair representa-tion of all segments of public interest.

Our examination of the membership of the Economic Council above also suggests the existence of the Tōdai–Yakkai–Zaikai complex. It may now be useful to test whether a similar coalition exists in another advisory council. Our choice was the extremely active Industrial Structure Council, which produces Japan's industrial policy. Industrial policy is clearly a subset of general economic policy. Once the overall plan is drawn up, its implementation is entrusted to different operating ministries. The industrial part of the plan is the jurisdiction of the Ministry of International Trade and Industry (MITI) and its Industrial Structure Council.

The Industrial Structure Council is the largest of all councils established for diverse economic policy purposes. It can have a membership of up to 130 persons, but actual membership has rarely approached 100. In 1983, it was 86. These are titular members. Other temporary appointees to numerous committees, subcommittees, and project groups would amount to several hundred. The size of the Industrial Structure Council prevents the exercise of individualized examination of its membership in the way that was possible with 27 members of the Economic Council. Table 9.5 summarizes the interest configurations, educational backgrounds, and bureaucratic connections of the counselors.

Table 9.5 indicates that the Industrial Structure Council is also dominated by business interests, the sum of members from private corporations, public enterprises, quasi-public organizations, and industry associations amounting to 61 out of a total of 86. In addition, almost half of the counselors are Tōdai graduates, and about a quarter graduates of the other Prestigious Four. Among the business counselors, the Tōdai graduates comprise nearly two-thirds, approximating the share of Tōdai graduates in the Economic Council membership. In contrast, there are only 3 Tōdai graduates among 25 non-business counselors. Again, it repeats the previously observed pattern that none of the labor counselors is a Tōdai graduate. Labor counselors with university credentials earned them at less prestigious private universities. The logic of prestige that apparently guides socioeconomic mobility in Japan directs the graduates of Tōdai and similarly prestigious universities to business. Further, *Who's Who*, gives full coverage to the business counselors of Table 9.5, but incomplete coverage to others ("no information" column). Among the 61 business counselors, 15 are former civil servants, and they are all with private and public corporations. On the whole, then, generalizations about the Economic Council apply to the Industrial Structure Council with a remarkable degree of regularity.

Table 9.5 Interest configurations and educational backgrounds of the Industrial Structure Council members, 1983

Education	Private corporations	Industry associations	Public and quasi-public corporations	Consumer organizations	Labor unions	Public interest	Total	Percentage
Tōdai	15	16	7	0	0	3	41	47.7
Prestigious Four	7	7	1	0	0	5	20	23.3
Other universities	4	4	0	0	3	4	15	17.4
No college education	0	0	0	1	1	1	2	2.3
No information[a]	0	0	0	1	4	3	8	9.3
Total	26	27	8	1	8	16	86	100.0
of whom former civil servants	5	5	5	0	0	0	15	17.4

[a] Refers to Council members who are not listed in *Who's Who*.

Sources: Shokuinroku (Staff Directory), 1983 (Tokyo, Ministry of Finance Press, 1983); *Jinji kōshinroku* (Who's Who), 1981.

Former civil servants in the private sector[6]

The substantial presence of former civil servants among private sector business leaders stimulates curiosity. This stems from the peculiarities of Japanese state civil service, which prematurely terminates the careers of a large number of high-level civil servants between the ages of 45 and 55. A rough breakdown of their second careers would be: one-third in private companies, one-third in public or quasi-public organizations (many of them "special corporations" – *tokushu* or *kōeki hōjin*), and one-third in other occupations like industry associations, universities, research institutes, independent practices, party politics, political offices, etc.

The only precise number known to the public is that of the retiring civil servants who move to private companies right away. These moves need official approval from the Personnel Administration Agency. In order to prevent potential abuse of the powers of office to secure favorable positions in the private sector, the law requires ministries and agencies to report on their retiring civil servants moving to the private sector and to prove that they are not moving to the companies they had directly dealt with during their active periods in government. "Direct" dealing is often narrowly construed, however. As a consequence, it is easy for civil servants to move to companies in the industries which generally fall within the jurisdiction of the ministries to which they belonged: e.g. Ministry of Finance officials move to banks and other financial companies, Ministry of Construction officials to construction companies, MITI officials to industrial companies, etc. According to Personnel Administration (Japanese Government, 1982), the number of civil servants who fell under the reporting obligations in 1982 was 266, a number considerably larger than ten years earlier.

Those who have risen to the positions of section chief or higher (like those high-level civil servants in Michio Muramatsu's study of bureaucracy mentioned earlier) are highly competent persons, easily matching their peers in the private sector in potential ability and promised performance. Through their offical duties, which involve "administrative guidance" of individual companies to make them conform to industrial policy, they have familiarized themselves with the details of the business they are taking up. Although they usually first move into staff positions or are attached to the new employers as "counselors" (*komon*), with a little reorientation and experience many of them prove qualified for taking charge of line operations. Freed from the long-term commitment of government employment, they are now on their own and can afford to be aggressive and mobile according to their qualifications, experience, and market opportunities.

A little numerical exercise may be useful to assess the importance of civil servants turned businessmen.

If 200 civil servants regularly move to private companies every year and if they have on average ten to twenty years of active life ahead, then over a period of twenty years there builds up a stock of 2,000 to 4,000 private business managers and executives who are former civil servants. Since the top managements of Japan's 400 major companies would add up to about 1,500 (as mentioned by Mannari), the estimated stock of former civil servants turned businessmen amounts to a formidable base for the supply of business leaders in these and other firms. Although not all retiring officials go into major companies, it is conceivable that these firms have the first pick of the ablest ones, if they wish. Yamamoto's non-exhaustive list (1972: 205–16) of retired highest-class civil servants (vice-ministers, bureau chiefs, and equivalent) by employer and position circa 1972 shows about 160 companies as their new employers. Some employers had two or three such former civil servants. They all occupied leading executive positions (board members, chairmen, presidents, vice-presidents, executive directors, comptrollers, counselors, etc.). Of the 169 companies to which civil servants had moved, 87 were mining–manufacturing companies. When these companies are checked against Henderson's list (1973) of the 100 largest mining–manufacturing companies of the same period (ranked by sales), 36 of them were among these 100 and, more remarkably, 7 of them were among the top 10. This is a very high rate of penetration of private business executive positions by former civil servants. According to the *Oriental Economist*'s survey (1984), in 1982 there were 30,192 top executives in all the 1,773 member firms of the stock exchange of Japan. These executives, who had moved into their present companies from outside, i.e. government, public enterprises, banks, or parent companies numbered 8,111, of whom those from government bureaucracies and public enterprises (former civil servants) were 1,232. When this number is compared with the maximum number of former civil servants in private companies, roughly 4,000 as mentioned above, the demonstrably high rate of success among civil servants in private business is impressive.

Civil servants' need for a second career arises from the rules and conventions of civil service employment. Up to the position of section chief, which is attainable around age 40, civil service tenure is secure with regular promotions. But beyond that, positions become fewer and civil servants with no more positions to be promoted to are compelled to move out of government. That is, after a tour of duty among several section chief positions, a civil servant is either promoted to bureau chief or removed from the civil service entirely. Once one of a cohort is promoted to a higher position, the whole cohort of civil servants who entered employment in the same year must be reshuffled so that no one is placed in the embarrassing situation of having to work for a superior of the same or younger age. The principle is that ranks in the civil service hierarchy must correspond to the age-graded seniority system.[7]

The highest position to which career civil servants can be promoted is that of administrative vice-minister, attainable in one's early fifties. After an average of two years in this post, they retire for good. But former vice-ministers are highly prized in the private sector.

Quite naturally, the level of private-sector jobs to which civil servants move roughly corresponds to the ranks at which they quit the civil service. But, after entry, how former civil servants will fare in private companies is a matter of opportunity and performance. Endowed with excellent qualifications, most perform well and many rise to top executive positions. It is some of these former civil servants, now successful business leaders, whom we encountered at the Economic Council and the Industrial Structure Council.

Ministries that handle placement services for their retiring civil servants never take their eyes off them during their second career. It is commonly acknowledged that placement strategies and decisions are in part motivated by policy considerations. For example, the government seeks to place former civil servants with firms or trade associations of major importance to its policy. These firms and associations also want former officials in their managerial ranks for precisely the same reason: if their economic prospects depend on how they stand in relation to policy, it is good for them to have the kind of people around who can relate to policy-makers and keep in touch with government thinking. Since "administrative guidance" (by means of persuasion, encouragement, coercion, arm twisting, legal threat, etc., depending on the quality of specific company–government relationships) is the instrument of policy implementation, former civil servants as managers can significantly contribute toward the lubrication, facilitation, and even exploitation of business–government relationships for the benefit of their new employers as well as for their own.

The need for a close calibration of industrial policy and business behavior is greater in proportion to legal controls on the economy. In the 1950s and 1960s, many economic activities were subject to controls: e.g. international trade, foreign exchange allocation, credit rationing, interest rates, technology induction, industrial location, etc. During this time, therefore, "administrative guidance" was a kind of law enforcement, and the authority of the bureaucracy was something to be feared. But, as the Japanese economy is now substantially liberalized and internationalized, MITI officials themselves acknowledge that "administrative guidance" has no legal threat behind it and that it is increasingly an art of diplomacy. Willing cooperation and skills to secure it on both sides are more needed than before. As former civil servants in managerial positions of private firms increase in number, these firms acquire bargaining strength *vis-à-vis* the civil servants on active duty, whose number remains constant and who by definition are younger than their former superiors now turned businessmen. Consequently, social power relations between business and bureaucracy are reversed: government officials must heed the interests of private firms in the formulation and implementation of economic and industrial policies. Furthermore, the relatively young high-level civil servants (45–55 years old) with an eye on entering private business must start pleasing their prospective employers (55–70 years old) at an appropriate time: the hierarchy of the civil service is recreated in the structure of personal relationships between former civil servants in business and incumbents in government on a national scale. State administration and major private companies, in effect, form an "extended government."

Elite consolidation through kinship and marital ties

The commonality or compatibility of educational backgrounds, ideological preferences, and socioeconomic statuses pull people together in closer working relationships. The same factors facilitate social relationships and often bring about groups of elite families linked by intermarriage. Just as a few hundred major companies can be said to control the economy, the forces of selection and integration in the social space of family, kinship, and marriage produce a few hundred prestigious family groups as a ruling class. Business leaders of major companies often turn out to be builders and managers of powerful family dynasties. In Japan, the traditional elites dating from premodern days have either transformed themselves into leading business groups or have been drawn into the reorganized upper class by marital ties with leading business families. The builder of a dynasty is an organizational entrepreneur who maximizes the chances for his own advancement in wealth, prestige, and power by deploying his kin over desirable positions and by forging marital alliances with other established families. Successful Japanese businessmen who are adept at utilizing the rules of the marketplace are also generally good at the use of the nonmarket networks of kinship and marital ties.

The existence of family groups bound by marital ties (*keibatsu*) as power bases for sociopolitical influence is a popular topic in all kinds of publications, from serious to frivolous. There are numerous examples to illustrate this point. One of the most amazing networks of families in recent history is the Nagano clan (Nagano ichizoku). For three decades, its central figure, Shigeo Nagano (1900–84), former President of the Japan Chamber of Commerce and Industry (Nissho) and former chairman of Nippon Steel, was also a powerful industrial and Zaikai leader until the moment of his death. Ozono (1983) summarizes the extent of power implied in the achievements of the Nagano men: 15 former presidents and chairmen of major companies with stocks traded in the prestigious First Division of the Tokyo Securities Exchange; 4 former administrative vice-ministers of state; 4 former or incumbent members of the National Diet, 3 of them having served as Ministers of State, and 1

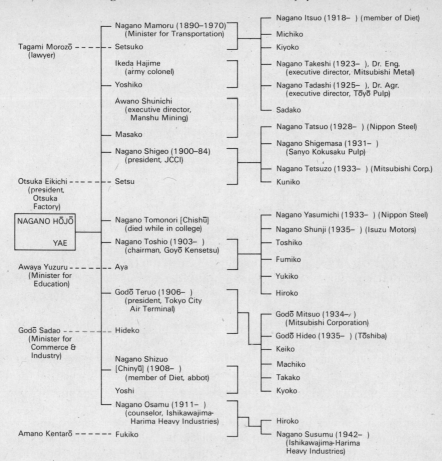

9.1   The genealogy of the Nagano clan, I. Note: The chart shows only the male line. The offspring of daughters married to other families are not shown. The solid lines show direct Nagano lines of descent. Broken lines show the other families who supplied spouses to the Nagano. For example, Setsuko paired with Nagano Mamoru is a daughter of Tagami Morozo. The paired men and women on this chart indicate married couples.

former prefectural governor. Most of the Nagano men are Tōdai graduates, while the Nagano women are graduates of well-known women's colleges. Thus, the Nagano clan represents a substantial cross-section of bureaucratic, business, and political elites. The illustrious genealogies of the Nagano clan vividly show how Tōdai degrees, political connections, business successes, social recognition, and marital nexus all converge to generate and perpetuate a family dynasty.

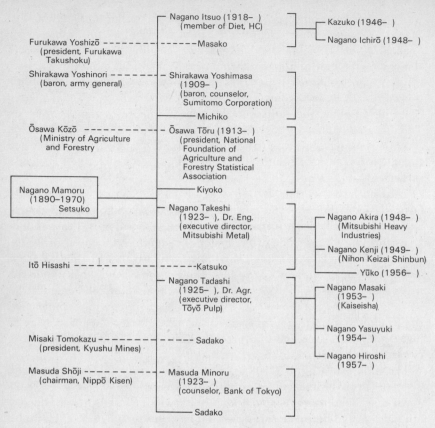

9.2   The genealogy of the Nagano clan, II.

The Nagano family was a local priestly dynasty until Shigeo's grandfather's time.[8] Shigeo's father, Nagano Hōjō (in the genealogical charts, names are noted in the Japanese way: surname first, followed by personal name), rebelled against the tradition and pursued a different career as a lawyer and justice in the new era of Meiji. Hōjō died at the age of 46, survived by his wife, seven sons, and two daughters. Mrs. Yae Nagano was an extraordinary woman. Despite poverty, she saw five of her sons through Tōdai and one through Tohoku University. A son who was to resume the priestly tradition of the family (Chishū in figure 9.1) died young while in a Buddhist college. The two daughters had good marriages: Yoshiko to an army colonel and Masako to the managing director of Manchurian Mines.

When Hōjō died, the first son, Mamoru (1890–1970), was a freshman at Tōdai. Shigeo (1900–84) was in the fourth grade of primary school. The seventh and youngest son, Osamu (1911–), was an infant. The grown-up son, Mamoru, shared the burden of supporting the family with his mother. Luck was on their side, however. Mamoru had a good friend at Tōdai, a son, Masao, of Japan's most celebrated business leader of all time, Shibusawa Eiichi (1840–1931).[9] Shibusawa pretended to "employ" Mamoru as his son's companion for study and research and paid Mamoru his monthly "salary," which Mamoru remitted to his mother back home in western Japan. Mamoru was a brilliant student, competing for first place with Kōtaro Tanaka, later Chief Justice of the Supreme Court. However, Mamoru Nagano, despite his Tōdai degree, shunned a governmental career and chose banking. After his success in business, he turned to politics and attained the portfolio of Minister of State for Transportation in the late 1950s. Shigeo's career was sketched earlier.

The fourth son, Toshio (1903–), was a high-level civil servant purged by General MacArthur after the war. He took up his second career in business and did very well, rising to the highest executive position of Penta Ocean Construction, which is one of the major companies of the Fuyō Group.

The fifth son, Teruo (1906–), first practiced law after graduation from Tōdai and joined Nippon Kōkan (Steel Pipes), the second most important major steel producer after Nippon Steel. He was a strong candidate for the Kōkan presidency but the Kōkan "natives" objected to his appointment on the grounds that it was not right to put two major steel companies of Japan under brothers of the same family. He then moved to Japan Air Lines and is currently with Tokyo City Air Terminal.[10]

The sixth son, Chinyū (1908–), a graduate of Tōhoku University, was "elected" by the brothers to rescue the family's priestly profession. He obliged and studied Buddhism at Ryūkoku University, which Chishū attended but did not finish due to his premature death. He has risen to a high position in the nationwide order of his denomination. The Nagano clan backed him fully when he successfully ran for the Upper House of the National Diet (the House of Counselors).

The seventh and youngest son, Osamu, a doctor of engineering (1911–), has had a typical technologist's career and retired as vice-president of Ishikawajima-Harima, one of the largest engineering firms of Japan and an affiliate of the Mitsui Group.

Figure 9.2 shows the occupational statuses and marital relations of the children of the oldest of the Nagano brothers, Mamoru. His three sons were all Tōdai graduates. The first son, Itsuo (1918–), became a member of the Upper House of the Diet. The second son, Takeshi (1923–), executive director of Mitsubishi Metal and the third son, Tadashi (1925–), executive director of Tōyō Pulp, are already among business leaders by criteria used by Mannari and illustrated in table 9.2. According to the age distribution of Japanese business leaders, Mamoru's sons born in the 1920s were, in the 1980s, waiting in the wings for top business leadership to be passed down from the generation of the 1910s.

292   Koji Taira and Teiichi Wada

It is noteworthy that the spouses of Mamoru's daughters have had distinguished careers and that one of them was a former aristocrat, Baron Shirakawa. It says something about social mobility in Japan that a country lawyer's granddaughter married into a noble family.[11] The husband of the second daughter, Kiyoko, is former Vice-Minister for Agriculture and former president of an important public corporation, Agriculture, Forestry and Fishery Corporation. The third daughter, Sadako, is married to a former Minister of State for the energy Resources Agency, currently a counselor for the Bank of Tokyo. Mamoru, former Minister for Transportation, certainly raised his family in a manner befitting his remarkable achievements and elevated position in Japanese society.

Mamoru's grandchildren belong to the postwar generation (born after 1945) and are either in search of a career or in the early stages of one. Among them, Takeshi's two sons, Akira (1948–), a Tōdai graduate, and Kenji (1949–), a Kyōto graduate, have started a typical business career as salaried employees of major firms, theoretically on the upward "escalator," as the Japanese would put it.

The children of Mamoru's younger brothers, most of them Tōdai graduates, are well on their way to distinguished positions as indicated by the organizations they are associated with. Information on how far they have come so far, however, is not available at time of writing, because they have not yet made their way into Who's Who in Japan.

The male lines of the Nagano clan alone have become quite complex in four generations. If the collateral families from which the wives of the Nagano men came or into which the Nagano daughters were married were to be taken into account, the family nexus would indeed be formidable. With abundant biographical data publicly available, patience alone is the constraint on any attempt to account for all the inter-connections of Who's Who-worthy families. For example, Yanaga (1968: 327–8) lists more than 100 families in a "marital network linking business, political, and academic elites with the imperial family and the former aristocracy." The list includes Mamoru Nagano, Shigeo Nagano, and Teruo Godō. Our geneological charts suggest nothing about the Nagano clan's marital ties stretching to the imperial family. But that is because we have limited our attention to the immediate families of the Nagano men and their in-laws. A more comprehensive research of the type that Yanaga has done should uncover the family trees of the Nagano in-laws, leading eventually to the imperial household.

To summarize how family connections develop and solidify, if more than 100 families can be linked with one family in this way, any one of the 100 families may also be linked to its own set of yet another 100. Eventually, all the family cells of a social matrix can be filled in by relating all elite families to one another by blood or marriage. In some parts of this matrix, interlinkages of families may be particularly dense due to their long dynastic histories. (The imperial dynasty has the longest history of any family in Japan.) But what is important is that even the new members of the business elite like the Nagano brothers are quickly integrated into the existing elite matrix through their own marital ties or those of their children and grandchildren. If there is that much elite integration despite the functional division of society into government, business, and various groups, too formal an analysis of business–government relations as intersectoral relations would overlook the all too prevalent shortcuts in communication and cooperation that exist between political, bureaucratic, and business leaders through the web of kinship and marital ties.

Conclusion

This chapter shows how Zaikai (organized business) and Yakkai (state bureaucracy) interact with each other through their leading members, who share common social origins and educational backgrounds. The educational backgrounds are predominately Tōdai, supplemented by four other prestigious universities. In light of the excellent performance of the Japanese economy, there is no denying that the T–Y–Z complex has been managing the economy very well. Although this chapter does not describe how politics fits into the picture painted here, it is well known that the continued supremacy of the conservative Liberal Democratic Party as a governing party of Japan is financed by the political donations of Zaikai and that the Zaikai-supported lawmakers in the Diet are content with a passive role of passing the bills presented to them by the state bureaucracy. Inspiration for good laws and the required technical expertise to handle legislation come from Tōdai education. In short, it cannot be denied that the T–Y–Z complex is also a collective governor of Japan's policy.

Nevertheless, "Who governs Japan?" is a popular research topic among Japan specialists in America. It is generally treated as a sort of multiple choice question: politicians (political parties), big business, bureaucracy, or none of the above. It is significant that the choice of answers is severely limited to begin with. For example, neither labor nor any ideological group figures to any noticeable extent as a potential governing force. Yanaga (1968) picks big-business as the force that governs Japan; Johnson (1975) offers bureaucracy. Treize (1976) takes a pluralist view. No American specialist on Japan seems impressed with Japanese politicians. Japanese journalists, however, for example, Nihon Keizai Shinbun (1983), tend to be impressed with the activities of the Liberal Democratic Party, which produces the prime minister and all other ministers of state who command the state bureaucracy and lead the political forces in the Diet. Interestingly, prime ministers and state ministers, especially more successful ones among them as "statesmen," have largely been Tōdai graduates and ex-bureaucrats (Murakami and Hirschmeier, 1979). The view that emerges from this chapter is that politics in Japan is largely symbolic or even cosmetic, and that there is some core of real governing–managing power shared among a few hundred men cohered in a network of intimate, supportive personal relations which we call the Tōdai–Yakkai–Zaikai complex. To this, one can add "Seikai" (politics). The men who are in it are bound by a sense of common destiny.

NOTES

The authors are professors of economics at the University of Illinois at Urbana-Champaign and at Waseda University, Tokyo, respectively. They are grateful to a number of people for information, suggestions, and comments; especially so to Professors Shozō Inoue, S. B. Levine, Hiroshi Mannari, Yoshikazu Miyazaki, Kazuo Tomoyasu, and Ronald Toby.

1 Clark (1979: 6) offers a version of "Japan, Inc." and rejects it as "a common misapprehension." He says: "The idea of 'Japan, Inc.' is partly an extension from persons to institutions of the ill-informed judgement that all orientals look the same. It is also partly a rationalization of Japanese commercial success, which becomes attributable to an advantage no Western businessman enjoys: the unconditional support of a sympathetic government. It is an absurd simplification." Although it is commonly believed that foreigners are responsible for fabricating the expression, Abegglen (1970: 33) says that he heard it from a Japanese businessman. In fact, Japanese writers generally use the term approvingly as a useful device for focussing attention on the essentials of Japanese-style business–government relations. The close business–government relations implied in "Japan, Inc." became a contested issue out of an ideological outrage felt by people who consider such relations unfair or even immoral. Once someone denounces a concept, someone else is bound to rise to its defense. Thus, there has been a whole series of serious, though somewhat unproductive, efforts to clarify whether Japan is really "Japan Inc." Examples of such efforts are discussions of the topic in Vogel, 1975; Patrick and Rosovsky, 1976; and Johnson, 1982. For a Japanese view of it, see especially an article by a former MITI official who was in a sense a manager of "Japan Inc.": Namiki, 1979.

2 This tripod that supports the dynamic Japanese economy is "Tokyo University, State Bureaucracy and Organized Business." *Tōdai* and *Zaikai* are familiar terms in Japan. But *Yakkai* for state bureaucracy needs a caveat. It is meant to be short for *Yakuninkai* (officialdom), which should pass as an alias for a more traditional *Kenkai*, which in turn can be considered short for *Kanryōkai* (bureaucracy). Professor Toby, who coined the word for us, says that *Yakkai* not only rhymes well in the context but evokes a humorous homonym, meaning "nuisance" as in "he made a nuisance of himself."

3 For exhaustive details of the Nikkeiren structure and operations, see Levine, 1984.

4 See a brief illuminating note on Dr. Ōkita and EPA economist-officials in Yamamoto, 1972: ch. 8.

5 Using all the officially established advisory councils related to economic matters, Sato also counts present and former civil servants, men from private corporations,

and others, reaching the conclusion that business interests dominate these councils. A recent official count of the extant councils as of August 1983 puts their total as 213 (*Shingikai Yōran*).

6 In this section, we draw liberally upon a very illuminating article on the subject by Johnson (1974). We would also like to gratefully acknowledge that we have benefited greatly from extensive personal correspondence with Professor Kazuo Tomoyasu of Nihon University on recent trends of occupational changes of high-level civil servants.

7 This applies to "career" civil servants who enter government employment by the standard civil service examinations. There are "non-career" civil servants who enter employment by different kinds of examination. The "non-career" civil servants have better job security than "career" ones so long as they can tolerate the indignity of blocked promotions and perpetual subservience to younger fast-track "career" superiors. This is another example of how the kind of examination that one takes determines lifetime opportunity in Japan. An upwardly mobile person should pass the Tōdai entrance exam and then the career civil service exam.

8 The narrative of the Nagano clan is based on Arima, 1980; Tahara, 1980; Ozono, 1983; and *Jinji Kōshinroku*, 1981.

9 On Shibusawa, see Hirschmeier (1964).

10 The reader may wonder why in figure 9.1 Teruo is not a Nagano but a Godō. His story illustrates an interesting aspect of the Japanese family dynasty. Teruo married a daughter of a former Minister for Commerce and Industry, Takuo Godō. Then the only Godō heir died without a successor. Teruo's father-in-law asked Teruo to succeed him in the Godō family. Teruo agreed and was adopted into the Godō family. If the adoption had been intended from the beginning, a normal process would have been for Teruo to marry into the Godō family, becoming a Godō at the outset. In this case, a Godō daughter was married out to the Nagano, and a Nagano man was adopted into the Godō. This means that the Godō daughter, once married out, was not "returning" to her original family. She came as the wife of an adopted son, not as a Godō daughter. The intricate legal maneuver was necessary and possible because the basic principle was absolutely legitimate: that the Godō family line had to be maintained. As a consequence, a classic dynastic alliance between Godō and Nagano family groups was effected.

11 This and other social events in Japan's "high society" are extensively collected and analyzed by Fujishima (1965). The mixing of the business elite and the aristocracy, of course, should surprise no one. The ultimate example of this social trend was Crown Prince Akihito's marriage to a daughter of the owner of the Nisshin Flour Milling Company (77th in sales ranking in 1971)

REFERENCES

Abegglen, James C., 1970. "The economic growth of Japan." *Scientific American*, 223, 3: 31–7
Arima, Makiko, 1980. "Nagano Shigeo to gonin no kyōdai" (Nagano Shigeo and five brothers). *Chūō kōron keiei mondai* (Central Review: Management Problems), 19, 1 (Spring): 390–406

Clark, Rodney, 1979. *The Japanese Company*. New Haven and London: Yale University Press

Fujishima, Taisuke, 1965. *Nihon no jōryū shakai* (Japan's High Society). Tokyo: Kōbunsha

Henderson, Dan Fenno, 1973. *Foreign Enterprise in Japan: Law and Policies*. Chapel Hill, N. C.: University of North Carolina Press

Hirschmeier, Johannes, 1964. *The Origins of Entrepreneurship in Meiji Japan*. Cambridge, Mass.: Harvard University Press

Japanese Government, 1982. *Eiri kigyō e no shūshoku no shōnin ni kansuru nenji hōkokusho* (An Annual Report on the Approval of Moves to Profit-Making Enterprises). Personnel Administration Agency

  1983. *Shokuinroku* (Staff Directory)

Jinji kōshinsha, 1981. *Jinji kōshinroku* (Who's Who), 31st edn., Tokyo

Johnson, Chalmers, 1974. "Re-employment of retired government bureaucrats in Japanese business." *Asian Survey*, 14, 11 (November): 935–65

  1975. "Japan: who governs? An essay on official bureaucracy." *Journal of Japanese Studies*, 2, 1 (Autumn): 1–28

  1982. *MITI and the Japanese Miracle*. Stanford University Press

Kakuma, Takashi, 1981. *Nihon no shihai kaikyū: Zaikaihen* (Japan's Ruling Classes: Zaikai). Tokyo: PHP Institute

Levine, Soloman B., 1984. "Employers association in Japan." In John P. Windmuller and Alan Gladstone (eds.), *Employers Association and Industrial Relations*. London: Oxford University Press, ch. 12

Mannari, Hiroshi, 1974. *The Japanese Business Leaders*. Tokyo University Press

Miyazaki, Yoshikazu, 1983. "Nihon no kigyō shūdan to paawa eriito" (Japan's enterprise groups and power elite). *Ekonomisuto* (Economist), May 10: 20–34

Murakami, Hyoye, and Johannes Hirschmeier (eds.), 1979. *Politics and Economics in Contemporary Japan*. New York and San Francisco: Kodansha International

Muramatsu, Michio, 1981. *Sengo Nihon no kanryōsei* (Postwar Japan's bureaucracy). Tokyo: Tōyō Keizai Shinpōsha

Namiki, Nobuyoshi, 1979. " 'Japan, Inc.': reality or façade?" In Murakami and Hirschmeier (1979), pp. 111–26

Nihon Keizai Shinbun (Japan Economic Journal), ed., 1983. *Jimintō seichōkai* (The LDP Agenda Investigation Committee). Tokyo

Okumura, Hiroshi, 1982. "Interfirm relations in an enterprise group: the case of Mitsubishi." *Japanese Economic Studies*, 10, 4 (Summer): 53–82

Ozono, Tomokazu, 1983. "Ningen renkanzu: Nagano Shigeo" (Networks of human relationships: Nagano Shigeo). *Will*, 2, 3 (March): 34–8

Patrick, Hugh, and Henry Rosovsky, eds, 1976. *Asia's New Giant: How the Japanese Economy Works*. Washington, DC: Brookings Institution

Sato, Hidetake, 1978. "Shingikai seido no kokuminteki kadai" (National problems of the institution of advisory councils). *Keizai* (Economy), no. 174: 123–50

Tahara, Soichiro, 1980. *Nihon no paawa errito* (Japan's Power Elite). Tokyo: Kobunsha

Taira, Koji, 1970. *Economic Development and the Labor Market in Japan.* New York: Columbia University Press

Tanaka, Yonosuke, 1979. "The world of Zaikai." In Murakami and Hirschmeier (1979), pp. 64–98

Toyo keizai (Oriental Economist), 1983. A special edition on Japanese economic planning, August 20

Treize, Philip H., 1976. "Politics, government, and economic growth in Japan." In Patrick and Rosovsky (1976), pp. 753–811

Vogel, Ezra (ed.), 1975. *Modern Japanese Organization and Decision-Making.* Berkeley, Calif.: University of California Press

Yamamoto, Masao (ed.), 1972. *Keizai kanryō no jittai: seisaku kettei no mekanisumu* (The Truth about Economist-Bureaucrats: The Mechanism of Policy Making). Tokyo: Mainichi Shinbunsha

Yanaga, Chitosi, 1968. *Big Business in Japanese Politics.* New Haven and London: Yale University Press

10

International bank capital and the new liberalism

Meindert Fennema and Kees van der Pijl

Introduction

This chapter deals with recent structural changes in the North Atlantic business system established in the period of American hegemony over Europe. In the era running from the closing stages of World War II to the early seventies, US political leadership, in meeting the global challenge of anti-capitalist forces, interacting with its economic primacy, worked to galvanize the states of North America and Western Europe into a single military–political bloc within which the American pattern of capital accumulation, developed in the New Deal and World War II, was extrapolated to the Atlantic level.

This process, which eventually eroded the initial American advantage over its Western European client states in terms of labor productivity, level of concentration and centralization of capital, and financial strength, can be analyzed for our purposes in terms of (1) the development of productive capital in the different component regions and in different industrial sectors; (2) the relation between productive and money capital as expressed in the power balance between industrial and financial firms; and (3) the overall structure of the profit distribution process, comprising several other distributive categories besides the main profit-takers mentioned under (2).

It is our contention that, whereas during the period of American hegemony and the Atlantic extrapolation of the mode of capital accumulation pioneered by the USA, these patterns were still primarily national (with a semblance of internationalism due to overwhelming US superiority), from the seventies on the acceleration of the internationalization of capital and the erosion of the US advantage have combined to create a truly international system, which is no longer an extension of a dominant national economy. Raymond Vernon, to whose product cycle analysis we shall return below, captured this transition when he wrote that

> by 1970, the product cycle model was beginning in some respects
> to be inadequate as a way of looking at the US-controlled
> multinational enterprise. The assumption of the product cycle
> model – that innovations were generally transmitted from the US
> market for production and marketing in overseas areas – was

Table 10.1 *Index of labor productivity in manufacturing in the main capitalist countries (1970 = 100)*

	USA	Japan	FRG	France	UK
1960	70	38	59	55	72
1965	85	54	76	70	83
1970	100	100	100	100	100
1975	118	132	127	120	118
1980	136	187	151	157	126

Source: Die Wirtschaft kapitalistischer Länder in Zahlen (IPW-Forschungshefte, January 1982), p. 102.

beginning to be challenged by illustrations that did not fit the pattern. The new pattern that these illustrations suggested was one in which stimulation to the system could come from the exposure of any element in the system to its local environment, and response could come from any part of the system that was appropriate for the purpose. (Vernon 1973: 110)

The process of the creation of the Atlantic business system under American auspices was characterized, on our three selected dimensions, by the superiority of US productive capital, notably in the most advanced industries; by the subordination of money capital to the requirements of productive capital; and by the tendential realization of Keynes' prescription of the "euthanasia of the rentier, the functionless investor" as the main characteristic of the profit distribution process. As we shall attempt to demonstrate in this chapter, the post-1970 Atlantic business system on the other hand is characterized by: (1) the much more even distribution of sectorwise industrial advantage among the leading centers in the capitalist world, at the expense of the earlier US position; (2) the resurgence of money capital *vis-à-vis* productive capital; and (3) the resurgence of rentier control.

As to the first element, the new prominence of European (and Japanese) industrial companies is to a certain extent a function of the rapid advance of labor productivity. As can be seen in table 10.1, labor productivity has increased most dramatically in Western Europe and Japan.

The second aspect, the resurgence of money capital, functioned as a pivot, not just of the structural changes in industrial production, but also of the overall change from a system composed of national states to a truly international one. Banks led the way in the transition from the system of political regulation of international exchanges in the period of American hegemony to economic regulation dictated by the breakdown of the Bretton Woods system and its replacement by the system of floating exchange rates and competitive financing of national deficits. Freed by the mid-1960s from the Keynesian controls imposed on them during the 1930s, banks in all the North Atlantic countries gravitated to a controlling position in the new, essentially liberal world credit economy taking shape as one aspect of the crisis of the industrial North Atlantic economy. Leaving behind them the system of central bank coordination and reciprocal currency supports, the banks functioned as key relays, translating the requirements of international reproduction into the various national economies.

"Rentier control" reemerged as part of the same development. But, if the rise to prominence of the banks in the Atlantic business system was accompanied by forms of appropriation of profit through the financial sphere rather than through productive or commercial activities, this did not simply amount to a "revenge of the rentier," as Jacob Morris (1982) has called it, since rentier income itself has been subject to concentration and socialization. It is through pension funds, life insurance companies, and investment trusts that rent, interest, and dividend income accrue to their recipients. The rentier perspective associated with a one-sided financial stake in business affairs had been reproduced in the new surroundings, however, and the reinforcement of those classes in society dependent on this growing income slice has been accompanied by the increasing adoption of this perspective as a formula of the general interest in a growing number of states.

The role of political strategy

The process of the formation of a US-led grouping of Western states in which the Atlantic business system was established, as well as the current process of globalization under the auspices of international money capital, has developed in constant interaction with the formation of transnational discussion platforms, business–government caucuses, and semipermanent consultative bodies such as the Bilderberg Conference and the Trilateral Commission. Through these bodies, competing economic interests have been constantly adjusted to overarching political strategies, and synthesized into a transcendent destiny for the West, a process similar to those described by Domhoff (1979) and Useem (1984). These bodies in our view are critical nodal points in shaping the actual course of political events, not by simply imposing their preferences but by marshalling the forces, thrashing out mutual differences, and developing effective political formulas necessary for inserting a particular fractional interest in the eventual "policy mix." It would be inaccurate to view the importance of these organizations in conspiracy terms. Rather we see fractions of the international business community in structural positions and we view these organizations as forums by which diverse fractions attempt to reach a common perspective and course of action.

In this chapter, we will operationalize the objective position in the economic structure according to the three dimensions mentioned above, i.e.

the region of location; its relation with productive or with money capital; and, finally, dependence on rentier income. In short, a capital fraction is a loosely organized grouping sharing a similar economic position (based on structural equivalence) and the ability to overcome economic and political constraints to reach a common strategic position formulated in terms of the general interest. Policy planning bodies, platforms for discussion on global problems, and networks of business communication all play important roles in reaching such a strategic consensus.

The restructuring of the Atlantic business system

The restructuring of industry

To understand the current process of internationalization of capital, the hitherto dominant view of the internationalization of industry, which still centers on the multinational corporation paradigm, has to be reexamined. In the product life cycle hypothesis (Vernon) it is assumed that as products pass from the infancy phase through expansion to maturity, the industry producing these products will standardize production processes and look for new markets to sell its products – which have become cheaper due to this standardization – and also for new labor markets where cheap and unskilled labor can be used in Taylorized production processes; hence the export drive in the expansion phase and direct investment into more backward regions in the phase of maturity (so-called runaway industry). It was assumed that American firms would first invest in Europe and eventually look for specific cheap labor markets in the Third World in what are by now known as newly industrializing countries.

The postwar experience of the overseas spread of industrial firms through direct investment apparently corroborated the validity of this hypothesis. In retrospect, the contingent articulation of this process with the establishment of a Pax Americana and the fact that the internationalization process was dominated by US firms warrant a reexamination of the concepts involved before the erosion of American predominance is analyzed in detail.

Raymond Vernon's *Sovereignty at Bay*, in which the product cycle model was presented, must be considered one of the key statements of the multinational corporation paradigm. This book indeed analyzes a series of developments which together contributed to the creation of the Atlantic business system linking the USA (with Canada) and Western Europe. Factors listed by Vernon which account for the US lead in developing manufacturing companies of a particularly dynamic type are: (1) the scarcity of skilled labor and the need to subdivide skilled jobs into semiskilled ones; the growth of science education in the USA, interacting with a dramatic rise of American primacy in the area of industrial inventions; and (2) the advances made by

American corporations in terms of organizational efficiency, from the primitive owner-run company through the functional management structure to the product or market divisional management structure. By exploiting the relative backwardness of Europe in these areas, the US consumer durables industry and more particularly the automobile industry performed in a way consistent with the mode: innovation, exports, and, finally, direct investment to exploit what remained of the advantage.

However, when European (and Japanese) industry had sufficiently caught up with their US counterparts to attempt to carve out a bigger market share in the Atlantic economy on the basis of the same products and processes, the result did not generally include the overseas spread of European (or Japanese) multinational corporations. Vernon himself, noticing the lack of European or Japanese direct investment in the USA at the time, acknowledged the fact that "the world may have to view the multinational enterprise as an asymmetrical phenomenon in which the American version is thought of as distinctive in scope and in strength" (Vernon, 1973: 114). In fact, Vernon had to acknowledge that the world economy in the seventies no longer behaved according to the product cycle hypothesis. In an article written in 1979 he referred to the existence of a truly global economy in which even a new product is not necessarily first produced in the country where it is to be marketed (Vernon, 1979). Empirical studies on the automobile sector indicate that patterns of foreign investment in the seventies contradict the product-cycle theses (Dankbaar, 1984).

As we see it, focussing exclusively on the multinational corporation may preclude acknowledging any symmetries in the international economy in the first place. True, in the late sixties there had been a distinct movement in Western Europe, publicized by Jean-Jacques Servan-Schreiber's *Le défi americain*, towards the formation of Western European firms capable of a multinational corporate strategy. As a result of this development, European firms in several branches were able to surpass their US counterparts who had been sector leaders a decade before. In chemicals, Du Pont de Nemours, industry leader in terms of sales in 1960, was second behind West German Hoechst in 1977; in the steel industry, British Steel and the Dutch–German combination, Hoogovens-Hoesch (recently dissolved again), made their appearance in the top ten, which in 1960 was practically an American preserve. In this case, the breakthrough of four Japanese steel firms was even more dramatic since no Japanese firm had been on the top ten list in 1960 (Maier, Melnikow, and Schenajew, 1980: 83–4). Chrysler's withdrawal from car production in Europe (taken over by Peugeot-Citroen in exchange for financial participation) and Volkswagen's major direct investment in the USA may also be cited as illustrations of an apparent trend to symmetry in a key sector.

However, the actual situation was not primarily one of symmetry in the sense of rival corporate giants developing multinational strategies for expansion. Rather, the leading companies on both sides of the Atlantic were part of national economies merging ever more into a wider world economy, abandoning the specific North Atlantic constraint as well as the features of internationalization typical of the multinational spread of US enterprise. As regards the form of internationalization, for instance, European states with national oil companies, attempting to emancipate international petroleum flows from Anglo-American control, sought to have the EEC coordinate refining activities and introduce a degree of protection. At the same time, against the background of the "Euro-Arab dialogue," bilateral barter agreements between these countries (notably France and Italy) and Middle East states were concluded, aimed at securing an independent supply of crude in exchange for advanced industrial equipment (Boers, Eisenloeffel, and van der Linde, 1984: 194).

Such forms of internationalization other than direct investment by single firms, of which many other examples could be cited, were much more numerous in Europe, and direct investment of European firms as such was also much more part of international trade strategies and other considerations. Not unexpectedly, in Europe, notably in French Marxist discussions, the critique of the concept of the multinational corporation was most pronounced and the quest for an alternative theory intense. For some time, a heated debate took place in these circles on whether the alternative concept should be the branch (automobile, steel, etc.), as Christian Palloix proposed (Palloix, 1973), or the sector (means of production, consumer goods, intermediate goods), on which his critics based their case (SIFI, 1974; Andreff, 1976). More recently, the notion of international regimes of accumulation, extending Henry Ford's prototypical system of subdivision of tasks and managerial control combined with mass consumption to the international level (hence dubbed neo-Fordism, Palloix, 1978), has been developed, again with French authors in the forefront (e.g. Lipietz, 1982; Andreff, 1982). In West Germany, the notion of the "new international division of labor" was developed by a group of authors at the Max Planck Institute to denote the same phenomenon (Frobel, Heinrichs, and Kreye, 1977).

From about 1970, new direct foreign investment as well as a host of other forms of exploiting labor power elsewhere (credit, subcontracting, barter, etc.) were aimed at specific pockets of cheap and/or easily manageable labor power in the context of this neo-Fordist division of labor. Within the advanced countries, employment in the manufacturing industries in the traditional centers decreased after 1970, while the number of workers employed in new, intensive-work/low-wage plants created by relocating production increased (Heinrichs, 1980: 188–9). In the periphery, the city-states of Singapore and Hong Kong, small countries like South Korea and Taiwan, and selected regions in big countries like Mexico and Brazil have attracted substantial segments of the globalized productive processes.

States, state-corporate joint ventures, and international public bodies take part in this process as well as the multinational business firms proper. Rather than picturing this process in terms of intercontinental competition between the USA, the EEC, and Japan, the primacy of the international economy over the national ones and its close relationship with the Western military system still dominated by the USA should be emphasized; shifts in the prominence of particular national capitals should be judged within this framework as secondary features, significant mainly in relation to political strategies.

This tendency towards internationalization can be illustrated by data from a study of international interlocking directorates performed by Fennema (1982). In Fennema's sample of 176 industrial firms and banks, there were 101 international interlocks (25 per cent) in 1970 and 152 in 1976 (31.5 per cent), whereas the number of national interlocks had progressed only marginally (Fennema, 1982: 186–7). Nationally Japanese capitalists and managers became less isolated from the hitherto exclusively Atlantic business system. In reference to the auto industry, Louis Wells writes:

> Although the president of one major European firm was still able to say that he knew personally the presidents of all American and European automobile firms but had never met a top manager of a Japanese manufacturer, that situation was changing. The Japanese were beginning to develop ties with American firms through joint ventures, and they were establishing some loose ties with European manufacturers. (Wells, 1974: 251)

In the network of interlocks, two Japanese firms actually became integrated into the Atlantic network in 1976. Other significant changes compared to 1970 in the prominence of specific national firms concerned the fact that the relative centrality of the New York banks (Morgan, Chase, Chemical) and the Dutch multinationals (Royal Dutch, AKZO) declined relative to the German firms (Mannesmann, Volkswagen, Daimler-Benz, Siemens, and Bayer) (Fennema, 1982: 191–2).

In the section on trilateralism we shall come back to these findings in order to explain some aspects of the formation of the Trilateral Commission as a key policy-planning body, its rise to prominence in the Carter administration and its failure since.

The resurgence of money and bank capital

The formative phase of the Atlantic business system under American auspices covered the postwar era up to the 1970s. During this period, the mode of accumulation developed in the USA (Fordism) encompassed the Western European economy as well as that of the USA. This articulation was largely orchestrated by international monetary institutions using the dollar as their yardstick. Under the Bretton Woods system as it functioned until 1971, Keynesian policies were national in form but international in content. The balance of payments served as the link between the national and international economy, in which the latter, as a consequence of dollar hegemony, coincided with the extension of the American national economy.

The growth of the Eurodollar market weakened the financial basis for the US international monetary monopoly. This market was not under direct control of American monetary authorities, nor was it monitored by any other national or international monetary authority. In the seventies, the Eurocurrency market (by then including other currencies besides the dollar) boomed as a consequence of OPEC petrodollars being recycled in the Western economies, and the shift from balancing to financing international payments deficits heralded the breakdown of the Bretton Woods system. Eurocurrency loans more than doubled between 1973 and 1978 (Ruffini, 1979: 238).

As the international credit system became independent from national or international monetary authorities, national economies became dependent on the vacillations of private international money flows. Interacting with the closing of the gap between the USA and Western Europe, industrial production throughout the Atlantic system stagnated and entire industries were liquidated and transferred to new zones of implantation. The existing relation between money capital and productive capital broke down and was replaced by a hypertrophy of the international circuit of money capital managed by the international banking system. Since monetary authorities were unable to maintain the Keynesian nexus between money capital and productive capital at the international level, the international economy was threatened by a compartmentalization into competing national economies. Once again, a monetary system in transition, operative in the context of excessively developed credit flows, tendentially forced the major capitalist states to subordinate all aspects of economic policy to the defense of the currency, thus fostering a climate of protectionism. As a West German banker wrote, "The leading western industrial countries reverted individually to a pre-Keynesian constellation similar to that at the beginning of the 1930s," with only the social security system preventing a spillover from economic to political crisis (Hankel, 1976: 52–3).

Under these conditions, the resurgence of money capital was evident on several levels. During the seventies, external financing, in which banks played a prominent role, increased. Except in the United Kingdom, the role played by banks in financing industrial investment tendentially increased between 1970 and 1978, particularly in Italy, Germany, and Japan. This can be seen in table 10.2.

Internationally, the banks are major modal points in the network of interlocking directorates. Between 1970 and 1976, the position of banks in the network analyzed by Fennema became even more important, a logical

Table 10.2 *Percentage of industrial investment financed by banks*

	1970	1975	1978
France	24.0	33.6	29.5
FRG	29.5	36.9	44.7
Italy	33.1	62.5	78.8
USA	27.9	28.7	30.2
Japan	31.6	29.5	38.5
UK	22.4	17.7	15.2

Source: Kessler and Israelewicz, 1981: 23.

Table 10.3 *Internationalization of banks belonging to the world top 50, 1971, 1976 and 1980*

	No. of banks			Assets in billion $			No. of foreign subsidiaries	
	1971	1976	1980	1871	1976	1980	1971	1976
USA	13	10	5	195	348	477	324	419
Japan	12	12	16	123	318	671	119	189
FRG	5	8	7	57	218	392	92	166
France	3	4	5	40	170	453	33	97
UK	4	4	4	58	102	279	77	169

[a]Foreign subsidiaries in advanced capitalist countries only and including participations, branch offices and representatives.

Sources: Transnational Corporations in World Development: A Re-examination (United Nations, New York, 1978)', p. 215; *The Banker* (June 1981).

development given the above discussion. The crisis is expressed in the liquidation and the devalorization of capital, and the transfer of large masses of capital in money form to new ventures. The deflationary policies of national governments, typical of the contemporary reaction to the world economic crisis, have furthermore led to a generalized contraction of domestic markets to the detriment of investment. Money capital therefore tendentially circulates in strictly financial circuits of a basically speculative nature.

In table 10.3, the internationalization of bank capital is documented for the years 1971, 1976, and 1980. As the table shows, the largest non-US banks expanded most markedly in the period between 1971 and 1976. Within the international network of joint directorates this is reflected in the changes with respect to the centrality of banks of various nationalities. The New York banks, J. P. Morgan, Chemical Bank, and Chase Manhattan, which together were linked to 65 different firms in 1970, had lost ground by 1976 to the Deutsche Bank (already central in 1970), the Dresdner Bank, the Canadian

Imperial Bank of Commerce and the Schweizerische Bankgesellschaft. The new prominence of these banks also has to be seen against the background of changing patterns of international investment and is part of a general tendency for German and Swiss firms to become more prominent in the Atlantic business system.

Compared to the large number of interlocking directorates established by banks, the limited number of interlocks between banks is striking. The interbank interlocks moreover are overwhelmingly international, with the exception of the British banks, National Westminster and Standard & Chartered, which can be explained by Westminster's interest in Standard & Chartered; and the Japanese banks, whose interlocks at the national level date from the Zaikai structure (Hadley, 1970).

The fact that in all other cases in the Fennema sample interlocks between banks of the same nationality are nonexistent, in combination with the considerable increase in international interlocks of the banks, gives rise to the assumption that the banks in the early seventies attempted to strengthen their position by seeking cooperation with banks from other countries. In turn, this would reinforce their position nationally. It might well be, then, that competition between national banks is conducted in the international markets, an idea suggested in 1971 by the Swedish banker, Lars-Erik Thunholm. According to Thunholm, increased competition in providing international services has its effects on the national market. The Eurodollar market, in his opinion, is "the most perfect competitive money market in existence, untrammeled as it is by legal and institutional regulations. Access to this market increases the banks' efficiency to serve their customers both in the national and in the international field" (Thunholm, 1971: 114).

Whereas national money markets are practically cartelized by state intervention, national consortia, and mutual agreements, the international money markets are ever less subject to such legal and institutional regulation. International activities were becoming more important for banks. In 1976, the ten largest US banks were dependent for more than 40 per cent of their income on foreign activities; in 1970, this was the case for only one of them. Although figures for European banks are not available, the pattern seems to be the same.

National legislation from the late 1960s on has been adapted to the need to meet international competition on the most favorable conditions. In several countries, the separation between various banking functions which in the 1930s served to put an end to the subordination of industrial investment to rentier control through financial firms, was repealed in the period between 1967 and the early seventies.

At the beginning of the seventies, increasing competition at the international level gave rise to the formation of international consortia. Banks from the same country shunned cooperation in the international arena. Instead, they looked for cooperation with banks from other countries who were competitors, actually or in terms of traditional interests and outlook, of their national rivals. Thus, when in 1967 the Dutch AMRO decided to participate in the Banque Européenne de Credit with the Deutsche Bank, Midland Bank, and the Société Générale (both the French and the Belgian banks of that name), the Algemme Bank Nederland reacted by participating in the Société Financière Europénne, together with the Dresdner Bank, Barclays, and the Banque Nationale de Paris. A survey of 125 consortia revealed that, except for some Japanese banks and a typical Commonwealth consortium, no two banks from the same country participated in the same consortium. This situation, however, also made for the consortia's inherent instability. Enemies of one's enemies' friends are not yet friends, and the banks' behavior as consortium members accordingly tended to be rather parasitic, reflecting the bank's own international strategy rather than a collective one (examples in Fennema, 1982). After 1975, the consortia entered a period of stagnation.[1]

Further analysis of the consortia showed that they were not simply defensive reactions of European banks, since American West Coast banks frequently participated in them. The New York banks, however, which were found to be central in the international interlock network, hardly participated. If, therefore, the formation of international consortia was a defensive reaction, it was a defensive reaction of both the American West Coast banks and the European banks against the New York financial establishment. This development was part of the centrifugal tendency affecting the financial order based on American hegemony and the Atlantic business system; a tendency also marked by the cropping up of new offshore Eurocurrency banking centers in such places as Hong Kong, Bahrain, the Bahamas, Singapore, the Netherlands Antilles, and Panama.

This expansion of bank capital, the increase in international bank activities, and the prominence of banks in the international network of interlocking directorates are reflected in a general movement from production to money capital in the profit distribution process. This is demonstrated in table 10.4.

It can be seen from the table that financial profits showed a steadily rising trend, even if the 1975 percentages, which are extraordinarily high due to depressed total corporate income at the height of the industrial crisis, are left out. In the USA non-financial profits soared after 1974 due to commercial and oil profits. Riding high on the waves of the rapidly expanding international credit business fueled by dollar inflation, oil profits, and the monetary equivalent of liquidated fixed capital throughout the Atlantic business system, banks were thus able to appropriate a growing share of the social surplus in the various countries. In order of make the step to the political corollary of this development, we have to briefly investigate the third aspect of the restructuring process, the resurgence of rentier control.

Table 10.4 *Savings of financial corporations and quasi-corporations as a percentage of total corporate and quasi-corporate income, 1965, 1970, 1975, and 1979*

	1965	1970	1975	1979
USA	14.6	40.1	15.1	27.6
FRG	25.4	43.3	75.5	50.7
France	0.7	10.9	24.6	27.0
UK	n.a.	9.6	62.7	28.6
Netherlands	n.a.	5.0	10.5	21.0
Japan	n.a.	19.0	a	42.9

[a] For Japan, total corporate income in 1975 was negative.

Sources: Calculated from (1965–75) OECD, *National Accounts of OECD Countries 1961–1978* (Paris, 1980), Vol. II, country tables; (1979), *ibid.*, *1963–1980* (Paris, 1982). Except for the USA and Japan, percentages for 1979 are not fully comparable to percentages for the earlier years due to the new OECD mode of calculation used in the 1982 edition. US and Japanese figures are all from this edition.

Table 10.5 *Households' property income (rent, dividends, and interest) in national income distribution (%), 1965, 1970, 1975, and 1980*

	1965	1970	1975	1980
USA	9.2	9.1	9.6	11.4
FRG	2.2	3.2	3.8	4.5
UK	7.9	6.3	4.3	4.7
France	4.2	4.3	5.4	5.4
Netherlands	17.4	13.9	9.9	12.4
Japan	7.3	7.1	9.1	9.9

Source: (1965, 1970) OECD, *National Accounts of OECD Countries 1961–1978* (Paris, 1980), Vol. II, country tables; (1975–80), *ibid.*, *1963–80* (Paris, 1982). UK and Japan figures are all from the 1982 edition.

The resurgence of rentier control

Rentier incomes, too, improved as part of the general movement terminating the Keynesian era. In table 10.5, the figures are presented for the main capitalist countries. The table shows that, even in traditional rentier states like the Netherlands, the movement toward extinguishing the rentier component in income distribution was halted after 1975.

The euthanasia of the rentier prescribed by Keynes and the "Revenge of the Rentier" enunciated by Jacob Morris (cf. also *Monthly Review*, 1982) merely denote the income distribution trends of the kind illustrated by the figures in table 10.5. Even in conjunction with the resurgence of the profit share accruing to back capital, rentiers' growing income slice would not be significant beyond the quantitative were it not for the coincidence of these trends with changes in the overall configuration of the Atlantic and world business systems.

In fact, during the period of Atlantic Keynesianism under US auspices banks were crucial links in the process of articulating money capital and productive capital in a way required by the Fordist mode of accumulation in which industry reigned supreme. But when industrial investment declined sharply in the 1970s, banks were forced into the international circuit of money capital as it had developed over the previous decades, engaging in currency transactions, the international public band trade, real estate investment, and other nonproductive ventures in order to keep afloat. Even industrial companies took part in this reorientation towards the financial sphere. In Germany, four industrial corporations (Siemens, Bayer, Daimler-Benz and Bosch) together held more than 20 billion DM in liquid assets in 1981; in 1982, Siemens alone cashed in almost 500 million DM in interest on its financial holdings (Welzk, 1983: 31). This shift from production to finance within industrial corporations was also apparent in several management changes. In one such shift, on September 4, 1984, Peugeot's engineer-president Jean-Paul Parayre was replaced by the banker Jacques Calvet.

As part of the same movement, the disintegration of the industry–trade union compromise supporting the Fordist order politically was replaced by bank power and rentier interests as the dominant interest group in the new configuration. Thus rentier interests – in the broad sense of the word – were crucial in the formation of a new power bloc which rose to political prominence after 1975. This was also reflected in changes in tax policy in several countries which shifted the tax burden away from financial companies. Only in the USA were tax levies on both financial and nonfinancial companies decreased.

Productive capital was linked to this power bloc in two ways: first, as part of a new trend in capital accumulation centered on the emerging electronics and other hi-tech industries. Here, banks served to channel savings of their clients as "venture capital" to new industries. Attracted by the whirlwind success of these industries, and aided by lowering of the capital gains tax in the USA, the money supplied by savers to US investment firms in 1978 was already equal to the total amount put at their disposal over the 1966–77 period (*Newsweek*, June 4, 1979). The second way in which industry was involved in the emerging international money economy was through its own investments to which we referred above.

We believe that the shift in power from the Keynesian industry bloc to the financial bloc constitutes a qualitative change for the Atlantic and world business systems. This may explain the general resurgence of an apparently nineteenth-century liberalism. With more wealth than ever circulating among

Table 10.6 *Direct taxes on financial and nonfinancial companies as a percentage of current business receipts*

	1968		1972		1976		1980	
	F	NF	F	NF	F	NF	F	NF
France	7.1	13.5	6.7	15.1	5.8	21.7	3.7	18.6
FRG	4.5	5.6	2.8	4.1	3.2	4.7	2.3	5.4
USA	8.7	30.9	7.9	25.7	6.7	25.3	5.2	19.4
UK	15.8	16.4	15.2	14.1	10.9	14.9	5.8	25.0
Japan	n.a.	n.a.	6.1	15.5	5.4	18.8	3.9	22.0
Netherlands	3.1	9.2	3.9	9.8	3.1	11.1	2.3	10.3

Source: Calculated from OECD, *National Accounts Statistics, 1964–1981* (Paris, 1983). These figures were kindly made available by Henk Overbeek from his dissertation material.

holders of intangible assets, state policy is geared to applying a deflationary "monetarist" recipe to the problem of overaccumulation. If the breakdown of the Bretton Woods system forces the individual states to do so in the first place, the shift from Keynesianism to rentier control marks the crystallization of a domestic power base for such policies. Cause and consequence are interwoven here, but to the degree that bankers and rentiers survive comfortably in a crisis-ridden economy, the principles of the free market economy of which they are the ardent champions assume new glamor. Of course, a world financial crisis would destroy this state of affairs, but as long as the main debtors and the biggest banks keep negotiating, the blame for having brought about the crisis can be passed comfortably to the trade unions, Keynesian government, and industry.

The rise and demise of trilateralism

Summarizing our exposition so far, we have argued that the structure of industry was characterized until the 1970s by the multinational spread of American corporations. After 1970, however, industry abandoned its Atlantic constraint as well as its foundation in a Keynesian class compromise, which centered on mass consumption and welfare statism. As the internationalization of a productive system passed beyond US hegemony, new forms and forces besides private direct investment by US firms became prominant as American preeminence dwindled. This is reflected in the growth of the number of international interlocks among the 176 banks and industrial firms in the Fennema sample for 1970 and 1976 from one-quarter to almost one-third, by the (still marginal) inclusion of Japanese firms, and by the growing prominence of German industrials in the network. Next, we argued that the resurgence of bank capital and the resurgence of rentier incomes, coupled with the hypertrophy of the international circuit of money capital, combined to replace the Keynesian order of the previous era by a new order of rentier control.

This section will be concerned with the question of whether actors who have a similar structural position in the Atlantic business system have tried to develop a common strategy in accordance with their structural equivalence. As we have pointed out in the introduction, mechanisms to develop such strategy are policy planning bodies, platforms for discussion on global problems, and networks of interlocking directorates. We will restrict ourselves to the Trilateral Commission and its impact on policy-making.

The era of Atlantic integration had produced its characteristic policy-planning bodies. The participation of the USA in World War II, which led to US hegemony over the postwar capitalist world, coincided with intensive discussions in wartime London concerning the eventual European order and its relation to the USA. Joseph Retinger, the advisor of the Polish General Sikorsky, worked from 1941 to organize Continental politicians in holding these discussions, out of which several crucial policy-planning bodies emerged, the most important of which was the European League for Economic Cooperation, one of the eventual constituent bodies of the European Movement and, as such, the one most closely connected with international business (Rebattet, 1962: 4–5). In 1954, when the "Free World" spirit suffered from rivalries between the Americans and the Europeans on the issues of colonialism and the nature of the Soviet threat, Retinger again appealed to the same personalities he had brought together in London. The result was the Bilderberg Conference in the Netherlands, perpetuated henceforth as a permanent body. Conceived as a forum for thrashing out mutual differences, the Bilderberg Conference brought together businessmen-politicians as well as representatives of the European Social Democratic opposition.

This setup, in line with the class compromise typical of the Keynesian era, allowed the Bilderberg conference to assemble the key decision-makers of the Atlantic world. Significantly, there was a distinct correspondence between the background of the personalities who were most prominent in the Bilderberg organization and the firms most central in the 1970 network of joint directorates analyzed by Fennema: the New York banks and the Dutch multinationals AKZO and Royal Dutch/Shell. If we consider these central firms not as centers of power but rather as nodal points where the sinews of power are most densely interconnected, then the prominence of the Dutch Prince Bernhard as chairman of the Bilderberg conference, Rijkens of Unilever and Meynen of AKZO as successive treasurers, and Van der Beugel, a network specialist on the ANB, S. G. Warburg, and other corporate boards as secretary succeeding Retinger, becomes clear given the aims of the Bilderberg conference.

The Trilateral Commission was launched as a reaction to the unilateral policy of the Nixon administration. Nixon's 1971 measures in the trade and monetary field aimed at restoring American economic primacy by meeting European and Japanese competition head-on. The Trilateral Commission, formed at the initiative of David Rockefeller and his advisor, Zbigniew Brzezinski, did not however bring together the internationalists of Pax Americana vintage. The composition of the Trilateral Commission diverged from its predecessor's, the Bilderberg Conference, in that it included Japanese businessmen and politicians, a change which was overtly expressed in the name of the Commission. It emerged at the critical moment when the Atlantic business system was slipping into an industrial crisis but the industrial point of view was still pertinent. As a consequence, the trilateralists succeeded in grasping the impact of the regional restructuring of industry but failed to contain the resurgence of rentier control.

The abandoning of the Atlantic constraint for a truly global business system, characterized by an intricate division of labor and the prominence of German industrials in the Atlantic network of interlocking directorates and its "opening" to the Japanese, both found their expression in the trilateral strategy: first, by the trilateral recognition of the primacy of international affairs over domestic affairs and the concept of global interdependence; second, by the trilateral rather than the bilateral Atlantic (and much less pronounced, Pacific) concepts of capitalist unity and the idea that the trilateral group of states would be led by the USA but no longer on the basis of American hegemony (Greiner, 1980: 162–5 and *passim*).

Political developments after 1974 show the impact of this trilateral concept as well as its demise due to, as we see it, its failure to incorporate the resurgence of rentier control into its doctrine. The Nixon policy had fostered centrifugal tendencies which had been operative from the mid-sixties. Pompidou, Brandt, and Heath had each, in his own way, sought to graft a new international policy onto this conjuncture. At this point, recognition that the postwar international order was in need of a basic reshuffling was widespread, but no consensus existed on how to achieve it. As Henry Owen wrote in the introduction to a Brookings Institution study published in 1973, "an old epoch is dying, but a new one has not yet come of age" (Owen, 1973: 3). In 1974, the annual report of the Council on Foreign Relations, one of the foremost US policy-planning bodies, stated that "the institutional components of the post-World War II era, such as GATT, IMF, and NATO, increasingly seem out of gear with changed conditions. The time is ripe for an attempt to analyze the characteristics of the kind of international system that would be suited to deal with the conditions and problems of the upcoming decade." The Council's "1980 Project" in this respect was projected to perform a task comparable to the seminal postwar planning conducted during World War II, and in the book by diplomat Harlan Cleveland, entited *Third*

Try at World Order, the undertaking was also compared with Wilson's League of Nations project (Shoup and Minter, 1977: 255).

While these debates were going on, the economic crisis acted as the great synchronizer. In terms of degree of elaboration and support, the trilateral concept seemed to hold out a plausible strategy in the circumstances. Between February and August of 1974, Heath, Brandt, and Pompidou were replaced by Wilson, Schmidt, and Giscard d'Estaing, while Gerald Ford took over the Nixon presidency in the USA. The transatlantic energy conflict which had lent Ostpolitik and the revival of Western European integration a distinct centrifugal aspect was shelved when Presidents Ford and Giscard d'Estaing reached agreement on this matter on the island of Martinique in mid-December. Thus the way was cleared for a first trilateral economic summit conference in 1975, held at the invitation of President Giscard d'Estaing in Rambouillet near Paris. Both the summit as a new form of mutual consultation and the leaders present (Giscard d'Estaing, Schmidt, Wilson, Ford, and Miki for Japan) testified to the impact of the trilateral idea, but the general tendency of economic policy, which was strongly deflationary in response to both the energy crisis and the wage demands of a still militant working class, prevented trilateralism from becoming operational at the government level.

In November 1976, Jimmy Carter was elected as President of the USA, and in Britain James Callaghan replaced Harold Wilson. Now the stage was set for a full-fledged attempt at executing the trilateral program of concerted economic growth, controlling the periphery in mutual consultation, and confronting the Soviet Union and its orbit peacefully by raising the theme of human rights. Boldly placing itself in a position of supreme authority on the observance of the dignity of man two years after finally withdrawing from Vietnam, the United States indeed demonstrated its determination to attempt one more "Try at World Order." From the President down, the Carter administration was stacked with members of the Trilateral Commission's American section, with Brzezinski himself acting as National Security Advisor.

The concept of US leadership without hegemony in an interdependent world could now be tested in practice. And although the representatives of the mass production industries of the previous era, unlike their counterparts in Europe and Japan, were hardly represented in their own trilateral section, the Carter administration took steps immediately after taking office to stimulate the American economy and to make the overseas partners do the same. The San Juan (Puerto Rico) summit of 1976, chaired by President Ford and attended by Schmidt, Giscard d'Estaing, Callaghan, Miki, and the Italian Premier Moro, had already decided upon an (unspecified) expansionary policy, but it took until the beginning of 1977 before this policy really began to materialize. In January, the new Japanese Prime Minister, Fukuda, at the prodding of the American President, announced a strikingly stimulative budget for the fiscal year beginning in April (*Newsweek*, January 31, 1977). In the USA, industrial growth had already resumed before the Carter election, and the administration's defense budget, growing in spite of the attempt to share out the armament expenses among the allies, further worked to sustain it. Manufacturing profits (minus petroleum and coal) as a percentage of total corporate profits had climbed from 38.9 in 1975 to 41.0 per cent in 1976 and remained at 40.0 per cent in 1977 before dropping sharply (*Economic Report of the President*, 1983: 238–9). At the 1977 and 1978 economic summits at London and Bonn, Carter, Fukuda, and the Western European leaders now joined by a representative of the EEC (Roy Jenkins) settled the US–German dispute on overseas sales of fast breeder reactors and worked out the policy of concerted economic growth, dubbed the "three locomotives" strategy.

The Western European "locomotive" was the first to grind to a halt. In 1976, there was still a growth rate of 4.5 per cent (compared to the 5.9 per cent US growth rate), but in the next few years growth rates subsided (OECD figures in *Handelsblatt*, July 17, 1980). Since the deflationary response to the crisis had already cut into the size of the markets of the metropolitan economies, their recovery had to be shared between domestic production and imports from relocated production in the context of the shift to a neo-Fordist division of labor and an international credit economy. Hence, the "trilateral" recovery of the second half of the seventies benefited industry only at a new, global level; within the metropolitan economies, expansionary economic policy hardly stemmed the tide towards the resurgence of money capital and rentier power. If the banks still had to yield some of the terrain conquered at the height of the crisis (cf. table 10.4), the relative improvement of rentier incomes was strongest in the period (cf. table 10.5).

In the USA, 1979 marked the end of the trilateral offensive. Apart from the trend toward money capital and rentier control, a specific factor here was the dramatic improvement of the share of oil companies in the profit distribution process. From 1978 to 1979, oil profits soared from $13.8 billion to 20.7 billion, and in 1980, with overall corporate profits falling, reached the sum of $28.0 billion (*Economic Report of the President*, 1983: 258–9). Several representatives of the trilateral East Coast establishment, such as Treasury Secretary W. Michael Blumenthal and HEW Secretary Joseph Califano, had to leave (so would, at a later stage, Cyrus Vance, the Secretary of State). At the Federal Reserve Bank, G. William Miller, the industrialist, who replaced Blumenthal at the Treasury in order to cover Carter's expansionary budget, was succeeded by banker Paul Volcker, an orthodox monetarist who had been Assistant Secretary of the Treasury under Nixon.

In Europe and Japan, the leaders subscribing to the trilateral strategy likewise lost ground in 1979. Fukuda was replaced by Ohira in Japan and Callaghan was replaced by Thatcher in Britain, both committed to a deflationary economic policy in line with the prevailing tendency towards rentier control, and ready to confront the working class head-on. Although not yet successful, in France and West Germany, right-wing forces, too, were stirring: the Chirac Gaullists were harassing Giscard d'Estaing on account of a bribery scandal and in West Germany Franz-Josef Strauss ran as candidate for the United Christian Democrat opposition against Chancellor Schmidt. In 1980, the politics of rentier control achieved hegemony when, at the Venice summit, an anti-inflationary policy was accorded priority as far as economic policy was concerned. Henceforward, successive summits one after another confirmed the monetarist strategy, while the shift to the right was completed when, at the Versailles summit in 1982, US President Ronald Reagan was able to insert a policy of military confrontation with the Soviet Union into economic policy by having a concerted embargo policy adopted. In short, the political effort to overcome the crisis by a rearrangement of the international order, but basing itself on the same principles as those of the period of American hegemony (internationalism and joint efforts to prop up industrial production), ran against the structural changes which were taking place. Although changes in the industrial structure had been taken into account, the Trilateral Commission was unable to deal with the changes in the structure of the international financial and monetary system. The contradiction between productive and money capital had become too sharp to be overcome by a neo-Keynesian internationalist strategy.[2]

Thus, the trilateral effort to overcome the crisis of the previous international order ran upon the fact that the restructuring of the Atlantic business system terminating the era of American hegemony was not confined to its regional and industrial aspect. The trilateralists operated on the assumption of the previous pattern of accumulation resuming, envisaging a geographical widening and more equitable organization of the productive system supporting it. But the deflationary turn of economic policy in the metropolitan centers, aimed both at deflating full employment pressures and at defending the currency in a context of monetary uncertainty, cut into existing markets and upset the hitherto intricate relationship between domestic mass production and consumption, welfare state arrangements, and the framework of international integration. Shifting production to new zones of implantation tended to reinforce the sectors producing investment goods for these new investment zones at the expense of the established mass production industries of consumer durables, while bolstering money capital and the rentier segment as a corollary to the financial and monetary channels prominent in the restructuring process. As rivalry for investment opportunities, rivalry over access to energy sources, and competitive deflation replaced the previous setting of mutual adjustment of international interests in the context of economic integration, the shared interest of the business community in the capitalist world was reduced to a minimal Cold War consensus. Befitting the rentier view of class struggle as a monstrous invention of leftist agitators and, internationally speaking, as a result of Soviet machinations, the politics of confrontation which emerged in the last years of the Carter presidency were elevated to the central theme of Reagan foreign policy and produced the new Cold War currently dominating international relations.

Today the arms race serves as the main context for technological innovation, increasingly absorbing industrial output in the absence of sufficient civilian markets and allowing the intense technological rivalries between the metropolitan countries to be camouflaged as contributions to the common defense effort and the cause of the Free World. As we have tried to demonstrate, it is the freedom accorded to international money capital which has contributed critically to this state of affairs.

NOTES

The main lines of analysis and empirical evidence are taken from the two books by the authors (Fennema, 1982; van der Pijl, 1985). The authors are indebted to Mark Mizruchi, Michael Schwartz, and Ad Teulings for critical comments on earlier drafts of this chapter.

1　The fact that these coalitions remained unstable suggests that structural equivalence might not be a sufficient basis for cohesive relations. This has implications for clique identification techniques based on grouping units together that are structurally equivalent. Our example suggests that group cohesion based on a specific structural equivalence may be counteracted by mechanisms based on other structural equivalence (in this case the nationality of banks). It may also be that a grouping based on structural equivalence will remain unstable if it lacks an articulated common strategy.

2　This failure is evidence against conspiracy theorists, according to whom historical developments are determined by the collusive behavior of politicians and business leaders.

REFERENCES

Aglietta, M., 1979. *A Theory of Capitalist Regulation: The US Experience*. First published 1976. London: New Left Books

Andreff, W., 1976. *Profils et structures du capitalisme mondial*. Paris: Calmann-Lévy

　　1982. "Régimes d'accumulation et insertion des nations dans l'économie mondiale." In J. L. Reiffers (ed.), *Economie-et finance internationales*. Paris: Dunod, pp. 104–30

Boers, J., G. Eisenloeffel, and C. van der Linde, 1984. "Olieraffinage en petrochemie in de Golfstaten en in de EG." *Economisch Statistische Berichten*, 69 (3444), February 22: 190–5

Burch, P. H., Jr., 1980/1. *Elites in American History*, 3 vols. New York/London: Holmes and Meier

Cleveland, H., 1976. *Third Try at World Order*. Princeton: Aspen Institute; Philadelphia: World Affairs Council

Dankbaar, Ben, 1984. "Maturity and relocation in the car industry." *Development and Change*, 15: 223–50

Domhoff, G. William, 1979. *The Powers that Be. Processes of Ruling Class Domination in America.* New York: Vintage Books

Economic Report of the President 1983. Washington, DC

Fennema, M., 1982. *International Networks of Banks and Industry.* The Hague/Boston/London: Martinus Nijhoff

Fennema, M., and K. van der Pijl, 1987. *El Triunfo del Neoliberalismo. Conflicto y Cooperacion en la economia mundial.* Santo Domingo: Editora Taller

Fennema, M., and H. Schijf, 1979. "Analysing interlocking directorates: theory and methods." *Social Networks*, 1: 1–36

Freitag, P., 1975. "The cabinet and big business. A study of interlocks." *Social Problems*, 23: 137–52

Frobel, F., J. Heinrichs, and O. Kreye, 1977. *Die neue internationale Arbeitsteilung.* Hamburg: Rowohlt

Greiner, B., 1980. *Amerikanische Aussenpolitik von Truman bis heute.* Cologne: Pahl-Rugenstein

Hadley, Eleanor M., 1970. *Antitrust in Japan.* Princeton University Press

Hankel, W., 1976. "A new order for American-European monetary policies." In E.-O. Czempiel and D. A. Rustow (eds.), *The Euro-American System.* Frankfurt/Boulder: Westview Press, pp. 51–69

   1982. "Shylock gesucht: Hockzinspolitik und internationale Kreditmarkte." *Blätter für Deutsche und internationale Politik*, 5: 591–605

Heinrichs, J., 1980. "Entwicklung des Arbeitslosigkeit und Arbeitsmarkpolitik in den Industrielandern." In *Strukturveranderungen in der kapitalistischen Weltwirtschaft.* Frankfurt: Suhrkamp, pp. 169–201

Helmers, H. M., R. J. Mohhen, R. C. Plijter, and F. N. Stokman, 1975. *Graven naar Macht. Opzoek naar de kern van de Nederlandse economie.* Amsterdam: Van Gennep

Kessler, D., and I. Israelewicz, 1981. "Eléménts d'interpretation de l'internationalisation du système de crédit." In *Internationalisation des banques et des groupes financiers.* Paris: CNRS, pp. 13–39

Koenig, T., 1979. "Interlocking directorates among the largest American corporations and their significance for corporate political activity." Unpublished PhD dissertation, University of California, Santa Barbara

Lipietz, A., 1982. "Towards global Fordism." *New Left Review*, 132: 33–47

Maier, L., D. Melnikow, and W. Schenajew (eds.), 1980. *Westeuropa in der heutigen Welt.* Cologne: Pahl-Rugenstein

Mills, C. Wright, 1959. *The Power Elite.* First published 1956. London/New York/Oxford: Oxford University Press

Mintz, B., 1975. "The President's Cabinet 1877–1972: a contribution to the power structure debate." *Insurgent Sociologist*, 5: 131–48

Morris, J., 1982. "The revenge of the rentier or the interest rate crisis in the United States." *Monthly Review*, 33 (8): 28–34

Owen, H., 1973. *Introduction to the Next Phase in Foreign Policy.* Washington, DC: Brookings Institution

Palloix, C., 1973. *Les firmes multinationales et le procès d' internationalisation.* Paris: Maspero

1978. "The labour process: from Fordism to neo-Fordism." In R. Panzieri, A. Sohn-Rethel, C. Palloix, S. Bologna, and M. Tronti (eds.), *The Labour Process and Class Strategies.* London: CSE Books, pp. 46–67

1982. "Crise et nouvelles formes de l'imperialisme." In J. L. Reiffers (eds.), *Economie et finances internationales.* Paris: Dunod, pp. 131–50

Pelkmans, J., 1984. "Economische topconferenties." *Internationale Spectator,* 38 (2) (February): 65–77

van der Pijl, K., 1985. *The Making of an Atlantic Ruling Class.* London: Verso/New Left Books

Rebattet, F. X., 1962. "The European movement 1945–1953." Unpublished DPhil dissertation, St Antony's College, University of Oxford

Ruffini, P. B., 1979. "Banques multinationales et systeme bancaire transnational." Unpublished doctoral thesis, University of Paris

Servan-Schreiber, J.-J., 1967. *Le défi américain.* Paris: Denoël

Shoup, L. H., and W. Minter, 1977. *Imperial Brain Trust. The Council on Foreign Relations and United States Foreign Policy.* New York/London: Monthly Review Press

SIFI, 1974. "Internationalisation du capital et processus productif: une approche critique." *Cahiers d'Economie Politique,* 1: 9–121

Thunholm, L. E., 1971. "Banking structure and bank competition." In *Banking in a Changing World.* Rome: Associazione Bancaria Italiana, pp. 99–120

Useem, M., 1978. "The inner group of the American capitalist class." *Social Problems,* 25: 225–40

1979. "The social organization of the American business elite and participation of corporation directors in the governance of American institutions." *American Sociological Review,* 44: 553–72

1982. "Classwide rationality in the politics of managers and directors of large corporations in the United States and Great Britain." *Administrative Science Quarterly,* 27: 199–226

1984. *The Inner Circle.* London: Oxford University Press

Vernon, R., 1973. *Sovereignty at Bay. The Multinational Spread of US Enterprises.* First published 1971. Harmondsworth: Penguin Books

1979. "The product life cycle hypothesis in a new international economic environment." *Oxford Bulletin of Economics and Statistics,* 41 (4): 255–67

Wells, L. T., Jr., 1974. "National policies in an international industry: the Europeans and the automobile." In R. Vernon (ed.), *Big Business and the State: Changing Relations in Western Europe.* London: Macmillan, pp. 229–55

Welzk, S., 1983. "Konzernentwicklung und Wirtschaftskrise." *Antrag an die Stiftung Volkswagenwerk* (November)

Index of authors

Subject index